THE RISE AND GROWTH

OF

THE ANGLICAN SCHISM.

THE RISE AND GROWTH
OF
THE ANGLICAN SCHISM.

BY THE REV.

NICOLAS SANDER, D.D.
c.1530 - 1581
SOMETIME FELLOW OF NEW COLLEGE, OXFORD.
ORDAINED TO THE PRIESTHOOD IN ROME CIRCA 1562.

PUBLISHED A.D. 1585 WITH A CONTINUATION OF THE HISTORY
BY THE REV. EDWARD RISHTON, B.A., OF
BRASENOSE COLLEGE, OXFORD,
MISSIONARY PRIEST OF THE SEMINARY OF DOUAI.

Translated, with Introduction and Notes,
BY
DAVID LEWIS, M.A.

TAN BOOKS AND PUBLISHERS, INC.
Rockford, Illinois 61105

Originally published in Latin in 1585 (Cologne) as *De Origine ac Progressu Schismatis Anglicani* ("Concerning the Origin and Progress of the Anglican Schism"). Issued in over 30 editions in various countries—in Latin, French, German, Spanish, Italian, Portuguese, and Polish.

This edition, the first edition in English, was first published in 1877 by Burns and Oates, London.

Republished in 1988 by TAN Books and Publishers, Inc. by arrangement with Burns & Oates Ltd., Tunbridge Wells, England.

Library of Congress Catalog Card No.: 88-50849

ISBN: 0-89555-347-3

Printed and bound in the United States of America.

TAN BOOKS AND PUBLISHERS, INC.
P.O. Box 424
Rockford, Illinois 61105

1988

CONTENTS.

BOOK I.

CHAPTER I.

CHAPTER II.

CHAPTER III.

CHAPTER IV.

CHAPTER V.

CHAPTER VI.

CHAPTER VII.

CHAPTER VIII.

CHAPTER IX.

CHAPTER X.

CHAPTER XI.

CHAPTER XII.

CHAPTER XIII.

CHAPTER XIV.

CHAPTER XV.

CHAPTER XVI.

CHAPTER XVII.

CHAPTER XVIII.

CHAPTER XIX.

BOOK II.

CHAPTER I.

CHAPTER II.

CHAPTER III.

CHAPTER IV.

CHAPTER V.

BOOK III.

CHAPTER I.

CHAPTER II.

BOOK IV.

CHAPTER VI.

CHAPTER VII.

CHAPTER VIII.

CHAPTER IX.

CHAPTER X.

CHAPTER XI.

CHAPTER XII.

INTRODUCTION.

By David Lewis

The earliest and the most trustworthy account which we possess of the great changes in Church and State that were wrought in the reign of Henry VIII. was written by the celebrated Dr. Nicolas Sander, and published in the year of our Lord 1585, at Cologne, with the following title :—

"Doctissimi viri Nicolai Sanderi, de origine ac progressu Schismatis Anglicani liber. Continens historiam maxime ecclesiasticam, annorum circiter sexaginta, lectu dignissimam: nimirum, ab anno 21 regni Henrici 8 quo primum cogitare cœpit de repudianda legitima uxore serenissima Catherina, usque ad hunc vigesimum septimum Elizabethæ, quæ ultima est ejusdem Henrici soboles. Editus et auctus per Edouardum Rishtonum. Præcipua capita totius operis post præfationem authoris' continentur. Coloniæ Agrippinæ, Anno Domini, 1585."

His work was sent to the printers after the death of the author, as may be gathered from the title-page, by the Rev. Edward Rishton, missionary priest, who added to it the Fourth Book.

Dr. Sander himself had made some progress in his account of the reign of Elizabeth, but as he had not perfectly arranged it for the press, Mr. Rishton thought it best to supply its place, as he has done, with the clear and accurate sketch, which is here called the continuation of the history.

Edward Rishton, the first editor of Dr. Sander's account of the rise of the Anglican Schism, was "descended," according to Tanner, "from an ancient and honourable family in the county of Lancaster—*familia antiqua et generosa in agro Lancastriensi oriundus*"—and entered Brasenose College, Oxford, in 1568, when Elizabeth was queen of England.

Having finished his course, he took his degree of B.A. in 1572, and in the following year entered the new seminary at Douai, then newly founded by William, afterwards Cardinal, Allen; for among those who, according to the register of the seminary, began to study theology on the feast of St. Remi, October 1, 1573, was Edward Rishton of the diocese of Chester.[1]

The seminary was an offence to queen Elizabeth and her ministers, who stirred up the heretics at Douai[2] to molest the English students whom Cardinal Allen had brought together. The molestations which the seminarists had to endure were so serious that it was resolved to remove into a more peaceful city. John Wright, B.D., and Edward Rishton were therefore sent to Rheims, November 10, 1576, to prepare the way for the migration thither of their brethren in Douai, if a place could be found for them, and if the University of Rheims were disposed to receive them with goodwill.[3]

On Easter Eve in the following year, April 7, 1577, Mr. Rishton was ordained priest at Cambrai,[4] and on the second Sunday after Easter, April 21, said Mass for the first time. He sang on that day the high Mass at

[1] Collegii Anglo-Duaceni Diarium, Diar. i. p. 5.

[2] See bk. iv. chap. viii. p. 298.

[3] Collegii Anglo-Duaceni Diarium, Diar. ii. p. 113.

[4] Ibid., p. 118.

the high altar of the parish church, according to the rite there in use; but the priests who were trained at Douai, *vexatione dante intellectum,* abandoned the local rites to which their forefathers had been accustomed in England, and said Mass according to the Roman rite, in obedience to the decrees of St. Pius V.[1] He left Douai August 2 of this year, and went to Rome[2] to perfect his theological learning. On the 18th of April 1580 he left Rome,[3] and on the last day of May was in the seminary, then in Rheims, together with the future martyr, Edmund Campian, of the Society of Jesus, and the celebrated Father Persons. Six other priests also were there on that day, two of whom, Ralph Sherwin and Luke Kirby, who had left Rome with him, not long after obtained the crown of the martyrs in England.[4]

Mr. Rishton left Rheims on the 5th day of June, and made his way to England; but "the feet swift to shed blood" overtook him, and he was seized, imprisoned, tried, and condemned to death.[5] That sentence, however, was not executed, but he was kept a prisoner in the Tower, out of which he was taken January 21, 1585, and placed on board a vessel, and cast ashore on the coast of Normandy, by orders of Elizabeth. He reached Rheims on the 3d of March, and then went to Paris, where he met his friend, who prevailed upon him to publish this work of Dr. Sander. But during his imprisonment in the Tower of London he kept a diary, in which he recorded from time to time the merciless tortures to which the Catholics within its walls were subjected by

[1] Collegii Anglo-Duaceni Diarium, Diar. ii. p. 118.

[2] Ibid., p. 126.

[3] Ibid., Appen., p. 297.

[4] Ibid., p. 166.

[5] See bk. iv. chap. ix. p. 313, note 2.

the ministers of Elizabeth. The diary was published after his death, at the end of the edition of Dr. Sander's work which was printed in Rome, 1587, and remains as a record of savage cruelty perpetrated by people who professed, and even practised, the utmost licence in matters of religion; but labouring, as is always the habit of people so professing, under the most perfect incapacity of allowing to others the same deplorable liberty, or even tolerating the only religion that is true. From Paris he went to Pont-à-Mousson, but did not remain there because of the breaking out therein of a grave disease, not, however, escaping the danger he hoped to avoid, for he became seriously ill at Ste. Ménéhould, where he departed this life to receive the reward of his good confession.

The day of his death, according to the Douai diary, was June 29, 1585, but it is not improbable that the report brought to the seminary at Rheims may have been inexact, or perhaps entered in the wrong place in the diary. Mr. Rishton has told the story of Alfield and Webley, who were put to death July 6 because they had brought into the country a book of Cardinal Allen. He must therefore have lived beyond the 29th of June. Still further, he has mentioned the deportation of priests in September of that year, and it may be that he lived even to see the beginning of 1586.

On the other side may be said that the positive testimony of the Douai diary is too clear to be set aside, for the printers in Cologne may have added the story of Alfield and Webley, and the deportation of the priests, in order to make the history complete down to the day in which they were printing the continuation of Mr. Rishton.

Nicolas Sander, the author of the work edited by Mr. Rishton, was descended from an ancient and honourable family, which in the reign of king John was settled in Sanderstead, in the county of Surrey. The head of the house at that time seems to have been William Sander, who, dying without issue, left his lands in that parish to the monastery of Hyde, near Winchester, and in the reign of Henry III. the monks entered into possession. In his other estates he was succeeded by his brother, and in the reign of Edward II. the family was settled at Sander Place, or Charlwood Place, in the parish of Charlwood, in the same county of Surrey.

In the beginning of the sixteenth century the head of the family was Nicolas Sander of Charlwood, whose son, Sir Thomas Sander, was high sheriff of Surrey, A.D. 1553. The high sheriff of the same county, A.D. 1556, was William Sander of Aston, a younger brother of Nicolas Sander, the father of Sir Thomas. William Sander of Aston married Elizabeth Mynes, who in her widowhood went into exile that she might keep the faith,[1] and of that marriage there was issue twelve children, of whom Nicolas Sander was one. Two daughters entered religion, and were professed in the monastery of Sion. Margaret, the elder, was prioress under Catherine Palmer,

[1] De Visibili Monarchia Ecclesiæ, p. 686, Wirceburg, 1592. "Nec mihi [Nicolao Sandero] fas est Elisabetham Gulielmi Sanderi patris mei olim uxorem, nunc viduam clarissimam matrem meam, hac eadem laude privare quæ præter me quem Christo ab infantia dedicavit, duas filias sanctissimo D. Brigittæ monasterio tradidit, ubi ambæ laudabiliter degunt, quarum natu major, Margareta sub Catherina Palmera sanctissima ejus conventus abbatissa priorissæ locum tenet."

who recovered possession of the monastery in the reign of Mary, and who was forced to abandon it under Elizabeth.

Another daughter was married to Henry Pits of Hampshire, and was the mother of John Pits, to whom we owe the great work "De Illustribus Angliæ Scriptoribus," printed in Paris, A.D. 1619.

Nicolas was born at Charlwood, A.D. 1527, and was educated in the famous school of William of Wykeham, in Winchester; from that school he went to the New College of its founder, in Oxford, of which he was admitted scholar, August 6, 1546, and then fellow two years afterwards, August 6, 1548. He applied himself to the study of canon law, and took his degree in that faculty.

In 1557 he gave public lectures as Shaggling[1] professor,[2] and in the next year—he must have been known as a theologian as well as a canonist—he was professor of divinity either in his own right or as the deputy of Richard Bruern.[3]

He resigned his fellowship and left England in 1561, never afterwards to set foot within it. Sir Francis Englefield, preferring banishment and the loss of his estates to the loss of the faith, went abroad, and took Nicolas Sander with him. And Sander was not un-

[1] à Wood (History and Antiquities of the University of Oxford, vol. ii. 901) says that the Shaggling lectures were "lectures that were extraordinary or temporary, allowed either by public authority, common consent, or recommendations. Their readers also were called Shaggling lecturers, and did receive—if they read not out of goodwill—allowance from the students of the university, or from colleges, or from the king, or from a bishop or bishops, or from a noble person, or others."

[2] De Visibili Monarchia, lib. vii. n. 1833, p. 676, ed. Wirceburg. "Nicolaus Sanderus, qui tanquam regius professor jus canonicum suo jure in Oxonio publice prælegit, ei loco et muneri ob fidem conservandam renuntians, et postea sacræ theologiæ professor factus hunc librum ad communem utilitatem conscripsit."

[3] à Wood, p. 849.

grateful, for he has left on record his great obligations to Sir Francis, who, he says, was his chief support for the twelve years which passed between his going abroad and the publication of his great book on the "Monarchy of the Church."[1]

On leaving England he went to Rome, where he was created doctor in divinity, and was ordained priest by Thomas Goldwell, the exiled bishop of St. Asaph.[2] In Rome he became known to the great Hosius, Cardinal Bishop of Ermland, who took him with him when he went as Legate of the Pope to Trent, and kept him also in attendance upon himself during his laborious mission in Poland, Prussia, and Lithuania.

Released from his attendance on the Cardinal, Dr. Sander went to Louvain, which was a true city of refuge to the English persecuted by the heretics, and was made regius professor of theology in that university. During his residence there he finished his great work, "De Visibili Monarchia Ecclesiæ, Lib. viii.," which was printed A.D. 1571, by John Fowler, like himself an exile, who had married one of the daughters of John Harris, once the secretary of Sir Thomas More.

In the early part of the year 1572, St. Pius V. sent for Sander from Louvain, and his friends believed that His Holiness was about to raise him to the purple. The Pope died on the 1st day of May, and it may be that Dr. Sander was sent for that he might proceed to Spain; for he was in Madrid in November 1573, as appears

[1] De Visibili Monarchia, 1892. "Pupillos Dei quos fovere, et suis opibus pascere nunquam destitit, meque in primis, cum et ductu ejus Angliam ab initio reliquerim, et sumptu ejusdem per hos duodecim annos potissimum alar et sustenter."

[2] Ibid., 1602. "Qui mihi manus presbyterii Romæ imposuit."

from a paper in the Record Office,[1] an extract from which has been most kindly furnished to the writer by the Rev. Father Knox, D.D., of the London Oratory.

At this time he was writing his history of the Anglican Schism.[2]

He was again in Spain in 1577 with the Nuncio Monsignor Sega, bishop, then of Ripa Tranzone, and afterwards Cardinal bishop of Piacenza.

From Spain he went as Nuncio of His Holiness Gregory XIII. to Ireland, where he landed in 1579, and where he is said to have died of want, hunted to death by the agents of Elizabeth, A.D. 1580, according to Pits; but A.D. 1583, according to Camden; and according to another account, in the woods of Clenlis, A.D. 1582. Lord Burghley, who in "The Execution of Justice" calls him "a lewde schollar"—he was as well born and well bred as his reviler—says that, "wandering in the mountaines in Ireland without succour," he "died raving in a phrensey."

The name and writings of Dr. Sander are in honour among all people except his own. There is no stain upon his character: he was honest, fearless, and spoke plainly, without respect of persons, according to the obligations of his state. His writings are grave, solid, and learned, without conceit or affectation, showing the simplicity and directness of his nature. Grave historians have been satisfied if they found a fact told by him; and it is not improbable that the reason why his country-

[1] Dom. Eliz. Add., vol. xxiii. n. 61. "Doctor Sanders cam from Rom to Madred yn November 1573."

[2] See below, p. 100.

men dealt so hardly with his name is founded on their conviction that his authority was too great to be overturned by any means except those which some of them too readily adopted—scurrilous railing. Thus Dr. Cox, tutor to Edward VI., and under Elizabeth bishop of Ely, writing to Rodolph Gualter, February 1572, speaks as follows of him :—

"There came out last summer an immense volume—*monstrosum volumen cujusdam Nicolai Sanderi*—by one Nicolas Saunders, who is, they say, a countryman of ours, the title of which is 'The Monarchy of the Church.' He appears to have been a mercenary employed by certain Cardinals, aided by the assistance of others, and decked out like Æsop's jackdaw." [1]

Dr. Cox thus wrote of the book in the fulness of his knowledge; for as late as August 26 in the following year, 1573, he says, "I have not seen the book of Nicolas Saunders about Monarchy : should I see it, and think it deserving of an answer, I will do as the Lord shall enable me." [2]

Then when men heard of his history of the Anglican Schism, they allowed themselves a licence, probably unparallelled, in dealing with the author. Francis Mason,[3] in his "Vindication of the Church of England," thus speaks of the book—his words are thus rendered by Lindsey :—

"Though in that libel of Sanders, concerning the schism, the number of lies may seem to vie with the multitude of lines."

[1] Zurich Letters, 1st series, No. 167, ed. Parker Society. The translation is by Dr. Hastings Robinson.

[2] Ibid., 2d series, No. 94.

[3] Vindiciæ Eccles. Anglican., lib. iii. c. 9. "Quamquam in famoso isto Sanderi de Schismate libello, mendaciorum numerus cum linearum multitudine certare videatur."

"He was the first man," says Camden,[1] "that broached that damnable lie concerning the birth of queen Elizabeth's mother, which no man in those days—though the hatred and malice of the Papists was then fresh against her, and might remember it—ever knew, England in full forty years after never heard of, the computation of time doth egregiously convince of falsehood and vanity, and he, forgetting himself, which a liar should not do, doth himself plainly confute. Yet are there some ill-disposed people who blush not at this day to beslur their writings with so impudent a lie."

Heylyn,[2] calling him Dr. Slanders, speaks of "his pestilent and seditious book, entituled 'De Schismate Anglicano,' whose frequent falsehoods make him no fit author to be built on in any matter of importance."

Strype, whose knowledge ought to have made him more careful of speech, uses the words, "Sanders, in his lying book of the English Schism;"[3] and in another place[4] he thus reviles him: "A most profligate fellow, a very slave to the Roman See, and a sworn enemy to his own country, caring not what he writ, if it might but throw reproach and dirt enough upon the reforming kings and princes, the reformers and the reformation." One "who made himself afterwards so famous for his slanderous accounts of the reformation, and for his zeal

[1] Annals of queen Elizabeth, ad an. 1583, in Kennet's History of England.

[2] Ecclesia Restaurata, pt. iii. p. 122.

[3] Life of Cranmer, bk. i. chap. xviii.

[4] Eccles. Memorials, ii. ii. p. 180.

in raising rebellions in Ireland against queen Elizabeth."[1]

"He was almost as bad an historian," says Collier,[2] "as he was a subject; but his falsehoods having been detected at large already, I shall refer the reader to that performance."

The "performance" to which Collier sends the reader is the "History of the Reformation," by Gilbert Burnet, D.D., bishop of Salisbury; moreover, a "performance" for which Collier had no respect himself.

"Liars by a frequent custom grow to such a habit," writes Burnet[3]—and there have been people who said that Burnet knew it well—"that in the commonest things they cannot speak truth, even though it might conduce to their ends more than their lies do. Sanders had so given himself up to vent reproaches and lies, that he often does it for nothing, without any end but to carry on a trade that had been so long driven by him that he knew not how to lay it down."

Dr. Sander, according to the same writer,[4] "intended to represent the reformation in the foulest shape that was possible; to defame queen Elizabeth, to stain her blood, and therefore to bring her title to the crown in question; and to magnify the authority of the See of Rome, and celebrate monastic orders with all the praises and high characters he could devise: and therefore, after he had writ several books on these subjects without any considerable success, they being all rather filled with foul calumnies and detracting malice than good

[1] Eccles. Memorials, iii. ii. p. 29. Oxford, 1822.

[2] Eccles. History, ii. p. 588.

[3] Hist. of the Reformation, v. p. 585, ed. Pocock.

[4] Ibid., iv. p. 583.

arguments or strong sense, he resolved to try his skill another way, so he intended to tell a doleful tale which should raise a detestation of heresy, an ill opinion of the queen, cast a stain on her blood and disparage her title, and advance the honour of the Papacy."

Dr. Sander certainly did commit to writing the horrible story of Anne Boleyn's birth, but it is not proved that he was either the first or the only one to do so, still less clear is it that he invented the "doleful tale." All that is certain and clear is that he believed the story to be true. In this he may have been in error, as other historians have been in error concerning many facts which they confidently related.

He says distinctly that Anne Boleyn was the daughter of Henry VIII., and he says also with equal distinctness that she was so considered during her lifetime. Now, as Dr. Sander could not have been more than nine years old at the utmost when Anne Boleyn came to her unhappy end, and when the story of her birth was published in the streets of Paris,[1] few people will venture to say with Camden that he was the first person —*primus omnium*—"that broached that damnable lie concerning the birth of queen Elizabeth's mother."

If Dr. Sander had been silent on one point, the morals of Anne Boleyn, it is probable that he might have been held to be an accurate historian. But as he has not been silent, his adversaries have been content to use the information he has supplied us, and to repay him with senseless abuse. The writers of a certain kind seem to agree in chanting the praise of Anne Boleyn,

[1] See below, bk. i. chap. xvii. p. 135, note 1.

and indeed Dr. Burnet admits that it is necessary to maintain the perfect honesty of that person, because the true story of her life "derogates so much from the first reformers."[1]

As to the reputation of Anne Boleyn, Dr. Sander did it no harm. It is true that the weight of his authority is added to the testimony of others, but he is neither the first nor the loudest in publishing the matters which make the life of Anne Boleyn so sad, for Simon Grynæus[2] speaks of her as a woman entitled to no respect. Mr. Pocock[3] has produced proofs that she was evil spoken of at a time when Dr. Sander had probably learned neither to write nor to read. The French ambassador did not spare her,[4] and the king's own sister, the duchess of Suffolk, is said to have uttered "opprobrious language" against her.[5]

The evil temper of Dr. Sander is supposed to have found satisfaction in decrying the person of Anne Boleyn; but even in this he is not singular, for in the Venetian Calendar of State Papers,[6] edited by Mr. Rawdon Brown, is a contemporary account of Anne, not more flattering than that of Dr. Sander.

"Madame Anne," says the writer, "is not one of the handsomest women in the world: she is of middling stature, swarthy complexion, long neck, wide mouth, bosom not much raised, and in fact has nothing but the English king's great appetite and her eyes, which are black and beautiful."

That is an account of Anne Boleyn in October 1532,

[1] See the passages quoted below.

[2] P. 26, note 2.

[3] Records of the Reformation, ii. pp. 468, 566.

[4] Le Grand, iii. 325.

[5] Venetian Calendar, Rawdon Brown, iv. 761.

[6] Ibid., iv. 824.

when she was living "like a queen at Calais," accompanied by the king "to Mass and everywhere, as if she was such."

Dr. Sander clearly was not writing without knowledge, nor was he the slave of his resentments or his passions. Others before him had written of Anne Boleyn as he has done. His praise of queen Catherine and his dislike of Anne Boleyn were not his own, for he has but faithfully represented the times he has described. In 1531 an eyewitness gives the following account of them:[1]—

"There is now living with him [Henry] a young woman of noble birth, though many say of bad character, whose will is law to him, and he is expected to marry her, should the divorce take place, which, it is supposed, will not be effected, as the peers of the realm, both spiritual and temporal, and the people, are opposed to it: nor during the present queen's life will they have any other queen in the kingdom. Her majesty is prudent and good, and during these differences with the king she has evinced constancy and resolution, never being disheartened or depressed."

Again Lodovico Falier, in his report to the Senate, November 10, 1531,[2] says:—

"The queen [Catherine] is of low stature, rather stout, with a modest countenance; she is virtuous, just, replete with goodness and religion; she speaks Spanish, Flemish, French, and English; she is beloved by the islanders more than any queen that ever reigned."

About the same time the French ambassador in Venice receives the following news:[3]—

[1] Venetian Calendar, Rawdon Brown, iv. 682.

[2] Ibid., iv. 694.

[3] Ibid., iv. 701.

"It is said that more than seven weeks ago a mob of from seven to eight thousand women of London went out of the town to seize Boleyn's daughter, the sweetheart of the king of England, who was supping at a villa—*in una casa di piacere*—on a river; the king not being with her; and having received notice of this she escaped by crossing the river in a boat. The women had intended to kill her, and amongst the mob were many men disguised as women; nor has any great demonstration been made about this, because it was a thing done by women."

These things were said and done when Dr. Sander was a baby, and by persons whom he probably never saw. The writers say that which he has said; and if they are trustworthy reporters of things seen and heard by them, it is not reasonable to say that Dr. Sander is not to be believed merely because he also reports the same doings and the same words.

Dr. Sander was not inventing, but at best repeating that which he had heard from others, seeing that the reader is referred by him to Rastall's Life of Sir Thomas More for the fact he puts on record in his history of the Anglican Schism. Camden seems not to have observed the reference, or if he did, to have passed over it in silence.

Dr. Burnet was a bolder man: he not only contradicts Dr. Sander, but denies also that Rastall ever wrote a Life of Sir Thomas More. The passage is not very short, but it deserves to be read. If the story of the birth of Anne Boleyn—

"Were true," writes Burnet,[1] "very much might be drawn from it, both to disparage king Henry, who pretended conscience to annul his marriage for the nearness of affinity, and yet would after that marry his own daughter. It leaves also a foul and lasting stain both on the memory of Anne Boleyn, and of her incomparable daughter, queen Elizabeth. It also derogates so much from the first reformers, who had some kind of dependence on queen Anne Boleyn, that it seems to be of great importance, for directing the reader in the judgment he is to make of persons and things, to lay open the falsehood of this account. It were sufficient for blasting it, that there is no proof pretended to be brought for any part of it, but a book of one Rastall, a judge, that was never seen by any other person than that writer. The title of the book is 'The Life of Sir Thomas More.' There is great reason to think that Rastall never writ any such book; for it is most common for the lives of great authors to be prefixed to their works. Now this Rastall published all More's works in queen Mary's reign, to which if he had written his life, it is likely he would have prefixed it. No evidence, therefore, being given for his relation, either from record or letters, or the testimony of any person who was privy to the matter, the whole is to be looked on as a black forgery, devised on purpose to defame queen Elizabeth."

Burnet's denial of the existence of the Life of Sir Thomas More, by William Rastall, seems to have had no weight with Tanner, for he in his "Bibliotheca Britannico-Hibernica," p. 617, assigns to Rastall a Life of Sir Thomas More. Pits, before him, mentions a Life of Sir Thomas More among the works assigned to Rastall, and as Tanner was not ignorant of the writings of Burnet, the agreement of Tanner with Pits is distinctly an act of disbelief in the confident declamation of Burnet; and be the history of Rastall's work what it may, it is clear that Dr. Tanner trusted to the authority of Pits, and admitted the existence of the book which Burnet had so rashly denied.

[1] Hist. Reform., i. p. 83, ed. Pocock.

Lord Herbert in his Life of Henry VIII. does not seem to have had any doubts of the existence of that Life of Sir Thomas More which Dr. Burnet has called in question. He says of the stories told of Anne Boleyn, that they were "foul calumnies," and he had therefore no interest in admitting that Dr. Sander was but relating that which he had learned from others and not invented himself.

"This author," says lord Herbert, meaning Dr. Sander, "though learned, but more credulous than becomes a man of exact judgment, reports out of one William Rastall, a judge, in his Life of Sir Thomas More, that Mistress Anne Boleyn was the king's daughter by the wife of Sir Thomas Boleyn, while *sub specie honoris* he was employed by the king, ambassador in France." Lord Herbert knew of no reason for denying that the Life of Sir Thomas More had been written by Rastall, and that it contained the story of Anne Boleyn's birth. Neither does he abuse Dr. Sander as a forger or liar; he thinks him indeed too credulous, but credulity is quite consistent with honesty; and he admits him to be a learned man, and therefore allows his readers to believe that Dr. Sander did take this story from the Life of Sir Thomas More, written by William Rastall.

Though the Life itself seems to be at present unknown, there is some evidence that it did once exist, for in the British Museum is a MS.,[1] the title of which is "Certain Briefe Notes appertaining to Bishop Fisher, collected out of Sir Thomas More's Life, written by Mr. Justice Rastall."

[1] Arundel MSS. 152, art. 3, fol. 264.

Now, if Dr. Sander was the forger he is said to have been, he must have been unwise in referring to any book at all, for no one will surely venture to say that he either foresaw or brought about the rarity of the MS. When Rishton prepared the history of the schism for the press, he too believed that there was other authority for the story than that of Dr. Sander, seeing that he either left on the margin, or inserted himself, the reference to Rastall. Rishton and his friend to whom he gave the book for publication are also more or less involved in the forgery, and deserve more severe blame than Dr. Sander, for they, without any excuse, made more public still the calumny said to be the offspring of spite.

Rishton was sent out of the country against his will, and hoped to return for the sake of preserving the faith among us, nevertheless he published this story. He could have done no greater harm to the Catholics he left behind, or to those who intended to enter the kingdom as priests, if the story was either unknown before or an invention of Dr. Sander, for it was carried into all lands; the book containing it went through many editions, and was translated into French, Italian, Spanish, and German while Elizabeth was still living. It was a wanton and utterly inexplicable insult not only to Elizabeth, but to all who acknowledged her as queen, whether subjects or allies, and under the circumstances a most grievous wrong done to the Catholics, whom Elizabeth and her ministers were daily harassing.

Rishton and others, driven out of the country, were thrown upon the charity of good people on the Continent, and it was necessary for him, as a priest, to have the countenance and support of bishops and priests and other honourable men; it is therefore not conceivable that he should thus do damage to himself, increase the vexations his countrymen were subject to, and disgrace the memory, hitherto held in honour, of Dr. Sander, whom he professes to respect, and whom he calls a saintly man. Certainly Rishton believed the story, and he also believed that Dr. Sander believed it.

Two years after the publication of Dr. Sander's book the same story concerning the birth of Anne Boleyn was published in Edinburgh by Adam Blackwood,[1] a lawyer, who lived long in France. He too repeated the tale of Anne Boleyn's tainted birth, and of her levity at the French court. In the next year, 1588, this book of Blackwood was printed again at Antwerp, and being written in French it can hardly be supposed that it was unknown in France. Yet no voice was raised in contradiction, and the story remained in possession. Now, whether true or false, it can hardly be said, under these conditions, that the history of Anne Boleyn's birth was the malicious invention of Dr. Sander.

Besides, Adam Blackwood was a lawyer defending the good name of Mary queen of Scots, whom Elizabeth had put to death against all justice, and we must give him credit—knowing nothing to the contrary—that he was possessed at least of the common sagacity of his profession. He could have done no good to the memory of the murdered queen by repeating a story which nobody believed, but he might have done harm, and

[1] Martyre de la Reyne d'Escosse. Edinburgh, 1587.

stirred up many to defend Elizabeth, by publishing a shameful story which was not true. He told the tale as if it were well known and undisputed, and if he did not believe it himself, and if others too did not believe it, he must have been more or less out of his mind when he wrote as he did.

But in the lifetime of Anne Boleyn herself, in the lifetime of her mother and reputed father, and when she was ostensibly the king's wife, and queen of England publicly crowned, common report at least hinted at the fearful stain of her birth. Mr. Pocock[1] has found a paper in the Record Office to which he has given the following most expressive heading:—

"Accusation brought against a priest named Jackson of having charged the king with adultery committed with Anne Boleyn and lady Boleyn, March 1533."

Nicholas Harpsfield,[2] archdeacon of Canterbury, writing in the reign of Mary, some twenty years before Dr. Sander wrote his book, and some thirty years before it was printed, says that he "credibly heard reported that the king knew the mother of the said Anne Bulleyne."

Mr. Brewer[3] has lately published a letter of Sir George Throgmorton addressed to Henry VIII., in which the writer recounts a conversation he had with Sir Thomas Dyngley, afterwards a martyr. Sir George confesses in his letter to the king that he had spoken of the king's criminal relations with lady Elizabeth Boleyn to the king himself. If he had not done so, it is not credible that he could have dared so to write to the king, nor is it credible that he invented the story. Certainly these

[1] Records, ii. p. 468.

[2] See p. 98, note 2.

[3] Letters and Papers, Henry VIII., vol. iv. Introduction, p. cccxxix.

reports may have been utterly false, and the fruit of malice or perverse imaginations, but it is also certain that they did prevail, and as they did prevail, it is certain that they were not the inventions of Dr. Sander, who at the time must have been a youth of ten or twelve years of age.

Mr. Brewer[1] has also found that the reputation of lady Elizabeth Boleyn was none of the best. "Mrs. Amadas, apparently the wife of the crown jeweller," whom he calls "a mad Welshwoman," was brought into trouble for saying that Sir Thomas Boleyn did not resent the corruption of his wife and his two daughters. Lady Elizabeth Boleyn, Anne's mother, "seems never to have been noticed by Katharine," the queen, is another statement of the same writer.[2] Now, if queen Catherine never "noticed" the wife of Sir Thomas Boleyn, there is nothing uncharitable in the supposition that the pure and devout queen had some grave reason for her neglect. Lady Elizabeth Boleyn was the sister of the duke of Norfolk, and the wife of a man high in the good graces of the king, nevertheless the queen kept aloof from her, and lady Elizabeth remained at the court, where she is found even after the trial in the Legatine court, and when the shame of her daughter could not be concealed, of the woman who was bent on the divorce of Catherine, and on taking her place on the throne. Cranmer,[3] writing to Sir Thomas Boleyn from Hampton Court, June 13, 1531, says, "The king his grace, my lady your wife, my lady Anne your daughter, be in good health, whereof thanks be to God."

[1] Letters and Papers, Henry VIII., vol. iv. Introduction, p. ccxxxii, note 2.

[2] Ibid., note 1.

[3] Jenkyns, Cranmer's Remains, i. p. 1.

Cranmer, the chaplain of the family, seems to have his conscience blunted early, and if nothing more had been heard of lady Elizabeth Boleyn than this report of Cranmer, it need surprise no one that her good name was gone. But this is not all. Mr. Pocock[1] has brought to light, from the Lansdowne MSS. in the British Museum, an account of Anne Boleyn, written during the reign of Elizabeth, agreeing substantially with the account given by Dr. Sander, namely, that she was the daughter of Henry VIII. Mr. Pocock's observation is, "Of whatever value the account given may be, it is plainly independent of Sanders' narrative." Mr. Pocock has so far, then, completely justified Dr. Sander from the undeserved charges of lies and forgeries which unscrupulous men had brought against him.

The very reverend M. A. Tierney, canon penitentiary of Southwark, showed to the present writer a copy of Cardinal Pole's book, "Pro Ecclesiasticæ Unitatis Defensio," in which a former possessor had written on the margin of p. lxxvii as follows:—

"Audivi dixisse hoc aliquando ducissam Somersetensem, et hodie fama est, Annam ipsam, non Thomæ Bulleni fuisse filiam sed ipsius Henrici 8[vi], qui illam ex Bulleni uxore dum vir peregre esset, generasset. Eaque ipsa de re regem a Bulleno admonitum antequam rex Annam duxisset sed frustra."

This book had been the property of the reverend Edmund Hargatt,[2] February 1, 1561, and Mr. Tierney's belief was that the note was in the handwriting of the

1 Records, ii. p. 373.

2 Among the priests who had taken refuge abroad mentioned by Sander (De Visibili Monarchia Ecclesiæ, p. 672, n. 1736, ed. Wirceburg), is Edmundus Hargattus.

then owner, who was a priest driven out of the country because of the change of religion.

It is not unreasonable to admit that this note was written some twenty years before the publication of Dr. Sander's book, and ten or twelve years before Dr. Sander began to write it. There is also no reason for imagining that Mr. Hargatt was writing deliberately that which was not true, so we may also admit with him that the story of Anne's unhappy birth was very well known at the time: "*hodie fama est.*" It was the common talk before the history of the schism by Dr. Sander was ever heard of.

Sir Thomas More refused to take the oath of succession as it was offered to him, though he was willing to take it provided he was not required to swear at the same time that the marriage of Henry and Anne Boleyn was valid. It may be imagined that his objection to that marriage rested on the fact that Henry had been married to queen Catherine, and that queen Catherine was still living. But that was not his difficulty, though it undoubtedly was a difficulty, at least it was not the whole. These are his words in his letter to Dr. Wilson:—

"Finally, as touching the oath, the causes for which I refused it, no man wotteth what they be, for they be secret in mine own conscience: some other, peradventure, than those that other men would ween, and such as I never disclosed unto any man yet, nor never intend to do while I live."

Sir Thomas More kept his secret to himself. It could not have been the bigamy of the king, for that was universally known, and any one might have guessed it. Still further, it is at least very probable, if not certain, that the secret reason was not the criminal relations of Henry with lady Elizabeth and her daughter Mary, the elder sister of Anne. Even if that story were false, it was not secret, for Sir George Throgmorton spoke of it to the king himself, who would be naturally the last person to hear it from a subject, if it had not been publicly spoken of, and treated as a notorious fact.

Archdeacon Harpsfield[1] refers to these words of Sir Thomas More, and to the reports about lady Elizabeth Boleyn and her elder daughter Mary, "of the which impediments," he writes, "Sir Thomas More was not by likelihood ignorant, and seemeth to touch them, *or suchlike*, in these words, among other things, to Dr. Wilson." Harpsfield seems to insinuate something further as being either known to or suspected by Sir Thomas. "*Them, or suchlike*," is a strange expression. He refers again[2] to the fatal marriage and its dissolution in these words:—

"You will perchance now ask me what was the cause that the king's marriage with the lady Anne was never good. Surely, the true cause was that the king married her, his true wife living, and so had two wives at once, which is by the civil law a thing infamous. If you will reply that that was not the cause that the king and Parliament found, I grant you, and the more pity."

About forty years after archdeacon Harpsfield wrote, a prebendary of Chichester, Dr. Thomas Stapleton, a learned, sober, and grave man, defending himself and

[1] Treatise of Marriage, bk. iii. p. 28, Eyston MS. [2] Ibid., p. 61.

his countrymen, whom Elizabeth publicly defamed as degenerate and seditious men of mean birth. These reproaches, said Dr. Stapleton, show weakness of mind; they are most unseemly in her mouth who utters them, for she is regarded as the cause of sedition throughout the world. She does not resemble the illustrious and Catholic race from which she is descended; nay, nothing can be more at variance with the laws of nature than her existence. She certainly knows who her mother was, but everybody does not who was her father.[1]

The sting of this answer of Stapleton on behalf of his outraged companions in exile lies in the words that the laws of nature had been departed from as far as it is possible, and that the reproach of that departure touched Elizabeth. That departure could mean nothing else but the story told by Dr. Sander, for the laws of nature were not violated, unless it be that her mother was the child of her father.

In the year 1533, Cranmer, in open court—styling himself Legate of the Apostolic See, even while usurping the jurisdiction of that see, contrary to the law—pronounced the marriage of Henry and Catherine a nullity, and, five days later, pronounced the marriage of Henry and Anne Boleyn, contracted before the divorce, to be lawful and good. But in 1536, when Anne Boleyn was about to pay in her death the price of her unlawful rank, the same Cranmer, sitting again, as he says, in

[1] Apologia pro rege Catholico, p. 161. "Sed cur tandem hos exules seditioses, degeneres et infimo loco natos esse denuntiat? Impotentis animi sunt hæc convitia et ineptissime a tali persona proficiscuntur, quæ ipse seditionum fons per totum Christianum orbem habetur et quæ a nobilissimis et Catholicissimis proavis, imo *et ab ipsis naturæ regulis quam longissime aberrat*. Quæ denique probe novit qua matre nata est, cum tamen de patre non inter omnes constet."

open court, in the palace of Lambeth, May 17, said that the marriage of Henry and Anne Boleyn was and always had been a nullity. Henry and Anne were never man and wife. He did not say why that marriage was no marriage—indeed he had been equally cautious in pronouncing the former sentence—but he grounded his sentence on something or other, which he called "true, just, and lawful reasons lately brought to his knowledge." [1] These reasons do not seem to have been ever made known, nevertheless the judge sitting in court pronounced a sentence of nullity of marriage upon grounds apparently known only to himself, and which may have been falsely suggested to him; which seem also to have been suggested to him, not in court, during the process of the suit, but elsewhere, and possibly before the suit was begun.

Cranmer was a very different man in his life and conversation from Sir Thomas More, nevertheless both seem to be of one mind touching the validity of the marriage of Anne Boleyn, and both keep secret the grounds of their opinion.

Lord Herbert in his Life of Henry VIII.[2] confesses his own inability to give any account of the matter. He accepts Cranmer's language, and there leaves it: these are his words:—

"The causes [of the dissolution of Anne's marriage] being not yet set down otherwise than they were declared, just, true, and lawful impediments of marriage: I know not how to satisfy the reader therein."

[1] Wilkins, iii. 804. "Ex quibusdam causis veris, justis et legitimis ad notitiam nostram jam nuper deductis."

[2] Page 420.

Lord Herbert, thus silent, but whether from ignorance or from policy, is left to the discretion of the reader, whom he cannot, or refuses to, satisfy.

According to Cranmer's account of the matter, given in the sentence he delivered in the palace of Lambeth, Cranmer had ascertained some time previously that the marriage was null from the beginning, for the word "lately" seems to exclude information given on the day on which he held the court. It is true he saw Anne Boleyn in the Tower, and may even have heard her confession sacramentally on the 16th of May,[1] which was the day before he pronounced the sentence; but even Cranmer must not be accused without clear proof of having made use, in a judicial process in the outer court, of any fact the knowledge of which he obtained under the seal of confession.

Besides, Cranmer does not say from whom he learned the facts which he considered sufficient to justify him in pronouncing the marriage never to have been good.

But the silence of Cranmer is broken in Parliament; the Lords and Commons, with the king, who had sanctioned the statute 28 Henry VIII. c. 7, say in that statute that the reasons were

"Confessed by the said lady Anne before the most reverend father in God, Thomas archbishop of Canterbury, metropolitan and primate of all England, sitting judicially for the same."

The parliamentary account might be accepted if the judicial process at Lambeth lasted more than one day,

[1] Sir William Kingston on that day thus writes to Cromwell (Cavendish, ed. Singer, p. 459): "The kyng's grace showed me that my lord of Cantorbury shuld be hyr confessar, and was here thys day with the quene."

and if the court sat also in the Tower, so that Anne might appear before it; but as there is no trace in the letters of Sir William Kingston either that Anne ever left the Tower after she had once entered it as a prisoner, or that the archbishop held his court for any time there, the declaration of Parliament remains unexplained, and is certainly at variance with the plain meaning of the statement of the archbishop that he had "lately" heard of the reasons; for even if the process lasted more than one day, the word "lately" would be out of place in the sentence.

Parliament, however, though it seems to contradict the sentence of Cranmer, to darken the matter and shroud it in a mist of uncertainty, makes one revelation, not of the facts, but of the difficulty or danger of making them known. Repealing the former act of succession, it thus speaks:—

"Albeit, most dread sovereign lord, that the said acts were then made, as it was then thought by your majesty's nobles and commons, upon a pure, perfect, and clear foundation, thinking the said marriage then had between your highness and the said lady Anne in their consciences to have been pure, sincere, perfect, and good, and so was reputed, accepted, and taken in the realm, **till now of** late that God of His infinite goodness, from whom no secret things can be hid, hath caused to be brought to light evident and open knowledge, as well as of certain just, true, and lawful impediments, unknown at the making of the said acts, and sithen that time confessed by the said lady Anne before the most reverend father in God, Thomas archbishop of Canterbury, metropolitan and primate of all England, sitting judicially for the same, by the which plainly appeareth that the said marriage between your grace and the said lady Anne was never good nor consonant to the laws, but utterly void and of none effect."

Now, if Anne appeared before Cranmer, and confessed, either personally or by her proctor, any impediment to the marriage, that impediment, according to her confession, was "unknown" at the time. But it was perfectly well known at the time that Henry had a wife then living, and so that cannot be one of the reasons. Neither can it be said that Henry or his advisers had found out by this time that the marriage with Catherine was good and valid, because the princess Mary is declared illegitimate; and that marriage, therefore, was still regarded as invalid from the beginning.

Parliament does not say to whom those reasons were "unknown," and it may therefore be understood to say that they were unknown to everybody except to Anne, who is said to have confessed them. Now the relations of Henry with Anne's sister and mother were not "unknown"—certainly they were not unknown about the court; and if they were "unknown" at any time, it was not for Anne Boleyn to confess them. These were matters which the king's proctors might have alleged in court, as admitted by the king, for he had already admitted some of them, seeing that he applied for a dispensation from the Pope to marry Anne at the time he hoped for the legal dissolution of his first marriage with Catherine the queen.

But if the impediments of which Cranmer and Parliament speak were "just, true, and lawful," it is difficult to find more than one reasonable explanation of the silence in which they have been buried. Henry made no secret of his reasons for getting rid of queen Catherine —though they were not the true reasons, but legal and pleadable reasons if true—and it might be expected that he should be equally frank in his conduct when he wished to dissolve the illegal marriage of Anne Boleyn with himself. But he was silent, his ministers are silent, the judge whom he allowed to do his work is silent, and the reasons why his marriage with Anne Boleyn was a nullity have never been divulged.

Some have proposed, by way of explanation, a contract of marriage between Henry Percy, afterwards earl of Northumberland, and Anne Boleyn, entered into by them when Henry Percy was in the household of Cardinal Wolsey and Anne about the court. If that contract had ever been made, it would have been an impediment to the marriage so long as it subsisted, and no longer; but it did not subsist, it was put an end to by the interference of the king, the Cardinal, the earl of Northumberland (the young man's father), and finally by the young man's marriage, "by means whereof," says Cavendish,[1] "the former contract was clearly undone."

But at the time of Anne Boleyn's disgrace, Henry Percy, then married—and his marriage too must have been a nullity, if that of Henry and Anne was a nullity —denied in the most solemn way conceivable that he had ever promised to marry Anne Boleyn. But if the pre-contract subsisted, and was the true, just, and lawful

[1] Page 129, ed. Singer.

impediment, it seems inexplicable why that was not said, unless it be that Parliament was ashamed to make an impediment *diriment* of that which was only an impediment *impedient.*

Even if the pre-contract subsisted, that is but one impediment, and it is not a sufficient explanation of the act of Parliament, which speaks of more than one impediment—"lawful impediments unknown." The precontract was but one, and it is not credible, if it ever subsisted, that it was unknown. Certainly it was not unknown to the king, if the account given by Cavendish be accurate; and most certainly it could never cause Anne's marriage to be null.

If there were any "certain just, true, and lawful impediments unknown" at the time when Parliament declared the marriage of Anne and Henry to be good, "undoubtful, true, sincere, and perfect ever hereafter, according to the just judgment of the said Thomas archbishop of Canterbury, metropolitan and primate of all this realm,"[1] they must have been secret in no ordinary way; for Henry was king of England, and his kindred known; Sir Thomas Boleyn was earl of Wiltshire, Anne his daughter marchioness of Pembroke, and lady Wiltshire was the sister of the duke of Norfolk: their kindred and condition being perfectly well known.

The impediments of matrimony are known also, and among them, for they were but twelve until the Council of Trent, there is only one, that of kindred, which can have rendered this marriage unlawful and void. It has never been said that Henry and Anne were of kin to one

[1] 25 Henry VIII. c. 22.

another by any public and lawful relation. The Tudor and the Boleyn families were not bound to each other by any ties of marriage on the male or female side. They were free to marry, nevertheless there was some bond which brought Henry and Anne within the forbidden degrees, and the impediment was diriment, seeing that the attempted marriage was never any marriage at all. If we do not admit this, we must admit that Cranmer in pronouncing his sentence, and Parliament in making a law, gave utterance to that which is not true, without the excuse of necessity; for the marriage was about to be dissolved in another way, namely, by the execution of Anne Boleyn.

We have now the confession of Cranmer, of the two Houses of Parliament, and of the king, that the impediments were not only diriment, but also unknown. Admitting, then, that the impediment was unknown—we must shut out from the question the relations of Henry with lady Elizabeth Boleyn, and with her daughter Mary, for they were not unknown—nothing remains but to accept the fearful story told, not by Dr. Sander only, nor by him before all others, and say that, at least, by the confession of the king and both Houses of Parliament, Anne Boleyn was Henry's child.

It has been pleaded, by way of objection to this dismal story, that it is disproved by the age of Anne Boleyn. But the plea rests on an assumption which has not been made good, and for which no evidence has been brought. It has been said that Anne Boleyn went to France in October 1514 as one of the attendants of the princess Mary, who was going thither to be married to the king of France. "If Mistress Anne Boleyn went to France," says lord Herbert,[1] "with Mary the French queen, as is proved by divers principal authorities, both English and French, besides the MSS. I have seen, . . . it must follow that she was born about or before 1498."

But lord Herbert has not found many who accept his account, and it is not admitted that Anne Boleyn was the "M." Boleyn who went with queen Mary to France in 1514. The common account is that Anne was born in 1507, but for that account there is no other authority —apparently Mr. Brewer knows of no other—than the herald and antiquary Camden, who also seems to have had no authority for his assertion. As Henry VIII. was born A.D. 1491, he was seven years older than Anne according to lord Herbert, and sixteen according to Camden. Both accounts are equally trustworthy, for they seem to be nothing but guesses, and perhaps guesses made for the purpose of furnishing some grounds for disputing the history of Anne as it was known to Dr. Sander.

Anne Boleyn was dear to Protestants, and they have spoken kindly and well of her. She had chaplains who rose to high places — Latimer, Shaxton, and Parker. Cranmer himself, her tutor and father's chaplain, was made archbishop at her request.[2] She was a woman notorious, if not famous, in Europe, and came to an untimely and miserable end. But notwithstanding, none

[1] Life of Henry VIII., p. 259.

[2] See bk. i. chap. xiii. p. 87, note 2. Dr. Sander is confirmed by the Venetian ambassador, see Venetian Calendar, Rawdon Brown, iv. 846. "His majesty has created Dr. Cranmer—who had been tutor to the marchioness Anne, and lately ambassador to the emperor—archbishop of Canterbury, this having been done by favour of said marchioness.

of those who spoke of her, or who had received benefits from her, seem to have taken the trouble to tell us how old she was. All we seem to gather is that she was certainly young even when she perished on the scaffold. The glimpses we have of her in the Tower, from the letters of Sir William Kingston, betray levity perhaps, but still it is the levity of a very young woman.

George Wyatt, defending her memory against Dr. Sander, refrains from telling her age, and is also silent about the story of her birth, and that silence is full of meaning. Foxe is equally silent; and Strype, who had so many opportunities, and who had consulted so many records of those days, seems to have found no clue to her age; and there is nothing known that can be opposed to the statement of Mr. Justice Rastall and Dr. Sander, which is certainly probable and consistent with itself.

It is hardly credible that Anne Boleyn—supposing her to have been born, as Camden says, in 1507—was one of the ladies in attendance on queen Mary of France in 1514, and to have been the only one allowed to remain when the king dismissed the Englishwomen in attendance on Mary.

There seems to be no fact clearly ascertained in the history of Anne Boleyn inconsistent with the supposition that she was born in 1510, or even 1511. Mr. Brewer[1] finds her about the court in March 1522, "present at one of those revels at court in which Henry delighted." But she may have been a child, acting in some pageant during the carnival, for Ash Wednesday in that year fell on the 5th of March.

[1] Letters and Papers, &c., iv. Introduction, p. ccxxxiv.

Anne, then, was at the court in 1522, and again when the son of the earl of Northumberland fell in love with her, and was not allowed to marry her, because he was already betrothed to a daughter of the earl of Shrewsbury. This affair with Henry Percy seems to have been serious, and Anne, according to Cavendish, hated the Cardinal because he meddled in the matter.

At that time also she seems to disappear from the court, and we hear no more of her in England till 1527. Dr. Sander, following Rastall, says that at fifteen she misconducted herself—at the time of her abandonment by Percy—and was sent by her father to France. If she was born in 1510, or early in 1511—for Camden's assertion is not of more value than that of Dr. Sander—she was then fifteen, and in 1527, when Henry resolved to divorce his wife for her sake, she was seventeen.

She spent two years in France, from 1525 to 1527, and nothing is known of her at variance with this account of Dr. Sander.

The divorce of Henry VIII. has been always regarded as the work of Cardinal Wolsey, but whether he himself, or the king's confessor, Longland bishop of Lincoln, by his advice, first broached the matter to the king, has been disputed. There has been no dispute about the Cardinal's desires and the bishop's service to bring it to pass. William Tyndale and the apostate Observant, William Roye, on the one hand, the queen herself and the emperor Charles V. on the other, agree in this, that the Cardinal of York was the well out of which the bitter waters of that great scandal issued forth. The Cardinal of York had been, as he believed, deluded and overreached by the emperor Charles V., the nephew of the queen, and too many people knew it. He desired revenge, and as he could not punish the emperor in person, he resolved to make him suffer in the honour of his family. The vain-glorious man had been hurt by the contempt of one whom he did not respect, and he was humbled in the presence of the queen, whose daily life was not like his. Bent upon revenge, he advised the king to put away his lawful wife. Hatred is a bad counsellor, and the Cardinal found out that he had given counsel against himself; the divorce was not to be had, and though the Cardinal desired it as much as the king himself, he could not bring it about. It is true he embittered the days of the queen, but he utterly ruined himself;

῾Η δὲ κακὴ βουλὴ τῷ βουλεύσαντι κακίστη.

The king, who, if he did not love his wife, most certainly held her in great respect, disliked at first the shameless advice of his minister, discerning its extreme unseemliness, if not its sinfulness, for he must have felt that at least there was something dishonourable in the wish to put away the mother of his child, and whom he had regarded as his wife for nearly twenty years. The tempter, however, had done his work, and the evil thought in the king's mind was never cast out again. The king consulted learned men, but with great secrecy, and began to read the writings of canonists and theologians on the doctrine of marriage. As he went on with his dismal studies he became aware that he cared less than he did for the queen, and that he should be glad to put some one else in her place. The more he read, the more clearly he saw that his marriage was not good; in the end he convinced himself that the Pope could never make it good, it being beyond his power to make lawful such a marriage as his. His agents in Rome were instructed, therefore, "if it be possible, to retain some notable and excellent divine, a friar, or other that may, can, or will firmly stick to our causes, in leaning to that *quod Pontifex ex jure divino non potest dispensare.*"[1]

But he saw also at the same time that the Pope only could set that marriage aside, for though he had persuaded himself that it was not within the power of the Pope to make it lawful, he nevertheless believed that it could not be safely made void without the Pope's consent.

It is not known when he began to entertain doubts about his marriage; but it is certain that he had made up his mind to desert the queen, and to sue for a divorce early in 1527, when Anne Boleyn reappeared at the court.[2] In May of that year Cardinal Wolsey, as Legate, held a court in his own house, and began a process *ex officio* against Henry, who was charged with the offence of living in the state of marriage with the widow of his brother deceased. It does not appear that the queen was aware of these doings, and the only defender of the

[1] Letter of Henry to Gardiner and the others, April 6, 1529, in Burnet, History of the Reformation, iv. p. 117, ed. Pocock.

[2] Letters and Papers, Brewer, iv. p. 111, 5774. Sir Thomas Boleyn made a deposition as a witness for the king in the suit for the divorce, July 15, 1529, that the king treated the queen as his lawful wife "till about two years ago, when he heard that the king was advised by his confessor to abstain from intercourse with the queen, so as not to offend his conscience." On the 25th of July 1527 he had not broken off with her, as appears by a letter of Sampson to Cardinal Wolsey, in Pocock, Records of the Reformation, i. 11.

marriage present in court was Henry VIII., who longed to hear it pronounced a nullity. That process was abandoned: probably the Cardinal saw that he could not attain his ends without dishonour to himself and the king; for the queen would have refused to be silent when deprived of her rank, and would have appealed at once, with the good wishes of all the world, under a wrong so treacherously done, to the sovereign judge, the Bishop of Rome.

In the meantime news came of the sack of Rome by the Imperialists under the duke of Bourbon, and there arose at once throughout Europe a cry of indignation and of shame that a Catholic emperor should do the work of the heretics. Though the faith was dying, perhaps even dead, in the minds of men in power, yet the habits which the faith had formed could not be laid aside at once; accordingly, out of reverence for the faith so shamelessly outraged, public prayers and supplications, with fasting, were had recourse to, bishops and kings agreeing together that at least the outward decencies must be respected. The people fasted, and made with the clergy solemn processions throughout the land, for as the shepherd was struck, they knew that the dispersion of the sheep must follow; and so it did.

The fast of three days having been ordered, the Cardinal and the king saw that they could make use of the public wrong done to the Pope. They would concert measures as publicly for his deliverance, and send a most solemn and pompous embassy to France—an open profession of zeal and devotion; but the embassy was a cloak for quite other designs.

"Neither was it long," says Harpsfield,[1] "but that the Cardinal was sent ambassador to the said French king, and it was thought that the king was moved for the marriage of his sister, and that it had gone forward, saving that the most virtuous lady had a special respect and regard that she would not marry the king to the great discomfort and undoing of queen Katherine. When this practice of the divorce came to the knowledge of queen Katherine, little marvel was it if she took it grievously, even to the very heart; considering after so long quiet and prosperous continuance, her great misery and calamity, immediately, if the divorce should take place, as indeed it did not many years after, which her infortunable and unlucky chance, it was thought the main and great tempest, wherewith she was tossed and tumbled by the ragious insurges of the wind and water, and often driven from the shore, before she could, at her first coming out of Spain, arrive, did many years before bode and portend. And as it hath been said, the queen herself by reason thereof mistrusted ever and feared some unlucky and unhappy chance impending upon her.

"The queen remaining in this great dolour, sorrow, and lamentation, the king did comfort her, and willed her to bear all things patiently, saying that all that was attempted tended only to the searching and finding out of the truth. Then was there nothing so common and frequent, and so tossed in every man's mouth, in all talk and at all tables, as was this matter, both in taverns, alehouses, and barbers' shops, yea, and in pulpits too: some well liking and allowing the divorce, some other most highly detesting the same. The king, that the matter might be more orderly and authentically heard, discussed, and determined, requested Pope Clement to send purposely some Cardinal into England with sufficient authority to end and decide the weighty matter, who sent Cardinal Laurent Campegius, that had been Legate in England ten years before, and did associate to him Cardinal Wolsey."

The queen herself, whom the divorce especially touched, was kept in ignorance of the plot devised against her as long as possible, and then when it was no longer in the king's power to hide from her that he had taken measures to put her away and make her marriage a nullity, she was told not the truth, but something else

[1] Treatise of Marriage, bk. ii. p. 95, Eyston MS.

—namely, that the king had been troubled in his mind, and was bent, not on divorcing her, but on searching out the truth concerning the validity of their marriage, the legitimacy of their child, and the right of that child to her father's inheritance, out of his deep concern for the peace and well-doing of his subjects, and the quiet of his own conscience, which had been disturbed by the opinions of learned men. It was considered expedient at this time by the duke of Norfolk also and his friends that the Cardinal should be absent from the court, and the Cardinal was therefore sent ambassador to France.

"Their intent and purpose was," says Cavendish,[1] "only to get him out of the king's daily presence, and to convey him out of the realm, that they might have convenient leisure and opportunity to adventure their long-desired enterprise, and by the aid of their chief mistress, my lady Anne, to deprave him so unto the king in his absence that he should be rather in his high displeasure than in his accustomed favour, or at the least to be in less estimation with his majesty."

The Cardinal, with a large train, left London, July 3, 1527, and in due time landed at Calais. He made three treaties with the king of France, by one of which the contracting parties agreed that no Bull or Brief of the Pope should be received in France or England during the captivity of the Pope.[2] "That during the said cap-

[1] Life of Cardinal Wolsey, p. 148, ed. Singer.

[2] "It is reported that the Cardinal of York," says Andrea Navagero, the Venetian ambassador in Spain, writing from Valladolid, July 27, 1527 (Rawdon Brown, Venetian Calendar of State Papers, iv. 142), "has arrived at Calais, and was to meet the most Christian king at Amiens. The imperial councillors of Valladolid say in secret that the Cardinal intends to separate the Church of England and of France from that of Rome, making himself the head of it, saying that as the Pope is not at

tivity of the Pope, whatsoever by the Cardinal of York, assisted by the prelates of England assembled and called together by the authority of the said king, should be determined concerning the administration of ecclesiastical affairs, in the said kingdom of England and other countries, being in the dominion of the said Henry, should—the consent of the said king being first had—be decreed and observed."[1]

Francis I. also took the like power to himself within his dominions, but it may be doubted whether he was quite as earnest in the matter as the Cardinal was, seeing that the latter proposed to ask the Pope to make him, Cardinal Wolsey, his vicar-general so long as the captivity lasted.

On this attempted usurpation of the Papal jurisdiction, and its subjugation at the same time to the civil power, the consent of which was required for its valid exercise, lord Herbert observes, "Here certainly began the taste that our king took of governing in chief the clergy, of which, therefore, as well as the dissolution of monasteries, it seems the first arguments and impressions were derived from the Cardinal."[2]

Cardinal Wolsey having persuaded four other cardinals to enter into his plan, wrote a letter from Compiègne, September 16, 1527,[3] which they signed with him, to the Pope, in which he asked him to intrust his

liberty, he is not to be obeyed in any way; and that even were the emperor to release him, he could not be considered free, unless all his fortresses and the whole of his territory, now in the emperor's hands, were restored to him. I cannot affirm whether this be true or reported with a view to alienate the Pope from the two kings."

[1] Lord Herbert, Life of Henry VIII., p. 209; Rymer, Fœdera, vi. pt. ii. p. 85.

[2] Ibid., *ut supra*.

[3] Le Grand, Hist. du Divorce, iii. p. 4.

whole authority into the keeping of him, Cardinal Wolsey. The Bull was also written ready for the seal of the Pope, in which the Cardinal proposed to take all the Papal power—"*omnem potestatis et ordinariæ et extraordinariæ plenitudinem*"—so that he might, as he said, be able to dispense even with the divine law, and do that which the Holy See had not been in the habit of doing; moreover, the Pope was also to promise never to undo the acts of the Cardinal, or cancel his powers so long as he remained a prisoner.[1]

While the Cardinal was asking for these powers from the Pope in prison, he and Francis I. were leagued together to respect no decrees which the Pope might make during his imprisonment.

It has been said that the Pope did grant the powers asked for; so says lord Herbert, on the authority of Hall. Strype,[2] too, who might have known better, after enumerating his titles, writes that the Cardinal "received one more from Pope Clement this year, that of vicar-general, whereby he was empowered to perform all that the Pope might have done himself."

This commission to be the vicar of the Pope serves but one purpose now; it unveils the deep-rooted immorality of the Cardinal of York, his contempt of justice, and his want of reverence for holy things. He has himself revealed the meanness of his mind, for he told the king that his reason for desiring to obtain the Papal powers

[1] Pocock, Records, i. p. 19. "Ad exercendum, exequendum et expediendum omnia ea et singula quæ nos de potestale vel ordinaria vel absoluta in remittandis, relaxandis, limitandis aut derogandis canonibus facere possemus absque aliqua restrictione etiamsi ad divinæ legis relaxationem limitacionem casus pertineat, fueritque ejusmodi in quo Sedes Apostolica non consueverat dispensare."

[2] Ecclesiastical Memorials, i. p. 107, ed. of 1822.

was that he might delegate judges to determine the question which the king had raised concerning his marriage, and on the queen's appeal, to take cognisance of the cause himself, and to decide it, without any appeal to the Pope from his sentence.[1]

But the Cardinal, before he left France, and before the Pope could even see the Bull which he had so carefully drawn up, took upon himself to execute the office which he intended to assume.

"In the morning that my lord," says Cavendish,[2] "should depart and remove, being then at Mass in his closet, he consecrated the chancellor of France a Cardinal, and put upon him the habit due to that order, and then took his journey into Englandward."

Cavendish was more learned in the ceremonial of the Cardinal's household than in the Rubrics of the Pontificate. That which Cavendish did not clearly understand, and which Fiddes[3] also describes in the same words, is explained in a Life of Cardinal Wolsey in the Vatican, a copy of which may be seen among the transcripts in the British Museum, and which Mr. Pocock[4] has published among his "Records of the Reformation." Clement VII. had promised, on the petition of king Francis, to make the chancellor of France a Cardinal, but he had hitherto, for certain reasons, put off the formal promotion. Wolsey, in his vanity, trampling on decency as well as law, undertook to do that which the

[1] Letters and Papers, Brewer, iv. pt. ii. 3400.

[2] Life of Wolsey, p. 185, ed. Singer.

[3] Life of Wolsey, p. 404.

[4] Records, ii. p. 88. "Unum e proceribus Galliæ, quam Clemens, petente rege, Cardinalem designaverat quidem, sed tempus renuntiandi eum disluteral, assumere honoris ejus insignia, seque per Cardinali habere jussit."

Pope himself had not yet done. He ordered the chancellor to put on the dress of a Cardinal, and to assume the dignity promised but not conferred. There was no consecration.

The Cardinal of York was a great man in England, but the selfishness to which he was a slave had killed in him all respect for those whom he thought he could overreach or master. He was insolent to the Pope, and contemptuous of the Cardinals, his brethren. In the year 1529, within a few months of his miserable undoing, he threatened to become a schismatic bishop if the Cardinals should insist on the payment of the ordinary fees due on his translation from Durham to Winchester.

If the Cardinals—for that is the meaning of his letter to Gregorio Casali and Peter Vannes, who in Rome solicited his Bulls—" will not grant the Bulls for 5000 or 6000 ducats, they have little regard to his merits, or to the profit which will accrue to them by his acceptance of Winchester. Has already the profits of the see by the king's grant, and can hold them with Durham *without any Bulls.* If it were not for the evil example, would not give a thousand ducats for the Bulls."[1]

The man was a cardinal as well as an archbishop, yet he so little regarded the sacred relations in which he stood to the Pope as to say that he could hold a bishopric without the sanction of the sovereign Pontiff.

It is not improbable that he may have suspected that his absence from England in the year 1527 might be an occasion of mischief. He protected himself, therefore,

[1] Letters and Papers, ed. Brewer, iv. pt. iii. 5313.

against the queen, whom he had least reason to fear; for a priest whom he had employed as his commissary in Tournai, and whom he had made dean of the chapel royal, was, it seems, directed to watch the behaviour of the queen. This man, Dr. Richard Sampson, wrote to him, July 25, as follows:[1]—

"The great matter is in very good train; good countenance, much better than was in mine opinion: less suspicion or little: the merry visage is returned not less than was wont. The other party, as your grace knoweth, lacketh no wit, and so showeth highly in this matter. If that I perceive otherwise or more, I shall not fail to advertise your grace with diligence."

On the 29th of July the Cardinal himself sends a letter to the king, in which he tells him that he, the Cardinal, was "daily and hourly musing and thinking" on the "great and secret affair" of the king, and "how the same may come to good effect and desired end."[2] In other words, how to accomplish the divorce and break a lawful marriage.

"Secret affair," or "the king's matter," was the accepted phrase which men now used in speaking of the divorce, and the words no doubt helped very much to deaden their conscience, because they were in themselves innocent, though the real meaning was evil. It was, no doubt, a "secret affair;" but it was not at this time a secret to the queen, who had been able, notwithstanding all the efforts of the Cardinal and the king, to send an account to her nephew, the emperor, of the mischief that was done, and of the greater mischief to come.

[1] Pocock, Records, i. p. 11.
[2] Letters and Papers, ed. Brewer, iv. pt. ii. 3311.

The Cardinal Archbishop of York, "daily and hourly musing" how to bring the "secret affair" to "good effect and desired end," wrote on the 1st of August to the king's ambassadors with the emperor, namely, the bishop of Worcester, and Edward Lee, the Cardinal's successor in York, and instructed them to tell the emperor that there was no intention whatever to disturb the marriage, but rather to confirm it, against any doubts that might be made about it.[1] The bishop and the priest were to say that to the emperor, who already knew all that had been done, and that the Cardinal had been the cause of that "scandalous proceeding."

It cannot be said in favour of the Cardinal that he yielded to the king only so far as was necessary for the discovery of the truth concerning his marriage. He knew the marriage was a lawful and perfectly valid marriage, and he also knew that the king under his teaching had made up his mind to break it. He was not shocked at this profanation of a sacrament, and he did his utmost to help the king. He knew, too, that others would think ill of him for his servility, and he therefore strove to the end to hide as much as he could the real purpose of the king. It was part of his service to be rendered in France to tell the French king that Henry VIII. was dissatisfied with his wife, and wished to be rid of her. "Nothing now remains," he writes to the king, August 16, "except to disclose your private matter, which I propose to do in so cloudy and dark a sort that he shall not know your utter determination."[2]

He was not so reserved in his dealings with the king

[1] Letters and Papers, ed. Brewer, *ut supra*, 3327. [2] Ibid., 3350.

of England, and he does not pretend to be ignorant of the king's purpose. When Henry had made up his mind to send some one to the Pope, and had chosen Dr. William Knight, secretary of state, and had informed the Cardinal of his resolve, the Cardinal, not thinking that Dr. Knight was a man fit for the purpose, but submitting to the king's choice, gave him such instructions as were suited to the evil intended "with less disclosing of the matter."[1] In the beginning of this affair of the divorce, the Cardinal hoped to attain his end by fraud, and to obtain from the Pope the implicit dissolution of the king's marriage without the Pope's knowledge of the meaning of his acts.

The secretary of state whom the king sent to the Pope was Dr. William Knight, at this time a prebendary of St. Paul's, of Bangor, and of Lincoln, as well as archdeacon of Huntingdon and of Chester. He became also, two years later, archdeacon of the East Riding of York, on the probably enforced resignation of Thomas Winter, the son of the Cardinal, then in disgrace, and near his most wretched end. Dr. Knight served the king faithfully, and never shrunk from any baseness; he received his reward in due time, and was made bishop of Bath and Wells, but in schism, and without the leave of the Pope—a heretic and a schismatic.

Dr. Knight left London instructed by the king to ask the Pope for a dispensation to have two wives at once, but the archdeacon does not hide from the king that in his opinion such a dispensation might be difficult to obtain.[2] Later instructions from the Cardinal reached the arch-

[1] Letters and Papers, ed. Brewer, *ut supra*, 3423. [2] Ibid., 3422.

deacon before he was admitted into the presence of the sovereign Pontiff. These instructions had been brought to him by the chaplain of Sir Thomas Boleyn, believed to be no other than Thomas Cranmer. The new instructions seem to have been less openly shameless, for it does not appear that the archdeacon prayed the Pope to sanction polygamy. The suggestion, then, that the king might have two wives living at the same time, did not come from the Pope, as some have said, but from Henry himself, and the men without honour and without faith in whom he had placed his confidence to his irreparable hurt.

According to the archdeacon's account, there was nothing illegal in his petition to the Pope, however suspicious it might seem.

"We desired His Holiness"—these are his words—"to commit the knowledge of the dispensation that was obtained in time of Juli, of famous memory, for matrimony to be had between the king and the widow, relict late of prince Arthur; and that he might have it in form as that was that your grace [the Cardinal] sent hither."[1]

There is something evil-sounding in a petition presented by a man to examine into the lawfulness of a contract into which he had entered, and by which he had profited; nor is it to his credit that he should attempt to direct that examination according to his own opinion. The king professed to have doubts about his marriage, and said that his conscience was ill at ease, because he was not living in lawful wedlock. Hence the necessity,

[1] Burnet, Hist. Reform., iv. 34, ed. Pocock.

he said, of ascertaining whether the dispensation granted by Julius II. was a sufficient justification. He did not now maintain that the marriage might not be made lawful, or that the Pope could not grant the dispensation: he wished to be sure that the dispensation already granted by the Pope was without flaw; that was all.

On the surface nothing could be more fair, nothing more worthy of an honest man, than to be secured against the disherison of his children and the dishonour of his wife. Henry VIII. was not careful only of his wife and child, but he was also afraid of offending God, and accordingly, as a good and pious Catholic, he went to the Pope for the solution of his doubts and the peace of his conscience, grievously disturbed.

As Henry and Catherine could not have been lawfully married without the permission of the Pope, so Julius II. had permitted their marriage. But now, after eighteen years of marriage, the Pope, Clement VII., is asked to examine and determine whether the dispensation of his predecessor was valid. A scruple so strange and so late in coming might be honest, but it might be also not honest.

His Holiness assented to the prayer of the king so far as it related to the searching out the validity of the dispensation, but he refused to accept the conditions which the king wished to lay those under who were to make that examination. He would not, without consulting the Cardinal *Sanctorum Quatuor,* issue the commission which the archdeacon desired to have in the form in which the archdeacon presented it.

The archdeacon was not alone in this embassy;

Gregorio Casali was with him, a skilful Italian, and apparently a much abler man than the archdeacon of Chester. They no doubt saw that the Pope had some suspicions of their master, and that he would not enter blindly into their toils. So they began to weave the web of iniquity elsewhere. This is the account which the archdeacon gives of their second attempt:—

"We, perceiving that the obtaining of our charges, after the king's and your grace's pleasure, depended much upon the advice of *Sanctorum Quatuor*, did prevent his going unto the Pope, and delivering your grace's letters with recommendations accordingly, we desired him to be good and favourable unto our requests in the king's behalf; and for the better obtaining of our desires, we promised to see unto him with a competent reward."[1]

This was said to Lorenzo Pucci, Cardinal Bishop of Palestrina. They then showed him the commission, which had been drawn up in England; but the Cardinal, though promised a "competent reward," told the archdeacon and his companion at once that the commission "could not pass without perpetual dishonour unto the Pope, the king, and your grace," *i.e.*, Cardinal Wolsey, by whom that very commission had been designed.

The commission had been contrived in a spirit of fraud, and in the expectation that the Pope would not discover the snare laid for him. "When the purport of that commission is well studied," so says the Cardinal himself to the king, "it will be found that nothing can

[1] Burnet, Hist. Reform., iv. 35, ed. Pocock.

be better suited to your purpose *with less disclosing of the matter*."[1]

Cardinal Pucci saw perhaps no fraud, for he saw too clearly all that was meant, and he may have regarded the commission so drawn up, and which he pronounced dishonourable, as the blundering of unscrupulous men without honour or shame. There was no help for it now, the king's agents must leave the commission with the Cardinal, and accept his corrections.

The Cardinal *Sanctorum Quatuor* drew up a commission in due form, and Mr. Secretary Knight sent it home, hoping that it would answer the purpose of his master; and that done, he believed that he had done all that was desirable to be done.

The commission being obtained, "though not in the form that was conceived in England," the two agents, "Mr. Gregory and I," says Dr. Knight in his letter to the king, "have rewarded with two thousand crowns" the Cardinal *Sanctorum Quatuor*, "of such money as your highness hath caused to be made unto Venice for the furtherance of your causes." The same person wrote also on the same day to Cardinal Wolsey in these words: "We have given unto my lord Cardinal *Sanctorum Quatuor* two thousand crowns, and unto the secretary thirty crowns."[2] The thirty crowns paid to the secretary were probably fees of that officer, but perhaps liberally discharged, and with an evil purpose.

Dr. Knight was an archdeacon, and therefore an ecclesiastical judge; on the road to a bishopric, and in

[1] Letters and Papers, ed. Brewer, iv. pt. ii. n. 3423.

[2] Burnet, Hist. Reform., iv. pp. 36, 39, ed. Pocock.

fact he travelled on it and obtained his reward, but out of the grace of God. He had no scruples about bribery, and did his utmost to corrupt a Cardinal of Holy Church. It is true he had been instructed to do so, and money had been provided for the very purpose of buying justice—provided, moreover, by a Cardinal, who to please the king, whom he professed to serve, shrank not, having dishonoured himself, from dishonouring his brethren the Cardinals of the Roman Church.

The archdeacon announces the corruption of Cardinal Pucci to the king and to the Cardinal of York, without any misgiving that either of them would be otherwise than glad over the fate of the Cardinal; and no doubt they were glad, but with the gladness of Annas and Caiphas when they were told that Judas had accepted the thirty pieces of silver.

He proclaimed the dishonour of the Cardinal on the 1st day of January 1528; but three months later, Gardiner and Fox and Gregorio Casali, the king's agents in this disreputable affair, in their letter to the Cardinal of York, made their confession in these terms: "It should be displeasant to his grace to understand that the said Cardinal hath refused to take the two thousand crowns offered by Mr. Secretary [the archdeacon] and Mr. Gregory [Casali], which his highness thought verily he had accepted and taken."[1]

Dr. Gilbert Burnet published these letters of the archdeacon of Chester, and might have read them; nevertheless, he thus expresses himself: "The Cardinal

[1] Pocock, Records, i. p. 102.

Sanctorum Quatuor got *four thousand crowns* as the reward of his pains, and in earnest of what he was to expect when the matter should be brought to a final conclusion."[1]

It is not so easy to excuse Burnet's rejoicing over the fall of a Cardinal; for he knew, or might have known, that the Cardinal had not accepted any money whatever, seeing that he has printed a letter of Cardinal Wolsey also in which the confession is made, perhaps not without regret, that the hands of Cardinal Pucci refused to touch the wages of sin.[2]

The archdeacon asked the Pope for a commission to try the validity of a certain dispensation; the Pope granted it, though not in the form in which the archdeacon had been instructed to obtain it. He also asked for a dispensation to enable the king to marry within the forbidden degrees of kindred and affinity. That too was granted. Both the dispensation and the commission were sent at once to England by the prothonotary Gambara, but as they were not according to the form in which they had been fashioned there, they were therefore insufficient for the king's purpose. Mr. Pocock has published a letter, drawn up by Peter Vannes, secretary of the Cardinal of York, before he entered the king's service, to be sent by the king to the Cardinal Pucci, in which this acknowledgment is made, and in which the Cardinal is entreated to be more indulgent to the king.[3]

[1] Hist. Reform., i. 94, ed. Pocock.

[2] Ibid., iv. 47, ed. Pocock. "Et quamvis munusculum illud olim oblatum recusaverit."

[3] Records, i. p. 60. "Accepimus deinde commissionem et dispensationem quæs sanctissimus dominus noster—vestra reverendissima dominatione plurimum juvante — pro causa nostra nobis benignissime concessit, easque etsi, ubi maturo prudentique consilio adhibito, omni ex parte perpendissemus, invenerimus pro nostro recte conficiendo negotio, nullius esse roboris validitatis et effectûs."

The dispensation for the future marriage of the king is couched in the most ample form, for he has leave to marry any one related to him in the second degree of kindred, and in the first degree of affinity, whether lawfully or unlawfully entered into. Moreover, he is not allowed to marry his brother's widow; and that is the marriage which he wished to make void.

Nevertheless, the dispensation was not regarded as sufficient, and the reason seems to be this. Dr. Knight was commissioned to sue out a dispensation to enable the king to have a wife *constante matrimonio*—in other words, to commit polygamy. Polygamy not being sanctioned, the dispensation was treated as worthless.

Mr. Pocock has printed this dispensation, and with it certain notes made in the margin of the same, one of which states directly that the dispensation, being conditional on the dissolution of the subsisting marriage, was not to the purpose. In the opinion of him who wrote that note the dispensation should have been unconditional, and without any relation to the dissolution of the marriage of Henry and Catherine.[1]

Certainly this seems to show that Henry VIII. and Cardinal Wolsey, while asking for a commission to examine into the lawfulness of the dispensation by which the marriage of the king had been sanctioned, were asking for another dispensation of the like nature to be granted at the same time. Now, if the Cardinal *Sanctorum Quatuor* had granted the commission, and then the dispensation, without any mention of the controversy about

[1] Pocock, Records, i. p. 23. "Hoc petere nihil pertinet ad præsentem dispensationem quam convenit absolutam esse, et cum decisione ac dissolutione præsentis matrimonii non conjungi."

the first marriage, is it quite certain that Henry would have waited for the divorce before he took advantage of the dispensation, if it had been drawn up in the terms proposed by him through the archdeacon of Chester? The archdeacon himself seems to have discovered the trick, if trick there was, or perhaps it had been explained to him, for he confessed that he did not think he should obtain the dispensation in the form in which he had been instructed to ask for it.

It may be that there was no plan laid for deceiving the Pope, but the facts, and the admission of the archdeacon, are more easily interpreted in a bad sense.

If the dispensation had been granted as it was asked for, namely, without conditions and without mention of Henry's marriage with Catherine, it would have been very easy to say, when the king married Anne Boleyn, that he did so with the implicit sanction of the Holy See. It would have been said that the Pope knew of the first marriage, and of Henry's denial of its lawfulness, and yet had granted him a dispensation to marry; that he must have regarded the first marriage as a nullity, and the dispensation therefore an implicit declaration of that nullity.

The first embassy ended in failure. In the beginning of the next year, 1528, it was resolved to send abler men to the Pope; accordingly the choice of the king and the Cardinal fell upon Edward Fox, the king's chaplain, afterwards, in schism, bishop of Hereford, and Dr. Stephen Gardiner, trained in the household of Wolsey. A fitter instrument could not be found than this latter ecclesiastic, a man greedy of power, insolent and overbearing, whose conscience seems to have been wholly under the dominion of his will.

Cardinal Wolsey, in commending Gardiner to the Pope, spoke of him as a man who was in all his secrets, and as his other half, and then protested, on his life and soul, that he, the Cardinal, would undergo any torments rather than further any wishes of the king which he did not know to be right, lawful, and just.[1] Now, the Cardinal knew, for he confessed it in his letters[2] to Gregory and John de Casali, that the wish of the king was to put away his wife.

In this embassy the first place had been given to Fox, who had been for some time in the service of the king, and the second place was given to Gardiner, who hitherto had been in the service of the Cardinal. But before they left England, the order of precedence was changed. Gardiner, who was the last, made himself first, and Fox accepted his position, probably unable to withstand the more resolute will and more ambitious temper of Dr. Stephen Gardiner. This is the account they both give of this their arrangement. They wrote a joint letter from Dover to the Cardinal, February 13, 1528, and thus explain the matter:[3]—

"And where your grace, among such articles as we required answers unto, maketh mention that because I, Edward Fox, am the king's servant and counsellor, and first named in the letters of his grace's own hand, if it were so thought convenient between us, should have

[1] Burnet, Hist. Reform., iv. p. 45, ed. Pocock. "Hujus regis precibus . . . quas nisi rectas sanctas ac justas esse scirem, omne prius supplicii genus ultro subirem quam eas promoverem, pro hisque ego vitam meam et animam spondeo."

[2] Burnet, Hist. Reform., iv. pp. 19, 53, ed. Pocock. The first written in December 1527, the second in February 1528.

[3] Pocock, Records of the Reformation, i. p. 74.

the former place, and I, Steven Gardyner, to have the speech and utterance as hereunto, albeit we both joined in this message as to be in all doings of one mind, will, and intent, endeavouring ourselves ever to that may be to the furtherance of the king's mind and purpose ; by reason whereof, without distinction of superiority, to that effect and purpose, we have been always, and be of such conformity, as we shall take in good part whatsoever shall be the king's and your grace's pleasure in that behalf; yet that matter referred to our discretion, forasmuch as in this journey and message we be both the king's servants, having equal charge and burden in this matter, we are between us agreed, resolved, and determined, that the pre-eminence both of place, speech, and utterance be always given to me, Steven Gardyner, without altercation or variance, as our old amity and fast friendship doth require."

Bonner, who knew him well, writing to Cromwell, to whom he, Bonner, owed his promotions in the Church, calls the attention of his patron to the overbearing temper of the bishop.

"I mislike in the bishop of Winchester," says Bonner, "that when any man is sent in the king's affairs, and by his highness' commandment, the bishop, unless he be the only and chief inventor of the matter, and setter-forth of the person, he will not only use many cavillations, but also use great strangeness in countenance and cheer to the person that is sent."[1]

Perhaps Dr. Gardiner meant to give the Cardinal a hint at the same time that he was no longer his servant,

[1] Foxe, Acts and Monuments, v. p. 154, ed. Cattley.

but one of "the king's servants," as he afterwards was, and, as the king's servant, unable, if not unwilling, to help his old master in his sore distress and utmost need.

Having informed the Cardinal of the order of precedence which they had established, the two priests went on their way to do their utmost to break a lawful marriage, and to minister to the passions of the king. They arrived at Orvieto on the night of Friday, March 20, 1528, and "came to the Pope's presence"—so they wrote on the 31st of March—the twenty-second day (mid-Lent Sunday), "and so daily from that time to the depeching of this post, were with His Holiness every day, three or four hours, consulting and debating."[1]

In their first audience the Pope told them that in the matter which they had to treat "he would give such resolution without tract or delay as" they "could reasonably desire, and as might be agreeable with law and equity, for justification of his doing and maintenance of his and the king's honour hereafter."[2]

And throughout this most painful business, notwithstanding the importunities of the king and the pressure which his agents put on the Pope, who was then, in the eyes of men, perfectly defenceless, Clement VII., in the midst of his sore anxieties, spoke no other language: he would do justice according to the law.

Henry VIII. had written a book[3] in his own defence, and this book, sent to Orvieto with the ambassadors,

[1] Letter of Gardiner and Fox, March 31; Pocock's Records, i. 92.

[2] Ibid., p. 95.

[3] The king in a letter to Anne Boleyn thus speaks of his book (Lettres de Henri VIII. à Anne Boleyn, Let. 16, Crapelet, Paris): "I am ryght wel comfortyd in so muche that my boke makyth substantially for mi matter: in lokyng wheroff I have spente above four ours this day."

was presented to the Pope by Gardiner and Fox on Tuesday, March 24, and this is their account of the matter in their letter to the Cardinal :[1]—

"The next day at afternoon we went, as was appointed, to the Pope's Holiness, and exhibited unto him the king's book; which His Holiness incontinently began to read; and standing awhile, and after sitting upon a form covered with a piece of an old coverlet not worth twenty pence, holding the book, read over the epistle before, and the latter part of the book touching the law, without suffering any of us to help him therein. Noting evermore the reasons as one succeeded another, and objecting that which His Holiness saw afterward answered. Which done, His Holiness greatly commended the book, and said he would for a day keep it with him, to the intent he might by himself at good leisure read, as well the first part, as also the second part again. And forasmuch as the epistle was directed to your grace and the other prelates, His Holiness demanded for the answer made thereunto, as the king's highness requireth in the end of his epistle. We said that none answer was made in writing, but of what sort the answer was His Holiness might perceive by your grace's letters, and such words as we had spoken unto him on your grace's behalf. And so seeming to be right well content therewith, His Holiness demanded whether the king's highness had at any time broken this matter to the queen or not. We said yea, and that she showed herself content to stand to the judgment of the Church." [2]

The Pope then told the two ambassadors that, as

[1] Pocock, Records, i. pp. 100, 101. [2] Ibid.

matters stood, Cardinal Wolsey could not be one of the judges, seeing that he was not indifferent in the matter, having already declared his mind, and thereby in a manner given sentence beforehand.

To this Gardiner replied that the Cardinal had given his opinion on one part of the question only, not on the whole question. He had said that the law was in favour of the king if the facts were as the king alleged, but he had never said that the facts on which the king relied were true; he was therefore an "indifferent" person, and might be left to examine and decide the question so far as the facts were concerned.

The Pope, seeing the meaning of Gardiner, pursued this matter no further, and was silent; and Gardiner says, "herewith His Holiness seemed satisfied."[1]

The commission, as before, under which judges were to try the validity of the dispensation by which the marriage of Henry and Catherine had been sanctioned, was drawn up in England ready for the Pope's assent, and was now in Gardiner's hands, but "it was then too late to read it. And His Holiness, willing us to leave it there with him, said he would in the morning read it by himself, and afterward send it to the Cardinal *Sanctorum Quatuor*," the bishop of Palestrina, whom Dr. Knight, archdeacon of Chester, reported as having accepted a bribe of two thousand crowns, and which Dr. Burnet magnified into four thousand.

The king's agents, dismissed by the Pope, went at once, as Casali had gone before with the archdeacon, to see the Cardinal *Sanctorum Quatuor*, in order to pre-

[1] Pocock, Records, i. p. 101.

pare him, and if possible to win him over to adopt the king's opinion.

The Cardinal received them courteously, and listened to their communications patiently, without directly contradicting anything they said, but without showing that he agreed with them. He contrived to break the force of Gardiner's attack by diverting the discussion to a question of form. He, the Cardinal, stood for the ordinary forms of the court; Gardiner preferred an older and disused form; and so far the Cardinal had the advantage. The next day, March 25, the ambassadors went to the Pope, but the Pope declined to speak or allow them to discuss the matter in his presence, because Cardinal Pucci, who was then ill, had not given his opinion.

At three o'clock the next day, March 26, the three agents of the king, on their admission to the Pope's chamber, found there with His Holiness the Cardinal Pucci and three other Cardinals. When they had all sat down, by direction of the Pope, the Dean of the Rota, Simoneta, was sent for—"a man of good gravity," says Gardiner, "and, as it seemeth, substantial learned." Dr. Stephen Gardiner found no good reason for changing that opinion.

The Cardinal *Sanctorum Quatuor Coronatorum* proved to be a stronger man than Dr. Gardiner, and now the question before the Pope was, not the substance of the commission, but the form in which it should issue. Accordingly this was now debated, and when Cardinal Pucci and the Dean of the Rota had spoken, the Pope bade Dr. Gardiner answer them. "And so I did," says

Gardiner, "to their good satisfaction;"[1] but the Cardinals may have had a different opinion.

It seems that for the present the Cardinals said no more, and Dr. Gardiner considered, because they were silent, that he was to have the commission drawn up in the form he proposed, but which was a form not then in use. And further, according to Gardiner's account, the Pope himself consented to adopt the old form, "and only rested to know the opinion of learned men whether the particular causes expressed in the commission may be justified to be sufficient for a divorce or not. And therefore willed the said Symonet to look his book, and to have conference with us."[2] But for all this, Gardiner is forced to say that, after "conference" with the Dean of the Rota, he had only "good hope that we shall somewhat remove the Pope's Holiness from the respect of the style."

Thus, then, on the 26th of March, after much disputation, Gardiner was not one step nearer his end. He had but "good hope," and he would not have had that consolation had he not been so overbearing and self-confident.

The next day was the day of the conference with the Dean of the Rota. "All this day," writes Dr. Gardiner, "from seven of the clock in the morning to dinner-time, and after dinner till it was night, the said Simonet, Dean of the Rote, hath been with us." But nothing was done, and the Dean of the Rota took his leave of them, having refused to yield in the slightest degree, notwithstanding their importunity; he would not change the ordinary processes of the court.

[1] Pocock, *ut supra*, p. 106.

[2] Ibid.

"On the morrow," says Gardiner, which was Saturday, March 28, "we went to the Cardinal de Monte," who was also most courteous, and praised Henry VIII., "much extolling the king's merits and your grace's towards the See Apostolic and them. . . . Finally he said what he might do in furthering the king's matter, which we showed unto him at length, it was his duty to do it, as a member of the See Apostolic." But he did not say what that was which he "might do." Gardiner was too sanguine, the Cardinal had promised nothing.

The next day was Passion Sunday, and the Pope having, after dinner, heard the opinions of the Cardinals Pucci and del Monte, and of the Dean of the Rota, admitted the king's agents into his presence, and "willed me, Stephen Gardiner, to ask what we desired." Gardiner spoke, and said in substance that he desired a commission to dissolve the marriage of Henry and Catherine. It was useless now to attempt to hide the real purport of their embassy to the Pope, as the archdeacon of Chester had been instructed to do. The archdeacon had asked for a commission to try the validity of the dispensation granted by Pope Julius II. As that commission was never executed, and was pronounced by Henry to be of no use to him, it became then impossible to hide, even under the processes of the law, the real nature of the king's demands. Gardiner now threatened to settle the matter in England without respect to the Pope,[1] and his insolence seems to have surprised even the Cardinals, who had already had some experience of him. "When I had thus spoken, with many more

[1] The words he confesses to have uttered may be seen in note 1, bk. i. chap. vii. p. 39, below.

words sounding to that purpose, every man looked on other, and so stayed." Well they might, for here was a priest in the presence of the Pope asking favours, and at the same time breaking out into unseemly threats against the jurisdiction, the powers of which he pretended to respect, and of which he professed to have need.

Cardinals Pucci and del Monte asked him "to be content with a commission containing no special causes, with promise of confirmation, which should serve the king's purpose. And therein should be no difficulty made."

The offer thus made by the Cardinals was not accepted by Gardiner, because his instructions required him to obtain from the Pope, not a commission to try the validity of the marriage, but a commission to dissolve it. Moreover, he was to obtain that dissolution from the Pope himself, not through the hands of Legates or other judges, from whose sentence, if adverse to her, the queen was certain to appeal. In that state of things the promise of confirmation could not be legally performed.

Gardiner in his letter assumes that the Pope and the Cardinals were ready to dissolve the marriage, and that they were restrained from doing so, not by any sense of justice, but by their dread of the emperor. He twisted a promise of confirmation of the sentence to be passed in England into "a plain confession," as he says, "that our cause was good, or else it ought not to be confirmed. Wherefore between our desire and their offer is only difference of time."

That is the way he justifies his importunities, as if the promise to confirm a sentence which is to be pronounced legally according to justice, and which all must presume, at least until delivered, to be an upright sentence, were the same thing with giving a sentence before the hearing of the cause. The promise of the Cardinals to confirm the sentence was a promise to confirm not an unjust sentence, but a lawful sentence, and Gardiner knew it to be so, for he refused the offer; such an offer was of no use to the king his master, because there was not the slightest intention in England to pronounce sentence according to justice.

On this day, Passion Sunday, Clement VII., with unwearied patience and the most generous forbearance, listened to the discussion held in his presence, and at the end said "that all that which with his honour he might do, he would do it gladly without tract or difficulty."[1] In other words, he would even change the forms of his court, and shorten the process; he would do everything but trench on the substance of justice.

But Dr. Gardiner—and if he had not confessed it himself, people might reasonably doubt the story—said in reply to the Pope these words:—

"That which was not honourable for His Holiness to grant, was not honourable to be desired on the king's behalf. So as in this matter, if honour should be touched, it should be touched in them both. And it is not to be supposed that the king's highness, who hitherto hath had such respect of his honour, conserved and defended the same above all other princes, would now, in conducing this matter to effect, do anything that should stain or blemish the same, or that your grace

[1] Pocock, i. p. 111.

[Cardinal Wolsey], who hath such consideration, both to the king's honour, as his subject, and to the See Apostolic, as member of the same, would be counsellor or minister in anything that should be dishonourable to both or either of them."

Dr. Gardiner wrote this to Cardinal Wolsey, who knew of the money sent to Venice for evil usage, and he said it in the presence of Cardinal Pucci, to whom he knew that two thousand crowns had been offered by way of bribe by the archdeacon of Chester.

The Pope hearing the king's ambassadors constantly saying that the only difficulty raised against the issuing of the commission was "the style and manner of late in every common cause used," said that he would "set apart all style and common course of the court which could be no law to him." The sovereign Pontiff is not bound by the forms of his own courts; he can change them when he will, and so when Gardiner urged upon him that he was asking for nothing unjust, and then said that his request was refused upon no grounds of justice, but of mere form, the Pope took him at his word, and said that if it be so, the forms of the court shall be changed.

"Finally, the Pope's Holiness said," writes Gardiner, "*if in the law* these causes may be ground just and sufficient to maintain a sentence of divorce, he will make such a commission, any style or use to the contrary notwithstanding. Adding thereunto, that if the emperor should grudge thereat, he cared not therefore, and having matter to defend *justiciam causarum*, he would by Breve signify to the emperor and the world that *in modo administrandæ justiciæ* he of duty ought to show all favour and grace to the king's highness for his manifold merits; and so he would. Wherefore His Holiness said he would hear what the Cardinal *de Monte* and the Cardinal Anconitane, unto whom he writeth in post, will say in these matters; and hearing their judgments, he would shortly satisfy our requests and desires. And then devise with us upon sending a Cardinal, and who should be most meet for that purpose."[1]

The Pope was willing to do all he could do for the king, but he would not do anything against the law under which the marriage had been made, for the queen had rights as well as the king. But if the forms of the law could be changed without wrong to the queen, the Pope said he would change them because Gardiner maintained in his presence that those forms kept the king from his just rights. Gardiner knew it was not so, and he pressed the Pope to make haste, but the Pope would not be hurried, "knowing of what moment and importance the matter is."

The Pope now dismissed them. They had been three hours pleading their cause before him, and so they sent home their account by "my lord Rochford's priest," the chaplain of Sir Thomas Boleyn, Thomas Cranmer.

This was the state of the question on Passion Sunday, March 29, 1528.

Cranmer left Orvieto on the following Wednesday, April 1, 1528, and on the same day Gardiner, Fox,[2] and

[1] Pocock, i. pp. 111, 112.

[2] According to Le Neve (ed. Hardy, iii. p. 683), Edward Fox was on this day elected provost of King's College, Cambridge, but according to Tanner, December 28, at the end of the year.

Sir Gregory went to the Pope and pressed him "to resolve himself without delay or difficulty," for they had sent to Cardinal Wolsey, they said, a letter, in which they announced the successful issue of their mission. They therefore claimed the performance of the promise which the Pope had made. Clement VII. knew as well as they did all that he had promised, and he knew too that he had not promised anything which favoured the king more than the queen. So he told them now that the matter "consisted in the knowledge of the law, whereof he is ignorant, and must needs therefore depend upon the resolution of them which be learned in that faculty."[1]

Gardiner urged haste, and a decision in his favour, but the Pope merely replied "he would do all things not contrary to justice."

The Pope had never promised to do that which Gardiner represented him as having promised; that is clear from Gardiner's letter. But the man had raised hopes in England which were not sure to be realised, hence the importunity. He made it even a matter of complaint against His Holiness that he had himself sent a report home too highly coloured. He "trusted His Holiness would give credence to the king's books," that is, he would have the Pope give sentence against the queen without hearing what she had to say in defence of her marriage.

Clement VII. always said that he would do all he could for the king; but he also always added, that he would do nothing beyond or beside the law. Catherine's claims upon his justice and his grace were as strong and

[1] A letter of Gardiner, Fox, and Casali, dated April 13, 1527, published by Mr. Pocock, Records, i. p. 120.

as clear as were those of Henry. His answer to Gardiner was that he must advise with those who were learned in the law; he would not make the law for the occasion; he was the common judge of all the faithful.

Gardiner finding him immovable in his resolve, tried to purchase justice by a promise of the "inestimable treasure of the king's good mind for recovery of the authority of the See Apostolic, with maintenance of the same." Clement VII. gently replied "he would do the best he could," and turned away from the priest, who did not remember to whom he was speaking. That very night Stafileo, who was believed in England to be in favour of the divorce, came to Orvieto. The next morning Gardiner and his colleagues called upon him and desired his help to obtain the commission, which was to "be directed to your grace [Cardinal Wolsey] alone, or jointly to you and another Legate."

Stafileo had received other instructions from Henry himself; it is probable that the king had discovered that the Cardinal was not so zealous for the divorce as he had been. Anne Boleyn and her friends were not friends of the Cardinal, and the Cardinal had none; the duke of Norfolk, her uncle, hated him, and others were then about the court ready to strike him if they had but the opportunity; but be that as it may, the king instructed Stafileo to obtain a commission directed not to Wolsey. Stafileo told the ambassadors that it was not in his instructions to ask for a commission directed to the Cardinal, "but expressly the contrary;" and the reason the king gave him for thus putting the Cardinal on one side was, that the queen "might and would" decline the jurisdiction.

On the 3d of April, "the Friday before Palm Sunday, the Pope's Holiness appointed *solemnem consessum* of the Cardinals de Monte and *Sanctorum Quatuor*, Staphileus, us, and the Dean of the Rota, to dispute and reason on the king's matter."[1] The Cardinals were still of the old opinion, and the Pope bade Dr. Gardiner answer their reasons, who, according to his account, showed them to be groundless, convincing even the Pope himself that justice lay with the king. But Gardiner's words and Gardiner's doings are not quite consistent, for he threatened the Pope if he did not consent, and laboured to terrify him, though he had convinced him. He also upbraided the Pope with the services of the king rendered to the Holy See, thus unrequited and despised. The Pope was patient under the insult, and the Cardinals kept silence; the effrontery of the speaker must have taken them by surprise. "These words were patiently heard of all parties," says Gardiner, "but nothing answered to them directly; and so the day being then spent, the Pope's Holiness did arise."

The next day, April 4, they "returned unto the Pope's Holiness, and spake roundly unto him." Their language must have been more insolent than on the day before, but they were speaking the language of Henry VIII. and Cardinal Wolsey, for Gardiner says that he spoke "as our instructions purporteth, and to that point that the king's highness would do it without him." This was said by a priest to the Pope: it was a threat of schism.

[1] Pocock, i. p. 124.

Clement VII. was patient even under this impertinence. According to Gardiner, his only answer was, "Would it were done, and to the other words nothing, but sighed and wiped his eyes." Gardiner was neither moved by the distress of the Pope nor frightened by his own disorderly demeanour. Nevertheless he seems to have understood the Pope, for he does not recommend the king to divorce the queen and marry another, knowing well that if that were done the process would be short, and the sentence certain, against his master.

At this time Clement VII. told the ambassadors in plain words, without any sort of disguise, that he could not grant their request, as, in fact, he never did. These are his words, according to the report of Dr. Gardiner :—

"In a matter *in qua vertitur jus tercii* he could do nothing without the counsel of them, and wished that it were in his power to give the king's highness somewhat depending only of his own particular hurt or damage, without touching any other man's right, with suchlike words; nothing sounding to the furtherance: but found ourselves in utter desperation."[1]

Gardiner and his friends at last understood that the Pope, however ready or even desirous to please the king, would not please him by wrong-doing. The queen had rights as well as the king, and the princess Mary had rights also, which were not to be taken away merely because it pleased her father to do so.

The ambassadors now changed their course. They had resolved, if they should fail to obtain the commission in the first form, to ask for a general commission; and so

[1] Pocock, i. p. 127.

Sir Gregory Casali, "speaking familiarly with the Pope's Holiness, said"—so he writes—"as of myself that I would know of my colleagues whether they will be content to take a general commission so His Holiness pass in secret manner the Decretal Commission." The Pope replied he might do so, and that he would himself "consider that matter."

The next day, which was Palm Sunday, they went again to the Pope, giving him but little time to consider the matter. However, when they were admitted to his presence they found that the Pope had considered it. He would not grant any commission that was to be kept secret; he must act openly, for if the commission was according to justice, it ought to be made public. Gardiner attempted to answer His Holiness as usual, without the least respect for him, but the Pope neither replied to him nor granted his request. "We could get none answer," he wrote to Cardinal Wolsey, "but so departed."[1]

The king's ambassadors having utterly failed to obtain the commission in the form they preferred, and which they had been instructed to press for, were now compelled to accept it in the form in which the Cardinals, whom the Pope consulted, were willing to grant it.

The difficulty had been foreseen and provided against in England, and Dr. Gardiner, driven to accept the general commission, set himself at once "to the devising of a general commission for a Legate, with such clauses as be contained" in his instructions. When he had done his work, he and his companions "showed the

[1] Pocock, i. p. 128.

commission" which he "had devised to Simonet, as the Pope's Holiness appointed" them. "For in these causes," he said, "His Holiness would of himself do nothing for anything we could do." The Dean of the Rota said the commission was good, "saving in the latter end," but it was too florid, and Gardiner expressed his willingness to correct his style.

The Dean of the Rota informed the Cardinal *Sanctorum Quatuor* of the commission, and on the next day, April 6, when the three ambassadors went to that Cardinal, they were told, even before they read it to him, "that it could not be granted." It was not for the sick man to tell the physician what remedies the latter should prescribe. But Dr. Gardiner insisted on it that the sick man knew his own disease in this case, and hath "knowledge in physic," and so "read unto him the commission by us devised." But as the Dean of the Rota objected to the latter part, so now the Cardinal *Sanctorum Quatuor* objected to the first part, and told the ambassadors that "it was ordered by the Pope's Holiness" that they should go to the Cardinal del Monte.

To the Cardinal del Monte they went, and with him they found the Cardinal *Sanctorum Quatuor*, the Dean of the Rota, and the prothonotary Gambara. They read the commission again, but they were not allowed now to dispute with the Cardinals. They were ordered to withdraw, the commission would be settled without them, and most certainly against them.

Gardiner and his companions now could do nothing: they were not allowed to dispute with the Cardinals or with the Pope. "All that afternoon," says Gardiner, "and the next day till it was night, we could not by any means possible know what they had done." Nevertheless they were not idle, and certainly they were not civil, for they "went now to the Pope, from the Pope to them;" but receiving no information, they "finally sent for Simonet, and desired him to show what was done. He said he was sworn he should show" them "nothing."

Late the next day, which was April 7, and "Tuesday after Palm Sunday, about two hours before night," they went to the Pope, who then showed them the commission as it would be issued. It did not please the ambassadors, and Gardiner insulted the Pope anew, saying that "His Holiness having mind to delude and delay us, had chosen these men as instruments." And he said this, he writes, "with as sore words as I could devise." Clement VII., unmoved by this insolence, replied calmly that he "must needs use other men's counsels."

Nothing could be more reasonable, for the Pope was not a lawyer versed in the intricate processes of the law, but being the judge, he would not let Gardiner filch the queen's rights from her when the queen could not speak in her own defence.

The Pope, however, offered Gardiner to accept the form which he had devised, if the Dean of the Rota would say that there "was nothing contrary to justice" in it. The Dean was sent for, and when he came was silent; he would not answer without consulting the Cardinals. "It was then two hours within night." The ambassadors had been four hours with the Pope. But Gardiner was not weary, so he disputed with the Dean, and "trusting by importunity to have obtained our purpose, tarried with the Pope's Holiness five hours within night, which after the counting of the clock there was one of the clock after midnight, at which time we departed with none other resolution but that the day following, before dinner, we should have a certain answer whereunto to rest."

On Wednesday, April 8, they went to the Pope "two hours before dinner-time," taking with them "books of the law" out of which they proposed to prove that their demands were lawful, and that the Cardinals who opposed them were unreasonable. At last the Cardinals consented to hear the commission as proposed by Gardiner read, and made their corrections, to which the ambassadors assented, "saving in certain points." At "two of the clock at afternoon" they went away, having received a promise that they should have a commission to their "good contentment." But that is the statement of Gardiner.

It is possible that Gardiner was too sanguine, and misinterpreted or misunderstood the Cardinals, for he has himself admitted that some of the corrections were not pleasing to him.

That night they went again to the Pope, "and then finding our minute altered," says Gardiner, "from that was agreed on before, began a new disputation with Simonet, the Cardinals being absent." Gardiner says here that the Cardinals had not kept their word; he doubtless thought so, but it is lawful for others to think that he has made a mistake, for in the course of this most disagreeable process there is no trace other than this, if this be one, of any double-dealing or unfairness of any kind on the part of the Cardinals and others with whom Gardiner had to treat.

In this "disputation" with the Dean of the Rota the differences were reduced to two words. "We differed," says Gardiner, "but in two words in the whole commission: as the sign universal *omnem* to be added to *potestatem*, and the word *nolente* to the clause *nolente aut impedito.*"[1] The Dean of the Rota would not give way to Gardiner's demands "without the advice of the Cardinals."

The Pope, willing to do all he could, and not regarding the impertinence of the ambassadors, though it was late at night, sent the Dean of the Rota and the prothonotary Gambara to ask the opinion of the Cardinals "upon those words." "The Cardinals," says Gardiner, "sent word that they were making collation, and on the morrow would look their books therein."

Hereupon Gardiner lost his temper, or pretended to do so, and told the Pope that the Cardinals whom he trusted had "nothing done in correcting the commission, of learning, but only of ignorance and suspicion;" and then insulted the Pope, saying that he (Gardiner) "took all this done as done by His Holiness' commandment, *qui oculos habet et non videt;*" and finally threatened the Pope with the loss of "the favour" of Henry VIII. and the ruin of the Holy See.

The Pope was greatly disturbed—so says Gardiner—and well he might; but his enemy has not recorded a

[1] The clause was as follows: "Vobis conjunctim, et, altero vestrûm nolente aut impedito, divisim, citra omnem personæ aut jurisdictionis gradum, omni recusatione et appellatione remotis, vices et omnem auctoritatem nostram committimus et demandamus."

single word uttered in haste on the part of Clement VII. His Holiness was patient and forbearing in the presence of most detestable meanness, and when he recovered himself from the distress into which the language of Gardiner had plunged him, he consented that the two words about which the dispute turned now should be put into the commission. It being then "an hour past midnight," the Pope was delivered from the presence of the king's ambassadors.

The commission, all disputing over, was drawn up and directed to Cardinal Wolsey, who was to be assisted in the execution of it by the archbishop of Canterbury, or any other of the English bishops; the word *omnem* was inserted in the clause *auctoritatem nostram committimus*, according to Gardiner's wishes, but the other word *nolente* was not inserted, because the commission was directed to Cardinal Wolsey, and because it was necessary that he alone should pronounce the sentence.

The commission was "not in all points" that which Gardiner desired, and as it had been drawn up by him in pursuance of the instructions he had received, nevertheless he thought it would answer the purpose. He had proposed to insert a clause in it to the effect that the Pope would confirm the sentence of the Legate, and refuse to call the cause up into his own court. But in this he failed.

The commission was sealed April 13, 1528.[1] Gardiner went at once to Rome to see Cardinal Campeggio, and Fox set out for England, carrying with him the

[1] Mr. Tierney has printed it from Rymer in his Dod., vol. i. p. 361.

commission which had been obtained with so much difficulty.

Fox landed at Sandwich on Saturday night, May 2, 1528. "The day following being Sunday," he says in a letter to Gardiner,[1] "I made all diligence possible towards Greenwich, where the king lay." And in Greenwich the first message from the king to him was "to go unto Mistress Anne's chamber."

The man went, he was a priest, and told Anne Boleyn that he had obtained the commission, under which the Cardinal of York was to dissolve the marriage of Henry and Catherine that Anne Boleyn might be queen of England, yet never the lawful wife of the king. Henry gave him time to tell his story, and then "came into the same chamber, after whose entry she [Anne] departed." Having welcomed his chaplain, he bade him at once "to show him what was done in his cause." The chaplain told him that the Pope would not say that the first marriage was invalid, but yet had granted a commission to the Cardinal of York to try the question, which he believed would satisfy the king; whereupon the king "made marvellous demonstrations of joy, calling in Mistress Anne, and causing me [Fox] to repeat the same thing again before her."[2] There was no shame in the palace of the king at Greenwich.

Whether the king was a better lawyer than Fox, or was more cautious, is not clear—anyhow he bade his chaplain tell his story to the Cardinal, for the king would have my "lord's grace's judgment in that weighty matter."

[1] Pocock, i. p. 141.

[2] Ibid., p. 144.

Fox, who had reached Greenwich at five o'clock, must now go on to London, for the Cardinal, who had spent the Sunday as usual in the court, had left two hours before the arrival of the chaplain. He reached Durham Palace at ten o'clock, and though the Cardinal was in bed he was admitted at once into his presence, and the Cardinal heard from him all that had been done at Orvieto. The Cardinal of York had more at stake in this matter than Fox had, and was not so easily satisfied.

"His grace seemed marvellously perplexed," says Fox, "thinking this commission to be of no better value than that was sent by Gambara."[1] The poor chaplain was dismissed, the Cardinal bidding him to "depart for the night, and to leave behind the said commission."

The Cardinal read the commission on the morning of Monday, May 4, 1528, and when he had mastered its meaning, "and his high wisdom well considered and pondered the same," he sent in the afternoon for his lawyer, "Master Dr. Bell," and Fox "to read the same before him, and in the presence of my lord of Rochford," who was the father of Anne Boleyn, and indecently earnest in furthering the divorce. They were all of one mind that the commission would do their work, and so they separated in good spirits.

But on Wednesday the Cardinal consulted more lawyers, "Dr. Wolman, Dr. Benett, and other," and the issue of that consultation was not so satisfactory as that was at which Sir Thomas Boleyn was present. The matter was not so clear now, and the Cardinal began to see and to feel that the burden was laid on his shoulders,

[1] Pocock, i. p. 145.

not on those of the Pope, where he had proposed to place it.

Fox thereupon was instructed to direct Gardiner to press for the Decretal Commission which had been first asked for, and which the Pope had absolutely refused to grant.

On Saturday the Cardinal's difficulties seemed to have grown, he by that time being "perfectly informed," says Fox, by some of her counsel, that the queen was about to renounce any advantage she might have by the second Brief of Julius II., "refusing to enter the disputation of the validity of the same," and to rest her cause on the first Brief only. In order to meet this, the Cardinal directed Gardiner to find out from men learned in the law whether the marriage might not be declared null, because the impediment of public decency was not in terms removed.[1] The Cardinal was bent on breaking the marriage, but he wished to do so with a good conscience, if that were possible, intending, says Fox[2]—

"In this cause of so high consequence, wherein dependeth the wealth or ruin of this realm, the conservation of his honour, or else immortal ignominy and slander, the damnation of his soul, or else everlasting merit, to proceed according to due order of justice, and to ground and firm his conscience upon so perfect and infallible rule of equity, that before God he may count himself discharged."

In this mind the Cardinal desired Fox to write to Gardiner, and direct him to ascertain whether the Cardinal, whom Gardiner had assured the Pope to be

1 Pocock, Records, i. p. 150. See the objection as put by the lawyers of the king afterwards, pp. 62, 96.

2 Ibid., p. 151.

impartial, could annul the marriage on the ground that the dispensation which made it lawful had been issued without the knowledge of the king. It is incredible that he can have been ignorant that the king's knowledge of the existence of the dispensation was an utterly irrelevant fact, perfectly immaterial to the issue. The Cardinal must have been by this time, even if he ever had any doubts, thoroughly aware that the marriage was simply unassailable, otherwise he could not have had recourse to these flimsy excuses for the doing of a great wrong. He knew he was shortly to sit in judgment in a public court as judge, nevertheless in the meantime he was the advocate of the plaintiff, searching out the means whereby he might deliver judgment in his favour, and against the defendant, who, though the queen of England, was then a helpless woman in the power of a merciless husband resolved to be rid of her at any cost. On this matter the king and the Cardinal were of one mind, and probably had no secrets from each other.

"Yesterday, to my great marvel," writes Fox to Gardiner,[1] "and no less joy and comfort, his grace [the Cardinal] openly, in presence of Mr. Tuke, Mr. Wolman, Mr. Bell, and me [Fox], made protestation to the king's highness, that although he was so much bound unto the same as any subject might to his prince, and by reason thereof his grace was of so perfect devotion, faith, and loyalty towards his majesty, that he could gladly spend goods, blood, and life in his just causes: yet sith his grace was more obliged to God, and that he was sure he should render an account *de operibus suis* before

[1] Pocock, i. p. 153.

Him, he would in this matter rather suffer his high indignation, yea, and his body jointly to be torn in pieces, than he would do anything in this cause otherwise than justice requireth; ne that his highness should look after other favour to be ministered unto him in this cause, on his grace's part, than the justness of the cause would bear. But if the Bull were sufficient, he would so pronounce it, and rather suffer *extrema quæque* than to do the contrary, or else *contra conscientiam suam*."

Cardinal Wolsey spoke thus to the king, who knew that he was the first to move in the divorce, in the presence of Fox, who knew that he desired it, and who was to repeat the words to Dr. Gardiner, privy to all the secrets of the Cardinal, and whom the Cardinal had recommended to Clement VII. as his "other half."

The more the commission was considered by the lawyers the less it was liked. There was one clause in it which filled them with fear: Cardinal Wolsey was directed to discharge his duties under the commission *prout animo conscientiæque tuæ juris ratio persuaserit*. Now *juris ratio*, said the lawyers, allows the queen the right to "appeal at her good pleasure and liberty from whatsoever decree or sentence, either interlocutory or definitive, she will," and thereby prolong the litigation, "and finally frustrate the king's expectation, to the utter and extreme peril of all those that have intermeddled them in this cause."

The result of this consultation was an order from the king to Gardiner to obtain ampler powers for the Legate, and to threaten the Pope with the revolt of England from the obedience of His Holiness if those powers were not granted. Then, to make matters certain, Dr. Gardiner was told that the king thought he had been negligent in his master's service; he must therefore, if he would recover the king's good graces, obtain the Commission Decretal, and also persuade the Pope to send a Legate to England, who with the Cardinal should give sentence in the king's cause.

But the Pope made no further concessions than this, he allowed Cardinal Campeggio, at the request of the king's ambassadors, to be one of the judges with Cardinal Wolsey; and now, in the new commission, the words for which Gardiner had so earnestly contended were inserted, thereby enabling either of the Cardinals in the absence of the other to give sentence in the cause. This commission was issued June 8, 1528, and in virtue of it the Legatine court was held in the following year.

But Cardinal Wolsey was not satisfied; he wished to have larger faculties granted, and also a promise on the part of the Pope that the sentence he should give would never be reversed. He could not obtain any such promise, and Cardinal Campeggio, after long waiting, came to London in the beginning of October 1528, to determine, as men believed, the great dispute in favour of the king, and enable Anne Boleyn to call herself queen of England.

More than this, it was believed also by those who were about the king that the Pope had himself determined the question, and that the Cardinal Legates, when the time came for them to open their court, would sit merely to pronounce the sentence which His Holiness had already pronounced, and recorded in the Decretal Commission, which was believed to be at this time granted, and in the safe keeping of Cardinal Campeggio.

This Decretal Commission, or, as it is also called, *Bulla decretalis*, was asked for in the very beginning of the process. The Cardinal of York begged for it with all earnestness, and it was generally regarded as a thing of the very last consequence, for the king and his ministers seem at times to confess that they had no means of attaining their ends if they could not obtain the Decretal Bull instead of the general commission.

Clement VII. had been most earnestly and pertinaciously asked to grant this Decretal Commission; and on his refusal, asked again to grant it "in secret manner," the king's agents promising not to publish it, "but in case your Holiness do not confirm the sentence;"[1] that is, promising not to publish it unless the Pope died before the end of the trial, for it is not to be supposed that they were asking a favour, and at the same time threatening to use it against the Pope who granted it.

Clement VII. was asked to do a dishonourable act, on the understanding that while he lived he should not be put to open shame. He told them in the beginning "that he must so do as the See Apostolic be not slandered,"[2] and he continued to tell them the same thing to the end.

If the Commission Decretal is a lawful commission, not trespassing on the rights of others, the Pope said he would grant it; but if it involved a breaking of the law, it should not be granted: and as for the secrecy, the Pope did not want that, nor indeed could there be any

[1] Pocock, Records, i. p. 127.

[2] Ibid., p. 106.

secrecy in the matter, so he told the king's agents that if it was to be done it must be done publicly.

Mr. Pocock in his "Records"[1] has printed a letter from Gregorio Casali, in which the writer says that the Pope had promised to grant the Commission Decretal if Cardinal Campeggio would be the bearer of it; that he (Casali) thereupon went to Campeggio, entrapped him to undertake that matter, and then excused himself to the Pope as well as he could for the astuteness of his proceedings. The letter was written June 15, 1528, before Cardinal Campeggio left Rome.

Mr. Pocock[2] has published also another letter on the same matter, written by Gregorio to the duke of Norfolk after the divorce, when his services were no longer wanted, and when he had found out that he had been serving a hard master, who would not, or could not, relieve him. In that letter he says, "I obtained also a Bull Decretal, which was delivered—as the Cardinal of York in the king's name commanded—unto the Cardinal Campegius."

Gregorio Casali magnifies his services to the duke of Norfolk, who had profited by the elevation of his niece and the ruin of the Cardinal of York. He had lost money by his labours, and his letter to the duke of Norfolk is the letter of a man boasting his skill and suggesting rewards. He claims the merit of having obtained the Decretal Bull, but he does not say that he ever saw it.

Now this Commission Decretal had been drawn up in England, and had been presented to the Pope by the archdeacon of Chester, Dr. William Knight, apparently

[1] Vol. i. p. 172.

[2] Records, ii. p. 517.

without a shadow of suspicion that he was the bearer of a most dishonourable request. He probably learned its true nature from Cardinal Pucci when he heard him say "that it could not pass without perpetual dishonour unto the Pope, the king," and Cardinal Wolsey.

Fox confessed to the king at Greenwich[1] that the Commission Decretal, for which he and Gardiner had pressed the Pope so hard, was of so strange a character that the process of the court in London ought not to be founded on it, but rather on the general commission, which left the question of the validity or invalidity of marriages so contracted undetermined. But they wanted to have the Decretal nevertheless, though it was "to be kept secret, and to be shown to no man but only the king's councillors."[2] Still it was to be shown for the furtherance of the king's secret matter, for, says Gardiner, "the said commission in the first form, shown to such as have been of contrary opinion, shall and must satisfy them, and be *regula* to them that shall be judges how to proceed, seeing *rescriptum Pontificis* determining the case. And the second commission shall be that whereupon the jurisdiction shall be grounded to make process in the matter. The said first commission, obtained in secret manner, having none other use but to be seen there privily, shall be *calculus et suffragium Pontificis* in the law, and also *pignus suæ voluntatis et auctoritatis*, that the sentence to be given conformably thereunto shall be confirmed."[3]

The Decretal, then, was a sentence of the Pope "determining the case;" in other words, releasing Henry from

[1] Pocock, Records, i. p. 143.
[2] Ibid., p. 115.
[3] Gardiner's letter, March 31, 1528, Ibid., pp. 115, 116.

the bond of wedlock, if certain facts were once proved. It was to be kept secret on the whole, but communicated to the judges, who were to decide the question before them "conformably thereunto;" that is, the Pope was to deprive the queen of her right by a sentence that she was never to hear, and by means of judges who were not to tell her why her marriage was null.

Gregorio Casali says in this letter that the Pope would grant the Decretal unwillingly—*Pontifex invitus concedet hanc commissionem*—and would have no man know of it, either publicly or privately—*non vult quod sciatur neque palam neque secreto.*

This was written June 15, one week after the issuing of the commission to the two Cardinals, Campeggio and Wolsey, under which they were to try the question between the king and the queen.

Gregorio Casali says that the Pope against his will promised to grant the Bull, and that the Bull was to be kept from the knowledge of all men. Now, if it was to be kept secret, it is difficult to see the use of it. Possibly Gregorio Casali may have written more confidently than he ought. The Pope had hitherto refused the Commission Decretal, and refused also to do anything that was not to be made public.

Three days before Cardinal Campeggio arrived in London, Cardinal Wolsey wrote to Gregorio Casali,[1] instructing him to obtain the Pope's consent to a publication of the Bull which was to be kept secret. He asked for leave to show it to some members of the king's council who were opposed to the Cardinal's doings. He

[1] Pocock, i. p. 174, October 4, 1528.

asked for the Bull, and in doing so promised to show it only to the king, because it was to remain a secret. Now he wishes to free himself of the conditions he had proposed—in a word, to publish the Bull, for if once shown to his adversaries the secret could never be kept. It is not improbable that his end and aim were the publication of the Bull.

It seems, from the Cardinal's words, that it was to him a matter of the utmost moment, not only to possess the Bull, but to be able to show it; for he is most earnest and pathetic in his prayer to do so, saying that he could not pray more fervently to save his life, promising so to use it as to bring no risk, hurt, or hatred to the Pope.[1] If, then, the Cardinal had no misgivings about the justice of his procedure in asking for the Bull, it is hard to find a reason for this fear that the publication of it would be an evil thing for His Holiness.

Cardinal Campeggio then arrived, but whether he had the Bull with him or not is a question; there is no question, however, about this, that he did not deliver it up to Cardinal Wolsey or to Henry VIII. John Casali, in the absence of Gregorio, had an audience of the Pope—he wrote an account of it December 17, 1528[2]—and in the name of Cardinal Wolsey complained that the Bull was not shown in England, though the Pope had promised that it might be shown to the privy councillors by the king and the Cardinal.

The Pope, when he heard this, forbade the speaker to touch upon that matter, for the Cardinal of York, whom he had trusted, had deceived him;[3] "he had given a

[1] Pocock, i. p. 177.

[2] Burnet, Hist. Reform., iv. 64, ed. Pocock.

[3] Ibid., p. 65. "Sub fide ejus se deceptum esse."

Decretal Bull to be shown to the king only, and then to be burnt forthwith."[1] The Pope did this, according to the account of John Casali, to save Cardinal Wolsey from certain destruction, but he never promised to give him leave to show it to any members of the council. Nothing more, he said, was asked of him, and he had the letters of the Cardinal of York to show that it was so;[2] besides, if anything beyond this had been asked, it would not have been granted.

According to John Casali, the Decretal of which Gregorio had obtained the promise was given, but it must be remembered that the words of the Pope are known to us through John Casali. It is probable, perhaps certain, that the Pope spoke in Italian, but the letter is written in Latin, and rests on the fidelity of the writer. The king's ambassadors were instructed from London to say to the Pope things that were not true, and it may well be that these men, in return, did not always tell the truth to their employers. The statement that the Pope granted the Decretal rests on the credit of Gregorio and John Casali, and against this, as will appear further on, is the declaration of Uberto Gambara, bishop elect of Tortona, that the Decretal never was granted.

There is another difficulty raised by this letter of John Casali. He asked leave to show the Bull, and the Pope replied that the Cardinal never asked for a Bull which was to be shown. Three days afterwards the writer makes the same request, and the Pope answers, according to him, in these words :—

[1] Pocock, i. p. 65. "Bullam decretalem dedisse, ut tantum regi ostenderetur concremareturque statim."

[2] Ibid. "Litteras ipsas reverendissimi Eboracensis proferre possum, quibus id tantum, quod dixi, petit."

"The Bull was not asked for on those terms, for it was to be shown to no one but the king and the Cardinal of York, and I hear now from Campeggio that he has done as much: that being so, the Bull, according to the agreement, must be burnt."[1] But the Cardinal's agent still pressed the Pope, and said that the Bull was granted to be shown to certain members of the king's council. The Pope's answer is again that it was not so, he had the letters of the Cardinal of York to show, and then added in his humility, "I am not telling lies."[2]

Even after this John Casali returns to the subject, but is told that the Pope will not allow it to be spoken of, and learns that the Pope had ordered all traces of it to be blotted out of the Papal registers. Again, the Pope is troubled by John Casali, who asked him to find a way by which the Decretal might be shown to some members of the privy council of the king. If all this be true, John Casali must have believed that the Pope had spoken falsely, and that Cardinal Campeggio had written a falsehood in his letters to the Pope. The Decretal, if granted, was at this time not in existence, for it had been burnt: so said Cardinal Campeggio, and so believed the Pope, according to the account of John Casali, who, notwithstanding, presses the Pope to allow a document to be shown to others which the Pope has said is burnt, and which the Pope could not then allow to be shown without convicting Cardinal Campeggio of lying and himself of dishonest dealing. Even now the

[1] Burnet, iv. p. 68. "Hanc Bullam non ea conditione petitam fuisse ut ostenderetur cuiquam, præterquam serenissimo regi et dominationi vestræ reverendissimæ, et Campegium nunc ad se scribere tantundem effecisse: quo facto ex conventione Bullam comburi debere."

[2] Ibid., p. 69. "Nec loquor mendacia."

answer of the Pope, according to John Casali, is, "It cannot be done, and I will not allow it."[1]

Edward Fox, the royal chaplain, wrote a letter at the Cardinal's direction to Dr. Gardiner, dated May 12, 1528, one whole month before Gregorio Casali entrapped the Pope to promise the Decretal, and in that letter are these words:[2]—

"Wherefore, and in consideration of the premisses, his grace [the Cardinal of York] willeth and desireth you that sith his grace intendeth never to make process by virtue thereof [the Bull Decretal], *ne that it shall at any time be published,* or showed to any person in the world, whereby may arise any the least slander, oblique damage, or prejudice to the See Apostolic, or to the Pope's person; with that also his grace intendeth nothing, *but by showing thereof to the king's highness* to acquire such authority and favour of the same as might turn to the singular advancement, inestimable benefit, and perpetual wealth of that See: of which thing his grace willeth also you make faith and promise *in animam suam,* under most sacred oath and obtestation unto His Holiness."

It is plain, then, even from this, that the Cardinal of York had deceived the Pope: he had asked for a Decretal to be kept secret, shown only to the king, and now he, thinking the Decretal had been granted, forgets his promise and the condition, and proposes to show it to many—in short, he proposes to publish it abroad.

Those who were in the service of Henry VIII. speak quite distinctly that the Decretal Bull had been given;

[1] Burnet, iv. p. 71. "Non potest hoc fieri; nec a me impetrari."

[2] Pocock, Records of the Reformation, i. pp. 148, 149.

on the other hand, the Pope speaks, according to the testimony of the king's agents, with less clearness. In the words attributed to him, even by the agents of the king, the existence of the Bull is not so much insisted on as the conditions under which it was asked for. There is no hint of it in the letters of Cardinal Campeggio, published by Laemmer and Theiner.

Then, again, it is not clear that the king ever saw it; but it is clear from his own words that he has given, on two different occasions, different accounts of its disappearance. At one time he says that the Cardinals stole it, at another, that it was burnt.

By an "order taken for preaching and bidding of the beads in all sermons to be made within this realm,"[1] published by Henry VIII. and Cranmer, A.D. 1533, after the marriage with Anne Boleyn, all preachers were to—

"Declare the false and unjust handling of the Bishop of Rome, pretending to have jurisdiction to judge this cause at Rome; which in the first hearing thereof, did both declare and confess in word and writing the justness thereof to be upon our sovereign's side, insomuch as by a Decretal delivered to the Legate here, then sitting for the same cause, he did clearly determine, . . . and so, *eo facto*, pronounced in the foresaid Decretal, the nullity, invalidity, and unlawfulness of their pretensed matrimony, which was by his law sufficient judgment of the cause; which Decretal, by his commandment, after and because he would not have the effect thereof to ensue, was, after the sight thereof, imbesiled by the foresaid Cardinals, and one which then was here his cubicular,

[1] Jenkyns, Cranmer's Remains, iv. p. 254.

contrary to all justness and equity: wherein he hath done our sovereign most extreme wrong."

This is probably the account of the Decretal Commission which the king wished people to believe, and which he regarded as favourable to himself. But he does not say that he himself ever saw the instrument.

Again the king, in a letter to His Holiness, written after the trial in the court of the Legates, thus writes:—

"Never was there any prince so handled by a Pope as your Holiness hath entreated us. First, when our cause was proponed to your Holiness, when it was explicate and declared afore the same; when certain doubts in it were resolved by your counsellors, and all things discussed, it was required that answer might be made thereunto by the order of the law. There was offered a commission, with a promise also that the same commission should not be revoked; and whatsoever sentence should be given, should straight without delay be confirmed. The judges were sent unto us, the promise was delivered unto us, subscribed with your Holiness' hand; which avouched to confirm the sentence, and not to revoke the commission, nor to grant anything else that might let the same: and finally, to bring us in a greater hope, a certain Commission Decretal, defining the cause, was delivered to the judges' hands."[1]

But the king did not say that he saw the commission—he saw the promise, of which more hereafter—and his not saying so is at least to be taken into account; in another part of the same letter he returns to this Commission Decretal, which, he says, the Pope gave "to

[1] Burnet, iv. 171.

the Cardinal Campege to be showed unto us; and after, if it so should seem profitable, to burn it, as afterwards it was done indeed, as we have perceived."[1] Still he does not say that he had seen it.

Cardinal Wolsey also complained, November 1, 1528, in a letter to Gregorio Casali, that Cardinal Campeggio would not trust him with the Decretal,[2] and April 5, 1529, instructed Sir Francis Bryan and Peter Vannes to "labour and insist that the king's highness, as need shall be, may use and enjoy the benefit of the Decretal, being already in my lord Cardinal Campegius' hands."[3]

Now, if the Cardinal of York had seen at this time the Commission Decretal, he could not have said that it was in the hands of Cardinal Campeggio, because he knew that it must have been burnt; for that was the condition under which it was asked for, so says John Casali[4] in his letter, which the Cardinal must have received in the very beginning of the year, and before he wrote this letter.

John Casali says something more: in his letter to Cardinal Wolsey, December 17, 1528, he tells him that the Pope would not listen to any observations about the Decretal, because he had been deceived by the Cardinal of York, who had asked for a Decretal Commission to be kept secret, but who now asked leave to show it to the king's councillors.

If the Decretal Commission, then, had been given at all, it was given before Cardinal Campeggio set out on his journey from Rome, for he was to carry it to England, show it to the king and the Cardinal, and then burn

1 Burnet, iv. p. 172.

2 Letters and Papers, ed. Brewer, iv. pt. ii. 4897.

3 Burnet, Hist. Reform., iv. p. 90.

4 Ibid., 65. "Bullam decretalem dedisse, ut tantum regi ostenderetur, concremareturque statim." See above, p. ci.

it forthwith. The Legate arrived in London, October 7, and if he had such a commission, it is not probable that Henry and Cardinal Wolsey would have allowed him to keep it from them, seeing that they knew the conditions, namely, that the commission was to be shown them and then burnt. If they saw it, it was burnt at once; but if they never saw it, it is probable that the commission never existed. It is not clear that the king ever saw it, and Cardinal Wolsey complained that Cardinal Campeggio would not trust him with it,[1] and he has not said that he ever saw it.

John Casali was instructed to say to the Pope that he (the Pope) had granted the Bull, and that it might be shown to the privy councillors of the king. To this His Holiness replied, that it was not asked for under that condition, but under the condition that it might be shown to the king and Cardinal Wolsey only; and now, says the Pope, according to John Casali, "I hear from Campeggio that he has done as much."[2]

The question here is, whether Cardinal Campeggio showed the Decretal Commission to the king, or satisfied the promise of the Pope in some other way.

Now, in January 1529,[3] Sir Francis Bryan and Peter Vannes, in quest of new Decretals, were at Bologna, entertained there by the prothonotary Gambara, then governor of the city. They asked him whether the Pope was likely to listen to them on the king's behalf, and "grant the most holy and most necessary prayer of

[1] Cardinal Wolsey's words, recited in his letter by John Casali, are (Burnet, iv. 69, ed. Pocock): "Nullo pacto adduci vult Campegius] ut mihi suo collegæ commissionem hanc decretalem credat."

[2] Ibid., p. 68. "Et Campegium ad se scribere tantundem effecisse."

[3] Pocock, Records, i. p. 198.

the king without thwarting it secretly." The prothonotary, replying probably to the latter words only, said there was not the slightest doubt of it. "Then," said Vannes, "if we shall find the Pope thus disposed, we shall secure the king's ends." Gambara answered, "I think you will obtain everything *except the Decretals.*" The answer of Vannes is, "If so, the Pope will do nothing, for the Decretals are necessary for the king." The prothonotary then told them that after the departure of Dr. Stephen Gardiner, who with Gregorio Casali had wrung from the Pope the promise of the first Decretal, His Holiness had consulted the Cardinals Pucci and Simonetti—he had done so throughout—and was by them advised that no such Decretal could issue. This is the account of Sir Francis Bryan and of Peter Vannes, given in their letter to Cardinal Wolsey.

The prothonotary had been in England, for he was the bearer of the first commission, obtained by Dr. Knight, and not improbably perfectly well acquainted with the progress of the king's affairs. He certainly believed that the Decretal Commission was never issued, and in the strength of that belief told Sir Francis Bryan that the new Decretals then applied for would also be refused in the same way.

But admitting that the Decretal Commission was at any time in the hands of Cardinal Campeggio, it was either held back by him, or if shown to the Cardinal of York, was found insufficient by that Cardinal for his purpose. The Cardinal complains that Cardinal Campeggio would not intrust it to him, and he does not say that he ever saw it. The king says that Cardinal Campeggio held it, and said that it was stolen and burnt, but he does not say that he saw it.

This, however, is clear, the Decretal Commission, if it ever existed, was so drawn up as to be useless to Cardinal Wolsey, for in April 1529 he entreats Gardiner, Sir Francis Bryan, and the others to devise some way to release him from his trouble by obtaining some instrument by which the Pope might be made a party consenting to the divorce. "And therefore," he says,[1] "at the reverence of Almighty God, bring us out of this perplexity, that this virtuous prince may have his thing sped to the purpose desired, which shall be the most joyous thing that this day on earth may chance, and succeed to my heart." Here, then, within one month of the trial, we have a clear confession that the Pope had granted nothing which could be twisted into any admission on his part that the king's marriage was otherwise than valid and lawful.

In the instructions[2] given to Sir William Paget, the king says that Clement VII. gave to the Legates "one other special commission, in form of a Decretal: wherein the said Bishop of Rome pronounced and gave sentence that the king's highness' matrimony was utterly nought and unlawful, and that therefore his highness might *convolare ad secundas nuptias.*"

If the Pope did grant the Decretal in the terms suggested by the king, the controversy is ended, and the marriage of Anne Boleyn was lawful. If the Decretal was ever drawn up in Rome, Gregorio Casali, who says

[1] Burnet, Hist. Reform., iv. p. 88, ed. Pocock.

[2] A.D. 1533. Ibid., vi. p. 96, ed. Pocock.

he obtained the promise of it from the Pope, must have known something of it. If Cardinal Wolsey saw it but for a moment, that was enough: he might have pronounced sentence of divorce without fear. If the king believed that Cardinal Campeggio brought over with him a Decretal Commission by which the Pope declared his marriage "utterly nought and unlawful," it is most difficult to explain the doings and sayings of the king and the Cardinal of York after the arrival of Cardinal Campeggio. They no doubt expected a Decretal, and they believed perhaps that Cardinal Campeggio brought it; but it is quite certain that they did not know the effect of it, and as certain that they applied for another commission with larger powers after the arrival of Cardinal Campeggio. The decretal, therefore, if it existed, was of no service; but if it had been of the kind described by the king, that was enough, the Pope had really determined the question, and the marriage of Henry and Catherine was never good. But then neither Henry nor the Cardinal ever acted as if that were true.

The Cardinal of York had not been "perfectly informed" by the queen's lawyer, who so far betrayed his trust that the queen would renounce all the advantage she had by the second Brief of Julius II. On the 13th day of October, four months after that information, she demanded the production of the Brief. On the 7th of November she renounced the benefit of a clause in it, but that was because it was not necessary, and because the clause was put in to all appearance *ex abundant cautela*, seeing that the queen protested always, and maintained on oath, and was never contradicted by the king, that she never had contracted affinity with him.

Now this second Brief of Julius II. was so clear that while it stood there was no way open to the Cardinal to his end. Hence it became necessary to say it had been forged, but after a time it was found impossible to assail the Brief in that way. Accordingly a letter[1] was written in London, in the name of the two Cardinals, Legates of the Holy See, in which confession is made that the Brief could not be touched, and that the Pope only could declare it a forgery.

That Brief left no means of escape. The Cardinal of York, therefore, denies that there were any traces of it in the records of the realm, and maintains the improbability that any one could have foreseen the dispute twenty years before, and have provided against it, as it is provided in the second Brief of Julius II. The Cardinal was unjust to the lawyers of Henry VII. Mr. Pocock[2] has printed a letter of Ferdinand, the queen's father, written at Barcelona, August 23, 1503, in which the king says that the English lawyers, for the sake of shutting the door against all discussion of the invalidity of the marriage, required the insertion of the words which covered the possible affinity of Henry and Catherine.

Though the Brief was unassailable in itself, the Cardinal of York need not have troubled himself about it if the Pope had granted the Decretal. This application, therefore, to the Pope, to be made by the two Legates,

[1] Burnet, Hist. Reform., iv. p. 102, ed. Pocock.

[2] Records of the Reform., ii. p. 427. "Ha parecido a los letrados de Ingleterra, . . . porquitar toda duda para adelante en la succession de los hijos . . . que agora seha asentado se deve dezir en la dispensacion que consumaron el matrimonio."

is another and perfect confession that no such Decretal was ever issued.

The second alleged grievance of the king, the violation of a promise, comes now to be considered. The king in his last letter to the Pope, already referred to, says that His Holiness had promised to confirm the sentence of the Legates, not to quash the commission, nor to stop the process before it came to its legal ending. Of this promise, he says that it was "delivered unto us subscribed with your Holiness' hand."

This is the "pollicitation" of which so much has been said, and by which it is believed that the Pope Clement bound himself to do the will of Henry VIII. The king himself instructs Sir William Paget to speak of it to the foreign powers to whom Henry sent him in these terms:

"And at time of sending of the said commission he [the Pope] sent also down unto the king's highness a Breve written with his own hand: wherein he did also approve the justice of the king's cause, in like manner as he did in his Commission Decretal; and promised unto the king's highness, *quam sanctissime sub verbo pontificis,* that he would never afterward advocate the said cause out of the realm of England, but would suffer it to have the due course and order of entreating of the same within the king's highness' realm; which his sentence and promise [notwithstanding], yet the said Bishop of Rome, contrary to his own conscience and knowledge, what was the very truth and justice in the king's highness' cause, and to the extent he might molest and trouble the same, decreed out sundry citations," &c.

Here the king says that the Pope sent him a "Breve written with his own hand;" and it may be supposed, though he does not say so, that the king received and saw the "Breve;" nevertheless there are reasons for doubting the accuracy of the statement thus made by the king, and it is certainly probable that he did not carefully consider the contents of the "Breve," or that he misunderstood it.

There remains, then, the "pollicitation," or promise of the Pope to confirm the sentence of the Legates, and as the sentence of the Legates is always taken to be in favour of the king, it is said that the Pope promised to annul the marriage. Now, if His Holiness made that promise in the terms of the "pollicitation," which lord Herbert[1] published and Burnet[2] copied from him, the king could not complain of the Pope, for in that instrument the invalidity of his marriage was so far secured for him that there was nothing left but the sentence of the Legates; and that once pronounced, there was the promise of the Pope not only to confirm that sentence, but to defend it. This promise was drawn up in London, but there is, however, no proof that this was the promise which the king received, "subscribed" with the hand of His Holiness, on the 23d day of July 1528, as the document purports to be.

But if that be the "pollicitation," and if the Pope signed it, Cardinal Wolsey did not think it sufficient, and it is not to be supposed that the Cardinal allowed a document to pass, which should prove worthless, after

[1] Life of Henry VIII., p. 249.
[2] Hist. Reform., vi. p. 26, ed. Pocock.

the Pope had signed it, and therefore it is most reasonable to believe that the "pollicitation" which the Pope signed was couched in other terms.

On the 21st of April 1529, Sir Francis Bryan sends an account of his doings to Henry VIII., and confesses that the Pope would not consent to do that which the king desired of him.

"Were I to write otherwise," says Bryan,[1] "I should put you in hope where none is; and whoever has told you that he [the Pope] will, has not done you, I think, the best service. There is no man more sorry to write this news than I am. No men are more heavy than we are that we cannot bring things to pass as we would. I trust never to die but that your grace will be able to requite the Pope and 'Popys,' and not be fed with their flattering words. I have written to my cousin Anne, but I dare not write to her the truth, but will refer her to your grace to make her privy to all the news."

This confession of Sir Francis Bryan is very plain; the writer despairs of the Pope, and dares not tell Anne Boleyn how hopeless is her cause. It is clear, then, so late as April 1529, and six months after the arrival in London of Cardinal Campeggio, that the Pope had done nothing to further the ends of the king.

And in May 1529, within a month of the trial, Cardinal Wolsey himself, having made no progress whatever in the cause, having failed to bind the Pope, and being left to face the law, according to which the marriage of Henry and Catherine was as lawful as that of Adam and Eve, supplicated most piteously the king's ambassadors

[1] Letters and Papers, ed. Brewer, iv. pt. iii. 5431.

and his own to press upon the Pope with all earnestness the great necessity of giving way to the king's desires. He had misled the king, and the burden he had laid on his own shoulders, of his own will, was so heavy that it threatened to crush him. He implied throughout his long letter, written within a month of the trial, that he had not been able to compromise the Pope, or to obtain anything from him that could be used to the damage of the queen. He pressed Dr. Gardiner and Sir Francis Bryan to obtain even new and more ample faculties for himself and Cardinal Campeggio, and then revealed the secret of his difficulties; he admitted "the large promises which he [Cardinal Campeggio] and I so often have made unto the king's highness of the Pope's fast and assured mind, to do all that His Holiness, *etiam ex plenitudine potestatis*, might do."[1] It seems, then, that the Pope had promised nothing, and that the promises made to the king were really made by the Cardinal of York, who now begs the Pope to rescue him out of the perils he had brought on himself by his fatal gift of self-confidence.

Hitherto, then, the Cardinal had not been able to get any promise from the Pope that was of any service to him in the trial which was so soon to take place before him; for that very promise or "pollicitation" which the king said he had received from the Pope, and which, he not being a lawyer, understood not—perhaps also the true meaning of it was kept from him—was in the eyes of the Cardinal not to the purpose; these are his words:—

"And amongst other things, whereas ye, with these last letters, sent the Pope's pollicitation for the non-inhibi-

[1] Burnet, Hist. Reform., iv. 97, ed. Pocock.

tion or avoking of the cause, *the ratifying and confirming of the sentence by us his Legates* herein to be given, and other things mentioned in the same, ye shall understand that the said pollicitation is so couched and qualified, as the Pope's Holiness, whensoever he will, may reserve: like as by certain lines and annotations which in the margin of a copy of the said pollicitation I send you herewith, ye shall perceive more at large." [1]

Here, then, is a plain confession that the Pope never did bind himself to confirm the sentence of the Legates absolutely. No such promise appears in Gardiner's correspondence, though he once said that such a promise was given him, and he was allowed to say so without rebuke by the Pope, who probably thought it unseemly to dispute with Gardiner.

The promise, then, or pollicitation, about which so much has been said, is no promise, for Cardinal Wolsey confesses that the Pope was never bound to leave the cause to be decided by his Legates.

There is more behind. Cardinal Wolsey having told the ambassadors that the commission already issued was not large enough for the purpose, and that the pollicitation did not bind the hands of the Pope, thus proceeds in his instructions:—

"After your other suits for the ampliation of the new commission, if any such may be attained, brought unto as good a purpose as ye can, ye shall by some good way find the mean to attain a new pollicitation, with such, or as many of the words and additions newly devised as ye can get."

[1] Burnet, Hist. Reform., iv. p. 98.

It is plain from this that the instrument which the king described as a promise to confirm the sentence of the Legates was in the eyes of the Cardinal not so efficacious as it pleased the king to represent it. He certainly is dissatisfied with it, and urges on the ambassadors the desirableness of obtaining another.

On the 4th of May Gardiner wrote to the king in a letter which Burnet[1] has published, these words:—

"All jointly, and I myself apart, applying all my poor wit and learning to attain at the Pope's hand some part of the accomplishment of your highness' desires, *finally have nothing prevailed.*"

Here, then, Gardiner admits that after all his cunning and his blustering he had obtained nothing. The Pope had not promised to change the law for the purpose of gratifying the king, and he had not decided that his marriage was unlawful.

Moreover, as for the "promises" which the Cardinal of York said were made to the king by Cardinal Campeggio, Gardiner in the same letter wrote these words:—

"But it seemed strange to us to read in Cardinal Campegius' letters that neither he ne Campanus made on the Pope's behalf any promise to your highness, but only in general terms."

The failure was so thorough, and the danger to the Cardinal was so great, that the archbishop of York, at this time bishop of Winchester also, Cardinal of the holy Roman Church, directed a priest, the man who succeeded him in the see of Winchester, to present himself before the Vicar of our Lord, without the truth upon his tongue.

[1] Hist. Reform., vi. p. 23, ed. Pocock.

"To show unto the Pope's Holiness, by way of sorrow and doleance, how your courier to whom ye committed the conveyance of the said pollicitation so chanced in wet and water in the carriage thereof, as the pacquet wherein it was, with such letters as were with the same, and amongst others the rescripts of pollicitation, was totally wet, defaced, and not legible, so as the pacquet and rescript was and is detained by him to whom ye direct your letters, and not delivered amongst the other unto the king's hands; and unless His Holiness, of his goodness unto you, will grant you a double of the said pollicitation, ye see not but there shall be some notable blame imputed unto you, for not better ordering thereof, to the conservation of it from such chance."[1]

It is to be observed that all this was not the truth. The pollicitation had reached England in a state of perfect preservation. The Cardinal had had it copied, for the purpose of writing "certain lines and annotations," which he considered pertinent, "on the margin" thereof. But for all this, the king's ambassadors were instructed to say to the Pope that the pollicitation "was totally wet, defaced, and not legible."

The intention of the Cardinal of York was dishonourable: he hoped to obtain by fraud the ample powers which he could not obtain honestly, for Dr. Gardiner was instructed to say to the Pope, provided His Holiness granted another pollicitation, that the new one would be as like the old as possible, while in truth Gardiner was to make it after the new device of the Cardinal. These are the directions of the latter:—

[1] Burnet, Hist. Reform., iv. p. 99.

"And thus coming to a new pollicitation, and saying ye will devise it as nigh as ye can remember according to the former, ye by your wisdoms, and namely ye, Mr. Stevyns, may find the means to get as many of the new and other pregnant, fat, and available words as is possible, the same signed and sealed as the other is, to be written in parchment; the politic handling whereof the king's highness and I commit unto your good discretions, for therein, as ye, Mr. Stevyns, know, resteth a great strength and corroboration of all that shall be done there in decision of the king's said cause, and as ye write may be in manner as beneficial to the king's purpose as the Commission Decretal."[1]

It appears, then, by the admissions of the Cardinal of York, that within a month of the trial the sovereign Pontiff, pressed and harassed as he was by the persistent importunities of the king, had granted nothing whatever beyond that which the law allowed to any suitor. The queen's defence had not been made even difficult by any act of the Pope; and the pollicitation itself, with the Commission Decretal, if ever issued, took nothing away from the legal rights of the queen. Even now the Cardinal confesses that the Commission Decretal was of no force when he tells Dr. Gardiner that the new pollicitation, if it could be had, may be "as beneficial" as that commission. If the pollicitation was not of greater efficacy than the commission, he needed it not, if he had received the commission, and therefore it is plain that the Cardinal, unable to obtain the "Commission Decretal," forced himself to be content with the pollicitation, which

[1] Burnet, Hist. Reform., iv. p. 99.

he does not appear to have ever obtained in the form he desired.

Besides, the Cardinal has not left the matter in the dark; he tells the ambassadors in very clear language that after all their efforts and his, Clement VII. had not done any one thing for which he had been importuning him so long. In spite of all the "pursuits, instances, and requests" which were made "for the furtherance" of the king's "great and weighty cause," and notwithstanding the "importance of this matter, the justness of the thing itself, reason, duty, respect to good merits, detecting of falsities used, evident arguments and presumptions," the Pope "neither dare nor will do anything displeasing to the emperor," so that "it were in manner all one to prosecute the same at the emperor's hands as at the Pope's, which so totally dependeth upon the emperor."[1]

It has been the custom of many generations now for men who have not been able to make the Pope their partner in sin, to say that he refused their request for some unworthy reason, such as either the fear of certain persons, or an excessive desire to please some one else. Cardinal Wolsey was labouring to break a lawful marriage—he knew it was lawful, if he knew anything—and would not allow that the sovereign Pontiff had any other reason for maintaining it than fear of the emperor. Unable to break the Pope, or bend him to his will, the Cardinal forced himself, against his will, to be content with the faculties he had received, and open the court with Cardinal Campeggio; but he did not wish the Pope

[1] Burnet, Hist. Reform., iv. pp. 93, 94.

to know it, hoping by concealing it from him to obtain more ample powers.

"Wherefore," he writes to the ambassadors, "to show you in counsel, and to be reserved unto yourselves, the king's highness finding this ingratitude in the Pope's Holiness, is minded for the time to dissemble the matter, and taking as much as may be had and attained there to the benefit of his cause, to proceed in the decision of the same here, by virtue of the commission already granted unto me and my lord Legate Campegius."[1]

This was written within a month of the trial, and it appears then by the confession of the Cardinal of York that His Holiness Clement VII. had neither done nor promised to do anything whatsoever contrary to the ordinary process of the law, and the rights of the queen had not been sacrificed to the importunities of her enemies.

There is a further testimony to the integrity of the Pope in the letter of Dr. Bennet, Casali, and Vannes to the Cardinal of York, written from Rome July 9, 1529. They in an audience of His Holiness say to him—having just received their letters from England with an account of the opening of the Legatine court and the appeal of the queen—that they knew nothing of the legal process then begun; they fully believed that it had not been begun, and that no sentence would be pronounced unless the king could be assured that it would be in his favour."[2]

[1] Burnet, Hist. Reform., iv. p. 94.

[2] Pocock, Records, i. p. 252. "Respondimus, nos quidem de processu nihil scire, et plane credere, processum nullum istic actum; aut sententiam ullam definitam iri, nisi regia majestas securissimum primo omni ex parte suæ causæ exitum habuerit."

It seems from this statement of the king's ambassadors that the king had obtained neither a Commission Decretal "defining the cause," nor a "pollicitation" binding the Pope to confirm whatever sentence the Legates might pronounce.

There is still further testimony to the integrity of the Pontiff; for after the trial and the admission of the queen's appeal, the bishop of Tarbes, undertaking the king's cause, asked the Pope whether he would "molest" Henry if he put an end to the matter by such means as his "conscience" approved of. That was no doubt the same thing as asking the Pope whether he would overlook the proposed bigamy of the king. The Pope said he would "consult" thereupon in his council; but when the bishop went further, and threatened the Pope "with a greater ruin in Christendom than he hath seen hitherto" if the king were not satisfied, the reply of Clement VII. was, according to Dr. Bennet, the king's ambassador,[1] that if these evils were to come, he would rather they

"Should follow for doing his duty than the like should follow for lack of doing his duty; and added unto it that he was utterly determined to proceed according to justice and the order of the law; and repeated again that he nother for your highness [the king], neither for the French king, nother for the emperor would transgress one hair of justice."

Harpsfield also, who saw the letters that were written in the matter of the divorce, says that

"The king made marvellous instant suit that either

[1] Pocock, Records, i. p. 453.

the Pope would sign a Decretal drawn out for his purpose, or give a new commission to the Legates that they might proceed, all manner of appellation set aside, and that he would by his handwriting send word to the king that he would not advocate the matter to Rome." *But nothing of all these things could be granted.*

Gregorio Casali is the man who wrung from the Pope the promise of the *Bulla decretalis,* or Decretal Commission, yet he as late as February 16, 1529, admits that the Bull was never granted, and that it was wasted labour to ask for it. He writes in that sense to his cousin, Vincent Casali:[1]—

"I do not know what to hope of Dr. Stephen [Gardiner]'s mission, and how far the Pope ought to pronounce the Brief produced by the queen a forgery. I think His Holiness will do nothing; and you may tell Wolsey so in the event of his desiring my opinion. I hear you have told him that if the Pope's fears were removed he would do everything for the king *licita et illicita.* But if you rightly remember, I told you that the Pope would do all that *could* be done; for there are many things which the Pope says he cannot do, *vetuti esset Bulla decretalis;* and so he will say of that Brief, that he can pass no decision on a Brief emanating from Pope Julius, in the event of its being brought from Spain."

This confession of his want of success made by Gregorio did not hinder him from boasting later that he had "so handled" the Pope as to have obtained the *Bulla decretalis,* which now he says is one of the things the Pope cannot do.

[1] State Papers, Brewer, iv. pt. iii. 5302.

While the king was pressing on the Pope the justice of his cause and the torment of his conscience, he did not wholly trust to that justice. In the first place, he threatened to depart out of the unity of the Church, if he could not obtain his desires, and he proposed to reach his end by either of three different roads. The first was, a Papal dispensation to have two wives at once; the second, to bring the person of the Pope into his power; and the third, to make Cardinal Wolsey Pope.

Among "the heads of instructions given" to Sir Francis Bryan and Peter Vannes in December 1528, which Mr. Pocock[1] has printed, is this:—

"*Quod possit duas ducere uxores cum legitimatione prolis ex secundâ.*"

It was thought possible in England that the queen might be persuaded or frightened to take the veil, and that the king might then be dispensed from the bond of matrimony and be allowed to marry. But when afterwards the queen was found to be immovable, the king then returning to the proposal sent through Knight, asked for a dispensation to enable him to marry while the first marriage subsisted—in other words, to have two wives at once. Harpsfield,[2] having "seen the very originals," thus recounts the facts:—

"There was also in the said instructions an advertisement that the said agents should perfectly and substantially instruct themselves against the coming of Mr. William Knight, the king's principal secretary, of certain questions, by the learning, experience, and knowledge of the best advocates they could get in the court of Rome, to be retained of the king's counsel, and to be of his grace's part made sure by secret rewards, pacts, and conventions that afterwards they should not be

[1] Records, i. 189.

[2] Treatise of Marriage, bk. ii. p. 114, Eyston MS.

allured or drawn to the adverse part: the questions were propounded in form following, whereof I will shife no part of the king's own words :—

"Whether, if the queen, for the great and manifold effects that may ensue thereof, can be moved and induced to take vow of chastity or enter into religion, the Pope's Holiness may, *ex plenitudine potestatis*, dispense with the king's highness to proceed thereupon *ad duas nuptias*, and the children to be procreate in the same to be legitimate.

"And it be a thing that per case the Pope may not do, standing such laws as be already, both divine and human, and using his ordinary power, yet whether His Holiness may do it of his mere and absolute power, as a thing that the same may dispense in above the law, must perfectly and secretly be understood and known, and what precedent hath been seen of like matter, or how the court of Rome shall define and determine, and what it doth use, or may do therein, so that it may perfectly and assuredly appear that no exception or scruple, question or doubt, can or may be found, or alleged hereafter in anything that may or shall be affirmed to be in the Pope's power touching the matter."

But as it was possible that the queen might refuse to resign her rights as the king's wife by entering into religion, Henry provided for that difficulty in the following way: his agents were to inquire of the lawyers whether he might not deceive the queen.

"The king's said orators"—thus Harpsfield witnesses—"shall therefore in like wise ripe and instruct themselves, by their secret learned counsel in the court of Rome, if for so great a benefit to ensue unto the king's succession, realm, and subjects, with the quiet of his conscience, his grace should promise so to enter religion or make vow of chastity for his part, only thereby to induce the queen thereto, whether in that case the Pope's Holiness may dispense with the king's highness for the same promise, oath, or vow, discharging his grace clearly of the same, and thereupon to proceed *ad secunda vota cum legitimatione prolis,* as is aforesaid."

The king having directed his ambassadors to ascertain the effects of the queen's entering religion of her own freewill, and the effects of her entering religion under the delusion that the king was bound by his proposed promise or vow, proceeds a step further, for there was another way, as he thought, out of the difficulty. If the ambassadors should be told, as undoubtedly they would be, that the bond of marriage could not be broken, and that the queen, whether she became a religious or not, would be still and always his wife,

"Then shall the king's said orators perfectly inquire and search whether the Pope's Holiness may dispense with his grace, upon the great considerations that rest herein, to have *duas uxores*, and that the children of the second matrimony shall be as well legitimate as those of the first."

Henry VIII. would not accept a dispensation to enable him to marry the widow of his brother as a sufficient safeguard of his conscience, but he was ready to accept a dispensation for bigamy, and believed that it was within the jurisdiction of the Pope to grant it.

The Cardinal of York was ready to accept bigamy as the way out of the troubles which he had created. In his letter to Gregorio Casali, November 1, 1528,[1] he desired him to obtain from His Holiness the necessary powers whereby he might, with Cardinal Campeggio, authorise the king, on the queen's taking the veil, to contract a second marriage, the children of which should be as legitimate as the princess Mary.

Mr. Pocock[2] has published the "Draft of a remon-

[1] Letters and Papers, ed. Brewer, vi. pt. ii. 4897.

[2] Records, i. p. 212.

strance to be made on a personal interview between the queen and the Legates, May 1529," and the contents are said to be "Allegations delivered by the king's highness." In that instrument the queen was to be told that she need not fear that the king would marry anybody if she should enter into religion, because by the law the king's highness may not take another wife during the lifetime of the queen; "neither yet the Pope's Holiness can [dispense] with his grace so to do."

If the king was sincere in this, it is difficult to discover why he wished the queen to take the veil; for his ambassador in Rome had written to him, on the 3d of March, to the effect "that the most learned of the advocates consulted thinks that the Pope cannot give a dispensation that the king may marry again on the queen entering a religion."[1]

The second plan, that of brute force, which was devised in the interest of the king, was to be carried out in this way: the king of England and the king of France were "to furnish the charge for one thousand, fifteen hundred, or two thousand men, to be in guard at the Pope's person."[2]

Harpsfield, who saw the letters of the Cardinal on this matter, thus speaks of the guard proposed to be furnished for the service of Clement VII.:—

"Neither think you that this our declaration touching this plan and presidye is impertinent to our principal matter, for the very mystery thereof you shall now hear out of the Cardinal's own letters sent to Mr. Secretary and Mr. Bennet, which words were written in ciphers,

[1] Letters and Papers, ed. Brewer, iv. pt. iii. 5344.

[2] Fiddes, Life of Wolsey, Collections, p. 165.

and purport thus: 'As you know, and as it was declared to you in council, one of the things noted to be much to the advancement of the king's cause was, that the Pope's Holiness, taking this presidye, should thereby be brought to have as much fear and respect towards the king as he hath now towards the ambassador [the emperor], and consequently be glad to grant the king's desire, though you were ordained to show the French king that it was done for his sake, and to the Pope for his, and, indeed, it was done for the benefit of the king's affairs.'"[1]

The Pope never accepted the guard, and was in all probability as perfectly aware of the Cardinal's intentions as was the Cardinal himself, who, blinded by his vanity, imagined that so plain a trick could not be seen through.

The third plan of the king was the election of the Cardinal of York to the sovereign Pontificate of Holy Church. While Cardinal Campeggio was in England Clement VII. fell ill, and it was reported, and for a time believed, that he was dead. Thereupon the king at once, February 6, 1529, directed his agents in Rome to use all their skill and diligence to bring about the election of the Cardinal Wolsey. Nor did he hide from them that the Cardinal's election was desired by him for the purpose of divorcing the queen, it being, he confessed, not unknown to them how "necessary, and in any wise expedient, it shall be for the perfection of the king's said great and weighty matter to them committed to have the

[1] Treatise of Marriage, bk. ii. p. 113, Eyston MS. Mr. Brewer has given an account of this in State Papers, Henry VIII., vol. iv. pt. iii. 5179 *ad fin.*

said lord Legate of York, and none other, advanced to the said dignity Papal."[1]

The king impresses upon them that for "the perfect conducing of the king's great matter, which suffereth no tract, delay, or negative, it shall be found that there is none other for this purpose but only the said lord Legate of York." Moreover, he instructs them to bribe the Cardinals.

The Cardinal of York also lays aside his humility, and directs Gardiner, his former secretary and his other half, to forward his election. On the day after the king's instructions were prepared, February 7, Cardinal Wolsey tells Gardiner that "it is expedient to have such one to be Pope and common father of all princes as may, can, and will give remedy to the premisses." Farther on he adds: "When all things be well pondered, and the qualities of all the Cardinals well considered — *absit verbum jactantiæ*—there shall be none found that can and will set remedy in the foresaid things but only the Cardinal Ebor."

The "premisses" and the "foresaid things" was the "king's secret matter."

But the Cardinal, now so near his fall, considered himself the sole and necessary man, and that the safety of the Church depended on his election to the Papal throne. These are his words:—

"For the achieving and attaining whereof, forasmuch as thereupon dependeth the health and wealth, not only of these two princes [Henry VIII. and Francis I.] and their realms, but of all Christendom, nothing is to

[1] Pocock, Records, ii. 593.

be omitted that may conduce to the said end and purpose."

As the king gave instructions for bribery, so the Cardinal Wolsey, to his everlasting shame, directed Dr. Gardiner to strain every nerve to obtain his election, to spend money without stint, and to make promises; he had full powers to treat with every one, and the Cardinal's word that the Cardinal and the king would ratify whatever he might do.[1]

It is most improbable that the instructions sent to the ambassadors by the king were not shown to Cardinal Wolsey. Perhaps the truth is that they were his work. In those instructions the ambassadors were told that "if the election cannot be had in the person of the said lord Legate of York," the French Cardinals, "knit together to the king's devotion, . . . must be instructed beforehand" to persist in pressing the election of the Cardinal; but if they saw no hope of succeeding, they were then to make a protest against the election of any other, "which protestation" was to be "couched and devysed" by the king's ambassadors.

"And thereupon the Cardinals of the king's,[2] and the French king's adherents, to depart the conclave, whereby repairing to some other place, they, with the residue of the Cardinals absent, may proceed to such an election as may be to God's pleasure, the weal of His Church and faith, and of all Christendom, any election that

1 The letter of Cardinal Wolsey to Dr. Gardiner was published by Foxe, Acts and Monuments, iv. 600, ed. Cattley; by Fiddes, Life of Wolsey, Collections, p. 169; but a more accurate copy is to be found in Mr. Pocock's Records, ii. 607.

2 In Harpsfield, Treatise of Marriage, bk. ii. p. 119, Eyston MS., the reading is "king's side."

thus by pertinacity may ensue at Rome notwithstanding."[1]

Upon this Harpsfield[2] observes, with perfect justice, as follows:—

"Touching the said Cardinal, we have declared before what fervent suit the king made to have made him Pope, being ready to rear a schism in the whole Church, and to set up an antipope against the true Pope, rather than he would have been defeated of his purpose. And all was by his authority, being once made Pope, to bring to effect the divorce that he so long sought for."

The king's resolve to create a schism seems to have been no secret, for the emperor, in a letter written at Toledo, February 16, 1529, expresses his sorrow at the news of the Pope's illness, and adds, "His death might create a schism in Christendom."[3]

But the illness of the Pope passed away, and Henry had to struggle for his ends by another way than that of a schism in Europe.

When at last he saw that the Pope could be neither frightened nor deceived, and that there was nothing more to be done but go to trial before the Legates, he submitted to his lot. The Legates held their court, and proceeded *ex officio* against him and the queen, whom they charged with living disorderly, contrary to the laws of Holy Church. The articles thus objected the king would have gladly confessed to be true, for he wished to be rid of his wife: the queen refused to answer them, declining the jurisdiction of the Legates, and appealing to the sovereign Pontiff.

[1] Pocock, Records, ii. p. 598.

[2] Treatise of Marriage, bk. iii. 121.

[3] Letters and Papers, ed. Brewer, iv. pt. iii. 5301.

Now, the acts and words of Henry after the queen had refused to submit the validity of her marriage to be determined in the court of the Legates, show most clearly that the Pope had made him no promise to confirm the sentence of the Legates, or to allow the question to be finally settled in London. For as soon as the queen appealed, the king ordered his agents in Rome to do their utmost to hinder the appeal from being admitted, and to persuade the Pope not to call the cause up before himself. The Pope had granted nothing to the king by which the legal rights of the queen might be hurt, and it was now plain to all that the efforts of the king and his ministers for nearly two years had been thrown away. Henry VIII. found the law in his path; the Pope was an impartial judge, who would not at his request deprive the queen of her right, or of the weapons of defence which were allowed by law. Even admitting the Decretal Commission about which so much has been said, and the "pollicitation" itself, Henry knew that these instruments were of no force whatever to stop the course of law. The queen had appealed to the Pope, and there was end to all the intrigues, devices, and tricks of the king's agents, for the Pope neither would nor could refuse justice to the meanest of his children. So when the king's agents in Rome were striving to persuade the Pope to turn a deaf ear to the cry of the insulted queen, they were honest enough to write home to the Cardinal of York that the Pope could not in justice reject the appeal.[1]

[1] Letter of Bennet, Casali, and Vannes, Pocock, Records of the Reformation, i. p. 259. "Asserit Pontifex ex justitia hanc advocationem non posse cuiquam, nedum cæsarianis a Se denegari."

The king wished much to delay the admission of the queen's appeal, for he hoped to hurry the cause in England before the Legates, and obtain a sentence in his favour. If he could have prevailed upon Cardinal Campeggio to proceed, and pronounce sentence, which he might have done according to law, it was believed that the king intended to marry Anne Boleyn at once, though he knew, as everybody else did, that the sentence of the Legates was not, and could not be, a final decision in the cause.

The Legates did not pronounce any sentence; they did not hurry the process, indeed they could not, for they had to receive and consider the depositions of many witnesses; and then there were the peremptory orders of the Pope, that they must not, for he would not open a door for the king to sin. The cause had been a trouble to the Pope for some two years, but he never once put any difficulty in the way of ending it. All the delay arose out of the king's demands, almost always unjust, and the time that was wasted was wasted in listening to these demands, which after all could not be, and were not, granted.

Clement VII. always said that as Henry VIII. had rendered great services to the Holy See, he considered himself bound to do him all the kindness he could. He did so; he was patient with him, forbearing and generous in all his dealings with him. He bore too with the Cardinal of York, and seems to have refused him nothing that he asked for in the way of favours and graces. But in all his doings he never trenched upon justice, and never gave away the rights of a third person; he was perfectly immovable whenever the rights of another were touched.

When Henry pleaded his conscience, and said that he was convinced his marriage was unlawful, though he would not take the necessary measures to obtain the decision of his doubts, or the confirmation of his belief, the Pope readily admitted the value of his learning and the sincerity of his convictions, but he could not help him, because the queen's convictions were entitled to equal consideration, and the law must be administered without respect of persons.

The scruples of the king were not realities, for when Cardinal Campeggio offered to obtain a fresh dispensation and a declaration on the part of His Holiness that the marriage was perfectly valid and lawful, Henry VIII. declined the remedy.[1] He was convinced that the marriage was void, and that the Pope had not the power to make it good.

But his belief in the unlawfulness of the marriage was also pretended, for he was told of an easy way out of his troubles. Gregorio Casali, January 13, 1528,[2] reported a conversation he had had with the Pope to Cardinal Wolsey. Clement VII., according to the writer, suggested a way by which the dispute could be settled without any delay. It was this: "the king is troubled in mind, but if his conscience tells him his marriage is null, and that he can lawfully do that which he wishes to do—there is no doctor in the world who can see into that so clearly as the king—let him begin the process, marry a wife, and demand sentence."

[1] Theiner, p. 572.

[2] Burnet, Hist. Reform., iv. p. 41, ed. Pocock.

Now if the king was so convinced of the goodness of his cause, the remedy suggested by His Holiness was the simplest and the easiest. There could be no delay in the process, for both he and the queen, and his new wife so married, would have pressed the matter on, and the suit might have been brought to a close in a few months, or perhaps weeks, for the Pope promised to pronounce the sentence at once. "*Statim feretur sententia quam Pontifex maturabit.*"

The king did not run the risk; he preferred, notwithstanding his convictions and the trouble of his conscience, to obtain from the Pope, before the trial, a definite promise that the sentence should be as he wished it to be, in his favour against the queen.

The Cardinal of York seems to have urged the divorce on the sole ground of policy; he admitted that grave divines and lawyers maintained that the Pope could not dispense with the impediments that were in the way of the king's first marriage, but he does not seem himself to have once doubted the perfect lawfulness of that marriage, the dissolution of which he had taken upon himself to accomplish for ends of his own.

In the instructions[1] given to Gardiner and Fox when they were sent to the Pope to sue for a divorce, the Cardinal of York screens himself behind "the greatest divines and lawyers."

"If God," he says, "has given any light of true doctrine to the greatest divines and lawyers of this realm, and if in this angle of the world there be any hope of God's favour, Wolsey is well assured, and 'dare put his soul,' that the king's desire is grounded upon justice."

[1] Letters and Papers, ed. Brewer, iv. pt. ii. 3913.

He may, certainly, have persuaded himself that the Pope could not make that marriage good, but it is most improbable, and his conduct throughout is at least a profession that he fully believed in the powers of the Pope. But the unutterable meanness of all ambitious men broke out, and in these very instructions the Cardinal of York, knowing all that he knew, and knowing also, as all others knew, that the raising up of Anne Boleyn to the royal throne would be his ruin, thus continues :—

"On the other side the approved excellent virtuous qualities of the said gentlewoman, the purity of her life, her constant virginity, her maidenly and womanly pudicity, her soberness, chasteness, meekness, humility, wisdom, descent of right noble and high thorough regal blood, education in all good and laudable [qualities] and manners, apparent aptness to procreation of children, with her other infinite good qualities, more to be regarded and esteemed," &c.

The Cardinal archbishop of York, who knew all that passed in the court of Henry VIII., could write thus of the woman then openly coveting the place of the queen, and receiving those coarse and filthy letters of her adulterous lover, which no one has ever ventured to defend.

This account of Anne Boleyn given by the Cardinal was not forgotten by the king, for in the year 1533, when he sent Sir William Paget to justify and explain his conduct to the princes of Germany, he inserted it nearly word for word in the instructions of his minister, to the praise of "his lawful wife, the noble lady, dame Anne marques of Pembroke."[1]

[1] Burnet, Hist. Reform., vi. p. 9.

Neither the king nor the Cardinal went willingly to the trial; they had been both disappointed, for they had hoped to force or deceive the Pope to be their accomplice in a grievous wrong. Clement VII. and the Cardinals whom he consulted never swerved aside, threats and flatteries were equally powerless to move them, and the Pope, sorely troubled and without material succours, stood immovable; his duty, he said, was to see that "the See Apostolic be not slandered," and throughout this most shameful process the See Apostolic was not slandered.

The writer's thanks are due to many who have given him the benefit of their learning and advice, but especially to Charles J. Eyston of Hendred House, Esq., for the use of his MSS., particularly the Treatise of Archdeacon Harpsfield on Marriage, from which so many extracts will be found, not only in this introduction, but also among the notes; and to the Reverend the Father Law, of the London Oratory, whose constant help and prudent counsel, with his patient labour in reading the sheets as they came out of the printer's hands, have made this translation of Dr. Sander's work less imperfect than it otherwise must have been.

D. L.

March 27, 1877.

THE RISE AND GROWTH

OF

THE ANGLICAN SCHISM.

EDWARD RISHTON TO THE READER.

On my arrival in France, whither I was lately banished out of an English prison, I understood from the conversation of many people that the works of Dr. Sander, because of the high esteem in which the learned held them, were everywhere sought after by the printers for the purpose of publication, more especially those which had not been hitherto printed, but which that saintly man, too soon taken from us by death, had either left in the care of friends or retained himself. Of these, I was told that a work on Justification in seven books was at that time in the press at Trier,[1] and that some other writings of the same author were sought after, but above all a certain remarkable book on the beginning and growth of the Anglican Schism; of which there were copies extant in manuscript—though very few—in Italy as well as in Spain, where he finished the book, bringing the history down to his own day.

This work on the Anglican Schism, divided into three books, but not perfectly finished to the satisfaction of the author, owing to his other occupations and his other writings, was left behind by Dr. Sander when, in

[1] De Justificatione contra Colloquium Altemburgense, sive de Lutheranorum dissidiis circa Justificationem. August. Trevirorum, 1585.

his great zeal for souls, he went from Spain to Ireland to help the afflicted Catholics who in that country were fighting for the faith. He was not long there, for continual labour and hunger, the unhealthiness of the climate, the utter absence of all the necessaries of life, with other hardships and anxieties, weighed him down, and he resigned his saintly soul into the hands of Him who made him.[1]

Last year in Paris, after my return from England, I met a very old friend, Jodocus Skarnkert of Cologne, whom I had known also in Rome, and as we were both of us interested in ecclesiastical history, we often spoke of such books as this. My friend very earnestly pressed me to give him a copy of this work of Dr. Sander, he knew I had read it, and believed that I possessed a copy. He added that if I did so, I should not only give a very great pleasure to himself and his friend the bookseller, but render also no slight service to the whole of Christendom; for it is impossible, he said, for people not to learn a most profitable lesson—he knew something of the contents of the books—from a record of the deeds of the heretics and schismatics.

I began by refusing his request, alleging as the reason that I had not a copy of the book, and that it could not be easily found. Then I doubted whether it would be wise to print the book, while they, for the most part, were still living whose actions are recorded, and whose foul deeds are brought to light. He, however, insisted on it that the public good was to be preferred to the

[1] In the margin are these words: "Mors Sanderi in Hibernia an. 1581."

advantage of private persons, and that there was no hope now of their ever becoming better men, seeing that they are daily adding sin to sin; that the author himself would have published it some years ago, if he had not been hindered, first by his occupations, and then by death; that copies of it were abroad, and it was certain that before long some one would publish the book, and perhaps incorrectly, unless some Englishman undertook the charge of it. He said that no one could do that better than I could, who had some experience in such matters, and that it would not be difficult for me, who for nearly four years had observed those things that were done in prison in London, to add, in the reign of Elizabeth, all that took place in England after the death of Dr. Sander.

Yielding to these and other reasons, I promised Dr. Jodocus to do all I could, and exerted myself forthwith to obtain a copy by the help of my friends, and succeeded without much difficulty. Then I read the whole book through, correcting certain passages which were faulty, either because the transcribers were careless, or not clearly expressed because the author was in a hurry. I have also left out some of the discussions which seemed tedious, in order to preserve more closely the order of the story, adding much, especially those things that took place after the death of Dr. Sander. And as the whole work is not very long, I included it all in one volume, and sent it thus corrected, together with this letter to my friend Dr. Jodocus, to be transmitted by him to the bookseller who so much wished to have it, with the single request that he would have it correctly printed, which I hope will be done ; if not, my goodwill at least has not been wanting, and I trust that the charitable reader will think so.

I pray God of His goodness to grant that the Christian world may gather all the fruit I desire from this admirable history, and learn to hate heresy and schism. Friendly reader, farewell ; and pray unto God for me.

PREFACE.

By the Rev. Nicolas Sander, D.D.

THE Britons are said to have been first converted to the faith of Christ by Joseph of Arimathia, then confirmed therein by Eleutherus, the Roman Pontiff—the twelfth in succession from Peter—who sent to them Fugatius and Damian, by whom Lucius king of Britain and a very large number of the people were baptized, so that Tertullian,[1] who lived so near to their times, wrote, "Countries of the Britons which no Roman ever trod are subject unto Christ." But when the Angles and the Saxons from Germany had overcome the Britons in war, and hemmed them in in the more distant part of the island, Gregory the Great sent to those very Saxons Augustin, Mellitus, and others, monks of St. Benedict, who made Christian a nation hitherto given to idols, and baptized Ethelbert king of Kent.[2]

From that day almost to the twenty-fifth year of the reign of Henry VIII.,[3] for about a thousand years, none other than the Roman Catholic faith prevailed in England, insomuch that the very kingdom, from the days of king Ina to those of Henry VIII., for nearly

[1] Adversus Judæos, c. 7. "Et Britannorum inaccessa Romanis loca, Christo vero subdita."

[2] A.D. 596.

[3] A.D. 1533–1534.

eight hundred years, paid by way of tribute a penny for every house to the Roman Pontiff, in honour of St. Peter; the which tribute was commonly called Peter's pence. But Henry VIII., solely for the reasons I am about to set forth, changed the faith of Christ, and severed the realm of England from the communion of the Roman Pontiff.

Arthur, the elder brother of Henry, married to Catherine, the daughter of the Catholic sovereigns of Spain, not only died without issue, but more than that, on account of his sickly youth, and because of his death, which soon ensued, never lived with his wife. Thereupon Henry, by Papal dispensation, for the preservation of peace between the Spaniards and the English, took Catherine for his wife, and having lived with her for some twenty years, put her away, seemingly, because she had been married to his brother, but in truth that he might put Anne Boleyn in her place, who was more nearly related to him, for she was the sister of one, and the daughter of another woman, both then alive, with whom Henry had been living in sin; besides, she was considered, not without many good reasons, to be Henry's own child.

Henry then, in order to marry this woman, put away Catherine, and apostatised from the Roman Church. He did not enter any other older Church, nor did he go to that of the Lutherans and Calvinists, newly begun, but he set up a new Church, of which he called himself the supreme head on earth. Anne Boleyn had sinned with many before marriage, and after her marriage with the king she sinned with her own brother. She was always a Lutheran. In the end she was found guilty of adultery and incest, Thomas Boleyn, her reputed father, being one of the judges, and Henry had her put to death.

The hypocrisy then of the king, pretending the fear of God when he put Catherine away; the incestuous marriage with Anne Boleyn, I say incestuous marriage of Henry, for if Anne was not his own child, she was the child of his mistress; the incest also of Anne Boleyn with her own brother; the ecclesiastical supremacy of the king, which Henry was the first to assume, are the foundations on which that religion is built and stands, which England held and professed under Henry, Edward, and Elizabeth. And yet that which Henry set up in matters of belief, after the divorce, when he had himself styled supreme head of the Church, was by his children, Edward and Elizabeth, overthrown and utterly destroyed, for they brought in another gospel altogether, and put it in the place of that which Henry had founded.

The marvellous and amazing things that God wrought in that kingdom, after the beginning of the schism, for the purpose of bringing back the hearts of the children to the faith of their fathers, can never be thoroughly understood without a history of the schism; that history, strange and surprising, I shall now tell in all sincerity as I have gathered it either from public records or from the testimony, oral and written, of men of the greatest consideration, or at least from my own knowledge and observation.

THE ANGLICAN SCHISM.

BOOK I.

CHAPTER I.

STATE OF EUROPE—MARRIAGE OF ARTHUR AND CATHERINE—THE DISPENSATION—THE BETROTHAL OF HENRY AND CATHERINE.

WHEN the Empire was governed by Maximilian,[1] Spain by Ferdinand[2] and Isabella the Catholic, England by Henry VII.,[3] the state of Christendom was to all appearance singularly prosperous; for both in peace and war no one was more distinguished than the emperor Maximilian, or more successful than the Catholic sovereigns: no one was more valiant or more prudent than Henry VII., who, victorious in all his wars, abounded in all manner of riches.

Divisions were creeping in among the Mahometans, for Ismael Sophi, whose mother was a daughter of

[1] Maximilian I., born March 22, 1459; elected king of the Romans, Feb. 16, 1486; crowned April 10 of the same year; acknowledged as emperor on the death of his father, which took place Aug. 19, 1493. He was never crowned, and remained emperor-elect, dying Jan. 12, 1519.

[2] Ferdinand, son of John II., king of Navarre and Aragon, became king of Castille in right of his wife Isabella, daughter of John II., king of Castille. Isabella was born April 23, 1451, and died Nov. 26, 1504, before her husband, who, as king of Aragon, died Jan. 23, 1516.

[3] Henry VII. became king Aug. 22, 1485, and died in the twenty-fourth year of his reign, April 21, 1509.

Hassoun Cassan, put forth a new explanation of Islam, and the people were the more ready to accept it because he had made himself king of Persia. The Saracens, who had held Andalucia for nearly eight hundred years, were driven out of Spain. The new world, opened to the Christian kings in the infinite compassion of God, had begun to obey the Gospel: the Portuguese carrying it towards the south, and the Spaniards towards the west, together with the renown of their respective nations, by authority of the Pope, Alexander VI.[1]

While matters were thus happily ordered, a treaty was made, in the year of our Lord's Incarnation 1500, between the most mighty princes, Henry VII. of England of the one part, and Ferdinand and Isabella of Spain of the other part, for the marriage of Arthur, the eldest son of Henry VII., and Catherine, the well-dowered daughter of the Catholic sovereigns. The treaty was carried into effect in the following year, and the marriage was solemnised in London, in the church of St. Paul, November 14th, a day in England kept in honour of St. Erconwald. That night the princes were conducted with ceremonious observances to the bridal chamber, attended by a grave matron, who remained with them,[2] by order of Henry VII., acting on the advice of the physicians; for prince Arthur, hardly arrived at his fifteenth year, was suffering from a lingering disease, worn out by which in less than six months he departed this life.[3]

[1] See the Bull *Inter cætera Divinæ Majestati*, dated May 4, 1493.

[2] Mr. Pocock, Records of the Reformation, ii. p. 426, has published a letter of king Ferdinand, written at Barcelona, Aug. 23, 1503, in which the same account is given: "La dicha princesa, nuestra hija quedo entera, y ahun que se velaron ella y principe Arthur, no consummaron el matrimonio."

[3] Arthur was born Sept. 20, 1486—he was therefore fifteen years old and nearly seven weeks when he married Catherine. He died in Ludlow Castle, where he lived as prince of Wales, April 2, 1502.

When the Catholic sovereigns, on the death of prince Arthur, demanded their daughter, Henry VII. made them the offer of another marriage for her, and after mature consideration the offer was accepted. That offer was to this effect, that with the consent of the sovereign Pontiff, sought and obtained, Catherine should be betrothed to Henry, the brother of prince Arthur, who was then in the twelfth year of his age.[1] The proposed marriage was first of all discussed at home by learned theologians and lawyers of both realms, whether it could be made with due regard to public morals; and then, when they were satisfied that the marriage could be made lawful, ambassadors were sent from Spain and England, first to Alexander VI., and next to Pius III. But before the matter could be settled both these Popes died.[2] It was then brought before Julius II., who having consulted the most learned men, decided that, for the sake of preserving peace between two such powerful kingdoms, which was a common good, the impediment to the marriage, created by human laws, and that the only one, had in this case no place, and gave his sanction to the marriage.

The theologians maintained that the divine law recorded in the Holy Writings, is so far from forbidding such a marriage, that under the law of nature the patriarch Judas commanded Onan, his second son, to marry Thamar, the widow of his elder brother, who had died without issue, that there might be children to succeed him. They said, too, that if we look into the law of Moses, the same commandment, even under pain of dishonour, is laid upon the surviving brother, and it

[1] Henry VIII. was born June 28, 1491.

[2] Alexander VI. died Aug. 18, 1503. Francis Cardinal Piccolomini was elected Sept. 22, and took the name of Pius III. He died within a month of his election, Oct. 18, 1503. Julius II. was elected Nov. 1, 1503.

never could be that God should not merely allow, but even command, the breaking of the natural law in any case, certainly not in the state of nature, seeing that He had given that law as a gift inseparable from that state, yea, even as its rule and guide.

If any one holds such an opinion, he must hold also that God created nature unchangeable, and at the same time changed and destroyed it Himself, and therefore that He contradicts and denies Himself. It is most unseemly to think thus of God, and therefore nothing is more certain than that the marriage of one brother with the widow of another brother dying without issue is in no wise forbidden by the eternal or natural law; but only by positive and ecclesiastical law, from the observance of which, on good grounds, a dispensation from the Roman Pontiff may be had.

It is true that the law forbids the marriage with a brother's widow, but in this instance the law is inapplicable, partly because the marriage of Arthur and Catherine was never perfected, partly because, even if that were not certain, Arthur was now dead, and besides, even if after his death people believed that he and Catherine had been really man and wife, the difficulty was not of such a nature as not to become insignificant when put in the balance against the general advantage of peace between the two nations.

When the theologians had established their opinion by most weighty proofs drawn from the Sacred Books and from the writings of the Holy Fathers, and when not a voice was heard in opposition throughout the Church among any people on the face of the earth, Henry and Catherine are betrothed, and only betrothed because of Henry's youth.[1]

[1] Henry was twelve years of age and six months when the Brief was obtained.

Meanwhile, before the marriage took place, Isabella, Catherine's mother, died in Spain, and in England Henry VII.[1] Henry VIII., in the eighteenth year of his age, handsome and majestic in person, not destitute of judgment, and free from all fear of his father's authority, who was now dead, made Catherine his wife. It is true that he once said he should not marry her;[2] but now, on fuller consideration of the matter, and after a solemn publication of the Brief of dispensation in the presence of the great men of the kingdom, without a word of doubt from any one, and according to the resolution of his council, the marriage was openly solemnised on the 3d day of June 1509;[3] and on the feast of St. John Baptist next following, June 24th,[4] he and the queen were crowned together, amidst universal rejoicing, in the Benedictine monastery, westward of London, in the abbey church of Westminster.

Henry and Catherine had five children, three sons

[1] Isabella died Nov. 26, 1504, and Henry, April 21, 1509.

[2] According to Lord Herbert, Life of Henry VIII., p. 276, "a deposition of Richard Fox, bishop of Winchester, taken by Dr. Woolman, April 5 and 6, 1527, was read" in the Legatine Court, A.D. 1529. From which it appears that the bishop "did not remember that Henry VIII. when he came to age did expressly consent to or dissent from the intended marriage, yet that he did believe that a protestation was made in the name of Henry VIII." that he would not marry Catherine. He also said that Catherine was present, but not Henry VIII., and that the protestation was made in Durham House. But, nevertheless, the protestation produced before the Legates, according to Lord Herbert, p. 277, was made at Richmond before Fox, the bishop of Winchester, by Henry himself, and it does not appear that Catherine was present or knew of it. Burnet has printed it among the Records, vol. iv. p. 17, from the Cotton Library, and Mr. Pocock in a note says that he has not found it there. It is dated June 27, 1505. If a protestation was ever made in that form, the bishop of Winchester had forgotten it.

[3] Stow, Annales, p. 487. "The 3d day of June king Henry in his closet at Greenwich married the lady Katherine, his first wife, who had been late the wife of prince Arthur, deceased, and was dispensed with by Pope July."

[4] Ibid. "On the morrow, being Sunday and Midsummer Day, the king and queen were crowned at Westminster in most solemn manner by the archbishop of Canterbury and other assisting."

and two daughters, of whom the eldest—he was called Henry—died in the ninth month after his birth,[1] and as the others also died in their infancy, Mary alone, born at Greenwich, February 18, 1516, in the seventh year of Henry's reign, was alive when Henry and Catherine were dead.

[1] Stow, Annales, p. 488. "On New-Year's Day, at Richmond, the queen was delivered of a prince, to the great rejoicing of the whole realm. He was named Henry, but deceased on the 23d of February next following at Richmond, and was buried at Westminster."

CHAPTER II.

PIETY OF CATHERINE—DISSOLUTENESS OF HENRY—THE PRINCESS MARY SOUGHT IN MARRIAGE—BETROTHED TO THE DAUPHIN.

THERE was some difference in age between Henry and Catherine, and a still greater difference in their lives. She was older than her husband in years, at the utmost five years, but more than a thousand years in character. Catherine used to rise at midnight in order to be present at matins sung by religious. At five o'clock she dressed herself, but as quickly as she could, saying that the only time wasted was the time spent in dressing. She was a member of the third Order of St. Francis, and wore the habit thereof under her royal robes. She fasted every Friday and Saturday, and on bread and water on the eves of our Lady's feasts. She went to confession every Wednesday and Friday, and on Sunday received communion. She said the office of our Lady daily, and was present every morning in church for six hours together during the sacred offices. After dinner, and in the midst of her maids of honour, she read the lives of saints for two hours. That done, she went to church, and generally remained there till it was time for supper, which was with her a very scanty meal. She always prayed on her knees, without a cushion or anything else between them and the pavement.[1] Can any

[1] Harpsfield, Treatise of Marriage, Eyston MS., bk. ii. p. 137. "There was in the said house of Bugden, a chamber with a window that had a prospect into the chapel, out of the which she might hear divine service.

one be astonished that so saintly a woman was to be tried in a greater fire of tribulation, so that the fragrance of her goodness might be the more scattered over the Christian world?

Meanwhile Henry was giving the reins to his evil desires,[1] and living in sin, sometimes with two, sometimes with three of the queen's maids of honour, one of whom, Elizabeth Blount,[2] gave birth to a son, whom Henry made duke of Richmond.[3] The king, indeed, admired the sanctity of his wife, but followed evil counsels himself. His daughter Mary was brought up in kingly splendour, and made princess of the Britons or the Welsh, a people by whom the island was first inhabited, and who gave it the name of Britain. They have a language of their own which hardly any Englishman understands.

The Germans call foreigners Welsh, and so the Anglo-Saxons—invited over from Germany to defend the island, having turned their weapons at last against the Britons and subdued them—in order to distinguish between the Britons and themselves, called the former

In this chamber she enclosed herself, sequestered from all other company, a great part of the day and night, and upon her knees used to pray, at the said window, leaning upon the stones of the same. There was [*sic*] some of her gentlewomen, which did curiously mark and observe all her doings, who reported that oftentimes they found the said stones so wet after her departure, as though it had rained upon them. It was credibly thought that in the time of her prayer she removed the cushions, that ordinarily lay on the same window, and that the said stones were imbrued with the tears of her devout eyes." Hearne, in his glossary to Peter Langtoft, under the word "saw," gives the passage.

1 Stow, Annales, p. 486. "Matter pertaining to the politic government of the realm, with the which at the first he could not well endure to be much troubled, being rather inclined to follow such pleasant pastimes as his youthful years did more delight in."

2 Elizabeth Blount, daughter of Sir John Blount, afterwards the wife of Sir Gilbert Talboys.

3 Henry Fitzroy, created earl of Nottingham, duke of Richmond and Somerset, and also lord high admiral, A.D. 1525. He died without issue in 1536; having had his education directed by Dr. Croke, who was so active in bribing the foreign doctors to pronounce against the validity of Catherine's marriage.

Welsh, that is, not Germans, but in relation to the Germans, strangers and foreigners. The government or direction of this province is given only to him who is the heir of the reigning sovereign. That which the title of Cæsar was among the Romans, of Dauphin among the French, is that of prince of Wales among the English.

Into Wales, then, which lies on the western side of the island, under the care of four bishops, was Mary sent, with distinguished councillors and a splendid household, to control and govern it in her own right. She was sought in marriage by the neighbouring kings and princes. Among the first was James V., king of Scotland; then the emperor Charles V., who offered to put her in possession of Belgium at once. Then Francis I., king of France, sought her in marriage for his two sons, either for the Dauphin or the duke of Orleans. When Henry rejected the suit on account of the youth of the princes, king Francis offered himself as her husband; nor was Henry disinclined, if the emperor should not forthwith restore the Pope to his liberty, whom at the time he kept prisoner. For the king, if the emperor persisted in detaining the Pope in prison, thought of giving his daughter in marriage to the French king, and of declaring war against Charles. At last Mary was certainly betrothed upon certain conditions to the eldest son of the king of France, and the betrothal was made at Greenwich in England in due form on the 8th day of October [1527]; and the bishop of Ely[1] went over into France, and made an eloquent harangue on the subject in the presence of Francis, king of France.

[1] Nicolas West, born in Putney, educated at Eton and King's College, Cambridge. He was chaplain to queen Catherine and dean of Windsor. Was made bishop of Ely by Pope Leo X., and consecrated at Lambeth Oct. 7, 1515. He incurred the anger of Henry VIII. for his defence of the marriage of queen Catherine, and died April 28, 1533.

Now, how constant and unvarying was the belief and confidence prevailing among all Christian princes in the validity of the marriage of Henry and Catherine, appears plain enough from this; for they would not have sought their child in marriage so eagerly if she could not have become queen of England, and she could have no right to the throne unless born in lawful wedlock. Let us now return to Henry.

CHAPTER III.

WOLSEY—LONGLAND—THE DIVORCE.

CATHERINE'S life was one of soberness and modesty, that of the king one of levity and wantonness. No two lives more contrary the one to the other could be found. Then the man, hating restraint and given to wantonness,[1] began to grow weary of the grave matron, and his dislike of her could not be long hidden from the courtiers. Among these was Thomas Wolsey, daring and ambitious beyond his fellows, whose life was more like that of the king than that of the queen; seeking every opportunity to please the former, ruin the latter, and further his own interests.[2] The man, not merely of low, but of mean birth, having made his way into the court, became one of the royal chaplains, and at last almoner, recommended by Richard, bishop of Winchester.[3] By-and-by, when the king had made himself

[1] Harpsfield, Treatise of Marriage, bk. iii. p. 113. "I credibly understand himself [Henry VIII.] was beaten of his own father saying, to Alcocke, bishop of Ely, then present and entreating for him, 'Never entreat for him, for this child shall be the undoing of England.'"

[2] Cavendish, Life of Wolsey, p. 80, ed. 1827. "He was most earnest and readiest among all the council to advance the king's only will and pleasure, without any respect to the case: the king, therefore, perceived him to be a meet instrument for the accomplishment of his devised will and pleasure, called him more near unto him, and esteemed him so highly that his estimation and favour put all other ancient counsellors out of their accustomed favour. . . . Who wrought so all his matters, that all his endeavour was only to satisfy the king's mind, knowing right well that it was the very vein and right course to bring him to high promotion. . . . So fast as the other counsellors advised the king to leave his pleasure, and to attend to the affairs of his realm, so busily did the almoner persuade him to the contrary."

[3] Richard Fox was one of the chief agents of Henry VII. when he was earl of Richmond, preparing

master of Tournai, he accepted the revenues of the bishopric[1] from the hands of the king. Shortly afterwards he was made a bishop himself; bishop of Lincoln first, next of Durham, and then of Winchester also. As archbishop of York he held together the two wealthiest sees, Winchester and York, and in the end was made chancellor of the whole realm. Still more, he was made Cardinal, and appointed Legate *a latere*, with jurisdiction over the whole kingdom.[2]

his way to the throne, and was rewarded by being made keeper of the Privy Seal, then secretary of State, and loaded with ecclesiastical benefices. Finally he was raised to the see of Exeter, and was consecrated April 8, 1487. Translated Feb. 8, 1492, by Innocent VIII. to Bath and Wells. Two years afterwards he went from Bath to Durham, and was bishop of that see from Dec. 12, 1494, till he was translated to Winchester in 1500, the temporalities of which see he obtained Oct. 17, 1500, within a fortnight of the death of Thomas Langton, the former bishop, and therefore before the Pope could have made the translation. He was godfather of Henry VIII., founded the College of Corpus Christi in Oxford, and died Sept. 14, 1528. Roper, Life of Sir Thomas More, p. 5, ed. Dublin, 1765, says that the bishop once gave some advice to Sir Thomas More, who, not satisfied with it, discussed it with Mr. Whitford, then chaplain to the bishop of Winchester, and afterwards one of the fathers of Sion. Mr. Whitford recommended Sir Thomas to disregard the bishop's counsel, "for my lord," said the chaplain, "to serve the king's turn, will not hesitate to agree to his own father's death."

1 Stow, Annales, p. 492. "On the 2d day of October the king entered the city of Tournai. . . . He made his almoner, Thomas Wolsey, bishop of Tournai, and then returned to Calais."

2 Thomas Wolsey was born in Ipswich in the year 1471, educated at Oxford, and a fellow of Magdalene College, having taken the degree of B.A. when he was fourteen years old. He became one of the chaplains of Henry VII., and ever afterwards remained in and about the court. He was consecrated bishop of Lincoln March 26, 1514, by William Warham, archbishop of Canterbury. In the following July Cardinal Bainbridge died, and Thomas Wolsey succeeds him in the see of York. The Cardinal died July 14th, and the Bull of provision—for the Cardinal died in Rome—is dated Sept. 15th of that year. On Sept. 7th of this year Wolsey is declared Cardinal, and his title assigned him, that of St. Cæcilia, Dec. 13th, and on Christmas Eve he takes the oath as chancellor of Henry VIII. In 1518 he receives the see of Bath and Wells *in commendam*, which, however, he resigns when he becomes bishop of Durham. In 1521 he becomes abbot of St. Alban's—that is, he takes the revenue, for he was a secular priest. Dec. 30, 1523, he becomes bishop of Durham, but resigns that see in 1529, when he takes possession of Winchester, made vacant by the death of Richard Fox, his friend and patron. Thus he had at once the revenues of York and Winchester, and those of the abbot of St. Alban's,

More still, he had a pension[1] from the French king and from the emperor, to say nothing of the wealthy abbeys the revenues of which he seized. But what is yet more important is this, the king himself was utterly in his power, ordering all things at his good pleasure.

And as if all this was too little for him, moved by Satan, he aimed at the first see in the Church, the throne of the sovereign Pontiff.[2] When the emperor, Charles V., saw this, he began to flatter the man, and thereby make his folly minister to his own designs; so he wrote to him often, and always with his own hand, subscribing himself, "Your son and cousin,[3] Charles." Moreover, he gave Wolsey great hopes of the Papacy whenever Leo X. died,[4] if he could persuade the king to enter into a perpetual league with the emperor, and to declare war upon the king of France. Wolsey performed his part of the bargain most readily; but the emperor was so far from fulfilling his part that he laboured, to his great praise, to secure the election of Adrian VI. Wolsey, thinking it

besides pensions from the emperor and the king of France. On his relinquishment of Durham, the king gave the revenues of that see for one year to Anne Boleyn. Angl. Sacr., vol. i. p. 782.

[1] The French pension was twelve thousand livres Tournois. That of the emperor was three thousand livres, counted in Flemish money, granted in the year 1517; and again, in 1520, was increased by two further pensions of five thousand and two thousand ducats. He also had a pension of ten thousand ducats from the duke of Milan. See Fiddes, Life of Cardinal Wolsey, Collections, pp. 12, 43, 46.

[2] Stow, p. 514. "Pope Leo died this year, whereupon Dr. Pace, dean of Paul's, was sent to Rome to make friends in the behalf of Cardinal Wolsey, who was brought into a vain hope, through the king's favour and furtherance, to be elected Pope. But Adrian VI. was chosen before Dr. Pace could come to Rome, and so that suit was dashed."

[3] A contemporary Life of Wolsey in the Vatican, published by Pocock, Records, ii. 89, contains these words: "Carolus Cæsar diu litteras aliter quam manu sua scriptas non dedit, in quibus se 'filium' subscribebat."

[4] Leo X. died Dec. 1, 1521, and Adrian VI. was elected Jan. 9, 1522, who dying Sept. 14, 1523, was succeeded by Clement VII., elected Nov. 19, 1523.

better to hide his disappointment, waited for Adrian's death. But even then, when Adrian died, the emperor forgot the Cardinal;[1] and besides, having made Francis a prisoner at the battle of Pavia,[2] and receiving his two sons as hostages, he wrote but seldom to the Cardinal; and when he did, the letters were no longer written by himself, and ended simply with the word "Charles." Wolsey on seeing this did not conceal his rage; he opposed the emperor with all his might, took the side of his enemies, and became a thorough partisan of the most Christian king.[3]

1 Cardinal Wolsey's instructions sent with the approval of the king to the king's ambassadors in Rome (Burnet, v. p. 289, ed. Pocock) show how ready he was to accept the Papacy. He says "that the mind and intention of the king's highness, and of me both, is to put our helps and furtherance, as much as conveniently may be, that such a successor unto him [Adrian VI.] may now by the holy College of Cardinals be named and elected, as may, with God's grace, &c. . . . Ye shall understand that the mind and entire desire of his highness, above all earthly things, is that I should attain to the said dignity [of Pope]." . . . Then the Cardinal tells the agents that they were to solicit the Cardinals "by secret labours, alleging and declaring unto them my poor qualities, and how I, having so great experience of the causes of Christendom, . . . not lacking, thanked be God, either substance or liberality to look largely upon my friends; besides, the sundry great promotions which by election of me should be vacant, to be disposed unto such of the said cardinals, as by their true and fast friendship had deserved the same." These agents in Rome, one of them being himself a bishop, Clerk of Bath and Wells, had "ample authority to bind and promise on the king's behalf, as well gift of promotions, as also as large sums of money to as many and such as ye shall think convenient." . . . Lastly, Wolsey writes himself with his own hand to the bishop, that he must be "not sparing any reasonable offers, which is a thing that amongst so many needy persons is more regarded, than percase the qualities of the person: ye be wise, and ye wot what I mean. . . . The king willeth you neither to spare his authority, or his good money or substance."

2 The battle of Pavia was fought Feb. 25, 1525.

3 Tyndale, Practice of Prelates, p. 321, ed. Parker Soc. "As soon as the Pope was taken, the Cardinal wrote unto the emperor that he should make him Pope. And when he had got an answer that pleased him not, but according to his deservings toward the emperor, then he waxed furious mad, and sought all means to displease the emperor, and imagined this divorcement between the king and the queen, and wrote sharply unto the emperor with menacing letters, that if he would not make him Pope, he would make such ruffling between Christian princes as was not this hundred years, to make the emperor repent—yea, though it should cost the whole realm of England."

Burning with wrath at the emperor's conduct, and seeing that the king was becoming more and more estranged from Catherine, and that his own ambitious temper was extremely offensive to the latter, he resolved to bring about the divorce of the king and queen. He considered that it would be advantageous to himself, not unpleasing to the king, hateful to Catherine, and most disagreeable to the emperor to see his aunt divorced.[1] He sends for John Longland,[2] the confessor of Henry VIII., and tells him how very much he thought of the king's salvation. He could not be silent any longer about a matter of such grave importance, nor did he think it right to speak of it to any one before he spoke to the king's confessor, who knew well all the secrets of the king. At last he spoke out, saying that he did not think the king's marriage was valid, and gave many reasons for his opinion. Longland thought the man was sincere in what he said, and did not venture to contradict him on account of his rank. He knew also that a divorce would not be disagreeable to the king, and so he answered merely that it was but just that a matter of so much importance should not be made known to the king by anybody but Wolsey him-

[1] The emperor, in his answer to Clarencieux (Le Grand, iii. 46), says that the divorce was the work of Wolsey, "who, out of greed and ambition, and because the emperor would not use his army in Italy to make him Pope by violence—according to the request made by Henry VIII., and by him in letters written by himself—and thereby satisfy his vanity, ambition, and greed, has often boasted that he would so embroil the emperor's affairs as to surpass any troubles known for a hundred years, even at the cost of the ruin of England." Thus the information possessed by Tyndale—in the foregoing note—is not inexact.

[2] John Longland was educated at Magdalene College, Oxford, and became one of the prebendaries of Lincoln in 1514. In 1517 he was dean of Salisbury, and canon of Windsor in April 1519. He was consecrated bishop of Lincoln at Lambeth May 5, 1521, by the archbishop, William Warham; and on the death of that prelate, succeeded him as chancellor of Oxford. He was with Cranmer at Dunstable when the latter, against law, pronounced the sentence of divorce.

self. Wolsey undertook to do so; and the king, as soon as he saw what he had come to speak about, interrupted him and said, "Beware of disturbing settled questions."[1]

Three days afterwards[2] Wolsey took Longland with him to see the king, but Longland merely begged the king to let the matter be examined. Then, as the king did not refuse this, Wolsey broke in and said that there was a woman of great beauty and nobleness in France, Margaret, sister of the most Christian king, formerly married to the duke of Alençon, and a fitting bride for the king. "We will speak of this hereafter," said Henry; "now silence is necessary above all things, lest the matter be bruited abroad before everything is ready, and leave a stain on our honour," for he knew well whom he should marry if he could once put queen Catherine out of the way.

[1] Harpsfield, Treatise, &c., bk. ii. p. 93, says that all this began with Cardinal Wolsey, "who first by himself, or by John Longland, bishop of Lincoln, and the king's confessor, put this scruple and doubt in his head. At the first hearing whereof, the king, somewhat astonished, held his peace awhile, not a little marvelling at this matter so moved unto him. At length he answered thus: 'Take heed, I beseech you, reverend father, and well consider what a great and weighty enterprise you take now in hand.' And speaking much in the commendation of his wife, said that his marriage was allowed by the most learned and virtuous bishops of the realms of England and Spain, and confirmed also by the Pope's authority."

[2] Polydori Vergil., lib. xxvii. p. 685. "At triduo post, Volsæus incredibili armatus audacia Lincolniensem convenit eumque ducit ad regem."

CHAPTER IV.

THE DIVORCE RESOLVED ON—THE BISHOP OF TARBES—THE CARDINAL SENT AS AMBASSADOR TO FRANCE—ANNE BOLEYN.

THE king having obtained a promise of secrecy, gave his whole mind to the divorce. He read and re-read, and compared together, with certain theologians, those passages of Scripture, especially those in Leviticus and Deuteronomium, which he thought most to the purpose. He also examined minutely the Brief of Julius II. issued in confirmation of his marriage with the queen. But after spending nearly a year in this secret examination of the question, he could find nothing for his purpose in the sacred writings, not a flaw in the Pontifical Brief. More than this, if he thought he had found anything amiss in the Brief of the Pope, he was met by another Brief obtained by king Ferdinand, in which the matter was more clearly and more distinctly expressed,[1] and so he and those whom he consulted came to the conclusion that the matter could be carried no further.

[1] The two Briefs have the same date—Dec. 26, 1503; and both may be seen in Burnet, Hist. Ref., iv. 15, 61, ed. Pocock. But it was pretended in England during the trial that the second Brief was a forgery, and that there was no trace of it to be found in the archives of the State. That pretence was a pretence; for a copy of it had been brought over to England by order of the Pope, and there is a letter in the Record Office of Sylvester de Gigliis, bishop of Worcester, to Henry VII., in which it is stated that the second Brief was issued for the consolation of queen Isabella, then upon her deathbed. See Letters and Papers, illustrative of the reigns of Richard III. and Henry VII., vol. i. p. 243. Publications of the Master of the Rolls.

There the question might have been left, and so in truth it would have been, if it had not been disturbed, partly by Wolsey, who would not allow the matter to rest, and partly by the king, who, grown weary of his wife, eager to marry Anne Boleyn, and therefore bent on having a divorce, allowed himself to be swayed by the most trivial reasons in the direction of his wishes.

It came to pass at this time that there was an embassy from France in England. Mary the princess of Wales had been formerly promised in marriage to the Dauphin, and now she was sought rather for the duke of Orleans, the second son of Francis I. In that embassy was the bishop of Tarbes.[1]

Henry then directed Wolsey to let the bishop know of the question that had been raised about the marriage, not indeed on the part of the king, but by Wolsey as a most faithful friend of the French alliance. He was also to say that king Henry, if the marriage could be set aside, would—and of that he had a certain expectation—make the sister of the French king his wife.

Wolsey did as he was bidden, and added that the question was one of such a nature that an Englishman should not be the first to touch it or bring it forward, for no subject could bear the burden of the hatred and illwill which he would incur if he impeached the marriage of the king, or raised a doubt concerning its validity. The best course to take was that he, the bishop of Tarbes, interested as he was in the welfare of both kingdoms, should, as the ambassador of the king of France, undertake the task himself.

[1] Gabriel de Gramont was consecrated bishop of Conserans in 1523, which see he left for that of Tarbes in 1524, and was in England in the year 1527. On the 24th Sept. in the year 1529 he was made archbishop of Bordeaux, and created Cardinal June 8, 1530. He became afterwards bishop of Poitiers, and in Oct. 1533 was archbishop of Toulouse. He died in the following year.

The proposal seemed fair to the bishop; so he took the advice of his companions, and before the council, in the presence of the king, spoke to this effect:—

"The English and the French are both alike persuaded that nothing is more desirable than peace for the two kingdoms; accordingly we have hitherto been settling the marriage of the duke of Orleans with her most serene highness Mary, princess of Wales, in furtherance of the blessing of peace—a marriage which, I do not doubt, will be to the advantage of both nations. But there is another way of attaining the same end, infinitely more convenient, were it permitted me to speak of it. But why should it not be? I have to do not only with Christian, but also with most excellent and wise men, who prefer the public good to any private advantage. How much better it would be if a marriage of this kind were contracted by grown-up persons rather than by children, by the sovereign rulers of their realms rather than by princes subject to them—in a word, by royal persons themselves rather than by their children. As for us in France, it is well known that the sister of the most Christian king, the duchess of Alençon, is to be had in marriage, and that she is not married because she is waiting for some one who shall increase and not lessen the royal splendour of her house. Now, if in England a certain chief personage—yea, even the first of all—were without a wife, why should we not try, to the great advantage of both kingdoms, to bring these royal personages together, and bind them in the bonds of wedlock?

"Your serene highness, most mighty king Henry—and I pronounce your name to do it honour—is free from the bonds of wedlock in reality if not in appearance, not in my opinion only, but in that of almost all the most learned men. For though Catherine be a most noble as well as a most saintly woman, I marvel much how you can have and keep her as your wife—the wife once of your brother, whom according to the gospel you may not have. I do not doubt at all that the gospel which the English, your subjects, believe, is the one which we also believe, though they may not speak their thoughts about your marriage openly till your highness gives them leave to do so.

"Foreign nations, indeed, have always spoken with greater freedom of this marriage, and are very sorry that your majesty in your youth was led to make such a mistake through the counsel of those whom you trusted. Now, if it be true that no man may marry his brother's wife, your highness has the best opportunity of throwing off as soon as possible the bonds of matrimony in which you are now held, and, by placing the sister of the most Christian king in the place of Catherine, of establishing a firm and lasting peace between these two most noble kingdoms. You will think in your wisdom more at leisure of this, it being enough for me to have spoken with Christian freedom of that which is at once advantageous and honourable."[1]

Henry feigned both displeasure and astonishment at this strange and hitherto unheard-of proposal, but as it touched his honour and his eternal salvation, he would take time to think of it. The bishop of Tarbes hurried back to France that he might be the first to give the king tidings, unexpected, of so joyful an event.

But the English, when they heard of the bishop's deed, spoke loudly against the ambassadors of France, and blamed in every way the intention of the king; for

1 Henry himself, in the presence of the Legates, in 1529, refers to this; but the bishop was the bishop of Bayonne, Jean du Bellay, unless it be a mistake of Cavendish, who in his "Life of Wolsey," p. 219, thus relates the fact: "I will declare unto you," says the king, "the special cause that moved me hereunto: it was a certain scrupulosity that pricked my conscience upon divers words that were spoken at a certain time by the bishop of Bayonne, the French king's ambassador."

everybody believed that the affair had been arranged and spoken of at his suggestion.

At this very time news arrived of the capture of Rome[1] by the Constable de Bourbon[2]—he had paid for his perfidy with his life—and of the sacking and burning of the city. The holy places were profaned, the sovereign Pontiff himself, Clement VII., besieged, yea, even kept as a prisoner.

Wolsey takes this opportunity of urging Henry VIII. to go to the aid of the Pope, saying that he could do nothing less than show himself the Defender of the Faith, for the king had lately received for himself and his descendants that title from the Apostolic See, because he had written a book against the heresies of Luther.[3] By helping the Pope, he said to the king, that he would lay him under a lasting obligation, would find him not only a favourable judge in the matter of the divorce, but also his earnest defender; besides, he would deserve well of the king of France, and especially of his children, whom he would thereby deliver out of the hands of Charles V., in whose power they were at the time.

The king was persuaded[4] to send the Cardinal to

[1] The troops of Charles V. entered Rome, May 6, 1527, and for two months the Holy City was subjected to the most grievous pillage and other wickedness of lawless men, most of whom were heretics from Germany; and among them was Thomas Cromwell, afterwards the vicar-general of Henry VIII., who thus began his life in murder and sacrilege.

[2] Charles duke of Bourbon, constable of France, born Feb. 28, 1489; slain before the gates of Rome May 6, 1527.

[3] The title of Defender of the Faith was granted to Henry by Leo X. Oct. 11, 1521. It had been asked for long before, but for some reasons there seemed to be an unwillingness to grant it, for even on May 22, 1516, Cardinal Wolsey complains of the delay to the bishop of Worcester—see Martene and Durand, Collect. Ampliss., vol. iii. col. 1274. The book which the king presented to the Pope as his own is now generally believed to have been the work of John Fisher, bishop of Rochester.

[4] According to Cavendish, the king sent Wolsey on this embassy by the persuasion of Anne Boleyn's friends, "that they might have convenient leisure and opportunity to adventure their long-desired enterprise, and by the aid of their chief mistress, my lady Anne, to deprave him so unto the king."—P. 148, ed. Singer.

France with two colleagues, and a sum of eighty thousand gold pieces. But besides the general instructions given alike to the three ambassadors, he gave others of a secret nature to Wolsey, which concerned the divorce of the queen, the marriage of the duchess of Alençon, and the deliverance of the two children of Francis, who were hostages in the hands of the emperor.

Wolsey set out on his journey[1] joyous and exulting, but to his astonishment, while halting in Calais, other letters are brought to him from the king. In these he is charged to say nothing of the marriage with the duchess of Alençon, and to speak only of the other matters. The reason of this was that the king had made up his mind to marry Anne Boleyn, if he could put queen Catherine away. Wolsey was angry, for his chief reason in pressing the divorce was that by the second marriage he might lay the king of France under an obligation, and thereby bind him to his interests. Wolsey, indeed, was not ignorant of the king's passion for Anne Boleyn, but he never imagined that the king meant to marry her; he persuaded himself that Henry would treat her as he had treated her sister and her mother before, who never had any expectations of being raised to the throne.

[1] In July 1527.

CHAPTER V.

SIR THOMAS BOLEYN—SIR FRANCIS BRYAN—EDUCATION OF ANNE BOLEYN.

ANNE BOLEYN was the daughter of Sir Thomas Boleyn's wife; I say of his wife, because she could not have been the daughter of Sir Thomas,[1] for she was born during his absence of two years in France on the king's affairs.[2] Henry VIII. sent him apparently on an honourable mission in order to conceal his own criminal conduct; but when Thomas Boleyn, on his return at the end of two years, saw that a child had been born in his house, he resolved, eager to punish the sin, to prosecute his wife before the delegates of the archbishop of Canterbury, and obtain a separation from her. His wife informs the king, who sends the marquis of Dorset[3] with an order to Thomas Boleyn to refrain from prosecuting his wife, to forgive her, and be reconciled to her.

[1] Sir Thomas Boleyn or Bullen was made viscount Rochford, June 18, 1525; earl of Wiltshire in England, and earl of Ormond in Ireland, Dec. 8, 1529. He died in 1538, having seen the dishonoured rise and the disgraceful ruin of his family.

[2] "In Francia legatum agente." Acting as ambassador, but not necessarily an ambassador; and the document, printed for the first time by Mr. Pocock, Records of the Reformation, ii. p. 573, agreeing substantially with this history, has the words: "A ce fois aux garres en France pour le roy." Here in the margin of the original is a note in these words: "Hæc narrantur a Gulielmo Rastallo, judice, in vita Thomæ Mori." William Rastall was a nephew of Sir Thomas More, and in the reign of Mary one of the puisne judges of the King's Bench.

[3] Thomas Grey, son of the first marquis of Dorset, and the father of Henry Grey, who was made duke of Suffolk. This duke of Suffolk married Frances, daughter of Charles Brandon, duke of Suffolk, and of Mary, sister of Henry VIII. Thomas Grey died in 1530, and all the honours of his family were forfeited by his eldest son, the duke of Suffolk.

Sir Thomas Boleyn saw that he must not provoke the king's wrath, nevertheless he did not yield obedience to his orders before he learned from his wife that it was the king who had tempted her to sin, and that the child Anne was the daughter of no other than Henry VIII. His wife then entreated him on her knees to forgive her, promising better behaviour in the future. The marquis of Dorset and other personages, in their own and in the king's name, made the same request, and then Sir Thomas Boleyn became reconciled to his wife, and had Anne brought up as his own child.

But his wife had borne Sir Thomas another daughter before this one, named Mary. Upon her the king had cast his eyes when he used to visit her mother, and now, after the return of Sir Thomas, he had her brought to the court, and ruined her. The royal household consisted of men utterly abandoned—gamblers, adulterers, panders, swindlers, false swearers, blasphemers, extortioners, and even heretics; among these was one distinguished profligate, Sir Francis Bryan,[1] of the blood and race of the Boleyn. This man was once asked by the king to tell him what sort of a sin it was to ruin the mother and then the child. Bryan replied that it was a sin like that of eating a hen first and its chicken afterwards. The king burst forth into loud laughter, and said to Bryan, "Well, you certainly are my vicar of hell." The man had been long ago called the vicar of hell on account of his notorious impiety, henceforth he was called also the king's vicar of hell. The king, who had sinned before with the mother and the elder daughter, turned his thoughts now to the other daughter, Anne.

[1] His office at court was master of the king's henchmen, *i.e.*, the king's pages. Le Grand (Histoire du Divorce, i. p. 79) thus writes of him: "Neveu de Norfolc, et cousin germain d'Anne de Boulen. On crût qu'avec cet apuy, il ne manqueroit pas de s'élever, et on le considera pendant quelque tems comme un favory naissant, mais il ne put se soutenir. Il aimoit à boire et etoit fort sujet a mentir."

Anne Boleyn was rather tall of stature, with black hair, and an oval face of a sallow complexion,[1] as if troubled with jaundice. She had a projecting tooth under the upper lip, and on her right hand six fingers.[2] There was a large wen under her chin, and therefore to hide its ugliness she wore a high dress covering her throat. In this she was followed by the ladies of the court, who also wore high dresses, having before been in the habit of leaving their necks and the upper portion of their persons uncovered. She was handsome to look at, with a pretty mouth, amusing in her ways, playing well on the lute, and was a good dancer. She was the model and the mirror of those who were at court, for she was always well dressed, and every day made some change in the fashion of her garments. But as to the disposition of her mind, she was full of pride, ambition, envy, and impurity.

At fifteen she sinned first with her father's butler, and then with his chaplain, and forthwith was sent to France, and placed, at the expense of the king, under the care of a certain nobleman not far from Brie.[3] Soon afterwards she appeared at the French court, where she was called the English mare, because of her

[1] "Colore subflavo." Simon Grynæus, quoted below, says she was "fuscula," and George Wyatt seems to admit the fact, when he says in the passage, part of which is given in the following note, "She was taken at that time to have a beauty not so whitely as clear and fresh above all we may esteem, which appeared much more excellent by her favour passing sweet and cheerful."

[2] Mr. Singer, in his edition of Cavendish, has printed a memoir of Anne Boleyn by George Wyatt, the grandson of Sir Thomas Wyatt, mentioned in this history, who admits this deformity in the following cautious and inconsistent terms: "There was found, indeed, upon the side of her nail, upon one of her fingers, some little show of a nail, which yet was so small, by the report of those that have seen her, as the workmaster seemed to leave it an occasion of greater grace to her hand, which with the tip of one of her other fingers might be and was usually by her hidden without any least blemish to it. Likewise there were said to be upon some parts of her body certain small moles incident to the clearest complexions."

[3] Blackwood (Martyre de la Royne d'Ecosse, p. 7. Anvers, 1588) says that the nobleman was a friend of Sir Thomas Boleyn: "Amy de ce père putatif."

shameless behaviour; and then the royal mule, when she became acquainted with the king of France. She embraced the heresy of Luther to make her life and opinions consistent,[1] but nevertheless did not cease to hear mass with the Catholics, for that was wrung from her by the custom of the king and the necessities of her own ambition.

On her return to England she was taken into the royal household, and there easily saw that the king was tired of his wife. She also detected the aims of Wolsey, how much the king was in love with herself, and how quickly he changed in his lawless affections. Not to speak of strangers to her family, she saw how her mother first, and then her sister, had been discarded by the king. What was she, then, to hope for in the end if she did not take care of herself at first? She made up her mind what to do. The more the king sought her, the more she avoided him, sanctimoniously saying that nobody but her husband should find her alone; nevertheless she did not think there was any want of modesty in talking, playing, and even in dancing with the king. In this way she so fed the fires of the king's passion that he became more and more determined to put away Catherine his wife, and to put a woman of such admirable modesty in her place.[2] The news was carried over into France, and there it became a common report that the king of England was going to marry the mule of the king of France.

[1] Sleidan, bk. ix. p. 170, Bohun's Trans.

[2] The author is more generous to Anne Boleyn than the Protestants were who strove to advance her. Simon Grynæus, an agent of the king, thus writes to Bucer (Original Letters, ed. Parker Society, Letter cclvi.): "Whether she has children by the king I do not know. She has not any acknowledged as such: they may probably be brought up in private, which, if I am not mistaken, I have heard more than once, though there are those who positively deny that the king has any intercourse with her, which in my opinion is not at all likely. But she is young, good-looking, of a rather dark complexion, and likely enough to have children."

CHAPTER VI.

SIR THOMAS BOLEYN WARNS THE KING — CONFESSION OF SIR THOMAS WYATT—INFATUATION OF THE KING—SIR THOMAS MORE — MARY BOLEYN — DISTRESS OF THE CARDINAL.

THOMAS BOLEYN, the reputed father of Anne, was at that time in France, detained there on the king's business with Sir Antony Brown.[1] But when he heard that the king was in love with his daughter, and wished to make her queen, he returned to England in great haste, and without the king's knowledge, thereby departing from the custom observed by ambassadors, to let the king know, while it was yet time, that which might prove hurtful to himself hereafter, if the king ever heard it from others. He applied himself to Henry Norris,[2] one of the king's chamberlains, begging him to make his excuses to the king for his unexpected return, and to obtain for him a secret audience.

Sir Thomas then, having obtained the audience, told the king everything; how Anne was born when he was in France, and how he for that reason would have sent his wife away if he, the king, had not interfered, and if his wife had not confessed without hesitation that Anne Boleyn was the king's child. Henry replied, "Hold your tongue, you fool, hundreds are compromised; and be her father who he may, she shall be my wife. Go back to your embassy, and do not say a word

[1] He was master of the horse to Henry.

[2] Groom of the stole, executed A.D. 1536.

of this." The king went away laughing, Sir Thomas being still on his knees.

To lessen men's surprise at the sudden arrival of Sir Thomas Boleyn, a report was spread abroad that he was the bearer of the picture of the duchess of Alençon to the king.[1] But afterwards, when Sir Thomas saw that the king was bent on marrying Anne, both he and his wife took every pains and trouble to help Anne, that they might not, by some mistake or other, miss the good fortune they expected. On the other hand, throughout England, every man of sense, modesty, and honour—every man who feared God, hated exceedingly the divorce of the queen and the marriage of Anne. Above all others, the members of the king's council thought it their duty to warn him. And as they would not meddle with questions of the divine law, for they were laymen, they resolved to speak only of Anne's licentious life, or rather of her reputation, which was of the worst; and that it might not be thought that they were influenced by idle rumours, they agreed that the whole matter should be investigated.

Among the courtiers was Thomas Wyatt, who being afraid, if the king discovered afterwards how shameless Anne's life had been, that his own life might be imperilled, went before the council, for his conscience accused him grievously, as soon as he knew it to be assembled for the purpose, and confessed that he had sinned with Anne Boleyn, not imagining that the king would ever make her his wife.

The council, furnished with this information, said that

[1] Stow, p. 530. "There arose about this time a brute in London that divers great clerks had told the king that the marriage between him and the lady Katherine, sometime wife to his brother, prince Arthur, was not lawful. Whereupon the king should sue a divorce and marry the dutchesse of Alanson, sister to the French king: the town of Calais this sommer, and thereupon viscount Rocheford had brought with him the picture of the same lady."

it was its duty to watch over not only the life, but also the honour and good name of the king; adding that Anne Boleyn was stained in her reputation, and that, moreover, so publicly as to make it unseemly in his majesty to take her as his wife. It also told the king all that Wyatt had confessed.

Henry was silent for awhile, and then spoke. He had no doubt, he said, that the council, in saying these things, was influenced by its respect and affection for his person, but he certainly believed that these stories were the inventions of wicked men, and that he could affirm upon oath that Anne Boleyn was a woman of the purest life. Thomas Wyatt was very angry when he heard that the king would not believe him, and so he said to some of the members of the council that he would put it in the king's power to see with his own eyes the truth of his story, if he would but consent to test it, for Anne Boleyn was passionately in love with Wyatt.[1]

Charles Brandon,[2] the duke of Suffolk, repeated the

[1] Harpsfield, Treatise of Marriage, bk. iii. p. 87. "Sir Thomas Wyatt the elder, understanding that the king minded to marry her, came to him and said, 'Sire, I pray your grace pardon me, both of my offence and my boldness. I am come to your grace of myself to discover and utter my own shame. But yet my most bounden duty and loyalty that I owe to your grace, and the careful tendering of your honour more than of my own honesty, forceth me to do this. Sire, I am credibly informed that your grace intendeth to take to your wife the said lady Anne Bulleyne, wherein I beseech your grace to be well advised what you do, for she is not meet to be coupled with your grace, her conversation hath been so loose and base, which thing I know, not so much by hearsay, as by my own experience, as one that have had my carnal pleasure with her.' At the hearing of this the king, for a while being something astonied, said to him, 'Wyatt, thou hast done like an honest man, yet I charge thee to make no more words of this to any man living!' This story have I heard the right worshipful merchant, Mr. Anthony Bonvise, rehearse; which thing he heard of them that were men very likely to know the truth thereof."

Dr. Nott (Surrey and Wyatt, ii. p. xviii.) says "the story is too absurd to need refutation," and in a note denies that Harpsfield had related the story of Wyatt. "A friend of mine," he says, "has gone over the whole of that MSS., and tells me that no mention of Wyatt's occurs in any part of it."

[2] Charles Brandon was "son to Sir William Brandon that bare king Henry VII.'s standard at Bosworth field, and was there slain."—Stow, p. 495. He was created viscount Lisle and duke of Suffolk, Feb. 2, 1514.

words of Wyatt to the king, who answered that he had no wish to see anything of the kind—Wyatt was a bold villain, not to be trusted. Why should I go on? The king told everything to Anne Boleyn, who shunned Wyatt; and that avoidance of him saved his life, for he too might have suffered death with the others when Anne's incest and adultery were detected.

When Wolsey had come back from France,[1] the king directed him to prosecute the cause of the divorce to the utmost of his power, and to press the Pope on the subject, chiding him somewhat sharply because of the slowness of his procedure. For if Catherine was to be put away—and on this Wolsey was of one mind with the king—why should he not be at liberty to marry an Englishwoman as well as a foreigner? It was not in Wolsey's power now to draw back from the enterprise on which they had entered; although he was in sore distress, he however put on a good face, and promised to exert himself.[2] He invites both the king and Anne to York House, where he entertains them at a sumptuous feast.[3]

[1] About the end of September or the beginning of October A.D. 1527, *i.e.*, not long before the courts sat in Michaelmas term, according to Cavendish, p. 186, ed. Singer, who says that the Cardinal, after visiting the king, "returned to his house at Westminster, where he remained until Michaelmas term, which was within a fortnight after."

[2] He then drew up the instructions for Sir Gregory Casali; the faculties which the Pope was to grant him for determining the validity or invalidity of the dispensation, and which the Pope—so he desired—was to sign blindly, trusting to Wolsey's honour. Sir Gregory was to say to the Pope, on behalf of the Cardinal, that he, the Cardinal, "pro re nullâ quantumque grandi, nullo favore aut commodo, quicquam effecturum quod aversetur officio meo, et erga Christum præstitæ professioni, neque unquam a recto, vero justoque tramite digressurum." But he insisted on being the judge, and in the same letter to Sir Gregory had said that the marriage was not lawful. The letter is printed by Burnet, Hist. Reform., iv. 19, ed. Pocock.

[3] Cavendish, p. 134, ed. Singer, 1827. "And yet the Cardinal, espying the great zeal that the king had conceived in this gentlewoman, ordered himself to please as well the king as her, dissimuling the matter that lay hid in his breast, and prepared great banquets and solemn feasts to entertain them both at his own house. And thus the world began to grow into wonderful inventions not heard of before in this realm."

Everybody was at this time talking of the divorce. All those urged it on in every way who thought that their advancement could be secured only by disturbances, for they saw a road open to the highest honours through the divorce. On the other hand, those who confessed the faith, loving only the truth, defended the cause of the queen, abandoned openly by men, as the most just. Books were everywhere written—some in defence of the marriage, others against it. One of the books attacking the marriage was presented to the king, and read in the presence of many bishops in the palace of Cardinal Wolsey, but most of the prelates dared say nothing either in favour of the truth or in condemnation of the king beyond this, that there were passages in the book which might reasonably make the king scrupulous about the marriage of himself and queen Catherine.[1] Every good man, and every learned man, was strongly against the divorce, and hardly anybody but the impious and the ignorant favoured it; nor was the king so dull as not to see that his cause met with grave opposition, and was in peril of being lost.

He sends for Thomas More, whom he knew to be a man of the highest ability, exceedingly learned and perfectly honest, and asks him his opinion about the marriage. More at the time was a member of the council, but he was not yet chancellor.[2] He answered candidly that he did not at all approve of the divorce.[3] Henry did not

[1] Sir Thomas More seems to speak of this (Strype, Mem., i. ii. p. 197) in his letter to Cromwell: "Which book was afterward at York Place, in my Lord Cardinal's chamber, read in the presence of divers bishops and many learned men. And they all thought that there appeared in the book good and reasonable causes that might move the king's highness, being so virtuous a prince, to conceive in his mind a scruple against his marriage: which, while he could not otherwise avoid, he did well and virtuously, for the acquiescing of his conscience, to sue and procure to have his doubt decided by judgment of the Church."

[2] Sir Thomas More received the seals Oct. 25, 1529, and took the oath of his office the next day.

[3] Sir Thomas More himself in a letter to Cromwell (Strype, Mem., i. ii. 197) speaks of this: "At which

like the answer, but he would leave no stone unturned to serve his purpose, so he promised the highest rewards to Sir Thomas if he would conform his view to that of the king, and then commanded him to take counsel on the subject with Dr. Fox, provost of King's College, Cambridge.[1] This Dr. Fox was the most zealous of all the promoters of the divorce. But so far from changing his opinion after the conference was More, that he would have urged the king with far greater freedom not to put away his wife, if he had the opportunity; but the king never touched upon the subject again, though in other affairs the services of More were regarded above those of all others. The king used to say that if Sir Thomas More were won over to his side, it would do more for him than the assent of half his kingdom.

About this time Mary Boleyn, the elder sister,[2] seeing that Anne was preferred to her, and that she herself was slighted not only by the king but by her sister, went to the queen, and bade her be of good cheer; for though the king, she said, was in love with her sister, he could never marry her, for the relations of the king with the family

time not presuming to look that his highness should anything take that point for the more proved or improved for my poor mind in so great a matter, I showed, nevertheless, as my duty was, at his commandment, what thing I thought upon the words which I there read. Whereupon his highness accepting benignly my sudden unadvised answer, commanded me to commune further with Mr. Fox, now his grace's almoner, and to read a book with him that then was making for that matter."

[1] Edward Fox, born in Dursley, Gloucestershire; educated at Eton and King's College, which he entered March 12, 1512. He was elected provost Dec. 27, 1528. He became also archdeacon of Leicester and Dorset. Soon after, he was made the king's almoner, and employed in the diplomatic service. He seems to have been a heretic very early, and accepted the bishopric of Hereford in 1535, retaining with it the provostship of King's College, and died in London May 8, 1538. He was consecrated by Cranmer, and without Bulls, therefore never a lawful bishop.

[2] It has been said of late years that Mary was younger than Anne. Mr. Brewer (Letters, &c., iv. Introd. p. ccxxvi) writes: "We must infer that Mary was the elder sister. Any doubt on that head is entirely dispelled by the petition presented to Lord Burghley in 1597 by Mary's grandson, the second Lord Hunsdon, claiming the earldom of Ormond in virtue of Mary's right as the elder daughter."

were of such a nature as to make a marriage impossible by the laws of the Church. "The king himself," she said, "will not deny it, and I will assert it publicly while I live; now, as he may not marry my sister, so neither will he put your majesty away."

The queen thanked her, and replied that all she had to say and do would be said and done under the direction of her lawyers.

But Henry was held back not so much by his respect for the laws of the Church as by his fear of the emperor Charles V.; for he knew too well that the emperor would not patiently endure the divorce of his aunt, and that his own subjects would be angry if he entered into new and questionable relations with the French, and deserted the ancient alliance of the house of Burgundy, with which they were bound by the gainful bonds of trade. He saw also that men loved and admired the queen for her goodness, while Anne Boleyn was everywhere regarded as a woman of unclean life, and that Wolsey, his chief minister, was not so earnest in the matter as he had been; and last of all, he remembered the account he had one day to give before the judgment-seat of God. The thought of this pursued him night and day; he could come to no decision, and was unable to sleep. Whether he had friends he knew not, but he was certain he had enemies; and besides this, his own conscience condemned him, and he regarded his life as joyless.

But when he could not indulge his passions except on the condition of making Anne Boleyn his wife, and was by some told that his marriage with Catherine was against law, knowing also that he had rendered such services to Pope Clement, in return for which he might confidently expect that the Pope would do for him all that he was asking him to do, and that both the neighbouring princes and his own subjects would yield before the authority of the Pope, he doggedly made up his mind, overcome by his passions, to put Catherine away, to make Anne his wife, and disregard the emperor, then at variance with France and Venice. And certainly if the Roman Pontiff were not he whom, because he sits in the see of Peter, the effectual prayer of Christ Himself has made strong in the faith,[1] there was every appearance that Clement would have yielded in everything to the wishes of the king.

While the king was thus tormented, Wolsey also was troubled in the same way, carried to and fro in the tumult of his thoughts. At one moment he was glad to see the emperor slighted by the king, at another grieved at the elevation of Anne Boleyn to the highest rank. At one time he was afraid the king would dismiss him with contempt and find other means to obtain the divorce, at another time he hoped that the king's passion for Anne Boleyn would die out, and that he might be persuaded to marry the sister of the most Christian king. Anyhow the Cardinal, domineered by his lust of power, forced himself to satisfy the desires of the king.

[1] St. Luke xxii. 32.

CHAPTER VII.

THE KING SENDS ENVOYS TO ROME—ANSWER OF THE POPE—DECISION OF THE CARDINALS—LEGATES APPOINTED.

THE king and the Cardinal resolved to send Stephen Gardiner[1] and Francis Bryan as ambassadors to the Pope.[2] Gardiner was one of the most learned lawyers of the day, and was now in the service of the king, having been hitherto of the household of Wolsey. These men, to make themselves the more welcome to the Pontiff, made efforts at Venice in the king's name to obtain the restitution of Ravenna to the Apostolic See: the Venetians, however, refused to do so then. From Venice they went to Orvieto, where the Pope was residing at the time.[3] When they came into the presence of His

[1] Stephen Gardiner, educated at Cambridge, master of Trinity Hall in 1525. In 1529 he was made archdeacon of Norfolk, of Worcester and of Leicester in 1531, at the end of which, Dec. 3, he was consecrated bishop of Winchester. He was deprived of the mastership of Trinity Hall under Edward VI., but was restored in 1556, and continued to hold the office with his bishopric for the rest of his life. Gardiner was one of the most zealous agents of the king in the matter of the divorce, and in the maintenance of his supremacy.

[2] Gardiner went first with Edward Fox, the king's almoner, and set out on his journey in the second week of Feb. 1528. Sir Francis Bryan went in November following, having as his companion Peter Vannes, then the king's secretary, but who, like Gardiner, had been trained in the service of the Cardinal.

[3] Clement VII. had then made his escape from Rome, and was in great distress, but Gardiner (Pocock, Records, i. 89) is so far from being touched at the sight of the Vicar of God in his poverty that he thus writes: "The Pope lieth in an old palace of the bishops of this city, ruinous and decayed, where, or we come to his privy bedchamber, we pass three chambers, all naked and unhanged, the roofs fallen down, and as we can guess, thirty persons, rif-raf and other, standing in the chamber for a garnishment. And as for the Pope's bedchamber, all the apparel in it was not worth twenty nobles, bed and all."

Holiness they congratulated him on his escape, and then laid their two proposals before him. The first was that His Holiness should join the league of the English and the French against the emperor; the second, that he should by his authority dissolve the marriage of Henry and Catherine, who, they confessed, was a most noble and virtuous lady, but the widow of the king's brother. Of this marriage they said that it was contrary to the law of nature, and that Julius II. was deceived into sanctioning it, seeing that he had no power to dispense with the divine law.

The scruples of the king, they avow, might have been removed at home by the English bishops; but the king, to give no ground for the emperor to suspect that the English bishops had arranged the matter in the king's interests only, preferred to have the question brought before the sovereign court of the whole Church. His Holiness could settle the matter most easily, for the divorce once agreed upon by the king and queen,[1] the queen, a saintly woman, desirous of a more austere life, would without difficulty withdraw into a monastery. No better judges for the settlement of the question could be assigned than the distinguished Cardinals Campeggio[2] and Wolsey[3]—the one at present in England, having a perfect knowledge of the matter; the other having been

[1] Gardiner, writing from Orvieto, March 31, 1528 (Pocock, Records, i. 101), says that the Pope asked him "whether the king's highness had at any time broken this matter to the queen," and that he answered, "Yes, and that she showed herself content to stand to the judgment of the Church."

[2] Lorenzo Campeggio succeeded his father as professor of law in Bologna, and on the death of his wife was sent for to Rome, made auditor of the Rota and bishop of Feltre A.D. 1512. In 1523 he was translated to Bologna, and in 1525 resigned. He was Cardinal Protector of England in 1524, and in the same year, on the king's petition, Clement VII. made him administrator of the see of Salisbury, and in 1535 Henry VIII. deprived him.

[3] Gardiner and Fox, writing to Cardinal Wolsey from Orvieto, March 31, 1528 (Pocock, Records, i. 104), say, "We thought Cardinal Campegius should be a very meet personage to be sent into England, who might, being there jointly with your grace, proceed in this matter."

at a former time in that country with the power of a Legate,[1] sent by Leo X., could not be wholly unacquainted with English affairs.

The Pope having thanked both the king and them, and explained why he could not enter into the French league, he wished them to lay the question of the divorce before certain Cardinals and theologians; if it could be shown that the king's petition could be lawfully granted, he would not only grant it, but would congratulate himself that he had an opportunity of showing how thankful he was to so great a prince, who, by the most learned work he had written in defence of the seven sacraments of the Church, had rendered such great services to the Church at large, and who also had lately come to the assistance of the Apostolic See, and, above all, had placed the Pope under infinite obligations by delivering him out of the hands of his enemies.[2]

The Cardinals and the theologians having heard the arguments and reasonings of the ambassadors, with one consent reported that the marriage of Henry and Catherine was valid and lawful, and forbidden by no divine law. The passage in Leviticus about the brother's wife must of necessity be interpreted so that it shall not clash with the law afterwards declared in Deuteronomium, by which the surviving brother is commanded to marry

[1] The peaceful entry of the Legate into England A.D. 1518 was purchased by Leo X. at a heavy price. Wolsey threatened to bar his passage unless his faculties were withdrawn, and he (Wolsey) made co-Legate with Campeggio. Leo X. gave way. If the Cardinal had indulged his ambition less, it would have been better for him and for England, for the Legatine faculties thus wrung from the Pope supplied the king with the means of his utter undoing twelve years later. See the Cardinal's letter in Martene et Durand, Ampliss. Collect., iii. 1284.

[2] Gardiner and Fox, writing to Cardinal Wolsey from Orvieto, March 31, 1528 (Pocock, Records, i. 111), say, "The Pope's Holiness said that all that which with his honour he might do, he would do it gladly without trait or difficulty." P. 113, "His Holiness said he gladly would do all things he might by his authority do." P. 95, "Agreeable with law and equity." But law and equity were understood in another sense by Henry and his counsellors.

the wife of his brother dying without issue.[1] These laws are perfectly in unison, the latter being only an exception to the first; or if they are contradictory, it is not the law in Leviticus that must prevail, but that in Deuteronomium, which repeals it. As for the words of St. John the Baptist, "it is not lawful for thee to have thy brother's wife,"[2] brought forward by the ambassadors, it is plain that the Baptist was speaking of a brother then living, the tetrarch of Iturea and Trachonitis,[3] to whom a daughter had been born; whereas Arthur, the king's brother, not only was not living, but had left no children of the marriage.[4] In a question so free from doubt, no judges should be appointed, least of all in England, where everything would be at the king's mercy; and above all, those should not be sent as judges who, having received great favours from the king, were therefore in a greater measure than others bound to serve him.

When this report was made known to Dr. Stephen,[5] he went back to the Pope, and said that there were theologians in Rome of another opinion, and added that the king, even if the marriage were not forbidden by the divine law, would make it plain that the dispensation granted by Pope Julius was by no means canonical or lawful; he was exceedingly surprised that the question was not referred to judges for its solution at the request of a king who had done such services to the

1 Levit. xviii. 16; Deuter. xxv. 5.

2 St. Mark vi. 18.

3 St. Luke iii. 1.

4 Tyndale (Practice of Prelates, p. 328, ed. Parker Society) argues in the same way: "I see no remedy but that a man must understand the text thus—that Moses forbiddeth a man to take his brother's wife as long as his brother liveth, . . . and therefore John rebuked Herod for taking his brother's wife from him, his brother being yet alive; . . . but if his brother die childless, then he ought to have her, and that she is bound to offer herself to the other brother, by the law of Moses; and that it is lawful now, though no commandment."

5 Dr. Stephen Gardiner. He is called Dr. Stephen or Steven as often, if not more frequently, than Dr. Gardiner.

Church, seeing that the like petition from private persons would not be refused: he expected a more favourable answer from His Holiness.[1] The Pontiff said, "What I can do lawfully for the king, that I will do.[2] This, however, is not a question of human law, but of a Christian marriage; and as that is a sacrament instituted by Christ, it is not in my power to change the law: you are asking for the dissolution of a marriage, when man cannot sever that which God has united; a marriage, too, entered into with the sanction of my predecessor, confirmed by a cohabitation of twenty years and the birth of children. Besides, does not the matter touch the honour both of Catherine the queen and of Charles the emperor? Who will answer for it, that such a divorce may not be the occasion of a great war? It is my duty to take care that no troubles that I can hinder shall rise to disturb the Church of God."

So spoke the Pope, but he referred the question again to other Cardinals and theologians. Among these,

[1] Gardiner (*ut supra*, p. 110) confesses that he threatened the Pope. "I said the king's highness would take very strangely, and would think his manifold benefits ill employed, if in the manner and form of obtaining justice there shall no more respect be had of his person and weight of his cause than *promiscuæ plebis;* ne obtain more here after so great charges, costs, and delay of time, than his majesty might have obtained at home. Not doubting but his majesty understanding hereof would use *domestico remedio apud suos.*"

[2] The Pope never spoke in any other sense throughout the progress of this suit. Gardiner and Gregory Casali threatened the Pontiff "that the king would do it without him." This was on April 1, 1528, before the Legates were appointed. The answer of the Pope was (Pocock, Records, i. 127), according to Gardiner, "He would it were done;" but that did not mean that he would approve of it, but that such an act on the part of Henry would bring the cause to a decision sooner; for the Pope adds, "In a matter *in qua vertitur jus tertii* he could do nothing without the counsel of them, and wished that it were in his power to give the king's highness somewhat depending only of his own particular hurt or damage, without touching any man's rights, with suchlike words, nothing sounding to the furtherance." Again, after the trial in London, Dr. Bennet, in a letter from Rome, Oct. 27, 1530, reporting the Pope's answer to his demands, says, "He said that he would do nothing in this matter, but that the law will, neither for your highness, neither for the French king, neither for the emperor; and other answer we could not get of him."

though some said it would be better to try the question in Rome, where justice was done to all, than to have it tried in England, where everything would be at the king's mercy, yet there were others who, fashioning ecclesiastical affairs for political ends, and complaining loudly of the heresies that had lately grown up in Germany, and of the excessive lukewarmness of other princes in the defence of the faith, were of opinion that Henry, a most zealous defender of the faith, should be more gently dealt with, especially as it was said, that the queen was willing to enter a monastery. It certainly seemed very hard, to them, that judges should not be appointed at the request of so great a king; it was possible that the king, during the progress of the suit, if at present somewhat perverse, might be brought by degrees to a better mind. Why stand in the way of a trial? It is in the power of the Pope to have the cause at any time brought before himself.

The latter opinion prevailed with the Pope, partly because he favoured Henry very much, and partly because he had no suspicion whatever that all that which had been said to him about the consent of Catherine, and of her desire to become a nun, was false. Accordingly Lorenzo Campeggio and Thomas Wolsey, Cardinals, priests, and bishops, were appointed judges in the cause.

CHAPTER VIII.

THE QUEEN PETITIONS THE POPE—CARDINAL CAMPEGGIO ARRIVES IN ENGLAND—HYPOCRISY OF HENRY—FIRMNESS OF THE QUEEN—ANNE BOLEYN AT COURT—INSOLENCE OF THE KING'S AMBASSADORS.

THOUGH nothing had been said to the queen about the embassy sent to Rome,[1] yet the moment she suspected that something of the kind was done, she wrote to the Pope begging him to send no Legates to try the question of the divorce in England, for that would be nothing else but to make the king a judge in his own cause. She wrote also to the emperor, and told him of Wolsey's intrigue and of the king's purpose, earnestly beseeching him not to abandon his aunt, who must endure these wrongs because of the hatred borne to the emperor.

The imperial ambassador complained to the Pope that the king of England had sent his agents secretly from England to Rome, and had kept the fact from the knowledge of the queen, who was chiefly concerned in the matter, and that judges had been appointed before the Pope had heard what the queen had to say in her own defence. "What scandals will arise," he said, "when the emperor defends his aunt against the wrong-doings of the king! What was to be looked for from

[1] The king was afraid of the queen's interference from the first, and there is a letter of his to the Cardinal, Sept. 1527 (Burnet, vi. 22, ed. Pocock), in which he says, "Lest the queen should prevent us by the emperor's means in our great matter."

England in its present state, where the most wicked men, because they encouraged the king in his evil courses, were raised to all places of honour, but where the good and faithful people, who, purely through the fear of God, defended the cause of the queen, were thrust out of every place of honour which they held ?"

Then the Pope, seeing that the information given him by the king was false, sent four messengers in all haste, by different roads, with directions to Campeggio to travel as slowly as he could,[1] and on his arrival in England, to make every effort to reconcile the king and the queen, and if he should fail, then to persuade the latter to become a religious.[2] But if in that also he should fail, he was at least not to pronounce the sentence of divorce without a fresh and clear command of the Pope. "This," said the Pope, "you must regard as the final and most serious injunction."

He wrote other letters also from Viterbo, in which he clearly showed that if the matter concerned only himself, he would have shrunk from no danger for the sake of the king, but now the king's wishes could not be satisfied without injustice and public scandal.

Campeggio[3] arrived in London October 7, 1528, and

[1] This is the explanation of the words of Campeggio—"Quanto alla negociatione mia ch' io vada adagio. Io l' ho fatto, et quanto mi sarà lecito lo faro por la cagione che ella scrive"—in his letter from Paris to Salviati, secretary of the Pope. According to Theiner, the letter is dated 16th Nov. 1528, doubtless a mistake for September, seeing that Cardinal Campeggio was in London during that month.

[2] In the letter of John Casali, Dec. 17 (Burnet, iv. 67, ed. Pocock; and Le Grand, iii. 117), in which the writer gives an account of an audience of the Pope, the fact is thus stated: "Ego, inquit [Pontifex], illi [Campegio] imposui ut divortium regi dissuaderet, persuaderet reginæ." See also the account of the interview between the Legates and the queen, given by Du Bellay, in Le Grand, iii. 195.

[3] He was lodged the first night in the house of the duke of Suffolk, in the borough, and the next day was to make his public entry into London. But as he was suffering from gout, he avoided the fatigues of that ceremony, and was carried in a boat towards evening to the palace of the bishop of Bath and Wells, where he remained. The next morning, Friday, he was visited by the Cardinal of York, and on the 22d was received

on being introduced to the king by Wolsey,[1] on behalf of the Pope, the Cardinals, the clergy, and people of Rome, he offered their services to Henry as the one whom they regarded as their deliverer. Fox then, on the part of the king, replied. That done, the king and the two Cardinals withdrew together, and had a long and secret conference on the question of the divorce. The arrival of Campeggio was most disagreeable to men of every rank in the kingdom, for it was commonly reported that he was come for the purpose of setting aside the marriage of the king with his saintly queen.[2] To her above all was it painful, and her nights and days were spent in mourning and in weeping.

Campeggio sent persons to her in secret, and made attempts to console her; but when he advised her to enter, of her own accord, some religious order, at least for the security of her life, she answered resolutely that she was determined to uphold the marriage to the utmost of her power, a marriage which the Roman Church

in public by the king. On the following day the king called on the Cardinal after dinner, and in answer to his proposal to obtain a dispensation to ratify the marriage, and thereby take away all scruples, the king answered, that to effect that he did not wish for such a dispensation, and insisted on the invalidity of the former, and the nullity of the marriage. —Theiner Monum. Hibernorum, p. 572.

[1] Stow, p. 541. "On the 9th of October he came from St. Mary Overy's by water to the bishop of Bath's palace, without Temple Bar, where he was visited by the Cardinal of York and divers other estates and prelates; and after he had rested him a season, he was brought to the king's presence, then being at Bridewell, by the Cardinal of York, and was carried in a chair between four persons, for he was not able to stand, and the Cardinal of York and he sat both on the right hand of the king's throne, and there one Francisco, secretary to Cardinal Campeius, made an eloquent oration in Latin, ... to the which oration Doctor Fox, provost of Cambridge, made a discrete answer."

[2] Harpsfield, Treatise of Marriage, bk. ii. pp. 99, 100. "Nothing was touched at this time openly of the king's great matter, but much and divers talk and rumour came abroad after the coming of the Legate. Neither would men spare to talk freely and frankly, that the king to serve his own appetite and pleasure more than for any just impediment in his marriage, had procured the said Legate to be sent for that he might be divorced from the queen, which almost universally was misliked, especially among the common people."

had once decreed as lawful. She would not acknowledge him as judge whose appointment to that office was not so much made by the Pope as wrung from him by manifest falsehood on the part of the king.

Campeggio understood her. He then wrote to the Pope, and told him of the queen's resolution and of the excessive pressing of the king to have the matter ended; he informed him also that Wolsey, whose name was before his in the commission, was wholly bent on pronouncing for the divorce,[1] and then begged His Holiness to tell him as soon as possible what he was to do. The Pope remained silent, for at this time his sole object was delay; and so nothing more was done in the matter for six months, from October 7, 1528, to May 28, 1529.

The king, seeing the indignation of the people[2] at his attempt to put away so noble a woman as his wife for the sake of a woman unclean of life, called peers and commons together on the 8th day of November, and in their presence declared upon oath that he had begun this process solely from conscientious scruples, and not

[1] Cardinal Campeggio, writing from London, October 17, 1528, says that the Cardinal Wolsey and the king "erano risoluti in questa materia di venire alla dissolutione del matrimonio," and that he could not shake in the least degree the determination of Wolsey, "allegando che se non si seguiva il desiderio del Re, il quale è munito et giustificato da molte ragioni, scritture et consigli di molti homini litterati et timorati di Dio, che ne seguirà presta et total ruina del regno, di sua Signoria reverendissima, et della reputatione ecclesiastica in questo regno."—Theiner, pp. 570, 571.

[2] Harpsfield, Treatise of Marriage, bk. ii. p. 100. "For the repressing of which talk the king assembled at his palace at Bridewell, in the month of November, his nobility, judges, and councillors, with divers other persons, to whom he declared the great worthiness of his wife, both for her nobility and virtue and all princely qualities to be such that if he were to marry again, he would of all women match with her, if the marriage might be found good and lawful. But her worthiness notwithstanding, and that he had a fair daughter by her, he said he was wonderfully tormented in conscience, for that he understood by many great clerks, with whom he had consulted, that he had lived all this while in detestable and abominable adultery, wherefore, for the settling of his conscience, and the sure and firm succession of the realm, he did advocate this Legate, as a man most indifferent, and said that if she by the law of God should be adjudged his lawful wife, there was never thing more pleasant and acceptable to him in all his life."

because he was in love with any other woman;[1] there was not a more saintly woman, or one of nobler birth than his wife, and he had no fault to find with her but that of having been his brother's wife. The people who heard him swear this were amazed at the impudence of the man: the lewdness and adulteries of his life crying out aloud that he was not so tenderly devout as to be much troubled by scruples of conscience.

Campeggio persuaded the king to allow the matter to be settled in a friendly way, and not by means of an unfriendly lawsuit. The king was pleased with the advice he gave, and the Cardinals with his consent went to the queen[2] to induce her to enter some religious order. But when they had said, by way of preface, that they had received a commission from the Pope to try the question of the validity of her marriage, she interrupted them at once, and told them that they were opening a question settled for ever—settled not only in the councils of two of the most prudent monarchs, but in the consistory of the Pope, Pope Julius. The matter is determined by a married life of twenty years, and by the birth of children, the congratulation and the sanction of Christendom. Then, looking at Wolsey, she added, "I am indebted for this sorrow to you alone, who persecute me with so much hatred, either because I have not been able to endure your ambition and your immoral life, or because my nephew the emperor took no pains to obtain for you the Papacy."[3]

[1] At this time Cardinal Wolsey had in his possession a letter written by both the king and Anne Boleyn, urging the hurrying on of the divorce. See Burnet's Hist. Reform., i. p. 103, ed. Pocock.

[2] The two Cardinals went to the queen, Tuesday, Oct. 27.—Theiner, 578.

[3] Harpsfield, *ut supra*, p. 101. "Not long after this both the Legates repaired to the queen and told her that they were appointed by the Pope judges to hear and determine the controversy lately risen touching her marriage with the king, and to give a final sentence whether it were consonant with the law of God or no. The queen, after the hearing of this, being abashed and aston-

Then, when they saw her great distress, and the tears which she could not control, they thought it better to refrain from further discussion and to do the rest of their work by the mouth of others.

The king[1] kept Christmas in great splendour, with jousts, banquets, and pageants, to which the Cardinals were asked, and made a display in the sight of all the people of his passion for Anne Boleyn. Wolsey warned him that he must be careful of his own honour at least, and leave Anne to her father's care till the end of the trial. At last the king consented, not without difficulty, that at least during Lent they should not see one another. But when Lent was over, he ordered Thomas Boleyn, whom he had already raised to the peerage as Lord Rochford,[2] to bring Anne back secretly to court. At the same time he wrote a letter full of love to Anne herself, and most tenderly begged her to return. But she would not go back to

ied, and pausing awhile, 'Alas! my lords,' saith she, 'that now almost after twenty years there should any such question be once moved, and that men should now go about to dissolve and undo this marriage as wicked and detestable,' imputing the original of all her trouble to Cardinal Wolsey and to his deadly feud against the emperor, whom he of all princes of Europe most maligned and hated, because he would not serve and content his immoderate ambition, aspiring to be made Pope. The Cardinal, on the other side, laid all the fault from himself, and declared that this thing chanced far against his will. He said he was by the Pope assigned to be a judge in this cause, and swore by his profession that he would, in hearing the same, minister justice and right indifferently."

[1] Hall, 756. "The king kept his Christmas at Greenwich with much solemnity and great plenty of viands, and thither came the two Legates, which were received by two dukes and divers earls, barons, and gentlemen, to whom the king shewed great pleasures, both of justs and tourney, banquets, masks, and disguisings. And on the twelfth day he made the lawful son of Cardinal Campeius, born in wedlock, knt., and gave him a collar of S.S. in gold. But the queen shewed to them no manner of countenance, and made no great joy of nothing: her mind was so troubled."

[2] Sir Thomas Boleyn was created Viscount Rochford June 18, 1525. On the same day Henry Fitzroy, the son of Elizabeth Blount and of Henry VIII., was created earl of Nottingham and duke of Richmond and Somerset. Sir Thomas Boleyn was made earl of Wiltshire Dec. 8, 1529. Du Bellay, writing to the grand master of France Dec. 26, 1527, says that there was a report at this time that Sir Thomas Boleyn was to be made duke of Somerset. —Le Grand, iii. 76.

him who had sent her so undeservedly away; nor could her mother persuade her by any means to go back to the king. But when Thomas Boleyn, who used to say that the king's wrath is the messenger of death, advised her to return as soon as possible, unless she wished to be the ruin of herself and of the whole house of Boleyn, she answered, "I will go, but when I shall once have that man within my clutches, I will treat him as he deserves." Then the king, to soothe her temper, forgetting all respect to his own name and honour, received her with greater magnificence than he had ever done before.

But as to the question of the divorce. When the king saw that all theologians and canonists were of one mind, namely, that the marriage would have been unlawful but for the authority of Julius II., who dispensed with the observance of the ecclesiastical law, he strained every nerve to break the force of that dispensation of the Pope.[1]

To that end special instructions[2] were given to Stephen Gardiner and Sir Francis Bryan, who were still in Rome, to spend money without stint, and to promise large presents to those Cardinals and theologians who might be of service to them. The king, too, by his ambassadors, asked the Pope to pronounce the dispensation

[1] The Cardinal in November 1528, and now one of the two judges before whom the cause was to be tried, instructed the ambassadors in Spain to find proofs of the forgery of the second Brief of Julius II., saying himself that he regarded that Brief as a forgery—"*Verum si falsum, quod arbitror*" (Pocock, Records, i. 187), and that it would be a most pleasing service to the king to throw more suspicion upon it—"*rem gravissimam et acceptissimam regiæ majestati faciet.*"

[2] The heads of these instructions have been published by Mr. Pocock, Records, i. p. 189. Among them are these: "Declaratio Pontificis per Bullam quod matrimonium ab initio . . . non esset verum. De trahendis amicis in partem regis verbis, pollicitationibus et aliis modis quibuscunque. De lucrandis et attrahendis cardinalibus in partem regis et præsertim Sanctorum Quatuor."

granted by Pope Julius a forgery, and therefore worthless; and secondly, for the settlement of the royal succession, to sanction the marriage of the princess Mary, the daughter of Henry and Catherine, with the duke of Richmond, the bastard child of the king.[1]

The third request was made in writing, and not by word of mouth: the king with his own hand wrote and subscribed a petition to His Holiness—who can temper and relax the ecclesiastical laws, by his Apostolic authority—in which he prayed the Pope to allow his marriage with Anne Boleyn, notwithstanding the impediment of the canon law,[2] which made it unlawful because of his criminal relations with Mary, the sister of Anne.[3]

That the king wrote that letter and made that request is hinted at by Cardinal Cajetan, and plainly asserted by Cardinal Pole,[4] who adds that even this last request would have been granted, if it could have been shown that Pope Julius had not the power to grant the dispensation which made the marriage of Henry and Catherine lawful.

[1] Cardinal Campeggio, in his letter written from England to Rome, says that this project was then discussed when he came over as Legate. Theiner, Vet. Mon., p. 571: "Et han pensato di maritarla con dispensa di S. S. al figliol naturale del re, se si potrà fare."

[2] Harpsfield, bk. iii. p. 57, Eyston MSS. "He sought to be dispensed to marry with her whose sister he had carnally known before."

[3] The dispensation to be granted by the Pope was drawn up in England, and contained this clause: The king to be at liberty to marry any woman, "Dummodo proptèr hoc rapta non fuerit, etiam si illa tibi alias secundo aut remotiori consanguinitatis, aut primo affinitatis gradu, etiam ex quocunque licito vel illicito coitu proveniente."—See Pocock, Records, i. p. 26, Dod. ed. Tierney, i. p. 357. The only person excluded by the king was the widow of his brother—"dummodo relicta dicti fratris tui non fuerit." The date of the desired Bull was Dec. 21, 1527. Mr. Pocock has taken his copy from the "form in which it appears in the Record Office."

[4] De Eccles. Unit. Defens., lib. iii. c. iii. "Quia eodem tempore quo Pontificis dispensationem de uxore fratris ducenda rejecisti, ab eodem Pontifice magna vi contendebas, ut tibi liceret ducere sororem ejus quæ concubina tua fuisset, idque ita impetrasti, si ante constitisset non habuisse jus Pontificem priore illa in causa dispensandi."

The course pursued with respect to the first request of the king was this: his ambassadors demanded the production, and then the quashing, of the decree of Pope Julius in confirmation of the marriage. That the matter might be properly and orderly dealt with, the Pope said he would ask the emperor, in whose keeping was the original Brief of Julius, to send it either to Rome or to the Legates in England. The king's ambassadors demanded that, unless the emperor produced the Brief within two months from that time, the Pontiff should pronounce it null and of no effect. This demand was, by order of the Pope, referred to the two Cardinals, Del Monte, and of the Four Saints, to the Bishop Simoneta, and to certain theologians, who having taken it into consideration, said that it was against all justice, seeing that too short a time was allowed the emperor, and that the decree which the Pope was asked to make was without precedent.[1]

Thereupon the Pontiff said that he should write to the emperor, from whom he did not think that more could be got by threats and legal pressure than by fair dealing. On the other hand, the ambassadors said that they cared nothing for the production of the Brief if not produced by a certain day.

Now, as this brought great trouble on the Pope, he wrote to Campeggio and blamed him for allowing such matters to be referred to Rome; they should have been settled in England, and he should not have allowed any one to think that he could obtain from the Pope that which ought never to be granted. The secretary of the Pope, John Baptist Sanga, ended the letter with a complaint against the king's ambassadors for the boldness

[1] The decree was drawn up in England, made ready for the signature of the Pope, who was instructed to say that an authentic Brief of his predecessor was a forgery. See the proposed decree in Pocock, Records, i. 184. "Ipsum Breve pro falso et nullo reputandum."

of their language and the threats they uttered against the Apostolic See, foreboding mischief if the Pope refused to grant the desires of the king.[1] As if His Holiness, he said, ought to fail in his duty, which he will not do to gain the whole world, or as if threats of this kind would not prove hurtful first of all to those who uttered them, as certainly they would, if the king, to gratify his passions, were to separate himself, as he has done at home from his wife, so abroad from the Apostolic See, the source and mother of the Christian Church. From all this it appears beyond all doubt that the ambassadors were well aware of the king's purpose to renounce the faith together with his wife, rather than live without Anne Boleyn.

[1] Gardiner used threatening language when he was baffled by the Roman lawyers (Pocock, Records, i. 133): he said to the Pope that if he did not grant the divorce, Henry VIII. would withdraw his favour from the Pope, "*ut inclinata jam Sedes Apostolica tota corrueret, communi consensu atque applausu omnium.* At these words, the Pope's Holiness, casting his arms abroad, bade us put in the words we varied for, and therewith walked up and down the chamber, casting now and then his arms abroad, we standing in great silence."

CHAPTER IX.

PERPLEXITIES OF THE KING—SITTING OF THE COURT IN BLACKFRIARS—THE KING AND QUEEN PRESENT—THE QUEEN APPEALS TO THE POPE.

THE king now heard from his ambassadors that none of his demands had been granted unconditionally by the Pope. Moreover, he was afraid that a general peace—the terms of which were then under discussion at Cambrai—might be established; which would make the Pope less dependent on him, increase the power of the emperor, and render his assistance less necessary to the king of France, to whom his children would be restored. Thus abandoned on all sides, he would be unable to put away his wife and marry Anne Boleyn without running into serious danger.

In this perplexity, having first taken the advice of Wolsey and his lawyers, he spoke to Campeggio. The Legate was holding back, most justly excusing himself on the ground that the Brief of Pope Julius had not been produced, and that the Pope had ordered him to proceed no further in the cause without fresh instructions. But in the end, by dint of threats, blandishments, presents, and importunity, the Legate, afraid for his own life if he did not satisfy the king, gave way, and, with Wolsey, opened the court, May 28, 1529, in the Refectory of the Blackfriars, London.[1]

[1] The king's licence for the sitting of the court, and thereby for the safety of the two Cardinals, who otherwise would have fallen under the penalties of Præmunire—for the Papal jurisdiction *in foro externo*

Before the Legates entered on their work the Papal commission was read. Then Henry is first summoned by name, and two proctors[1] appeared on his behalf; and after him the queen.[2] She presented herself in person, and protesting that she did not accept them as judges in her cause, appealed to the Pope; but as the Legates would not allow the appeal unless the queen could show by a rescript from the Pope that their powers had been withdrawn, the queen presents herself again on the next sitting of the court,[3] and gave in her objections in due form of law, as well as her reasons for appealing to the Pope, among which were these :—

The first, that the trial was held in a place where she could not hope for justice, she being a Spaniard by

had been suppressed by Parliament for nearly two hundred years—was granted May 20th, and on the 28th the two Cardinals began to constitute the court; and on the 31st that being done, the Bull of their commission was read before them, and they undertook to execute it, decreeing the citation of the king and the queen for the 18th day of June.

1 The king was represented by Dr. Sampson, dean of the chapel, afterwards bishop of Chichester, and finally of Lichfield and Coventry. He began his life in the service of Wolsey, and was for the greater part of his course a bitter enemy of the Papal jurisdiction. The other proctor was Dr. John Bell, who succeeded Latimer at Worcester. Neither Sampson nor Bell was properly a bishop, for they were both made in the schism, and without Bulls. Dr. Petre and Dr. Tregonnell were also counsel for the king.

2 Cavendish (Life of Wolsey, p. 213) represents the proceedings of May 31 and June 18 as one act. "The court being thus furnished and ordered, the judges commanded the crier to proclaim silence, then was the judges' commission, which they had of the Pope, published and read openly before all the audience there assembled. That done, the crier called the king by the name of 'king Henry of England, come into the court,' &c. With that the king answered and said, 'Here, my lords.' Then he called also the queen by the name of 'Katherine queen of England, come into the court,' &c., who made no answer to the same, but rose up incontinent out of her chair."

Campeggio (Theiner, p. 583) says that the commission was read "the last day of the past month," *i.e.*, May 31. Harpsfield also (see note at the end of this chapter) says that the king did not appear in person, but by two proctors, on the day when the court called him by name to appear. Mr. Pocock has printed the appeal of the queen in his Records, ii. p. 609, and in vol. i. 219, another appeal, in which, declining absolutely the jurisdiction of the Legates, the queen protests against the legality of the citation decreed against her, June 18, and commits her cause to the Pope.

3 June 18, 1529.

birth and a foreigner; and that Henry, who began the lawsuit, was the king of all England.

The second, that the judges were in their own persons not only under obligations to the king, but also in his power: Wolsey holding the bishopric of Winchester, the archbishopric of York, and many abbeys; Campeggio holding the see of Salisbury, given him by the king.

Finally, she declared solemnly on her oath that nothing but fear, most justly grounded, moved her to decline in that place, and in that cause, the sentence of the judges.

Though the judges, to please the king, would not admit the appeal of Catherine, nevertheless, because they would not pronounce the sentence of divorce, the king did not think that they had done him any service. Accordingly, standing before the court himself, he made a public declaration that in these proceedings he was not urged on by any dislike of the queen, but by scruples of conscience and the judgment of most learned men; though the Cardinal of York was at hand, a Legate *a latere*, to whom singly the power of deciding the question might have been delegated, yet he, to avoid all occasions of harsh judgments, had prevailed upon the Roman Pontiff, the sovereign head of the Church, to appoint judges to try the question, by whose decision, whatever it might be, he called all men to witness he would abide.

When the king had spoken, the queen insisted on the allowance of her appeal. The judges refused. Thereupon the queen, who was sitting on the left side of the court, rose from her place and went up to the king, who was sitting under a canopy on the other side. Falling upon her knees before him, she most humbly prayed him, who was at home in his own kingdom, to allow her, a foreigner, to prosecute her appeal in Rome, before the common father of all Christians, and also the judge whom the king himself acknowledged. The king rose from his seat, and looking at the queen with the utmost affection, declared that he gave her leave. The people present in court, seeing the faces and the demeanour of both husband and wife, could not refrain from weeping.

The queen thereupon went out of the court, and immediately afterwards was told that the judges and the king required her presence. "I will obey my husband," said the queen, "but not the judges." But her lawyers warned her that if she returned into court, her return would be taken as a withdrawal of the appeal, and damage her cause. She sent her excuses to the king, and returned to Castle Baynard, from which she had come to the court. When she was at home, she said to her lawyers, "To-day, for the first time, not to damage my cause, I disobeyed my lord the king; but the very next time I see him, I will go on my knees, and ask him to forgive my fault."[1] A woman worthy of a better husband! but it was by persecution of this kind it

[1] Harpsfield, Treatise of Marriage, bk. ii. p. 102. "The 28th of May following, the Legates sat solemnly at the Blackfriars, where the king by his two proctors, the queen personally appeared, with the said four bishops and others of her counsel, refusing to stand to the Legates' judgment, as judges incompetent, and appealing from them to the See of Rome. The Legates proceeded notwithstanding, and cited the king and queen to appear again the 18th June, upon the which day both of them made their appearance personally. At which time the king declared openly the great unquietness, vexation, and trouble wherewith he was grievously cumbered for his marriage, so that he could scarce intend any matter touching the necessary affairs of this realm, wherefore he desired that the matter might be, according to justice and right, quickly and speedily determined. He commended also at the time the queen's womanhood, wisdom, nobility, and gentleness. When the king had ended, the queen made her protestation, and did put in her *libellus recusatorius*, and renewed her provocation, alleging cause to be advocated by the Pope's Holiness, *et litis pendentiam coram eodem*, desiring to be admitted for probation thereof, and to have a term competent for the same. Whereupon day was given by the Legates till the 21st of the same month for the declarations of their minds and intentions thereunto. At which day both the king and queen appeared in person. And notwithstanding the said

pleased God to prepare for Catherine the crown of glory that never fades.

Legates declared as well the sincerity of their minds directly and justly to proceed without favour and affection or partiality, as also that no such recusation, appellation, or term might be by them admitted, yet she nevertheless persisting in her former mind laid in her appeal, which by the said Legates was also refused, and they minding to proceed further in the cause, the queen would no longer make her abode to hear what the said Legates would further discern [decern], albeit the king requested and commanded her to tarry, wherein afterwards she seemed to have some remorse of conscience, as it were for some disobedience towards her husband. And she reported afterwards to some that were of her council—by whom I had intelligence of it—that she never before in all her life in any one thing in the world disobeyed the king, her husband, neither now would have done, but that the necessary defence of her cause did force her thereto. Her proctor, notwithstanding, made answer for her, and said that she would stick to her appeal. But the Legates caused her to be thrice preconisate and called eftsoons to return and appear, which she refusing to do, was denounced by the Legates *contumax*, and a citation decerned for her appearance the Friday following to make answer to such articles as should be objected unto her." The king's own account (Burnet, Hist. Reform., iv. 118, ed. Pocock) agrees even verbally with this of Harpsfield, and Harpsfield had seen the king's letter.

CHAPTER X.

OBJECTIONS OF HENRY'S LAWYERS—ANSWER OF THE QUEEN'S LAWYERS.

HENRY indeed for the moment granted the request of the queen, but it was done in order that he might not seem uncourteous; for he urged the Legates in every way to pronounce sentence at once, and pronounce the Brief of Pope Julius null and void. His proctors therefore, when the Papal dispensation was produced in court, maintained that on many grounds it was not a sufficient justification of the marriage of Henry and Catherine, asserting that—

1. The Brief speaks of the marriage only, and makes no mention of betrothal; but as Henry and Catherine were first betrothed, and the marriage is against the canons, the dispensation for the marriage must not be taken as allowing the betrothal.

2. Nothing is said in the Brief of the age of Henry, who was then only twelve years old, and therefore not marriageable.

3. Moreover, that when Henry had reached the marriageable age, he protested that he would not wed Catherine.[1]

4. Besides, that this marriage was allowed for the purpose of preserving peace—the final cause of the dispensation—between Ferdinand and Isabella of Spain on

[1] Harpsfield, Treatise of Marriage, bk. ii. p. 47, Eyston MSS. "But there was never any such just and sufficient protestation lawfully before any judge proved." See above, note 2, p. 5.

the one hand, and Henry VII., king of England, on the other hand; but Henry VIII., not then of age, never thought of peace, and Henry VII. and Isabella were dead when the marriage was solemnised.

5. That the petition presented to the Pope was the petition of Catherine and Henry by name, and yet they had given no instructions on the subject, in virtue of which their parents could lawfully act on their behalf. A false recital vitiated the whole grant.

6. Lastly, that there were two impediments to the marriage—one of affinity, arising out of the former marriage of Catherine and Arthur; the other resting on what is due to public decency, the consequence of the contract of marriage, though the marriage may never have really taken place. Pope Julius by his Brief removed the impediment of affinity, but he said nothing about removing the other impediment of public decency. That being so, they asserted that because this second impediment had not been removed, the marriage of Henry and Catherine was not lawful and not valid.

That was what the king's lawyers said. Though the queen would have nothing more to do with the two judges, her lawyers,[1] nevertheless, lest they should be considered as having no legal defence, either in law or equity, replied immediately to all the arguments of their adversary.

They said that Pope Julius, when he removed by his pontifical authority the impediment created by the ecclesiastical law, destroyed at the same time every con-

[1] Harpsfield, Treatise of Marriage, bk. ii. p. 96, Eyston MSS. "The king in the meantime licensed queen Katherine to choose councillors whom she would, and she among other chose William Wareham, archbishop of Canterbury, and Nicholas West, bishop of Ely, doctor of laws, John Fisher, bishop of Rochester, and Henry Standish, bishop of St. Asaph, doctors of divinity, with divers other, whereof some played very honest parts, and stood stiffly and fast to her cause: some played the prevaricators, and fled from her to the king's side."

sequence of that impediment, so that the betrothal as well as the marriage of Henry and Catherine fell under the common law. Whenever, for grave reasons, an act is permitted to be done, all other acts without which it could not be done are at the same time made lawful also, otherwise the permission would be illusory. Henry was then under age, and betrothal only was lawful for him. The marriage has taken place with the leave of the Pope, and yet the lawyers on the other side foolishly maintain that there is a doubt whether the parties to it could be betrothed. Betrothal is only a promise of a future marriage, and is in nowise necessary to make any marriage valid; but if it has taken place, it is no hindrance to the marriage; on the contrary, it is most favourable to it. Now the marriage being allowed, the betrothal is allowed by implication, and is therefore valid. But even if it were not valid, it can do no harm whatever to the marriage afterwards solemnised, for the marriage subsists of itself without respect to betrothal, and unnecessary acts can never invalidate that which subsists independently of them.[1]

Nor is the marriage against the ecclesiastical law; on the contrary, it has so much to recommend it that the author of the law, had he but thought of it, would have taken the pains to declare that, in view of the public good, it should be lawful for the surviving brother to marry the widow of the deceased. Moreover, in a case that cannot be regarded with favour, when the marriage itself has been permitted, the betrothal, which is only a beginning of marriage, cannot be considered as forbidden.

There was no reason for referring to the want of age on the part of the king, for that alone, touching the

[1] L. Unica. Cod. de rei uxoriæ actione. "Si enim cum una in instrumento stipulatio valida inveniatur, allis etiam inutilibus suam noscitur præstare fortitudinem."—Note on the margin.

person or the matter, is necessarily to be spoken of which is against the law, and the mention of which is demanded by the principle on which the law is grounded. The matter in this case was not the want of age on the part of the king, for that was a natural defect which the Pontiff could not remedy, but affinity, that was an impediment to the marriage, and was set out in the Brief.

Besides, as to marriage nothing is necessary but the capacity of the persons, and certainly he is not unfit who is only twelve years of age. St. Jerome[1] tells us that Solomon and Achaz were fathers, the one in his eleventh, the other in his twelfth year. Even among private persons the Papal Brief would have been good though no mention had been made of the age of the parties to it for whom the dispensation was asked; for so slight and unimportant a matter as that of ages, if it had been mentioned, would never have moved the Pope to refrain from the furtherance of some greater good. How, then, can we imagine, that in a matter touching most powerful sovereigns, the Pope, who is the guardian of peace, would for this one thing, namely, that Henry was only twelve years old, put difficulties in the way of obtaining so great a blessing as the public peace of many kingdoms. The Pope is rightly very indulgent to kings, for God Himself seems to free them from the observance of human laws.[2]

As for the declaration[3] made by the king when he came of age, but of which Catherine was never informed, that could not be pleaded against her; for any declaration, however solemn, was done away with by the subsequent celebration of the marriage itself. It is extremely absurd now, after the marriage has taken place, to object that

[1] Ad Vitel. Ep. 72. "Quare Salomon et Achaz undecim annorum filios genuisse dicantur."

[2] 1 Kings viii. 11.

[3] See above, p. 5, note 2; and also p. 56, note 1.

Henry at one time declared he should not marry Catherine. He did say so, but then he married her. We must rely on the notorious fact, not on a secret declaration, and that more especially as the fact is both later in point of time, and a sacrament of Christ, confessed and ratified by the intercourse of so many years, and the birth of children.

They say that Henry being then a youth, could not have had any thoughts about peace; but why should they deny that he was capable of good thoughts and of holy desires, when about twelve years of age and close upon manhood? Certainly he was able to do wrong, and might have been found legally guilty of most grievous crimes. He might commit murder, and deserve everlasting death; and yet he was incapable of thinking of the public good, or of those things which belong to everlasting life! It is a foolish and impious opinion, condemned by good manners, and put aside by just laws; upright judges will not accept it, even if one were to bring forward witnesses and records to prove it. Besides, if the child had no wish to preserve the public peace, the father, in whose control he was, had; and he had that wish in his interest, as he had believed, on his behalf, when he procured the sacrament of faith for him, being still an infant.

When the Pope granted the dispensation, he did not consider Isabella of Spain and Henry of England as private persons, but as public and royal persons with public and royal duties, which did not come to an end with their lives, but which passed on to their heirs, Henry VIII. and Catherine, together with the right to the crown of England. Peace is not the good of certain persons only, but rather of the whole community. The people and the state do not die. We go further. It is enough for us that Henry and Isabella were alive when the dispensation was obtained, for matters of grace, the moment they are granted, derive their strength and completeness from the sole will of the grantor. At the same time we must not forget that the Catholic king Ferdinand was living when the marriage itself took place.

The children, themselves, it is said, did not authorise their parents to seek this dispensation; be it so, that is nothing to the purpose. The Pope may if he likes reject a petition presented to him on behalf of another, when it does not appear that the person presenting it has authority to do so; nevertheless, if he does not reject it, and grants the prayer, the grant is valid, and no further question can be raised concerning the person who presented it, but only whether the grant has been made. This applies with greater force to parents when they present petitions on behalf of their children. The law of nature itself teaches parents to lay up treasures for their children, and kings especially observe this law and custom, being wont to obtain through their ambassadors many graces for their children.

Nor is there any false statement in the clause, "a petition was lately presented to Us on your behalf." A petition was really presented according to the statement, on behalf of Henry and Catherine, for it is certain that all that was asked for tended wholly to their advantage. It can never be admitted that parents, to whom God has given their children, are without any authority from their children when acting in matters concerning their children's good, for the very existence of their children and nature itself is a perpetual cry unto parents to do all they can for the good of their children; "for if any one cares not for his own, especially those of his house, he has denied the faith, and is worse than an infidel."[1]

[1] I Tim. v. 8.

Let us now go to the last point in which our opponents think their greatest strength lies. In the petition presented to the Pope are the following words: "Some time ago a marriage had taken place between the lady Catherine and prince Arthur, the brother of Henry." Well, is not the impediment of public decency set forth with sufficient distinctness, seeing that it springs from the mere contract itself? Then we have in the same petition this clause: "The marriage was perhaps consummated." Does not this expression set forth the impediment of affinity? The word "perhaps" was brought in for the purpose of making the marriage valid under all conditions, even if the first marriage had been complete, which in truth it never was.

When the Pope saw—the facts were before him—that at the utmost there were but two things that stood in the way of the marriage of Henry and Catherine—the former marriage with Arthur the brother, and the possibility of its having been perfected,—when the Pope, I say, with the full knowledge of the case, removed, by his own authority, not only the impediment of affinity generally, but also that of the special affinity which might have subsisted between Henry and Catherine, did he not also at the same time remove the impediment of public decency which springs from the contract alone? For if Henry was allowed to marry the widow of his brother—the consummation of the marriage notwithstanding—how much more easy it was to allow him to do so, when the marriage was only celebrated and not completed. Thus spoke the lawyers of the queen.

The king's lawyers now alleged certain slight presumptions, when this question of the completed marriage was raised, in favour thereof, and maintained that the word "perhaps" was superfluous. They spoke of the youth of Arthur and Catherine, their supping together, their being shown late at night into their chamber, of their great love for each other, of the celebration of the marriage publicly, and finally alleged certain words said to have been uttered by the prince in jest the day after, as tending to prove that which the lawyers maintained to be a fact.

On the other hand, the queen's lawyers brought many and most strong reasons against these presumptions. In the first place, Henry VII., on account of the illness of the prince at the time, had placed him and Catherine under the charge of a discrete matron; and secondly, her most serene highness the queen herself had deponed upon oath,[1] in the presence of John Talcarne, public notary, before many bishops and other witnesses, that the marriage had never been completed; and again, when the queen had repeated her declaration in court publicly, in the presence of the king himself, Henry did not contradict her, and in so grave a matter it must be taken for granted that the king assented to the statement which he did not deny.

In addition to this allegation of the lawyers, let us give also a remarkable proof taken from a book of Cardinal Pole, written in the lifetime of Henry, and dedicated to him. In that book the Cardinal declared that Henry, at the time not dreaming of a divorce, admitted of his own accord to the emperor Charles V. that the statement of the queen was true.[2]

Again, the king's lawyers produced a letter of Cardinal Adrian, formerly the Papal collector in England,

[1] This she did Nov. 7, 1528, at Bridewell, in the presence of the archbishop of Canterbury, William Warham; Cuthbert Tunstall, bishop of London; John Clerk, bishop of Bath and Wells; John Fisher, bishop of Rochester; and Henry Standish, bishop of St. Asaph. The record of the act, attested by John Talcarne, has been reprinted from a rare book, by Mr. Pocock, Records, ii. p. 431.

[2] Pro Eccles. Unitatis Defens., lib. iii. c. iii. "Tibi autem, princeps, an credis? Si credis tu ipse hoc fassus es, virginem te accepisse; et Cæsari fassus es, cui minime expediebat, si tum de divortio cogitares, hoc fateri.

in which the Cardinal said that he heard Pope Julius declare his inability to grant the dispensation for the marriage of Henry and Catherine.

But the queen's lawyers produced in court a letter of the Pope on the subject written to Henry VII. at his request. In that letter were the following words: "As for the dispensation, We have never refused it, nor have We given any occasion for any one to suspect that We shall refuse it, as some persons have said, but not according to truth. But Our answer has been that We are waiting for a more favourable opportunity for granting it, in order that it may be made with more mature deliberation for the honour of the parties whom it concerns as well as for that of the Holy See."[1]

The lawyers who undertook the defence of her most serene highness the queen were the greatest and most learned men in England. Foremost among them was William Warham,[2] the archbishop of Canterbury, accompanied by five bishops—Cuthbert Tunstall,[3] then of London, afterwards of Durham; Nicolas West[4] of Ely; John Clerk[5] of Bath and Wells; John Fisher[6] of

[1] The letter is to be seen in Herbert, p. 275; and in Pocock, Records, i. p. 5, a fuller copy, taken from the Record Office.

[2] William Warham, educated at Winchester and New College, Oxford, where he took his degree in law. He was one of the lawyers of the Court of Arches. In 1494 he was made master of the Rolls; consecrated bishop of London September 25, 1502. Pope Julius II. translated him, December 29, 1503, to the church of Canterbury.

[3] Cuthbert Tunstall studied in Oxford, Cambride, and Padua; vicar-general of archbishop Warham in 1508; ordained priest in 1511, and made judge of the Prerogative Court, then archdeacon of Chester; master of the Rolls in 1516; keeper of the Privy Seal in 1523. He was consecrated bishop of London October 19, 1522, and translated to Durham March 25, 1530. He deserted the queen, and went over to the side of the king.

[4] See note, p. 9.

[5] John Clerk, a Cambridge doctor, archdeacon of Colchester October 22, 1519, and dean of Windsor in the following month. He was made also master of the Rolls in Oct. 1522, and in Rome, Dec. 6, 1523, according to Mr. Stubbs, consecrated bishop of Bath and Wells.

[6] John Fisher, educated at the grammar school of his native place, Beverley, in the East Riding of Yorkshire, and afterwards at Cam-

Rochester; and Henry Standish [1] of St. Asaph. Four others, theologians, were added to these, namely, Abel,[2] Fetherston,[3] Powell,[4] and Ridley.[5]

bridge, was elected chancellor of the university in 1504, and Nov. 24th of the same year was consecrated bishop of Rochester.

[1] Henry Standish, a native of Lancashire, and a Franciscan friar, provincial of his order, and consecrated at Oxford, July 11, 1519, bishop of St. Asaph. Though he pleaded for the queen now, nevertheless, in the Convocation House, where he was not an advocate but a judge, he gave sentence for the king in favour of the divorce.—Wharton, Hist. de Episcopis Assavens., p. 358.

[2] Thomas Abel, M.A., Oxford, was one of the queen's chaplains, and by her presented to the rectory of Bradwell-near-the-Sea, in Essex. He suffered martyrdom July 30, 1540.

[3] Richard Fetherston wrote a book against the divorce, and suffered martyrdom July 30, 1540.

[4] Edward Powell, born in Wales, fellow of Oriel College. He was rector of Bleadon, Somersetshire, in 1501, prebendary of Lincoln and of Sarum. He wrote against Luther as well as against the divorce, and in 1540 was martyred in Smithfield.

[5] Ridley, Cavendish's Life of Wolsey, p. 213. "There was also another ancient doctor, called, as I remember, Dr. Ridley, a very small person in stature, but surely a great and an excellent clerk in divinity."

CHAPTER XI.

THE BISHOP OF ROCHESTER PLEADS FOR THE QUEEN—DR. RIDLEY—THE DUKE OF SUFFOLK—CARDINAL CAMPEGGIO ADJOURNS—THE POPE RECALLS THE POWERS OF THE LEGATES—FALL OF WOLSEY.

THEN, when all the arrangements had been made which are necessary for the discussion of questions of the ecclesiastical law, John Fisher, bishop of Rochester, stood forth.[1] He was the light not of England only but of Christendom, a model of holiness, the salt of the people, and a doctor of the Church. He presented to the Legates a book he had written—and a most learned book it is—in defence of the marriage, addressing them at the same time with great gravity, and warning them against searching for difficulties where none existed, or allowing either the plain truths of Scripture, or the laws of the Church, which in this matter were abundantly clear, to be set aside. Still further, he begged them to consider carefully the great mischief likely to follow upon the divorce; the enmity between Henry and the emperor Charles and the princes who took their part; wars, not foreign only but civil; and, worse than all, dissensions in matters of belief, schism, heresies, and sects innumerable. "As for myself," said the bishop, "as I have taken great pains in the matter, I am bold enough to say, and I have not only proved it clearly in my book, on the authority of the Scriptures and of the

[1] June 28th, when the fifth session of the court was held.—Theiner, 585.

holy Fathers, but I am also ready to seal my testimony with my life's blood, that there is no power on earth that can break the bond of this marriage, which God Himself has made."[1]

When the bishop of Rochester, who was a man famous for his learning, remarkable for his holy life, deserving all honour on account of his episcopal dignity, and for his grey hairs venerable, had thus spoken, four doctors of canon and civil law produced a book they had written, and in which they had made it plain that the marriage of Henry and Catherine had been duly contracted according to the laws of the Church. Then three books were produced, each written by a bishop, namely, Clerk, bishop of Bath and Wells; Cuthbert Tunstall, bishop of London,[2] but at the time in Cambrai with Sir Thomas More on the business of the king; and Nicolas West, bishop of Ely.

After the bishops came the four theologians, Abel, Powell, Fetherston, and Ridley, who declared that, moved by the love of God and the truth, they had said nothing in defence of the marriage but that which they knew, to the best of their knowledge, to be in agreement with the gospel and the sacred writings; the judges themselves would admit it to be so, if they would condescend to read, as no doubt they would, the books they had written.

[1] Theiner, Monumenta, p. 585. The bishop on the 29th of June appeared in court, and said he was bound in the interests of truth, "per dirli, affermarli et con vive ragioni dimostrarli che hoc matrimonium regis et reginæ nulla potestate humana vel divina potest dissolvi, pro qua sententia asseruit etiam se animam positurum . . . et in fine obtulit libellum a se conscriptum super hac re. . . . Questa cosa di Roffense fu inexpectata et improvista, et pero tenuit omnem personam in admiratione."

[2] Pocock, Records of the Reformation, ii. p. 571. Tunstall afterwards abandoned the cause of the queen, and even told her so, when he, with the archbishop of York, on the part of the king, pressed her to accept the sentence which Cranmer had pronounced. "I had now changed my former opinion, and exhorted her to do the semblable, and not to usurp any more the name of a queen."

But Ridley, a sound and devout Catholic, to whom all flattery was hateful, complained in open court of the injustice of the Legates, who had exacted an oath of the queen's lawyers, and of the queen's lawyers only, that they would neither say, nor write, nor do anything in the cause otherwise than in strict accordance with the ecclesiastical laws. "For," said he, "if the like oath had been exacted of the king's lawyers, the process would have been already ended, and our opponents would not have denied that the truth is on our side. He would suffer any punishment they pleased if the king's lawyers, on being compelled to take such an oath, did not range themselves on the side of the queen." All the king's lawyers held their peace, and by their silence seemed to confess the truth of his words. Wolsey, in a most unseemly manner, resented the freedom with which Ridley spoke.[1] Neither he nor Cardinal Campeggio saw his way to go on with the cause, for the proofs of the validity of the marriage were all so clear and beyond doubt. Nevertheless, the king, as usual, was pressing them to pronounce sentence at once in his favour. Cardinal Campeggio then seeing that anything he could say would have no weight with the king, and not venturing in the face of evidence so clear, against the undoubted will of the Pope, and in spite of Catherine's appeal, to pronounce the sentence which the king demanded, at last spoke out with courage and freedom, and said that he had been a lawyer for many years, and for many years one of the twelve judges of the Rota in

[1] Cavendish, Life of Card. Wolsey, p. 224. "'Then,' quoth one Doctor Ridley, 'it is a shame and a great dishonour to this honourable presence, that any such presumptions should be alleged in this open court, which be to all good and honest men most detestable to be rehearsed.' 'What,' quoth my Lord Cardinal, '*Domine Doctor, magis reverenter?*' 'No, no, my lord,' quoth he, 'there belongeth no reverence to be given to these abominable presumptions, for an unreverent tale would be unreverently answered.'"

Rome, but had never known such hurry before, not even in matters of little moment, still less in a cause so weighty and important as this. Besides, the custom is, when the cause is ready for sentence, to leave the judges thirty clear days to weigh the arguments and the evidence; but in this, so many days have hardly gone by since the cause has been publicly pleaded. And what a cause! how important! How much scandal and trouble are sure to come out of it, unless, indeed, any one thinks that the sudden rupture of a lawful engagement, the hurried dissolution of a marriage which has been held valid for twenty years, the wretched bastardising of a noble and even royal issue, the provocation offered to a most powerful monarch, the sowing of discord among Christians, the contempt of the Papal power of dispensation, to be matters of little or no moment. He was resolved, for his part, to proceed not in hurry and haste, but slowly and safely, in so grave a question.

When Campeggio had spoken, men betrayed their astonishment in their countenances. Some were glad because he had spoken so clearly; others, on the contrary, were very much grieved, for they hoped to rise in the world by means of these disturbances. Some, however, were secretly glad, but pretended to be sorry, among whom was Cardinal Wolsey, who, though he was supposed to agree with Campeggio, nevertheless pressed for the delivery of the sentence without delay.

Campeggio would not pronounce any sentence, and suggested daily new reasons for delay; he also lengthened the process, contrary to all expectation, so that when the end of the month of July had come he announced that it was the custom in Rome for the courts there to be closed till the month of October.[1] When the

[1] Harpsfield, Treatise of Marriage, bk. ii. p. 107, Eyston MS. "But the Legates made no great haste, and Campegius pretended cause why they

king saw this he sent the dukes of Norfolk [1] and Suffolk [2] to the Legates. The two dukes, attended by many noblemen, presented themselves before the Legates during the sitting of the court on the 30th of July, and then, in their own and in the king's behalf, very urgently required the Legates to keep the king's conscience no longer in doubt, and to put an end to the cause by a definite and final sentence. Wolsey, however, though he was the first in the commission, held his tongue, for he was very much alarmed. But Campeggio declared that he was bound to be true to God and to the Roman Church, the custom of which was, in the court of which he was a member, to carry on no lawsuits between the end of July and the 4th day of October. Anything done in disregard

could not proceed until October following, whereof the king hearing complained to the dukes of Norfolk and Suffolk, and other nobles of his council, which noblemen were in hand with the Legates, sitting the 30th day of July, that day or the next to give final sentence in the matter. Campegius swore on his honour and faith that he bore to the Church of Rome, that the course of the courts there is, at the end of July to suspend all matters till the 4th day of October, and that all judgments given in the mean season were void; wherefore he required the king to bear with him until that day—before the which they could sit no more—trusting that then they should make an end to the king's contentation. The which answer did greatly offend the noblemen, and the duke of Suffolk giving a great clap on the table with his hand, did swear that there never was Cardinal that did good in England, and forthwith departed in great anger, with the residue of the nobility."

[1] Thomas Howard, duke of Norfolk, succeeded his father A.D. 1524, and complied with all the measures of the king; nevertheless, he was imprisoned and attainted in 1546, and from the Tower wrote a letter to the king (Herbert, p. 630), in which he said, "As for all causes of religion, I say now, and have said to your majesty and many others, I do know you to be a prince of such virtue and knowledge, that whatsoever laws you have in times past made, or hereafter shall make, I shall to the extremity of my power stick unto them as long as my life shall last." At the same time he begged the Peers that he "might have a ghostly father" sent to him, and that he "might receive" his "Maker." But also, in the same petition (Herbert, p. 631), is this: "Licence to send to London to buy one book of St. Austin, 'De civitate Dei,' and of Josephus, 'De Antiquitatibus,' and another of Sabellicus, who doth declare most of any book that I have read how the bishop of Rome from time to time hath usurped his power against all princes, by their unwise sufferance." If the king had lived a few hours longer, the duke would have been executed. He was left in the Tower during the reign of Edward, and set free by queen Mary.

[2] Charles Brandon. See note at the end of chapter v. of book ii.

of that custom would have no legal force whatever. If, however, the king will have patience till then, everything, no doubt, will be as he desired. The two dukes again insisted on the immediate delivery of the sentence, either then or at the utmost on the following day. Campeggio again replied that he could not do it. Thereupon Charles Brandon, duke of Suffolk, striking the table with great violence, cried out, "By the Holy Mass, no Cardinal or Legate ever brought any good to England." Whether it was a sudden fit of fury, or a mean desire to flatter the king, that moved him to speak thus, we know not, but certain it is, that by means of the king and his children, but above all by the offspring of the marriage which they so much desired, God did punish these noblemen for their pride and flatteries: witness those calamities which afterwards overtook them and their families.

The two dukes quitted the court in great wrath and indignation, and the king, already inflamed by passion, became still more furious at their instigation. But in the meantime the Pope had allowed the appeal of the queen, which was founded on justice,[1] and having publicly forbade Wolsey and Campeggio to meddle further with the cause, referred it to Paul Capisucchi, auditor of causes in the Sacred Apostolic Palace, and dean, with instructions to examine the question and report thereon to him. The auditor was also directed to appoint a day for the trial, and to summon the king and queen, by

[1] The queen's lawyers had lodged their appeal in Rome, and as soon as it came before the Pope, there was nothing to be done but to call up the cause out of the hands of the Legates. Dr. Bennet, the king's agent in Rome, writes thence to Cardinal Wolsey, July 9, to inform him that the Pope is about to supersede him.—Burnet, iv. 123, ed. Pocock. Dr. Bennet represents the Pope as saying, "God is my judge: I would do as gladly for the king as I would for myself; . . . but in this case I cannot satisfy his desire, but that I should do manifestly against justice, to the charge of my conscience, to my rebuke, and to the dishonour of the See Apostolic, . . . he cannot of justice deny it." The Cardinal and the king laboured with all their strength to deprive the queen of the means of defence which the law allowed her, namely, to appeal unto the Pope.

their attorneys duly appointed, to plead before him. This decree[1] of the Pontiff was published not only in Rome, but also in Bruges and Tournai, as well as in other churches of the neighbourhood in Flanders. It was also sent to her most serene highness the queen, that she might bring it to the knowledge of the king and the Legates.

The queen sent to the king Sir Thomas More,[2] an illustrious member of the House of Commons, famous for his natural gifts, his piety and learning. Sir Thomas was to say that the Pope had withdrawn from the Legates their commission, and had summoned him and the queen to plead by their attorneys in the court of the Rota, and that she sent word of this to the king for the purpose of learning from him whether he wished the summons to be sent him by an officer of the court or not.

The king's annoyance was very great, but as he had not had time to consider the matter, he concealed his vexation, and told Sir Thomas More that all this had been known to him for some time; he did not wish to have the summons served upon himself in person, but he would not hinder its being served on the Legates in the usual way; he was very much pleased that the cause was to be tried in a place which belonged to the queen as much as to himself, and he would do his utmost to have it settled in Rome.

So he spoke, but he hoped to bring about, by means of fresh ambassadors to the Pope, the renewal of the commission of the Legates, and so he submitted with the less repugnance to that which had been done.

After this, many of the queen's lawyers, but only one

1 Published by Le Grand, iii. 446, and in Tierney's Dod, i. 366.

2 Sir Thomas More, son of Sir John More, puisne justice of the Common Pleas, was born in Mill Street, in the city of London, A.D. 1480, and educated at Cambridge. He became a lawyer, and was made chancellor of the duchy of Lancaster, and on the fall of Wolsey, chancellor.

of the king's, went, with two notaries, to announce to the Legates that their powers had been recalled. They were then in the country together, about twelve miles out of London.[1] The lawyer sent by the king at the same time[2] declared in the presence of them all that the king wished nothing further to be done in England, all the pleadings would be carried on in Rome. The Legates respected the Papal order, and hopes were entertained that the king would listen to better counsels, when Campeggio received letters from the Pope ordering him to return to Rome immediately.

Then the king, for the first time losing all hopes that the question would be decided in his favour, burned with unutterable rage, and throwing the blame of the whole process deservedly upon Wolsey, who was the original cause of it, showed in unmistakable ways that he meant to do him a mischief. Many of the chief personages observing this—they had long regarded Wolsey with envious eyes, for his will was supreme in the administration of the state—took counsel together, and drew up very grave charges against him, which they reduced to writing, signed, and presented to the king.[3] The king showed them that he was pleased. Meanwhile, however, he concealed his purpose until Campeggio should have left the country, which he did September 7,[4] and had his baggage searched by order of the king.

[1] At the Moor, a house belonging to the abbey of St. Alban's, and which Wolsey inhabited as the abbot of that monastery.—Theiner, p. 587.

[2] The notice was served on the two Cardinals Sept. 6, 1529.—Theiner, p. 587.

[3] Hall, p. 759. "When the nobles and prelates perceived that the king's favour was from the Cardinal sore minished, every man of the king's council began to lay to him such offences as they knew by him, and all their accusations were written in a book, and all their hands set to it, to the number of thirty-and-four, which book they presented to the king."

[4] Sept. 7 may have been the day on which the Cardinal's departure was fixed; he did not leave London before October 5. He crossed the Channel October 26.—Theiner, p. 588.

That search was made chiefly for the purpose of seizing any letters of Wolsey's; none, however, were found.[1]

But Wolsey, knowing nothing of that which had been contrived against him, had gone to the king, then staying in a place near St. Alban's, where, with him and his council, he discussed many things that would have to be done in the trial to be held in Rome. Stephen Gardiner[2] was also there, one of the king's secretaries, who knowing himself to be suspected of having been the cause of the divorce, asked Wolsey openly to declare in the interests of truth, publicly before the king and the council, who they were who had been the first movers in the matter. "I will never deny," said Wolsey, "that I alone have done it;[3] and I am so far from regretting it, that if it had not been begun, I would have it begun now." These latter words, everybody understood, were meant for the king. Though he certainly was the first who raised the question, yet, when he saw the king's passion for Anne Boleyn, the man who loved the glory of men more than the glory of God, was sorry for the counsel he had given, when it was no longer in his power to undo it. At that time, however, the king remained silent.

[1] The officers of the customs (see Chapuys', the Spanish Ambassador's, letter, Oct. 25, 1529, Pocock, Records, ii. 69) asked the Cardinal to open his baggage for their inspection, and then, on his refusal, broke the locks themselves. When they had done their work, he told them they were silly people to suppose that he who had not been corrupted by the many presents of the king, could be bought by Cardinal Wolsey.

[2] He returned to England from Rome, June 24, 1529; the king had written to the Pope, May 20, to say that he had recalled him, and that Dr. Bennet would take his place. —Theiner, pp. 563, 585. He was secretary July 28, 1529, as he writes himself to Vannes.—Pocock, Records, i. p. 265.

[3] The French ambassador, writing from London, October 21, 1528, says that the Cardinal had urged the divorce for reasons of his own, it seems, and not because the marriage of Henry and Catherine was unlawful.—Le Grand, iii. 186. "Les premiers termes du divorce ont esté mis par luy en avant, afin de mettre perpetuelle separation entre les maisons d'Angleterre et de Bourgogne."

But after the departure of Campeggio, when Wolsey went again to resume his attendance at court, the king refused to speak to him. He then saw that the king was unfriendly. Not long after that, he was arrested, at the king's command, by Thomas duke of Norfolk, and compelled to resign, first the chancellorship,[1] which was given without delay to the illustrious Sir Thomas More, and next the see of Winchester, which Stephen Gardiner accepted at the king's hands. He had built himself a magnificent palace, York House,[2] and this too the king seized with all its furniture.[3] Lastly, he was stripped of almost all his goods,[4] and

[1] Wolsey, says Cavendish, "when the Term began, went to the hall in suchlike sort and gesture as he was wont most commonly to do, and sat in the Chancery, being chancellor. After which day he never sat there more." The dukes of Norfolk and Suffolk demanded of him the great seal, which he at first refused to surrender, but in the end he gave it up.

[2] York House was hardly furnished when the Cardinal was deprived of it. In a letter of Fox to Gardiner, May 12, 1528 (Pocock, Records, i. 145), we read thus: "The hall of York Place, with other edifices here, being now in building, my lord's grace, intending most sumptuously and gorgeously to repair and furnish the same." "The king" (Pocock, Records, ii. 68) "went to see his new wealth with Anne Boleyn and her mother secretly from Greenwich, and found the treasure surpassed his expectations."

[3] The Prevarication of the Church's Liberties, chap. iii. s. 2, Eyston MS. "For immediately after queen Catherine's appeal in the twenty-first year of his reign, he fell first upon York House, the ancient London seat of the archbishops of York, by the attainder of the Cardinal Wolsey in a præmunire — who for his own private ends was the first author of scrupling the king's conscience about his marriage with queen Catherine—and compelled the Cardinal before a judge of record to acknowledge the same—being then by him most sumptuously built and furnished—to be the king's right, and called it Whitehall. Then in the twenty-second year he took the hospital of St. James into his hands, together with all the meadows and pastures thereunto belonging, as commodious for his house of Whitehall, made a park thereof, built a fair palace thereon, and enclosed all within a brick wall."

[4] Cardinal Wolsey, Oct. 22, 1529, confessed himself guilty of the charges laid against him by the king touching the statutes of provisors and præmunire, and that "he deserved perpetual imprisonment at the king's will, and to forfeit to the king for ever all his lands, tenements, offices, fees, pensions, annuities, goods, and chattels which he has or may have; in consideration of which offences he grants to the king all his said possessions, with all the revenues arising from his archbishopric of York, bishopric of Winchester, abbey of St. Alban's, and his other spiritual benefices and promotions."—Chronol. Cat. of materials for the new edition of the Fœdera, p. 168.

banished at first to Esher,[1] then sent to his diocese of York.[2]

[1] Esher was a house of the bishop of Winchester, and at this time belonged to the Cardinal as bishop of that see.

[2] Cavendish, p. 298. "My lord of Norfolk said to Master Cromwell, 'Sir,' quoth he, 'methinketh that the Cardinal your master maketh no haste northward; show him that if he go not away shortly, I will, rather than he should tarry still, bear him with my teeth. Therefore I would advise him to prepare him away as shortly as he can, or else he shall be sent forward.'" Chapuys, writing to the emperor from London, Feb. 6, 1530 (Pocock, Records, ii. 76), says that the duke of Norfolk, on hearing that the Cardinal hoped to return to the court, "commencat très fort a jurer, que avant que souffrir cela, il le mangeroit tout vif."

CHAPTER XII.

FOREIGN UNIVERSITIES — BRIBERY — REGINALD POLE — WRITERS ON THE DIVORCE — LETTER OF THE PEERS TO THE POPE.

WHO would not imagine that the king would have wished now to abandon his evil purpose? But be astonished, O heavens, upon this![1] The very sin for which he punishes Wolsey so severely is the very sin in which the king obstinately persists. Therefore, O king, art thou inexcusable; for wherein thou judgest another thou condemnest thyself, for we know that the judgment of God is according to truth against those who do such things.[2]

Now the king, on the one hand, sends certain men—one of them being Thomas Cranmer,[3] afterwards arch-

[1] Jerem. ii. 12.

[2] Rom. ii. 1, 2.

[3] Cranmer, a native of Northamptonshire, was educated at Cambridge, and became a fellow of Jesus College. He forfeited his fellowship because, according to Strype, "he married a gentleman's daughter;" but according to Harpsfield, who had better means of knowing the facts, she was "a wanton maid at the sign of the Dolphin, that was wont to set young scholars their breakfast. . . . It chanced not long after that she died, and then became he a priest, and afterwards chaplain to Thomas earl of Wiltshire, father to the lady Anne Bulleyne, at the time that the king went about to make a divorce with queen Katherine, of the which matter the earl had oft talk with the said Cranmer, who was very forward to help forth the said divorce."

In the answers to the interrogatories ministered to him at Oxford, in the reign of Mary, we have these facts confessed by him, according to Foxe, viii. 58: "That he, the aforesaid Thomas Cranmer, being free, and before he entered into holy orders, married one Joan Black or Brown, dwelling at the sign of the Dolphin, in Cambridge. Whereupon he [Cranmer] answered that whether she were called Black or Brown he knew not, but that he married there one Joan, that he granted. 2. That after the death of the aforesaid wife, he entered into

bishop of Canterbury—to plead his cause in Rome; on the other hand, searches throughout all France for theologians and lawyers to maintain in writing that his marriage with Catherine was invalid. His object in this proceeding was that he might be able to dazzle men's eyes by a show of authority, that of universities, on his side, if, as seemed most probable, the Pope should pronounce against him. The king meant to produce, in the name of the universities—as if so many bodies of most learned men were ranged on his side—the opinions of a very few men therein, and they not only not the

holy orders, and after that was made archbishop by the Pope. He received, he said, a certain Bull of the Pope, which he delivered unto the king, and was archbishop by him. 3. Item, That he, being in holy orders, married another woman as his second wife, named Anne, and so was twice married. To this he granted. 4. Item, In the time of Henry VIII. he kept the said wife secretly, and had children by her. Hereunto he also granted, affirming that it was better for him to have his own than to do like other priests, holding and keeping other men's wives. 5. Item, In the time of King Edward he brought out the said wife openly, affirming and professing the same to be his wife. He denied not but he so did, and lawfully might do the same, forasmuch as the laws of the realm did so permit him. 6. Item, That he shamed not openly to glory himself to have had his wife in secret many years. And though he so did, he said, there was no cause why he should be ashamed thereof." He was archdeacon of Taunton in 1525, and in Italy on the affair of the divorce in the beginning of 1528, Foxe (viii. 6) says that Cranmer was the person who advised the king to consult the universities and learned men abroad, and Strype adopts the story. But Dr. Fiddes (Life of Wolsey, p. 444) shows that this device had been suggested before the trial, see Cavendish, p. 207. Nor can it be true that the king heard of Cranmer for the first time in August 1529, according to Foxe and Strype, seeing that he was chaplain to Sir Thomas Boleyn, and actively promoting the divorce for at least eighteen months previously.

Cardinal Campeggio, writing from London, June 4, 1529, says that he had heard rumours to the effect that the theologians of Paris were to be consulted; and Harpsfield (Treatise of Marriage, bk. ii. p. 96) says, "There were in the meanwhile sent by the king divers learned persons—some to Italy, some to France, and among others Dr. Stokesley and Dr. Fox; some into Germany, as the bishop of Hereford—to learn and know the censure and judgment as well of private men as of whole universities." This took place before the arrival of the Legate, and even before the Legate was appointed. "My lord Rochefort's priest" was in Italy in the beginning of 1528, carrying letters of the king, and busy in the affair of the divorce.—See Pocock, Records, i. 57.

most learned, but for the most part corrupted by royal bribery.[1]

This affair was at first placed in the hands of Reginald Pole,[2] whose noble birth vied with his honourable life and admirable learning, and afterwards in those of William Langey, a Frenchman.[3] But when Pole would not meddle in so foul a matter,[4] Langey,[5] preferring the king's money to his own reputation, brought over to his side all the poor lawyers and theologians he could.

Pedro Fernandez, a Brazilian bishop,[6] was at this time

[1] Harpsfield, bk. ii. p. 152. "I have heard a doctor and countryman of our own, that said he was joined in commission beyond the seas with others about these affairs, report that mules were well laden with English angels that flew far and wide among the learned men of France and Italy."

[2] There is a letter of Pole in Pocock, Records, i. 541, on the subject; but he does not seem to have done anything more than inform the king of what the doctors of Paris had done. In his letter to Edward VI. he gives the same account of his services.

[3] Cardinal Pole, in his letter to Edward VI., sec. 12: "Itaque delata mihi res est, addito collega Guillielmo Langeio, viro non tam nobilitate qua præstabat, quam litteris claro." He then says that he escaped the danger of being involved in the affair of the divorce: "Hic non dicam quibus modis evaserim ne me illa tempestas obrueret." William Langey was a brother of Du Bellay, bishop of Bayonne, afterwards cardinal, and at this time the French ambassador in London.

[4] Harpsfield, bk. ii. p. 147, Eyston MS. "He modestly excused himself as one unmeet, for lack of learning and experience, for such a purpose, neither yet could he with this answer quite rid his hands; but yet he gained so much, which was somewhat to his contentation, that the king did associate unto him a colleague, whom Mr. Poole was well content to suffer to despatch those affairs all alone, himself in the mean season remaining quiet and nothing intermeddling." Pole went to Paris on this business apparently in October 1529. See Le Grand, iii. 367.

[5] He seems to have been employed by the king as early as 1527, according to Stow, who writes, p. 531: "Monsieur de Langie was a gentleman greatly favoured, as well in the universities of Italy and Germany as in the universities of France, and brother to the Cardinal Bellay, then bishop of Paris. He was at that time travelled withal to procure the opinions and judgments of the doctors and chief learned men, subscribed with their hands and confirmed with their seals, of the chief universities, as of Paris, Orleans, and other of France, and of Padua, Vienna, and Bolonia in Italy, declaring by the same that the Pope could not dispense with the said marriage, as being by God's law prohibited, which afterwards was procured by the said Mons. de Langie, travelling in person to every the said universities with the king of England's commission, who had the French king's letters of singular commendation to the uttermost aid therein."

[6] Pedro Fernandez Sardinha; he was the first bishop of Bahia, San Salvador.

in Paris. In the preface to the book of Alvarez Gomez on the marriage of the king of England with his brother's widow, which he wrote, he says that he was an eyewitness of the bribery then wrought in Henry's name in Paris. "Certain theologians," so he wrote, "debasing the Word of God and seeking the favour of men, corrupted by gifts and largesses of angelets[1]—a coin well known among the English—fell into the toils of Satan, and helped the king's faction, contrary to their own convictions. And I am not afraid to speak so plainly, for I have seen it with my own eyes."

An attempt also was made, by a like profusion of money, but in vain, in the university of Cologne, to obtain a favourable opinion. Peter of Leyden[2] tells us of it; and while he praises the theologians of that university for their rejection of the king's money, he does not hide from us that some other universities were guilty of the basest flattery. These are his words: "Nothing has undermined your integrity, weakened your authority, overcome your constancy. So lately, when a certain king, mighty and powerful, hoped by heavy sums of money to purchase the opinion he wished to obtain, your rejection of him and his gold made him sensible of the unconquerable resolution of your minds. It makes one ashamed to reflect on the opinions he obtained in the meantime, by fraud and bribery, from some other universities, though they were all in vain while you refused your assent. So high is your authority, and such is your candour and discretion."

One, Croke,[3] indeed is spoken of as having spent pro-

1 Angelet, a gold coin, worth about five shillings.

2 Petrus Blomevenna, born in Leyden 1494, prior of the Carthusians of Cologne, in his preface to the first volume of the "Commentaries on the Sentences of Dionysius Carthusianus," Cologne, 1535. The prior died in 1536.

3 Richard Croke, admitted scholar of King's College, Cambridge, April 4, 1506. Soon afterwards he migrated to Oxford, and then went abroad at the expense of Warham,

fusely the king's money in other countries, so that the pestilence attacked not only the universities of Paris, Orleans, Angers, Toulouse, and Bourges, but also those of Padua and Bologna. Cardinal Pole,[1] to whom all this was perfectly well known, bitterly bewails it, and says that he could not marvel enough at the folly of the king spending such heavy sums of money to brand himself with shame; to make people believe that he had been for twenty years living in incest.

Others I pass by who complained of these things; even Sleidan,[2] who praises Anne Boleyn especially because she encouraged the heresy of Luther, says, nevertheless, that Henry had obtained the approval of his divorce not without suspicion of bribery.

Well, even in his own kingdom, Henry could get no theologians to say freely and without money that the divorce was just.

archbishop of Canterbury, where he remained about twelve years, during which time he visited Paris and Leipsic, where he was professor of Greek, as well as at Louvain afterwards. He returned to Cambridge, and was made public orator in 1522, then professor of Greek, on the departure of Erasmus. The king sent him to Italy in 1529—he being then tutor of the duke of Richmond—where he procured the opinions of divers men in favour of the divorce. On his return in 1532, he was made canon of Christ Church of the first foundation. In 1545 he migrated to Exeter College. He was vicar of Long Buckby in Northamptonshire, and died in London, 1558. Croke says of his doings (Pocock, Records, i. 404): "I never gave any man one halfpenny afore I had his conclusion with your highness without former prayer or promise of reward for the same. . . . And, gracious lord, I have laid out in your highness' cause above five hundred crowns." In a letter before this from Venice (Burnet, iv. 135) he said, "If that in time I had been sufficiently furnished with money, albeit I have, beside this seal, procured unto your highness one hundred and ten subscriptions, yet it had been nothing in comparison of that that I might easily and would have done."

[1] De Eccles. Unit. Defens., lib. iii. c. iii. "Ac primum in eo ipso quod modo retuli, cum sic auctor tuæ infamiæ esses, cum legatos ad omnes provincias mitteres, ubi litterarum gymnasia esse scires, ut præclarum hunc honoris titulum referrent, te non scortatorium aut adulterum sed incestuosum contra legem naturæ per viginti annos fuisse. Potuitne aliquod magis contra naturam accidere quam ut quispiam tanto studio, tantis suis sumptibus quantos tu fecisti hac una de causa perpetuæ turpitudinis notam sibi et labem imponendam curaret, pro qua si casu aliquo contracta esset eluenda generosissimo quisque animo libenter mortem oppeteret."

[2] Sleidan, Hist. Ref., lib. ix. p. 170 of Bohun's Translation.

Now, not to speak of Cambridge, where the king found more to favour him in some measure, it is certain that the common seal of the university of Oxford, often refused with the general assent of its most learned men, was at last obtained partly by force and partly by fraud. Some eight men at the utmost assembled by stealth, and having broken the doors of the church in which the common affairs of the university were settled, and public documents were sealed, put the seal of the university to the letter drawn up in favour of the divorce. They said that they acted thus in the interests of the university, for the king, if nobody gave him satisfaction, might become angry and destroy the university, abounding as it was in every kind of learning.[1]

Many Englishmen also throughout the realm wrote in defence of the marriage of Henry and Catherine. Among those whose names I know were John bishop of Rochester, Reginald Cardinal Pole, John Holyman,[2]

[1] Lord Herbert of Cherbury, in his Life of Henry VIII., inserted a document which he calls a "decree" of the university of Oxford, made April 4, 1530. But Antony à Wood thus speaks of it (Annals, ii. 44) in a note: "But upon my perusal of the University Register of Congregation and Convocation for that time, as also the Register of the Acts of the Chancellor's Court, I find no such act, which my lord Herbert produceth, inserted, therefore what he saith as to that matter must be looked upon as false. Such an act may be drawn up, but not allowed to be registered, because it did not pass."

Harpsfield thus speaks (Treatise of Marriage, bk. ii. p. 141): "It is not unknown how earnestly the proctors of both universities were laboured, and what rewards they had, to travel and work with the convocations of the said universities to get their consent and seal. And it is not unknown how oft it was denied, and that when all was done, all had not been obtained, partly some men had not shrunk out of the way for fear, and the very opportunity of the time had not been purposely espied when such men were away as were known would gainsay the matter. It is not unknown what a number of learned men did publicly in the universities stand with the queen's marriage, as Dr. Kirkam, Dr. Roper, Dr. Holyman, Mr. Moreman, Mr. Bayne, with divers others, of the which men and their doings many things might be here inserted worthy of observation and immortal remembrance."

[2] Born at Cuddington, Bucks, and educated at Winchester. He became a fellow of New College, Oxford, in 1512, and sometime afterwards a Benedictine monk in Reading. Consecrated bishop of Bristol Nov. 18, 1554—the only Catholic who sat in that see—he died Dec. 20, 1558.

bishop of Bristol, Abel,[1] and those seven priests already mentioned.[2]

In Spain the marriage was defended by Francis Royas, Alfonso de Virues,[3] Alfonso de Castro, and Sepulveda;[4] in Portugal by Alvarez Gomez; in Germany by Cochlæus;[5] in Flanders by Louis de Schore;[6] in France not by many, it is true, but Eguinard Baron,[7] Francis Duarene,[8] and [Francis de] Connan[9] gave their opinions on the question; in Italy by the Cardinal Cajetan;[10]

[1] Harpsfield, bk. ii. p. 131, Eyston MS. "In the mean season and the next year also, being the twenty-third of his reign, the queen's marriage was defended as well in divers open sermons, as also by printed books, especially one made by Mr. Thos. Abel, the said queen's chaplain."

[2] Chapter x. p. 67.

[3] Alfonso Ruiz de Virues, bishop of the Canary Islands, died in 1545.

[4] Johannes Genesius de Sepulveda.

[5] Harpsfield, Treatise, bk. ii. p. 153, Eyston MS. "Our countryman Mr. Morison doth grievously inveigh against Cochlæus for that book, and saith that he did not write it for the zeal and love of justice and truth, but stirred up with malice, envy, and hatred against the king, and for other corrupt affections; whose accusation the said Cochlæus refuting, protesteth, and most religiously sweareth and taketh God to witness, that this accusation was untrue, and that he was not solicited either by the Pope or emperor to write, nor anything at any time promised to him in their name for any such doings. Howbeit, he saith he was on the other side promised no small reward, in the year of our Lord 1531, if he would either himself write against the marriage, or procure some such censures and judgments from some universities of Germany as had proceeded from the universities of France and Italy. Yea, the very Lutherans were solicited and earnestly moved by the bishop of Hereford—not without fair liberal promises, as was to be thought—to give their judgment for the setting forth of the divorce, whereto they could by no means be induced."

[6] Professor of canon and civil law in the university of Louvain, of which he became rector in 1521, and in 1540 president of the Privy Council of Charles V. He published at Louvain, in 1534, "Consilium super Viribus Matrimonii inter Henricum VIII. et Catharinam Austriacam."—Paquot, i. 363.

[7] Eguinard Baron, born at Leon in Brittany, and professor of law in the university of Bourges. He died Aug. 22, 1550, aged fifty-five.

[8] Francis Duarene, of St. Brieu in Brittany, one of the most learned lawyers of his day. He was professor of law at Bourges, where he died in 1559, being then about fifty.

[9] Francis de Connan, a most learned jurist, master of requests to the king of France. He died in the forty-third year of his age, A.D. 1551.

[10] Thomas de Vio, Cardinal bishop of Gaeta, his native place, a Dominican. He wrote a letter to Henry VIII., dated Rome, Jan. 21, 1534; and before this a report on the pleadings of the advocates on both sides, presented to Clement VII., dated Rome, May 13, 1530. They may be seen as Tractatus 13 and 14, in the third volume of the Opuscula of the Cardinal. Lugduni, 1562.

and in other countries many other men of very great learning defended the marriage.

A letter also of Philip Melancthon was in many men's hands, in which he recommended the king to keep his wife, but to treat Anne Boleyn as a concubine. The king, too, and certain noblemen wrote to the Pope, begging him, as it was a matter of great moment that there should be a male heir to the kingdom,[1] to have the question speedily decided, so that the king might take another wife.[2] The answer of the Pontiff was that he would do his duty, but it was not in his power to promise the birth of a male child to any woman in the world.[3]

[1] Harpsfield, Treatise of Marriage, bk. ii. p. 85. "The crown of England also, for defect of issue male, is intrusted to the female. This discourse was not very seemly for an Englishman, neither was it seemly for any Christian man to devise and practise ways for a prince whereby he might put away his lawful wife for lack of issue male, neither was it to be thought that God would fortunate and bless such an unlawful divorce with any happy issue male. And indeed so it fell out, for albeit the divorce at length proceeded, yet had the king by the lady Anne Bulleine no issue male; and though he had such issue afterwards by another wife, yet had the realm thereby small comfort or commodity."

[2] The letter is printed by Lord Herbert (p. 331), who assigns to it the date of July 30, 1530. The writers threaten to find a remedy elsewhere if the Pope refused: "Hoc autem si non vult . . . ut aliunde nobis remedia conquiramus." It was signed by Cardinal Wolsey, archbishop Warham, the bishops of Chichester, Carlisle, Lincoln, and Menevia, the dukes of Norfolk and Suffolk, the marquises of Dorset and Exeter, the earls of Arundel, Oxford, Northumberland, Westmoreland, Shrewsbury, Essex, Derby, Worcester, Rutland, Cumberland, Sussex, Huntingdon, and Kildare, twenty-five barons, twenty-two abbots, eight knights of the shire, and doctors; among whom was Dr. Stephen Gardiner.

[3] Lord Herbert, p. 335. The Pope's letter is dated Sept. 27, 1530. The words paraphrased in the text are: "Sed pro Deo non sumus ut liberos dare possimus."

CHAPTER XIII.

DEATH OF CARDINAL WOLSEY—OF THE ARCHBISHOP OF CANTERBURY—CRANMER'S DISHONESTY—THE ROYAL SUPREMACY—THE MARRIAGE BEFORE THE DIVORCE.

In order to ensure success, the king judged it well to alarm the Pope.[1] Accordingly in the month of September [1530] he issued a proclamation[2] to the effect that none of his subjects, whether English or Irish, should without his leave present any petition to, or receive any letter from, the court of Rome. Then, when he heard that Cardinal Wolsey was living in great state in York, giving sumptuous feasts with all the pomp of his rank, and demanding the restoration of his precious mitre,[3] which the king held, he, considering all this to be something that he ought not to suffer, ordered the man to be arrested by Henry earl of Northumberland,[4] and then

[1] Harpsfield, bk. ii. p. 130. "Then was there the next year following, in the month of September, a proclamation that no person should purchase from Rome, or use, or put in execution anything in a year past purchased, or to be purchased afterward, to 'the let, hindrance, or impeachment of the king's noble and virtuous intended purposes;' which proclamation was thought to be principally devised to put the queen in some fear to take benefit of anything she had obtained, or should obtain, from Rome. It might also, all under one, serve against the Cardinal, in case he had or would procure any curse or other thing from the court of Rome against the king, to be restored to his former dignity, authority, and jurisdiction."

[2] The substance of the proclamation is printed in Lord Herbert's History, p. 330, and dated Sept. 19, 1530. But Mr. Pocock (Records, ii. 49) gives the whole proclamation, and there the date is Sept. 12, 1530.

[3] Polydori Vergilii, lib. xxvii. p. 688. "Non dubitabat scribere ad Henricum ut sibi commendaret mitram et pallium, quibus alias solebat, rem divinam faciendo, uti."

[4] Henry Algernon Percy, whose engagement to marry Anne Boleyn was broken by the Cardinal himself at the king's desire. The earl died in 1537. See Cavendish, Life of Cardinal Wolsey, p. 128.

to be brought to London.[1] But the Cardinal died on the road, at Leicester, on the 28th of November [1530],[2] and reports were spread abroad that he had taken poison.[3] This, however, is certain, that on being arrested for high treason he said, "Oh that I had been as guiltless of treason against His Divine Majesty! Now, indeed, while intent only on the serving the king, I have offended God, and have not pleased the king." Wolsey, of a truth, received in this world the reward due to his servility and pride, in order, as we trust, to escape the penalties thereof in the world to come.

But as Henry did not glorify God in the great gift with which He had endowed him, but became vain in his thoughts,[4] preferring Anne Boleyn to his everlasting salvation, and even to God Himself, God gave him up to the service of his passions, which he worshipped instead of God, in order that he who despised the everlasting reward might not be deprived, at least, of the reward of corruption. Accordingly God called to Himself William Warham, archbishop of Canterbury,[5] a good man, who

1 The installation of the Cardinal was fixed for Monday next after the feast of All Saints, but the earl of Northumberland arrested him on a charge of high treason on the Friday before the feast.—Cavendish, p. 343.

2 "Quarto Decembris e vita migravit," corrected in the following editions thus: "4 Calendas Decembris." According to Cavendish and others, he died on the 29th, the vigil of St. Andrew, and "had upon him" (Cavendish, p. 395), "next his body, a shirt of hair, besides his other shirt, which was of very fine Holland cloth; this shirt of hair was unknown to all his servants being continually attending upon him in his bedchamber, except to his chaplain, which was his ghostly father."

3 Cavendish (p. 368) tells how the apothecary of the Cardinal gave him, at his request, "a certain white confection," from the effects of which he never recovered." Chapuys, writing to the emperor, Dec. 4, 1530 (Pocock, Records, ii. 87), says it was rumoured that the Cardinal "apprins quelque chose pour haster ses jours."

4 Rom. i. 21.

5 The archbishop died Aug. 23, 1532. Harpsfield (Treatise of Marriage, bk. ii. p. 96) says: "Many ways were attempted to draw him to the king's side, and at length he fell in the king's high and grievous displeasure, and it was thought he should be appeached of treason for concealing the matter of the nun Elizabeth Barton, for his enemies had spread abroad rumours that he was privy to her doings. And Cromwell, that after the fall of the Cardinal grew in high estimation and credit with the king, scornfully said that if the king would be ruled

had earnestly pleaded the cause of the queen; and thereupon Henry, not willing that a place of honour so high should be fruitless to himself, determined to bestow it upon no one that would not minister with all his might to his passions. There was no one in the whole kingdom comparable to Reginald Pole, and to him therefore the king made the first offer of the archiepiscopal dignity, but on the condition of a distinct promise beforehand on his part to further the divorce with all his might.[1] Pole heard of this dishonourable condition, and refused to sit in the chair of pestilence.

When this came to the ears of Thomas Boleyn, the reputed father of Anne, he went to the king and said to him: "I have had for some time in my family a certain priest, grave, learned, and modest, whose fidelity to your majesty has been abundantly shown in the business on which he was sent to the Pope. He had been then for some time my chaplain, and I know him to be so well affected to the divorce that I will answer for him, if your majesty will make him archbishop, he will do whatever may be asked, or even desired, from any subject."[2]

by him, because he was an archbishop, he should be hanged on high, that he might with his heels bless all the world."

Harpsfield (*ut supra*, bk. ii. p. 97) tells the following story of the archbishop: "He charged upon his blessing the right worshipful Sir William Warham, knt., his nephew and godson, being then a young gentleman and waiting upon him in his chamber, that if ever after his death any should succeed in that see called Thomas, he should in nowise serve him, or seek his favour or acquaintance, for there shall, saith he, one of that name shortly enjoy this see, that shall as much by his vicious living as wicked heresies, dishonour, waste, and destroy the same, and the whole Church of England, as ever the blessed bishop and martyr St. Thomas did before beautify, bless, adorn, and honour the same. This I heard not long since out of the mouth of the said Sir William, who yet liveth." Harpsfield has told this in his "Historia Anglic. Eccles." also, p. 623.

[1] This and the foregoing sentence were omitted in the second and following editions.

[2] Harpsfield, bk. iii. p. 123. "When the king understood by the earl the great towardness of Cranmer to advance so much his desired purpose, little caring whether it were by right or wrong, and done by

The proposal pleased the king, more especially because Anne Boleyn made the same request. Cranmer is therefore nominated, on the condition that, being archbishop, he will, though the Roman Pontiff should give sentence in favour of the marriage, give sentence against that sentence, and that Catherine must be put away.[1]

But as Henry had not yet withdrawn from the communion of the Holy See, Cranmer must obtain from the Pope the confirmation of his dignity. He saw at once that every avenue to his consecration was closed against him if he did not declare upon oath, according to the canons, that he would never depart from the communion of the Roman chair; but he saw also into the intentions of the king, who would reject that communion utterly rather than not be married to Anne Boleyn. Under these circumstances the wily man would try by the most profound hypocrisy to serve two masters issuing contradictory commands.

lawful authority or no, he thought him a very meet man to serve his turn, and began daily more and more to be advised by him, being desirous to advance him to some high dignity ecclesiastical, that he might the better work his purpose by him. And shortly after, Dr. Warham being dead, he bestowed upon him the archbishopric of Canterbury; . . . and thereupon accordingly, being at a bear-baiting, and Cranmer also, called the said Cranmer unto him, and there told him that he gave him the archbishopric of Canterbury, which thing being heard abroad, was an heavy boding to good and wise men of some great and evil mishap hanging upon the Church and realm of England."

[1] Cranmer, in his examination at Oxford before the bishop of Gloucester, was thus addressed by Dr. Martin (Jenkyns, Cranmer's Works, iv. 92; Foxe, viii. 55): "You declare well, by the way, that the king took you to be a man of good conscience, who could not find within all his realm any man that would set forth his strange attempts, but was enforced to send for you in post to come out of Germany. What may we conjecture hereby, but that there was a compact between you, being then queen Anne's chaplain and the king's. 'Give me the archbishopric of Canterbury, and I will give you licence to live in adultery.' To this Cranmer replied, 'You say not true.'" Cardinal Pole (letter to Cranmer, Le Grand, i. 302) says that Cranmer was made archbishop for no other end but that of giving an appearance of right and justice to the divorce, and that but for the divorce Cranmer himself would never have imagined that he could be made archbishop, and certainly no one else thought him a fit man for such a place.

He was fond of the king from his heart, because he was very like himself, and the Pope he regarded only with fear;[1] and so the impious man, to please the king, determined to commit perjury, deliberately of his own free-will, that he might the more grievously at a later time hurt the Pope, not suspecting anything of the kind. Accordingly he sends for a public notary and tells him that he is about to take the canonical and accustomed oath of obedience to the Roman Pontiff, but before doing so it was his will and wish that the notary should place it on record in a public document that he took the oath on compulsion, and that nothing was further from his thoughts than to keep faith with the Roman Pontiff to the damage of the king.[2]

When this declaration had been made—and lest, perchance, the king might have some doubts about his breach of faith, in the presence of witnesses recorded and sealed—he took the solemn oath of obedience to the Pope as his predecessors had done, and at the same time took possession of the archbishopric like a thief.[3]

[1] He said so in a sermon preached in the cathedral of Canterbury, and admitted that he so said in a letter to Henry VIII. (Jenkyns, Cranmer's Remains, i. 170), "These many years I prayed unto God that I might see the power of Rome destroyed; and that I thanked God that I had now seen it in this realm." Nevertheless he accepted the archbishopric from the Pope, and took the oath to maintain the authority and power of Rome.

[2] Harpsfield, bk. iii. p. 126. "But before he took the said oath, early in the morning, he called to him certain of his friends, and among others Master Goodriche, that was afterwards bishop of Ely, and said to them, 'Sirs, bear me witness that, albeit I shall swear this day to be obedient to the See of Rome, yet I shall swear but with my outward lips, and not with my inward heart and mind; neither do I intend to keep promise with the Pope that is absent, but to blind and breare the eyes of the people here present.' And this protestation he required might be—doubtless to his perpetual shame—enacted and registered."

[3] Cranmer's Bulls were obtained in Rome in the usual way; his proctor taking the oaths in his name and in his behalf. But Cranmer in England, by his own account (Jenkyns, iv. p. 116), said that the proctor "should do it *super animam suam*," and that he, Cranmer, would not be bound by the promises made in his name and confirmed upon oath. Of this reservation the Pope and his officers knew nothing. He accepted the Bulls thus fraudulently obtained, and on the day of his consecration made a protest before a notary that he would take himself the same oaths, but without the intention of keeping

By these doings he made himself acceptable to the king, and it might have been said that the cover was really meet for the cup.[1] There were people who many years afterwards heard the king say that Cranmer, the archbishop of Canterbury, was one who never thwarted him in anything.[2]

During the arrangements about the archbishopric, Henry, like a mighty hunter, resolved to subject to his authority the first-born of the kingdom of heaven, that is, the servants of Christ, and the whole of the chief part of His lot. By an act of tyranny never heard of before, he had all the clergy[3] indicted for having

them (ibid., p. 248)—"Non est nec erit meæ voluntatis aut intentionis . . . me obligare ad aliquod"—against the king or his laws. And further, that he never meant to authorise his proctor to bind him, though his proctor by his authority had, so far as words have any meaning, most solemnly done so. Having made this protest, he went up to the altar, said Mass, and then said to those in the secret of his sin, when about to take the oath of obedience to the Pope, that he took it under the protest he had already made. The consecrating bishops may, or may not, have known of this dishonesty, but there is nothing in the records of it to show that they were his accomplices. Even if they knew of it, there is no excuse for Cranmer, for he and they knew that there was no authority in England to dispense Cranmer from the oath, or to allow him to take it in a new sense of his own. The Bull of the Pope recited the oath to be taken by Cranmer, and in the same Bull it is distinctly said that if Cranmer did not take the oath, both he and the bishop who consecrated him without that oath, were both suspended and forbidden the administration of their sees respectively, both in temporals and spirituals: "Volumus autem et auctoritate prædicta statuimus et decernimus quod si, non recepto a te [Cranmero] per ipsum antistitem prædicto juramento, idem antistes munus ipsum tibi impendere et tu illud suscipere præsumpseritis, dictus antistes a pontificalis officii exercitio, et tam ipse quam tu ab administratione tam spiritualium quam temporalium ecclesiarum vestrarum suspensi sitis eo ipso." Cranmer, then, it seems, never was archbishop of Canterbury, and all his acts were null except against himself.

[1] Harpsfield, bk. iii. p. 126. "Such an archbishop, so nominated, and in such a place, so, and in such wise consecrated, was a meet instrument for the king to work by—a meet cover for such a cup." The same saying is to be found also in Latimer's Sermons, ed. Parker Society, p. 181, "Such a cup! such a cover!"

[2] Cranmer said as much of himself. In his letter to Cromwell (Burnet, vi. 128, ed. Pocock) he says, "Against whose highness [the king's] he [Gardiner] knoweth right well that I will maintain no cause, but give place, and lay both my cause and self at my prince's feet."

[3] Gardiner, writing to the Protector from the Fleet, Oct. 14, 1547 (Foxe, vi. 43): "Now, whether the king may command against an act of Parliament, and what danger they

acknowledged and maintained, contrary to the king's will, the power of the Legates of the Roman Pontiff, a foreign power, as men then began to call it.[1] For this offence all their goods were forfeited and at the mercy of the king's exchequer.[2] The terror inspired by this most iniquitous charge crushed the clergy and bowed them down to the ground. They were to lose all their property, be deprived of their liberty, and put in prison for the rest of their days. Seeing no hope of relief anywhere, they gave up the battle as lost, and allowed themselves to be trodden under foot as salt that has lost its strength.

Accordingly, assembled in their House of Convocation, almost all the clergy of all ranks with one voice petitioned the king—offering him at the same time a hundred thousand pounds—of his goodness to forgive them and spare them the rest of the penalty. They asked him to do so in virtue of that supreme power, not only over the lay people, but also over the clergy within his

may fall in that break a law with the king's consent, I daresay no man alive at this day hath had more experience, what the judges and lawyers have said, than I. First, I had experience in mine old master the Cardinal, who obtained his legacy by our late sovereign lord's request at Rome, and in his sight and knowledge occupied the same, with his two crosses and maces borne before him, many years. Yet, because it was against the laws of the realm, the judges concluded the offence of the præmunire, which conclusion I bear away and take it for a law of the realm, because the lawyers so said, but my reason digested it not."

[1] Cranmer, when he was offered the archbishopric by the king, confessed that he must receive it from the Pope, "which," he said (Jenkyns, iv. 115), "he neither would nor could do," because the archbishopric "appertained to his grace, and not to any other foreign authority, whatsoever it was. . . . That he would accept it and receive it of his majesty, and of none other stranger who had no authority within this realm, neither in any such gift nor in any other thing."

[2] Stow, p. 559. "The clergy of England, being judged by the king's learned counsell to be in the præmunire, for maintaining the power Legatine of the Cardinal, were called by process into the King's Bench to answer, wherefore in their convocation they concluded a submission, wherein they called the king supreme head of the Church of England, according to the law of God, and not otherwise, and were contented to give the king £100,000 to pardon their offences touching the præmunire."

dominions, which they now for the first time recognised in him. It is said that the words used in that petition furnished the occasion for the king to style himself the supreme head of the Anglican Church.[1]

Then was heard everywhere, out of every man's mouth who was living a corrupt life, that the Pope had nothing to do with the kingdom of England, unless it pleased the king to allow him any authority in it; for, said they, every soul must be subject to the royal power, not only in civil but also in spiritual things. All this, it is true, was invented, maintained, and scattered abroad for the purpose of keeping people from imagining that the king had got rid of his wife without lawful authority.

After this nothing more was wanting for the marriage of the king with Anne Boleyn but a public sentence of divorce, and the king had no expectation that the Roman Pontiff would ever pronounce it. But he knew for certain that Cranmer, his tool, would shortly pronounce it, and then, lest he should be regarded as having made a person of low condition his wife, on the 1st day of September he created Anne Boleyn marchioness of Pembroke.[2]

The king, now impatient of further delay, though everything had not yet been duly prepared, determined to marry Anne Boleyn secretly on the 14th of the fol-

[1] The convocation of the province of Canterbury, March 22, 1531, adopted this formula in addressing the king: "Ecclesiæ et cleri Anglicani, cujus singularem protectorem unicum et supremum dominum, et quantum per Christi legem licet, etiam supremum caput, ipsius majestatem recognoscimus." — Wilkins, Concil., iii. p. 742. According to Parker (De Antiquit. Brit. Eccles., p. 487), Cranmer and Cromwell were the men who suggested this iniquity to the king: "Hujus consilii Cranmerus et Cromwellus clam authores fuisse existimabantur." And he adds that Henry, disliking the qualification "so far as the law of Christ allows it," sent Cromwell to the convocation to tell the clergy that if that clause were not withdrawn, the penalties of the præmunire would be inflicted. The clergy in their terror withdrew it, and accepted the king instead of the Pope.

[2] Stow, 560. "The 1st of Sept. [1532] the lady Anne Bologne was made marchioness of Pembroke at Windsor, and then was given her by the king one thousand pound by year out of the bishopric of Durham."

lowing November.[1] He must marry her, for in no other way could he accomplish his will; and the marriage must be secret, because he and Catherine had not been separated by any judicial decision. Accordingly the king sent for Rowland Lee,[2] then a priest, and whom afterwards he made bishop of Lichfield, and bade him say Mass according to the Catholic and Roman rite. To him the king declared that at last sentence had been given in his favour in Rome, and that it was lawful for him to take another wife. Lee, considering that it was not usual for kings to tell a lie, was at first silent, but immediately afterwards his conscience smote him, and he said to the king, "Your majesty, I hope, has the Pontifical Brief." The king made a sign to that effect, and the priest turned to the altar. Again the priest, being in doubt, and afraid that he might be doing something that was wrong, said to the king, "The sacred canons require, and it is of the utmost concern to us, that the Papal letters be read and published." Thereupon the king asserted that he really had the Papal Brief, but that it was in a very secret place, where he only could find it; it was not seemly that he should then go for it by himself, for it was not yet daylight. Rowland Lee made no further resistance, and having

[1] Hall, 794. "The king after his return married privily the lady Anne Bulleyn on St. Erkonwald's Day [Nov. 14], which marriage was kept so secret that very few persons knew it till she was great with child at Easter after."

[2] A native of Morpeth, and a Cambridge doctor. He was consecrated bishop of Lichfield at Croydon by Thomas Cranmer, April 19, 1534, assisted by Longland, bishop of Lincoln, and Thomas Chetham, bishop of Sidon.

No Bulls had been either asked for or obtained from the Pope, nevertheless Rowland Lee was consecrated, but in schism, and on taking possession of the bishopric, he took also the oath of supremacy, and accepted the spiritual jurisdiction from the king. These are the terms of his oath (Burnet, vi. 291, ed. Pocock): "I acknowledge and recognise your majesty immediately under Almighty God to be the chief and supreme head of the Church of England, and claim to have the bishopric of Chester wholly and only of your gift, and to have and to hold the profits temporal and spiritual of the same, only of your majesty, and of your heirs, kings of this realm, and of none other. . . . So help me God, all saints, and the holy evangelist."

said Mass, gave to Henry a second wife, the first being not only still alive, but not even divorced from him by any decision pronounced in any ecclesiastical court, or anything of the kind whatsoever.[1]

[1] Harpsfield, bk. iii. p. 24. "The which marriage was secretly made at Whitehall, very early before day, none being present but Mr. Norris and Mr. Heneage of the privy chamber, and the lady Barkely, with Mr. Rowland the king's chaplain, that was afterwards made bishop of Coventry and Lichfield, to whom the king told that now he had gotten of the Pope a licence to marry another wife, but yet, to avoid business and tumult, the thing must be done, quoth the king, very secretly, and thereupon a time and place was appointed to the said Mr. Rowland to solemnise the said marriage. At which time Mr. Rowland having come accordingly, and seeing all things ready for celebrating of Mass and to solemnise the marriage, being in a great dump, and staggering, came to the king and said, 'Sire, I trust you have the Pope's licence, both that you may marry and that I may join you together in marriage.' 'What else?' quoth the king. Upon this he turned to the altar and revested himself, but yet not so satisfied, and troubled in mind, he cometh eftsoon to the king and saith, 'This matter toucheth us all very nigh, and therefore it is expedient that the licence be read before us all, or else we run all, and I more deep than any other, into excommunication, in marrying your grace without any banns-asking, and in a place unhallowed, and no divorce as yet promulged of the first matrimony.' The king, looking upon him very amiably, 'Why, Mr. Rowland,' quoth he, 'think you me a man of so small faith and credit, you, I say, that do well know my life passed, and even now have heard my confession; or think you me a man of so small and slender foresight and consideration of my affairs, that unless all things were safe and sure I would enterprise this matter? I have truly a licence, but it is reposed in another sure place, whereto no man resorteth but myself, which, if it were seen, should discharge us all. But if I should, now that it waxeth towards day, fetch it and be seen so early abroad, there would rise a rumour and talk thereof other than were convenient. So forth, in God's name, and do that which appertaineth to you. I will take upon me all other danger.' Whereupon he went to Mass and celebrated also all ceremonies belonging to marriage." Le Grand (ii. 110) gives an extract from an account of the divorce presented to king Philip and queen Mary, which agrees with this extract from Harpsfield, but it does not say when the marriage took place.

CHAPTER XIV.

VALIDITY OF THE FIRST MARRIAGE — IMPEDIMENTS OF MATRIMONY—SHAMELESSNESS OF HENRY—SENTENCE OF THE POPE.

HENRY VIII. pleaded an impediment to his marriage with Catherine which he knew had no existence, having at the same time knowledge that this very impediment subsisted against the marriage with Anne Boleyn ; for it is plain that, under the circumstances, there were only two possible impediments to the marriage of Henry and Catherine. One of them might have been that of affinity, if the marriage of Arthur, the brother of Henry, with Catherine had been perfected; but the king knew that it had not, and said so to the emperor Charles V.[1] Catherine herself always maintained that it had not, and that with the solemnity of an oath.[2] Moreover, the health of prince Arthur was so frail at the time, and there was therefore no ground for insisting on the impediment of affinity.

Still further, even if the impediment did once subsist, it had been removed by the power of the keys of the kingdom of heaven in due form of law, in view of a

[1] See note 2, p. 63.

[2] Cardinal Campeggio (Theiner, p. 574) says that the queen persisted in this statement; and, according to Cavendish (p. 215), she asserted the fact again in the court of the Legates, saying publicly there to the king, "Whether it be true or not, I put it to your conscience." The king, thus challenged, did not contradict the queen, and in the whole course of the trial there is no hint given by the king, or his agents on his behalf, that the queen told anything but the truth. Attempts were made to prove the contrary, but her statement was never contradicted on any other ground than inferences drawn from the statements made by the king's witnesses.

greater good—the preservation of the public peace. Henry, it is true, maintained that the Pope could not dispense in the matter of that impediment; but he was in the wrong, for if, under the law of Moses, which was the ministration of death and damnation, and which was made void,[1] there was a power not only of dispensing with, but also of commanding, the marriage of a widow with the brother of the husband dying without issue, how much more certain is it that such a power, strong and stable, belongs to the keys of the Church of Christ, to the ministration of the spirit and of justice, and which have not been made void by any other testament, but remain to the end of time, and that a Christian, for the common good of the Church, may by that power be allowed to marry the widow of his brother deceased? There was no impediment of affinity of any kind to hinder the marriage of Henry and Catherine; and granting even that it did once subsist, the keys of Peter had taken it duly away.

As for the impediment of public decency, which is the only one that remains to be considered, it is admitted by all that it rests on ecclesiastical, not on any divine or natural law. Neither the lawyers of the king nor the king himself ever denied the sufficiency of the power of the keys for its removal. Then as there was no affinity, and as the impediment of public decency was taken away by the Brief of Pope Julius II., there remained no hindrance to the marriage or to perseverance in it. If any one were to say, by way of objection, that a man is forbidden by the law of God to marry the widow of his brother, the answer is ready, that the very same law of God makes an express exception: when the brother shall have died without issue,[2] as prince Arthur had done. But we must not forget

[1] 2 Cor. iii. 9–11.

[2] Deut. xxv. 5.

that the words of the divine law in the very same place are preceded and followed by certain considerations which utterly destroy the cause of the king. We read thus: "No man shall approach to her that is next of his blood,[1] to reveal her turpitude." And a little further on: "The turpitude of thy brother's wife thou shalt not reveal, because it is the turpitude of thy brother."[2] The marriage of a brother's widow, therefore, is forbidden for no other reason than this: She had become of kin to the brother, because she had been the wife of the brother who is dead. Man and wife are one flesh, and therefore the widow of my brother is as near in blood to me as my brother is, who is my next in blood; in the first degree of relationship.

Therefore, then, if we were to grant that God spoke in that place not only of an unlawful approach, but also of marriage—which many think is not the case—and that by "brother's wife" is meant not only the wife of a brother still living—as some of the holy Fathers maintain—but also the wife of a brother deceased; and still further, even, if we grant that the law in question was not ceremonial, but the expression of certain conclusions drawn from the law of nature, nevertheless, as the principle on which the law rests has been expressed more than once, and as that principle is nearness of blood, the result of consanguinity or of marriage consummated, which begets affinity, there was no tie of consanguinity or affinity to bind Henry and Catherine, seeing that the marriage of his brother was never consummated; and so we come to the conclusion that the marriage of Henry and Catherine was not forbidden by the divine law.

But, on the other hand, it is most certain that the impediment of affinity stood in the way of the king's

[1] Lev. xviii. 6. [2] Lev. xviii. 16.

marriage with Anne Boleyn, and that the king knew it, seeing that in a letter to Clement VII. he confessed that he had committed adultery with Mary Boleyn, the sister of Anne, and was therefore of kin to the whole Boleyn family, according to the words of St. Paul,[1] "He who is joined to a harlot is made one body." Now, as Mary Boleyn was related to Anne in the first degree of consanguinity, being her sister, born of one and the same mother, so Henry, because of his relations with Mary, stood in the first degree of consanguinity to all the brothers and sisters of Mary, and therefore to Anne Boleyn. It is come, then, to this: he who disturbed the world to obtain a divorce from Catherine on the ground of affinity, when there was none in truth, is not afraid to marry his kinswoman. He who said that the authority of the Pope could not justify him in keeping Catherine as his wife, now, not only without respect to that authority, but even in the very teeth of it, makes Anne Boleyn his wife, who was his near kinswoman. The king kicked against the goad in vain. God laid bare his hypocrisy, and revealed to the whole world the falsehood of his heart.

That is not all. Henry had sinned with the mother of Anne Boleyn,[2] and there was, therefore, that relationship between them which subsists between parent and child. But it is never lawful for a father to marry his own daughter, for marriage is never allowed between descendants and ascendants in the straight line.[3] Besides, the

[1] 1 Cor. vi. 16.

[2] Harpsfield, bk. iii. p. 28, Eyston MS. "Yea, I have credibly heard reported that the king knew the mother of the said Anne Bulleyne, which is a fourth impediment, and worse than the precedent. Of the which impediments Sir Thomas Moore was not by likelihood ignorant, and seemeth to touch them, or suchlike, in these words which he wrote to Dr. Wilson: 'Finally, as touching the oath, the causes for which I refused it, no man wotteth what they be, for they be secret in my own conscience: some other, peradventure, than those that other men would ween, and such as I never disclosed unto any man yet, ne, nor never intend to do while I live.'"

[3] Scotus, 4 Sent. dist. 40, qu. unic. "Non intelligitur tantum de patre proximo, sed de quocunque in linea recta, ita quod si Adam hodie viveret non posset ducere aliquam uxorem."

state of marriage is one of almost equality. Eve was taken out of the side of Adam ; and children are bound to honour their parents, and to acknowledge themselves to be so much their inferiors that they can never be on an equality with them. That being so, it was therefore a much more difficult matter to dispense with the marriage of Henry and Anne Boleyn, seeing that he had sinned with her mother. Besides, the affinity thus contracted touches the essence of marriage too nearly to be decently disposed of by a dispensation, especially if the sin be known to many.

Henry, therefore, who, against the law of nature in a certain sense, dared to marry the daughter of the mother he had defiled, was simply shameless when he pretended that he durst not keep his wife Catherine because he feared to sin against God; shameless also when he feigned to believe that it was not in the power of the Pope to sanction his marriage with Catherine.

Still further. It is clear from what we have already said that Henry was told in no doubtful way that Anne Boleyn was his own child, and yet he married her, he who was afraid to keep his wife because she was the widow of his brother, though there were not, and though there could not be, any issue of that marriage. This was rashness not to be believed, hypocrisy unheard of, and lewdness not to be borne; but it was the hypocrisy and the rashness and lewdness of one man. Nor is it to be much wondered at that a man should fall into sin, or that he should be contemptuous when he comes into the depths of it;[1] but this is marvellous and astonishing, that multitudes of men should endure patiently, not their own lewdness, but that of another—not only endure it patiently, but respect it, praise and honour it, and

[1] Prov. xviii. 3.

honour it so far as to build upon it their belief, their hope and salvation.

Now, all English Protestants—Lutherans, Zuinglians, Calvinists, Puritans, and Libertines—honour the incestuous marriage of Henry and Anne Boleyn as the wellspring of their gospel, the mother of their Church, and the source of their belief. Three years have hardly passed by since an English Calvinist in London presented to queen Elizabeth—Matthew Parker, the pretended archbishop of Canterbury, standing by—two books, but without his name, printed by John Day, in the latter of which, speaking of the marriage of Henry and Anne Boleyn, he says, "Oh, truly blessed and providential wedlock! birth and child divine, by which the country was rescued and delivered out of slavery and darkness worse than those of Egypt, and brought back to the true worship of Christ."[1]

Henceforth let no one be surprised at the ancient Cainites, people who worshipped Cain the murderer as the son of a mighty power; or at the Ophites, who, according to Tertullian,[2] reverenced, as the source of the knowledge of good and evil, the serpent, by which Adam and Eve were deceived in Paradise. For why should we not believe that such people once lived, when we see so many millions of heretics now treat with respect the marriage of father and child? These assign their deliverance from slavery worse than that of Egypt

[1] "De visibili 'Rom.' anarchia contra Nich. Sanderi Monarchiam προλεγόμενον, libri duo, Georgio Acwortho legum doctore."—Londini apud Johannem Dayum, 1573, p. 134. Matthew Parker himself was not behindhand with Dr. Acworth, for in his Life of Cranmer (De Antiquitate Britannicæ Eccles., p. 492, ed. Drake) are these words: "Ex his piis nuptiis edita est ad diuturnum Anglicani regni imperium atque patrocinium, æternumque Papalis dominationis excidium, Deo sacrata virgo domina Elizabetha, septimo idus Septembris."

[2] De Præser. Hæret., sec. 47. "Ophitæ, . . . serpentem magnificant . . . ipse enim, inquiunt, scientiæ nobis boni et mali originem dedit."

to this marriage, and boast that it has brought back the true worship of Christ.

Certainly it is true that this marriage has opened a door to every heresy and to every sin. Oh, the infinite goodness of God! He would not suffer these heresies of yours to come forth in any other way than through this incestuous marriage, thereby showing them to be the fruits of darkness, and that they could not be had but by deeds of darkness. The child must sin with the father, the sister with the brother—for Anne Boleyn sinned with her brother, as we shall soon see—in order to give birth to that evil thing which banished out of the land, and declared unworthy of life and the light of day, the Carthusian fathers and others, who, following the counsel of Christ, had made themselves eunuchs in order to gain the kingdom of heaven.[1] This was not all: it saw that the Church which, according to the words of our Lord, teaches and baptizes those who believe among all nations, is not the Church of Christ; that the Church of Christ is something else, lurking in secret places, in the caves of wild beasts, shunning the light, barren, unknown, without priesthood and without sacrifice; that it is not under the one shepherd who gathers together the sheep, dispersed throughout the world, into the one fold of Christ; that it has not the promises of God made to the city built on the mount which cannot be hidden—made to the children of light, not to those of the night—to the sheep of Peter, to the fish within his net, not to those who stray from the fold, or those by whom the net is broken.

Let us return to the subject of this book. The Roman Pontiff, after the most rigid examination of the question between Henry and Catherine, declared them bound

[1] St. Matt. xix. 12.

together in the bonds of lawful wedlock beyond the power of man to sunder. The sentence was as follows :—

"Clement Pope VII.—Whereas the validity of the marriage contracted by Our most dearly beloved children in Christ, Catherine and Henry VIII., king and queen of England, has been disputed, and the cause brought before Us, and by Us, in a consistory of the most reverend Cardinals, committed to Our beloved son, Paul Capisucchi, auditor of causes in the Sacred Apostolic Palace, and dean ; and whereas the aforesaid Henry, while the cause was still pending, hath put away the said Catherine, and *de facto* married one Anne, contrary to Our commandments, and in contempt of Our prohibitions contained in Our letter *in forma Brevis*,[1] and sent forth after counsel had with Our brethren the Cardinals of the Holy Roman Church, thereby temerariously disturbing the due course of law ;—

"We, therefore, in the fulness of that power given Us, unworthy as We are, in the person of the blessed Peter, by Christ the King of kings, sitting on the throne of justice, and looking unto God alone, do, by this Our sentence, which We pronounce, by Our duty constrained, and with the advice of Our venerable brethren, the Cardinals of the Holy Roman Church, in consistory assembled, declare that the casting out of the said Catherine the queen, and the withholding of her wifely rights and royal dignity, whereof she stood possessed when the suit was begun, and also the marriage contracted by the aforesaid Henry and Anne—all manifest and notorious deeds—to be what they are and were, null and unjust and contrary to law, to have been and to be tainted with the defects of nullity, injustice, and contempt of law ; and We further declare by the same sentence that the children, born or to be born of that

1 See the Brief in Le Grand, iii. 444, and also in Tierney's Dod, i. 366.

marriage, are and have always been bastards: We also declare that the said Catherine the queen is to be restored to, and reinstated in, her former rank, and quasi-possession of her wifely rights and royal dignity, and that the king aforesaid must put away and remove the aforesaid Anne from his house and quasi-possession of wifely and royal rights, and by this sentence in writing We restore and reinstate, put away and remove, the aforesaid persons respectively.

"Moreover, by this same sentence, after due deliberation had, in virtue of Our office, We pronounce the aforesaid Henry to have fallen, to his own damnation, under the censure of the greater excommunication, and to have brought upon himself the other censures and penalties in the aforesaid Brief expressed, because of his disobedience thereto, and contempt thereof, and We command all the faithful to avoid him.

"Nevertheless, as a father tender of heart, We wish to deal gently and mercifully with the said Henry, and so We suspend the effects of this sentence from this day to the end of September next, that he may the more easily obey Our sentence and decrees aforementioned.

"And if within that time he shall not have submitted himself, and shall not have reinstated the said Catherine in her former rank, in which she was when the lawsuit began, and if he shall not have put the aforesaid Anne from his house and her quasi-possession of the rights of wife and queen, and if he shall not have effectually purged his contempt, then We will and decree that this present sentence shall take effect now as then.—So We say."

CHAPTER XV.

APOSTASY OF HENRY — THE DIVORCE PRONOUNCED BY CRANMER — CORONATION OF ANNE BOLEYN — SIR THOMAS MORE—THE OBSERVANT FRIARS—THE ROYAL SUPREMACY.

HENRY regarded the sentence as a wrong done to himself, and then, to be avenged of the Pope for his vexation, took measures for the abolition by Parliament of the oath which the English clergy took to the Pope;[1] and, as was done of old by Julian the Apostate, creating himself Pope, ordered a new oath to be taken, in the terms of which the clergy and people acknowledged him as the supreme head on earth, next to Christ, of the English and the Irish Church.[2] Thus Henry cut off and

[1] Hall, p. 787, says that the king sent for the Speaker of the Commons on the 11th May, in the twenty-fourth year of his reign, which was A.D. 1532, and gave him a copy of the oath taken by the prelates, saying of them that they were but "half our subjects, yea, and scarce our subjects." Now the king knew well that the bishops, for more than two hundred years, had been renouncing all clauses in their Bulls which they were pleased to call "prejudicial or hurtful" to the king "their sovereign lord," and professing to accept the temporalities of their churches from the king. Lord Herbert (p. 363) says, "Whereupon these two oaths by the king's command being read and considered, the Parliament so handled the business, as it occasioned the final renouncing of the Pope's authority about two years after." In the twenty-sixth year of the king, A.D. 1535, an oath was to be taken by all persons to this effect (26 Henry VIII. c. 2): "In case any oath be made, or hath been made by you to any person or persons, that then ye to repute the same as vain and annihilate."

[2] The oaths of the bishops at this time may be seen in Foxe, v. 70–73. Each bishop acknowledges the king to be the supreme head of the Church of England "immediately under Christ," and from "this day forward I shall swear, promise, give, or cause to be given to no foreign potentate, . . . nor yet to the bishop of Rome whom they call Pope, any oath or fealty, directly or indirectly; . . . but at all times, and in every case and condition, I shall . . . maintain . . . the quarrel and cause of your royal majesty and your successors. . . . I

severed both himself and his people from the fellowship and communion of the Roman Church, in which ever since the days of Joseph of Arimathia all those kings and people had lived, who in these islands, each in his own generation, followed the Catholic faith of Christ; and they were the Irish, the Angles, the Normans, the Danes, and, the most ancient of them all, the Welsh.

We all know, O king, that thriving and glorious Church which you have abandoned and left: the Church founded by the great apostles Peter and Paul, which has prospered and endured under two hundred and thirty successors of St. Peter,[1] which the bishops, the kings, and people of all Catholic nations have confessed and honoured, which shuns and condemns the impious teachings of all heresies and all heretics, which abounds in fathers and doctors that cannot be numbered, and which is made glorious by the works of God truly marvellous and unceasing. But tell us, we adjure you by that supreme authority which you have assumed, whither did you go when you went out of the Roman Church? For if you would remain a Christian, you cannot do so without being in some Church. It is indeed true that the apostle Paul went out from among the Jews, Dionysius from the Areopagus, Justin the Martyr from the philosophers, and Augustin from the Manichees, all from the errors of the nations; but then every one of these, before he abandoned those with whom he had hitherto dwelt, saw first another society older than himself to which he could go. Paul went to Ananias, and to the others, the faithful of Damascus; Dionysius to

profess the Papacy of Rome not to be ordained of God by Holy Scripture, . . . that the said bishop of Rome . . . is not to be called Pope or supreme bishop, . . . but only bishop of Rome. And I shall firmly observe . . . laws and acts of this realm . . . enacted and established for the extirpation and suppression of the Papacy, and of the authority and jurisdiction of the said bishop of Rome."

[1] This was written in the Pontifical of Gregory XIII.

Paul and his companions; Justin to the Church of Christ in Palestine; Augustin to Ambrose of Milan and the Catholic Church.

But you, O king, when you deserted the Roman Church, to what other Church did you go? Did you go to the Greek Church? Certainly not, for you have not denied the Procession of the Holy Ghost from the Son. Did you go to the Æthiopic Church? No, for you have not submitted to the rite of circumcision. Did you go to the Armenians? No, for you have not denied original sin, nor, as they do, the salvation of all who died before the Passion of Christ. But at least, then, you went to Wicliffe, Luther, Zuinglius, or Calvin? Well, if you found any in your kingdom holding the errors of these men, you persecuted them with fire and sword. Whither, then, did you go when you went out of the Roman Church? Whither, indeed? It was to yourself. Well, then, you are Christ; for He alone has the authority necessary for the founding and gathering of the Christian Church together. He it was who said to Peter, "Thou art Peter, and on this rock I will build my Church."[1] What, I ask you, does He mean by "mine," if He does not mean the Christian Church? Christ, therefore, sends us to Peter, that is to say, to His Vicar; and you? you take us away from Peter, and call us to yourself. Then you are Antichrist, as it is written, "Beware that no man seduce you, for many will come in my name, saying, I am Christ, and will seduce many."[2] To come in the name of Christ, or to say, "I am Christ," is nothing else but a man's making himself, without signs of an apostolate, without lawful and orderly mission, the head of the Church, as if the care of the sheep of Christ had been originally and principally committed to him. Had the Church, then, died out of the world—had the

[1] St. Matt. xvi. 18.

[2] St. Matt. xxiv. 4, 5.

prophecies and promises of Christ failed before Henry and his child, had in incest, begotten a new Church of Christ? But if the Church of Christ has not failed, she must have been older than you. And if older than you, and yet not the Roman Church, you, when you left the Roman Church, should have gone to that which in your senseless decision is the truer; you should have made yourself a member of it by some sacrament, or at least by the mere laying on of hands, that we by that may know the society to which you belong, and the faith you profess. But now you have made yourself to your subjects the supreme head of the Church, you who were not even the lowest member of her.

Matters being thus arranged, the time had come when archbishop Cranmer, released, by the authority of a lay assembly,[1] from the obligations of the oath he had taken to the Roman Pontiff, felt himself at liberty, even against the orders of the Roman Pontiff, to separate Henry and Catherine by a sentence of divorce. Accordingly, with Henry's leave,[2] he took with him certain bishops, proctors, advocates, and notaries to the town of Dunstable, not far from the royal residence of Ampthill, where the queen was living at the time. He summoned the queen more than once to appear in his court,[3] and when he had waited, but in vain, for a fortnight, he

[1] 24 Henry VIII. c. 12, the statute by which appeals to the Pope were forbidden.

[2] Cranmer asked leave of the king to put an end to the suit between the king and his wife, though the cause was then in due course of law, beyond all mere episcopal jurisdiction, pending in the court of the Pope. The king gave him leave in these terms (Collier, Eccles. Hist., ii. Records, No. 24): "Albeit we being your king and sovereign, do recognise no superior in earth, but only God, and not being subject to the laws of any other earthly creature, yet because ye be under us, by God's calling the most principal minister of our spiritual jurisdiction, within this our realm, . . . will not therefore refuse—our pre-eminence and authority to us and our successors in this behalf nevertheless saved — your humble request. . . . Wherefore we inclining to your humble petition, ... do license you to proceed in the said cause."

[3] Herbert, p. 375. "With him came the bishop of London [Stokesley], Winchester, being Stephen Gar-

made his preparations for pronouncing the sentence of divorce.[1] Before this, he had warned the king, as one who in some measure shrunk from the divorce—that was done by agreement between them—no longer to retain his brother's wife contrary to the laws of the gospel; and if he did not obey, he said he must, however unwilling, because of the office he held in the Church of God, proceed to ecclesiastical censures against the king.[2]

diner, Bath [Clerk], Lincoln [Longland], and many great clerks." The bishop of Bath and Wells had been one of the queen's counsel, and Longland now completed his first sin. An account of this proceeding is to be found in Pocock, Records, ii. p. 473.

[1] Cranmer, in his letter to archdeacon Hawkins (Jenkyns, Cranmer, vol. i. p. 27), thus speaks of his proceedings: "It was thought convenient by the king and his learned counsel that I should repair unto Dunstable, which is within four miles unto Ampthill, where the said lady Katherine keepeth her house, and there to call her before me to hear the final sentence in the said matter. Notwithstanding, she would not at all obey thereunto, for when she was by Dr. Lee cited to appear by a day she utterly refused the same, saying that inasmuch as her cause was before the Pope, she would have none other judge; and therefore would not take me for her judge. . . . We examined certain witnesses which testified that she was lawfully cited and called to appear, whom from fault of appearance was declared *contumax:* proceeding in the said cause against her *in pœnam contumaciæ*, as the process of the law thereunto belongeth, which continued fifteen days after our coming thither. And the morrow after Ascension Day I gave final sentence therein, how that it was indispensable for the Pope to license any such marriages."

But the proceedings were clandestine. Cranmer confesses in his letter to Cromwell, Dunstable, May 17, that he wished his doings at Dunstable to remain secret, for fear the queen should hear of them, and counsel appear on her behalf. "If the queen appeared," says Cranmer, "I should be greatly stayed and let in the process, and the king's grace's counsel here present shall be much uncertain what shall be then further done therein." The letter is in Jenkyns, Remains of Cranmer, i. p. 26. Thus the archbishop, who had perjured himself to obtain the archbishopric, made a mockery of justice, consulting with the lawyers of the plaintiff, and preparing to give the sentence which the king desired, but which he could not pronounce according to any jurisprudence ever heard of, the cause being at the time in the court of appeal with the consent of the plaintiff.

[2] Jenkyns, Cranmer, i. p. 22. "I would be right loth, and also it shall not become me, forasmuch as your grace is my prince and sovereign, to enterprise any part of my office, in the said weighty cause, touching your highness, without your grace's favour and licence obtained in that behalf." Cardinal Pole, in his letter to Cranmer (Le Grand, i. 298), thus addresses him: "Was it not a mockery of the king to exhort him by pompous discourses to put away his wife, when everybody knew that he was doing all he could for that end? And to make your mockery the more complete, you threatened him with the censures of the Church, as if you were afraid he would not

The king's flatterers[1] cried out: "Oh the marvellous freedom of speech in a subject! Now indeed we see how great is the difference between the religion of Papistry and the true gospel of God. This bishop, if he were not sent of God, would not have dared thus to remind the king of his duty. Oh blessed day, which first brought us this heavenly light!"

Moreover, Thomas Cranmer, from the household of Anne Boleyn, was chosen as judge by the plaintiff in the suit on the condition of pronouncing the sentence of divorce. He never heard a word from the defendant, and boldly declared that the king was bound by the divine law to put Catherine away, and that he was free to marry again.[2] But Henry himself, holding the judge and the sentence in his own hand, and knowing well what the end would be, had already married Anne Boleyn,

listen to you, and at the same time everybody was well aware that on no considerations, human or divine, would he consent to retain his wife."

[1] Pocock, Records, ii. 529. "Articles devised by the holle consent of the kynges most honourable counseyle, &c. Art. 8: Our good bishop of Canterbury . . . apperceiving when he came to his dignity that his prince and sovereign lived in unlawful and unfitting matrimony, according to his duty did admonish him, and therein also reproved him, exhorting him to leave it, or else he would do further his duty in it, so that at the last, according to God's laws, he did separate his prince from that unlawful matrimony. In which doing, we think that every true subject should much the better esteem him, because he would execute God's commandment and set this realm in the way of true heirs."

[2] Prevarication of Holy Church's Liberties, bk. i. ch. i. s. 24, Eyston MS. "Moreover, the proceedings made before archbishop Cranmer were done *coram non judice*, for that he was not indifferently chosen by the king and queen. . . . Beside, the judge was a man chosen out of the family of Anne Bullen's reputed father, to whom he was a chaplain: he was much affected to Anne, desirous to advance her, yea, and obliged thereto, as recommended by her and Sir Thomas Bullen for a man fit to comply with the king in the matter of the divorce, to which end he was simoniacally preferred upon condition to sentence the divorce, and therein became capable of a premeditated perjury in swearing canonical obedience to the Apostolic See, and immediately prevaricating the same. . . . The Pope having admitted the queen's appeal, hath thereby closed the hands of Cranmer, or any other spiritual judge whatsoever, from any proceedings in the cause of the appeal, especially as the law stood at the time of the queen's first appeal, and therefore the said divorce was made *coram non judice*, viz., by Cranmer, that had no lawful authority for the same."

though he had put off the solemn celebration of the wedding till Easter Eve. Anne therefore was on that day, the day kept in honour of our Lord's burial,[1] the 12th of April [1533], brought forth before the world as the king's wife,[2] and on the 2d of June next following[3] was crowned, and on the 7th day of September, in the same year, in the fifth month after the marriage was publicly celebrated, gave birth to Elizabeth, Henry's child. It is clear, therefore, that there must have been a secret marriage.

Elizabeth was baptized at Greenwich, and then the king[4] called upon every bishop, and upon every person in orders, upon all the nobles, and upon every Englishman whatsoever of full age, to take an oath that Elizabeth was the next and the lawful heir to the kingdom of England. At the same time he robbed Mary, the daughter of Catherine, as being the issue of a marriage that was unlawful, of her right to the throne. That oath was tendered to John Fisher, the bishop of Rochester, and to Thomas More.[5] The latter seeing the

[1] Wriothesley, Chronicle of England, p. 17, Camden Soc. "The 12th day of April, Anno Domini 1533, beinge Easter Eeaven, Anne Bulleine, marques of Pembroke, was proclaymed queene at Greenwych, and offred that daie in the kinges chappell as queene of England. And the Wednesdaie before the good queene Katherin was deposed at Hanthille by the duke of Norfolke."

[2] Hall, 795. "The king perceiving his new wife queen Anne to be great with child, caused all officers necessary to be appointed to her, and so on Easter Eve she went to her closet openly as queen, and then the king appointed the day of coronation to be kept on Whitsunday next following."

[3] It seems to be universally admitted that Anne Boleyn was crowned on Whitsunday 1533, *i.e.*, June 1st, and the author consequently must have erred in saying that she was crowned June 2d.

[4] The Parliament that met at Westminster Jan. 15, 25 Henry VIII., and which sat till March 30, 1534, made a law, c. 22, called the Act concerning the Succession, to the effect that "all the nobles of your realm spiritual and temporal, as all other your subjects, now living and being, or hereafter that shall be at their full ages, . . . shall make a corporal oath" to hold as invalid the marriage of Henry and Catherine, and to hold as valid the marriage of Henry and Anne Boleyn, and that Elizabeth was born in lawful wedlock, and heir to the crown.

[5] On the 13th of April 1534, at Lambeth, by Cranmer, Sir Thomas

king rushing headlong into all wickedness, had not long before resigned the chancellorship.[1] They refused to take the oath, and were thrown into prison. As Sir Thomas More was led into the Tower of London, the warder of the prison was standing at the gate, and as usual demanded the upper garments of the prisoner. Sir Thomas, who was always cheerful, took off his cap and handed it to him at once; but the warder said, "I do not mean this, but the cloak which you have on." "Surely," said Sir Thomas, "the cap is the upper garment, for it covers the upper part of the body." Thus this saintly man, at the very doors of the prison, which to most men is full of terror, amused himself as if he were at a feast. He used to say that the world at large, into which man was driven when banished out of Paradise because of sin, was nothing else but a prison, out of which men are called every day to answer for themselves. His prison was smaller than the prisons of other great men, and he thanked God for it, for of those things which are not pleasant the least is preferable. His blessed soul cheered itself with thoughts of this kind.

At this time the name of the nun Anne Barton[2] was

Audley, then lord chancellor, and Thomas Cromwell, secretary of state. Sir Thomas More was the only layman summoned that day.

[1] He resigned May 16, 1532.

[2] Prevarication of the Church's Liberties, ch. iv. s. 3, Eyston MS. "The nun Elizabeth Barton, famous for virtue and the gift of prophesying, because she foretold, as afterwards it came to pass, that the lady Mary, then debased under the lady Elizabeth, should reign in her own right before the same lady Elizabeth, was by Parliament attainted, and with her Richard Masters, Edward Bocking, John Dearing, Hugh Rich, Richard Forisby, and Henry Gold, all priests—whereof two were seculars, two Benedictines, and two Franciscans—were executed. All the Observant friars of Greenwich, Canterbury, and Richmond, Newark and Newcastle, being houses of the foundation of Henry VII., only because they wholly stood for the cause of queen Catherine, were all of them driven and cast out of their monasteries; and the authority of the Pope, because he could not in justice be for the divorce of queen Catherine, was not only abolished, but the very name and word Pope or Papa was persecuted, insomuch as by proclamation he caused it to be blotted out, defaced, or erased in all

in all men's mouths. She said that Henry was no longer a king, because he reigned not of God;[1] that Mary, the daughter of Catherine, then regarded as one born out of lawful wedlock, would ascend the throne in her own right. For these sayings the nun was attainted, and by an act of Parliament[2] condemned and put to death, together with two Benedictines and two Franciscans,[3] all of whom believed her to have spoken, moved by the Spirit of God.

Sir Thomas More, among others, had carefully tested the spirit of the nun, and was unable to discover in it any trace of that fanaticism which was maliciously laid to her charge at the time.[4] What is certain is this, that she said that in due time things would come to pass which were at that time regarded as impossible; for Mary, who then was made to give way to Elizabeth, came afterwards to the throne before her, and in her own right.

Out of all the clergy, none withstood the divorce with greater freedom than the Friars minor, commonly called the Observants.[5] They, indeed, both in public disputa-

almanacs, calendars, yea, and in the books of all scholastic writers and doctors of the Holy Church, which is the cause why in so many old Latin and English books, printed or manuscript, we may all this day behold the said word Papa or Pope to be scraped or dashed out."

[1] Osee viii. 4. "Ipsi regnaverunt sed non ex me."

[2] 25 Henry VIII. c. 12.

[3] Stow, p. 570: "After Christmas the Parliament began wherein the forenamed Elizabeth Barton and other her complices were attainted of heresies." P. 571: "The 20th April [1534], Elizabeth Barton, a nun professed, Edward Bocking and John Deering, two monks of Christ's Church in Canterbury, and Richard Risby and another of his fellows of the same house, Richard Master, parson of Aldington, and Henry Hold, priest, were drawn from the Tower of London to Tiborne, and there hanged and headed; the nun's head was set on London Bridge, and the other heads on the gates of the city."

[4] Sir Thomas in his letter to Cromwell (Burnet, v. 485, ed. Pocock) says, "Howbeit, of a truth, I had a great good opinion of her, and had her in great estimation, as you shall perceive by the letter I wrote unto her."

[5] Harpsfield, bk. ii. p. 142. "There was then among the Observant friars at Greenwich a man of a good house and family, called Peto," who, preaching before the king on the history of Achab, said,

tions and in their sermons, most earnestly maintained that the marriage of Catherine was lawful; and the two fathers, Elston and Peto,[1] made themselves more remarkable herein than the rest. For this the king so hated all the friars of the Observance, that on the 11th of August he drove them out of every monastery of their order;[2] and speaking to Elston, threatened to throw him

"'Your preachers resemble the 400 preachers of Achab, in whose mouths God had put a lying spirit. But I beseech your grace to take good heed lest, if you will needs follow Achab in his doings, you incur his unhappy end also, and that the dogs lick your blood as they did his, which God forbid.' What moved this father to speak these words God knoweth, but that so it came to pass a very strange event did afterwards show; for at what time his dead corpse was carried from London to Windsor, there to be interred, it rested the first night at the monastery of Sion, which the king had suppressed. At which time, were it for the joggings and shaking of the chariot, or for any other secret cause, the coffin of lead wherein his dead corpse was put, being riven and cloven, all the pavement of the church was with the fat and the corrupt putrefied blood dropped out of the said corpse foully imbrued. Early in the morning those that had the charge of the dressing, coffining, and embalming of the body, with the plumbers, repaired thither to reform the mistake, and lo! suddenly was there found among their legs a dog lapping and licking up the king's blood, as it chanced to king Achab before specified. This chance one William Consett reported, saying he was there present, and with much ado drove away the said dog."

[1] Stow, p. 562. "The first that openly resisted or reprehended the king touching his marriage with Anne Boloigne was one Friar Peto, a simple man, yet very devout, of the Order of the Observants. . . . The king being thus reproved, endured it patiently, and did no violence to Peto; but the next Sunday, being the 8th of May, Dr. Curwin preached in the same place, who most sharply reprehended Peto and his preaching, and called him dog, slanderer, base beggarly friar, closeman, rebel, and traitor. . . . 'I speak to thee, Peto, which makest thyself Micheas that thou mayest speak evil of kings, but now thou art not to be found.' . . . Whilst he thus spake, there was one Elston, a fellow friar to Peto, standing in the Roodloft, who with a bold voice said to Doctor Curwin, 'Good sir, you know that Father Peto, as he was commanded, is now gone to a provincial council holden at Canterbury, and not fled for fear of you, for to-morrow he will return again. In the meantime I am here as another Micheas. . . . Even unto thee, Curwin, I say, which art one of the four hundred prophets into whom the spirit of lying is entered, and seekest by adultery to establish succession, betraying the king unto endless perdition, more for thy own vainglory and hope of promotion than for discharge of thy dogged conscience and the king's salvation.'" Stow (p. 560) says that Curwin preached on the 28th May. Dr. Curwin was made dean of Hereford in 1541, archbishop of Dublin in 1555, and in 1567 was transferred by Elizabeth to Oxford, being then an avowed Protestant.

[2] Lord Herbert's Life of Henry VIII., p. 407. "The 11th of August this year, our king, as he was watchful over the voice and

into the bottom of the sea if he did not hold his tongue.[1] The friar replied, "I never had any misgiving about going to God as quickly by water as by land." Ordered to leave England immediately, he retired into Flanders, where he remained till queen Mary came to the throne, when, having returned, he slept in peace in the monastery of his order in Greenwich.[2]

In the month of November[3] Parliament assembled, and Henry, for the purpose of revenging himself still more upon the Pope, took away from him all jurisdiction and power over the English and the Irish, and declared every one who should henceforth acknowledge the Pope's jurisdiction guilty of high treason.[4] He

affection of his people, or for the finding out how they would take his design of putting down religious houses, began with the remove of some, and therefore suppressed at Greenwich, Canterbury, Richmond, and other places the Observant friars, noted to be the most clamorous against him."

1 Stow assigns this threat to the earl of Essex, Henry Bourchier, who died A.D. 1539. His title and estates were given to Cromwell.

2 Harpsfield, bk. ii. p. 145. "After a day or two they were called before the council, and after many rebukes and threats, a nobleman told them that they deserved to be thrust into a sack and to be thrown and drowned in the Thames, whereat Friar Elstowe, smiling, said, 'Make those threats,' saith he, 'to the courtiers; for as for us, we make little account, knowing right well that the way lieth as open to heaven by water as by land.' Of this sermon and answer myself have heard the said Father Elstowe report. In fine they were banished, neither they two only, but all the Observants also, because they were of the same judgment, and could not find in their hearts to soothe and flatter the king with his false prophets. But see the providence of God; for as they were the first that at the commencement of the schism were banished and exiled, so the same, being practised by our gracious king and queen, they were the first of all other that were called home and restored, after twenty-four years, to their old and dear habitation."

3 Stow, p. 571. "The 3d of November the Parliament sat at Westminster, wherein the Pope with all his authority was clean banished this realm, and order taken that he should no more be called Pope, but bishop of Rome, and the king to be taken and reputed as supreme head of the Church of England."

4 The king in his proclamation, June 9, 1534 (Foxe, v. 69), made it known that "the bishops and clergy, . . . by word, oath, profession, and writing under their signs and seals, have confessed, ratified, corroborated, and confirmed" the king's title of supreme head, "utterly renouncing all other oaths and obedience to any other foreign potentates, and all foreign jurisdictions and powers, as well of the said bishop of Rome as of all others, whatsoever they be." In the course of the next year all the bishops were made to surrender

made an onslaught on the word Pope, and gave orders that for the future the Roman Pontiff should be called, not the Pope, but the bishop of Rome only.[1] He himself, the king alone, was to be considered supreme head of the Anglican Church, to whom above all others it belonged, by his full authority, to correct all errors, heresies, and abuses in the Church of England.[2] The first-fruits of all benefices were to be paid to him,[3] and also the tithes of all ecclesiastical dignities.[4] The king had the laws executed with such severity that a man might be condemned to death if he left unerased the name of the Pope in any book belonging to him. The

their Bulls, that they might henceforth be bishops by the grace of the king.

[1] The king, according to the same proclamation (Foxe, v. 70), ordered the bishops "to cause all manner of prayers, orisons, rubrics, canons, mass-books, and all other books in the churches, wherein the said bishop of Rome is named, or his presumptuous and proud pomp and authority preferred, eradicated and rased out, and his name and memory to be never more—except to his contumely and reproach—remembered, but perpetually suppressed and obscured.

[2] 26 Henry VIII. c. 1. "That our said sovereign lord, his heirs and successors, kings of this realm, shall have full power and authority, from time to time, to visit, repress, redress, reform, order, correct, restrain, and amend all such errors, heresies, abuses, offences, contempts, and enormities, whatsoever they be, which by any manner, spiritual authority, or jurisdiction, ought or may be lawfully reformed."

[3] 26 Henry VIII. c. 3.

[4] Ibid., § 19. "The king's majesty, his heirs and successors, kings of this realm, for more augmentation and maintenance of the royal estate of his imperial crown and dignity of supreme head of the Church of England, shall yearly have, take, enjoy, and receive, united and knit to his imperial crown for ever, one yearly rent or pension, amounting to the value of the tenth part of all the revenues, rents, farms, tithes, offerings, emoluments, and all other profits, as well called spiritual as temporal, now appertaining and belonging, or that hereafter shall belong, to any archbishopric, bishopric, abbacy, monastery, priory, archdeaconry, deanery, hospital, college, house collegiate, prebend, cathedral church, collegiate church, conventual church, parsonage, vicarage, chauntry, free chapel, or other benefice or promotion spiritual, of what name, nature, or quality soever they be, within any diocese of this realm, or in Wales." This followed upon the petition of the clergy in convocation, in which they prayed the head of the Anglican Church to deprive the Pope of the first-fruits, and if the Pope refuse to issue the Bulls to the bishops in consequence, to "ordain in this present Parliament, that then the obedience of him and the people be withdrawn from the See of Rome, as in like case the French king withdrew his obedience of him and his subjects from Pope Benedict XIII. of that name."—Wilkins, Conc., iii. 761.

name of the Pope was blotted out of all calendars, indexes, the fathers, the canon law, and the schoolmen. People were forced to write in the beginning of their copies of the works of St. Cyprian, St. Ambrose, St. Jerome, St. Augustin, St. Leo, St. Gregory, and St. Prosper, that if the books contained anything in defence or confirmation of the authority of the primacy of the Roman Pontiff, they rejected that word, opinion, or reason at once, and would not be guilty of so great a crime.[1]

Most of the bishops and the other prelates whose duty it was to withstand these things, from the first thought it best to give way for a time till the king changed his mind, or some Catholic prince came to the rescue of the Christian religion. But they waited in vain for the emperor or any other, for they had sinned so grievously against God and their neighbour. Still there was a holy remnant left in the land, which had utterly refused to bend the knee before Baal.[2]

[1] Jenkyns (Cranmer's Remains, i. 269–271) has printed a formal complaint from Oxford, made to Cranmer, of the retention of the Pope's name in books. One man says another "should make satisfaction for the putting out of the word 'Pope' in St. Gregory's works in our library." Again, "Pope was written into a calendar of a book in our college chapel after it had been once put out." One is accused of saying "it is not necessary to put out 'Pope' out of profane books." Cranmer in a letter to Cromwell, June 12, 1538 (Jenkyns, i. 247), says, "I lodged at my house in Croydon, when certain of my chaplains by chance went into the church there, and as they looked in certain books, they found the names of bishops of Rome not put out according to the king's commandment, wherefore I sent for all the priests of the church, and their books also, and showed them the place where such names were, and also commanded them that they should amend their said books, and I discharged the parish priest of his service at the same time." Again (ibid., 279), "I have committed two priests unto the castle of Canterbury for permitting the bishop of Rome's name in their books." Anton. Wood, Annals, ii. 59, 60: "The generality, though Roman Catholics, did, out of fear of the king, deny him, promising withal under their hands that none of them would call him by the name of 'Pope.' . . . So zealous were many against the Pope that all memory of him they obliterated, whether it were by pictures in glass windows or on signposts, or whether by name in printed or written service-books or parchments or other things."

[2] 1 Reg. xix. 18; Rom. xi. 4.

CHAPTER XVI.

MARTYRS—THE CARTHUSIANS—THE BISHOP OF ROCHESTER —SIR THOMAS MORE.

On the 29th day of April five most saintly men entered the glorious lists for Christ. Of these, three were priors of three monasteries of the Carthusians:[1] John Houghton,[2] prior of London; Robert Laurence, prior of Beauvale; and Augustin Webster, prior of Axholme.[3] They would not acknowledge the impious supremacy claimed by Henry VIII. in the Church, and for their refusal they obtained the palm of martyrdom.[4]

[1] The three priors, in their simplicity, went to Cromwell when they knew how angry the king was, and begged him to help and obtain for them some mitigation of the oath. The vicar-general of the supreme head of the Church of England ordered them forthwith into the Tower. After a week's detention Cromwell arrived with some members of the privy council to demand the oath, the acceptance of the royal supremacy, and the renunciation of the Pope. They promised to do everything permitted by the law of God. "I will have no exceptions," said Cromwell, "it must be done whether the law of God allows it or not." The priors replied that the Catholic Church held and taught a contrary doctrine. "What do I care for the Church?" cried Cromwell; "will you take the oath or not?"—Chauncy, Passio xviii. Carthusianorum, cap. x.

[2] John Houghton was born in Essex, and educated at Cambridge. He hid himself with a devout priest to avoid the state of marriage proposed to him by his parents. On being ordained priest, he returned to them, and obtained their forgiveness. He went to the Carthusians when he was twenty-eight years old, and the rest of his life was spent in peace and holiness till he was singled out for martyrdom. He was tried in Westminster Hall April 29, and martyred May 4, 1535, with the other two priors.

[3] Foxe, v. 101. "Besides and with these priors suffered likewise at the same time two other priests, one called Reginald, brother of Sion, the other named John Haile, vicar of Thistleworth [Isleworth]. Divers other Charterhouse monks, also of London, were then put in prison, to the number of nine or ten, and in the same prison died."

[4] The charge was that they said, "The king our sovereign lord is not supreme head in earth of the Church of England." They were

To this blessed company was added [Richard] Reynolds, a Brigittine monk of the abbey of Sion,[1] a great theologian, who, as he had often before edified the people by his most eloquent sermons, so did he edify them now by his example and patient endurance.[2]

He, when he heard his sentence, which was that of death, said, "I believe I shall see the good things of our Lord in the land of the living;"[3] and at the place of execution he begged the people to make continual prayer to God for the king, that he who was like Solomon in wisdom and goodness when he began to reign, might not, through the blandishments of women, fall away like Solomon at the end of his life.

The fifth priest who suffered at the same time was John Hale,[4] who having striven lawfully, obtained the reward of the heavenly calling.[5]

tried at Westminster, April 29, 1535, and found guilty. See Third Report of the Deputy Keeper of the Records, App. ii. p. 238.

[1] The monastery of Sion, near Isleworth, was founded by Henry V., 1414. On the dissolution it passed into the hands of the duke of Somerset, from whom it passed to the duke of Northumberland, who set up Jane Grey as queen. The nuns returned to Sion under queen Mary, but under Elizabeth they were forced to depart.

[2] Burnet, who did not know him, says contemptuously of him (Hist. Reform., i. p. 562) that he "was esteemed a learned man for that time and that order." But the writer of the "Expositio Fidelis de Morte Thomæ Mori," who knew him, says, "Vir angelico vultu et angelico spiritu sanique judicii, quod ex illius colloquio comperi, quum in comitatu Cardinalis Campegii versarer in Anglia."

[3] Ps. xxvi. 13. He asked the judges to give him two or three days to make his preparation for death, and was told that it rested with the king, upon which he made the observation in the text.—Illust. Eccles. Trophæa, sig. D. Monachii, 1573.

[4] Baga de Secretis, pouch 7, bundle 1, Third Report of the Deputy Keeper. John Hale, late of Isleworth, clerk, was indicted under the act for the establishment of the king's succession, and pleaded guilty, April 29, 1535, and judgment was given as usual in cases of high treason. Stow, p. 571: "The 29th of April, John, prior of the Charterhouse of London; Augustine Webster, prior of Bevall; Thomas Laurence, prior of Exham; Ric. Reginalds, doctor, a monk of Sion; and John Haile, vicar of Thistleworth, were all condemned of treason, who were drawn, hanged, and quartered at Tyborne the 4th of May, their heads and quarters set on the gates of the city, all save one quarter, which was set on the Charterhouse at London."

[5] Philip. ii. 5.

These were the first-fruits of the martyrs in the new schism of Henry VIII.

On the 18th day of June[1] following, three other Carthusians—Humfrey Middlemore, William Exmew, and Sebastian Newdigate—bore witness to the faith in the same noble way.[2]

They had been, for fourteen days before they were put to death, forced to stand upright, without the possibility of stirring for any purpose whatever, held fast by iron collars on their necks, arms, and thighs. These three were dragged on hurdles through the streets of London to the place of execution—together with William Horne[3]—and when they had been hung for awhile, were cut down, being yet alive. Then the executioner mutilated their persons,[4] and threw into the fire that which he had cut off. That done, he laid their bodies open with a sword, wrenched out the entrails, and threw them into the fire before their eyes. Finally, he cut off their heads, and divided their bodies into four quarters, which were first boiled, and then hung up in divers places to be seen of the people.

[1] According to Chauncy (Passio xviii. Carthusianorum, cap. xi.), it was the 19th of June.

[2] They were tried and found guilty of treason, June 11, 1535. And their crime was saying (Third Report, &c., p. 240), "I cannot, nor will, consent to be obedient to the king's highness, as a true, lawful, and obedient subject, to take and repute him to be supreme head in earth of the Church of England under Christ." Stow, p. 571: "The 18th of June three monks of the Charterhouse at London, named Thomas Exmew, Humfrey Middlemore, and Sebastian Nidigate, were drawn to Tiborne, and there hanged and quartered for denying the king's supremacy."

[3] William Horne was a lay brother. He was sent to Newgate, May 29, 1537, with the others mentioned below, who were literally starved to death. William Horne bore the hunger and thirst better, and when his companions had given up their souls to God, received better treatment, for he lived four years in prison, and was martyred Nov. 4, 1541.

[4] This insulting cruelty seems to have been inflicted on a priest in Ireland as late as 1777. These are the words, in a letter to Cardinal Castelli, of Dr. James Butler, second archbishop of Cashel of that name (Dr. Reneham, Collections, p. 331): "Sacerdotes Catholicos, quorum unus ex nostra provincia ad patibulum, capitisque ac membrorum abscissionem damnatus, infamem cruentamque hanc mortem perpessus est."

John Rochester and James Walver—they also were Carthusians—obtained favour in the eyes of the king, for they were sent to heaven, being simply hanged.[1]

Now, whether the tyrant was ashamed of so much slaughtering done in the sight of the people, or of slaughtering Carthusians only, he had the death of nine other Carthusians brought about by the foulness of the prison in which he held them, that they might not triumph publicly over him. These were John Bere, Thomas Greenway, John Davis, William Greenwood, Thomas Scriven, Robert Salt, Walter Person, and Thomas Reding.[2] So far as to the Carthusians; for though they did not all suffer death on the same day, yet I did not like to keep asunder in my story those whom the same faith and the same order had joined together.

The bishop of Rochester and Sir Thomas More were still in prison: two most shining lights of all England, and towards whom men's eyes and thoughts were directed. Henry was well aware of this, and was therefore the more desirous of winning them over to his side, especially Sir Thomas More, who, being a layman, was more in favour with lay people, and for very good reasons, because no such layman had ever been born in England. Henry, too, liked laymen better, and was more afraid of them.

Sir Thomas was born in London of a very honourable house, well instructed also in the Greek and Latin

[1] They had been sent from the Charterhouse of London, in which they had made their profession, to Hull; from Hull they were taken to York, where, in the presence of the duke of Norfolk, they were hung in chains, May 11, 1537, till every bone in their bodies fell detached from the rest to the ground.—Chauncy, c. xiii.

[2] The author has omitted one of the nine whose names he meant to give, namely, Thomas Johnson. Their companion already mentioned, William Horne, outlived them. John Bere, Thomas Johnson, and Thomas Greenway were priests, John Davis a deacon, the rest being lay brothers. Their sufferings in prison may be gathered from the "Life of Mother Margaret Clement," published by the Rev. Fr. Morris in his "Troubles of our Catholic Forefathers," 1st Series.

tongues, and conversant with public affairs for nearly forty years. He had discharged the honourable duties of ambassador, and had filled with the applause of all men the highest offices in the state. Though he was twice married, and was the father of many children, he was never careful about increasing his means; and he never added even twenty pounds a year to his patrimony. Henry sent many of the nobles to him, but to no purpose; and unable to make up his mind whether it would be more to his advantage to let so illustrious an enemy of his adultery live on, or to brand himself with shame for putting out so shining a light of the Christian world, he resolved at last to put to death the bishop of Rochester first, to see whether More afterwards could be made to change his opinion. He had heard by this time that the bishop had been made a Cardinal,[1] and as for breaking his resolution, there was not the slightest hope that he could ever do it.[2]

There was not in England a more holy and learned man than John Fisher, bishop of Rochester. He was now worn out by age, and though he had been offered more than once a better endowed see, he could never be persuaded to leave the poor church to which God had first called him. He would not acknowledge the ecclesiastical supremacy of the king,[3] and for that refusal was

[1] He was made a Cardinal by Paul III., May 21, 1535, by the title of St. Vitalis.

[2] George Wyatt, Memoir of Queen Anne Boleyn, App., Cavendish, ed. Singer, p. 438, says, "It is here to be noticed, that of her time—that is, during the three years she was queen—is found by good observation that no one suffered for religion, which is the more worthy to be noted for that it could not be said of any time of the queens after married to the king." But Harpsfield (Treatise of Marriage, bk. iii. p. 60, Eyston MS.) speaks otherwise of Anne Boleyn: "This woman, which at such time, as with her playing, singing, and dancing she had best opportunity, never ceased—as the other dancing damsel that craved St. John Baptist's head—to crave the good bishop's and Sir Thomas More's heads, which thing at length, to their immortal glory, she compassed. Ere the year turned about, to her perpetual shame and ignominy, she lost her head also, as did the foresaid dancing damsel."

[3] Baga de Secretis, *ut supra*, p. 239. "That John Fissher, late of

tried[1] and condemned, and led forth to death, June 22d. As soon as he came in sight of the place where he was to be conqueror in the glorious contest, he threw his staff away, saying, "Now my feet must do their duty, for I have but a little way to go." Having reached the place of his martyrdom, he lifted up his eyes to heaven and said, "*Te Deum laudamus, Te Dominum confitemur.*" When he had finished the hymn he bowed his head beneath the sword of the executioner, gave up his soul to God, and received the crown of justice. His head, fixed on a pike, was exposed to the sight of all on London Bridge, but was afterwards taken away, because it was said that the longer it remained the more ruddy and venerable it seemed to grow.[2]

The day on which the bishop was to die had, by order of the king, been kept secret from Sir Thomas More; nevertheless he was told of it, and then, overcome by a great fear that he was not to gain the crown of martyrdom himself, began to pray, saying, "I confess to Thee, O Lord, that I am not worthy of so great a crown, for I am not just and holy as is Thy servant the bishop of Rochester, whom Thou hast chosen for Thyself out of the whole kingdom, a man after Thine own heart; never-

the city of Rochester, in the county of Kent, clerk, also called John Fissher, late of the city of Rochester, bishop; treacherously imagining and attempting to deprive the king of his title as supreme head of the Church of England, did, 7th May, 27 Henr. VIII., at the Tower of London, openly say and declare, in English, 'The king our sovereign lord is not supreme head in earth of the Church of England.'" He was tried June 17, 1535, and found guilty. Chronicle of the Grey Friars, London, p. 38: "Also this yere, the 22d day of July, was the byshoppe of Rochester, John Fycher, beheddyd at Towre hill, and buried in the churchyard of Berkyne, by the northe dore. And the 26th day of the same month, was beheddyd at Towre hill Sir Thomas More, sometime chaunsler of Yngland; and then was tayne up the byshoppe agayne, and both of them burryd within the Tower."

1 The bishopric had been declared by act of Parliament vacant from January 2d, and he was arraigned not as bishop, but as John Fisher, clerk, and because deprived of his barony, was not tried by the Peers, but by a jury.

2 The fact is recorded also in the accounts of Fisher and More, published by Mr. Pocock, Records, ii. 556.

theless, O Lord, if it be Thy will, give me a share in Thy chalice."

He wept while uttering these words and others of a like nature; his countenance also, at other times so calm, betrayed the sorrow he could not hide, and the children of this world imagined that he was afraid of death, and might therefore be won over to obey the king. Many of the chief nobles went to see him, for the purpose of winning him over; but when they could not succeed in the slightest degree, they intrusted the matter at last to Alice, his wife,[1] who was to persuade her husband not to give up herself, his children, his country, and his life, which he might still enjoy for many years to come. As she harped on this, More said to her, "And how long, my dear Alice, do you think I shall live?" "If God will," she answered, "you may live for twenty years." "Then," said Sir Thomas, "you would have me barter eternity for twenty years; you are not skilful at a bargain, my wife. If you had said twenty thousand years, you might have said something to the purpose; but even then, what is that to eternity?"

When it became clear that Sir Thomas More was not to be shaken in his resolution, he was deprived of all his books,[2] which were regarded as instrumental in withdrawing him from the love of this world, and kindling within him the desire of everlasting life. Thereupon he closed the windows of his prison, and spent the whole of his time with God in holy meditation. The jailer asked him why he sat in the dark; he replied that there was nothing else for him to do, for the "shop must be shut when the goods are gone." By goods he meant his

[1] Alice Middeton. She was the second wife of Sir Thomas, and was herself a widow when he married her.

[2] This was done by Rich, the solicitor-general, who was afterwards made Lord Rich, Sir Richard Southwell, and Mr. Palmer, employed by Cromwell.—Roper's Life, p. 65. Dublin, 1765.

books, and truly Sir Thomas had opened a shop in his prison, where he purposed to sell all that he had, that he might possess himself of heaven with the price. He wrote two books during his imprisonment—one in English, "Comfort in Tribulation;"[1] the other in Latin, on the Passion of Christ. When he had written the story of the Passion as far as those words of the gospel, "They laid hands on Jesus,"[2] hands were laid upon him, and he was not allowed to add another word.

In the course of his trial he was asked in court what he thought of the law—enacted after his imprisonment—by which the whole authority of the Pope was set aside, and by which the supreme power over the Church was vested in the king; he replied, that he did not know of any law of the kind. The judge interposed and said, "But we tell you that such a law exists, what do you think of it?" More replied, "If you treated me as a free man, I would have believed you on your word when you tell me that there is a law to that effect; but you have cut me off from your community, and you have shut me up in jail, not as a stranger but as an enemy. I am civilly dead; how is it that you question me concerning the laws of your state, as if I were still a member of the community?" The judge lost his temper and said, "Now I see, you dispute the law, for you are silent." Then said Sir Thomas, "If I am silent, that is to your advantage, and that of the law; for silence is consent." "Then," said the judge, "do you acknowledge the law?" "How can I do that," answered Sir Thomas, "seeing that no man can acknowledge anything of which he is ignorant?"

Sir Thomas More framed his answers in this way on purpose, that he might not deny the faith on the one

[1] A Dialogue of Comfort against Tribulation.
[2] St. Matt. xxvi. 50.

hand, nor on the other hand court his death; for though he had a great longing for martyrdom, he never forgot that it was a grace from God. In the uncertainty he was in, as he often said, whether God would give him this grace, he answered modestly as I have shown.

When at last the judge called on the twelve men in whose province it lies to decide the question of life and death, these men brought in a verdict of death against Sir Thomas More. Thereupon he, now more sure of his state, told them frankly what he thought of that law. "I," said he, "have by the grace of God been always a Catholic, never out of the communion of the Roman Pontiff, but I had heard it said at times that the authority of the Roman Pontiff was certainly lawful and to be respected, but still an authority derived from human law, and not standing on a divine prescription. Then when I observed that public affairs were so ordered that the sources of the power of the Roman Pontiff would necessarily be examined, I gave myself up to a most diligent examination of that question for the space of seven years, and found that the authority of the Roman Pontiff, which you rashly—I will not use stronger language—have set aside, is not only lawful, to be respected, and necessary, but also grounded on the divine law and prescription. That is my opinion; that is the belief in which by the grace of God I shall die."

He had hardly ended his answer when they all cried out that More was a traitor and a rebel.

On his return from the court he was met by his daughter Margaret, whom he loved so much, whom he had taught both Greek and Latin, and to whom he had often written when he was in prison. She had come to bid him her last farewell. The father stood, and not only did not refuse the kiss of his child, but gave her his blessing. The wife[1] of John Harris, who had been secretary to Sir Thomas More, was there with Margaret, and being afraid that Sir Thomas would go away after kissing his child, and that she should not be able to say farewell herself, suddenly seized the head of Sir Thomas, as he was leaning over his daughter's shoulder, and with great affection kissed her master before all the people, upon which Sir Thomas said to her, "Kindly meant, but not politely done."

He was led to the place of execution on the 6th day of July. When he came to the foot of the scaffold, and saw that it would not be easy for him to mount, he called to one of the attendants, and said, "I beg you will help me to get up; as for coming down, you may leave me alone for that." When he had ended his prayer, had called the people to witness that he was going to die in the Catholic faith, and had said the psalm *Miserere*, the executioner came forward, and, according to the custom, asked him to forgive him. That done, he struck off the head of justice, of truth, and of goodness. All England mourned the dead, regarding the blow as having fallen not so much upon the martyr of Christ as upon itself.[2]

1 Dorothy Colley.—Fr. Morris, Troubles of our Catholic Forefathers, p. 5.

2 Cromwell thus defends the king's conduct (Burnet, Hist. Ref., vi. 117, ed. Pocock): "And concerning the executions done within this realm, ye shall say to the said French king that the same were not so marvellous extreme as he allegeth. For touching Mr. More and the bishop of Rochester, with such others as were executed here, their treasons, conspiracies, practices secretly practised, as well within the realm as without, to move and stir dissension, and to sow sedition within the realm, intending thereby not only the destruction of the king, but also the whole subversion of his highness' realm, being explained and declared, and so manifestly proved afore them, that they could not avoid nor deny it; and they thereof openly detected and lawfully convicted, adjudged, and condemned of high treason by the due order of the laws of this realm, it shall and may well appear to all the world that they, having such malice rooted in their hearts against their prince and sovereign, and the total destruction of the commonwealth of this realm, were well worthy, if they had had a

Early in the morning of that day his daughter went about from church to church, and gave large alms to the poor. When she had given all that she had, and was at prayer in church, she said to her maid, "Ah me! I have forgotten the shroud for my father's body." She had heard that the body of the bishop of Rochester had been laid in the ground without cross or lights, unattended by a priest, and that no one came to bury the holy martyr. Indeed no one dared to render him that service, for the fear of Henry's cruelty had fallen upon all. Margaret took care that her father should not be treated in the same way.

Her maid recommended her to provide herself with linen at the nearest shop. "How can I do that," she replied, "when I have no money left?" The maid said, "They will trust you." "I have no money," was the answer of Margaret; "and though I am far from home, and the people here do not know me, yet I will try them." She then entered a shop in the neighbourhood, asked for as much linen as she thought was necessary, and settled about the price. Then, as if looking for her money, she put her hand in her purse, in order to be able to say that to her great disappointment she had none; however, if they would trust her, they should be paid without delay. But lo! she who knew too well that a few minutes before there was nothing in her purse, now found in it the price of the linen, neither more nor less than the sum she was then bound to pay. Comforted by the miracle, she took up the linen, wrapt her father's body therein, and honourably buried the martyr of Christ. No one disturbed her in her pious

thousand lives, to have suffered ten times a more terrible death and execution than any of them did suffer." It is plain that Cromwell understood his business as well as any modern minister of state.

duty, for they respected the woman, especially the child.[1]

[1] The trial took place on the 1st of July 1535, and (Stow, p. 572.) "the 6th of July Sir Thomas More was beheaded on the Tower hill for the like denial of the king's supremacy : and then the body of Doctor Fisher, bishop of Rochester, was taken by and buried with Sir Thomas More, both in the Tower." Stow probably copied the Grey Friars' Chronicle ; see the latter part of note 3, p. 122.

CHAPTER XVII.

VISITATION OF THE RELIGIOUS HOUSES — SUPPRESSION OF THE SMALLER MONASTERIES—DEATH OF QUEEN CATHERINE—EXECUTION OF ANNE BOLEYN—FATHER FOREST—LAMBERT—MARTYRS—ST. THOMAS BECKETT—ANNE OF CLEVES—CROMWELL.

In the month of October following [A.D. 1535], Henry, as supreme head of the Church, determined to make a visitation of the religious houses. One Lee, therefore, a doctor of the civil law, but not in holy orders, was sent to make inquiries into the life and conversation of monks and nuns.

For the making of this visitation, instructions [1] were given that any one under four-and-twenty years of age might be compelled to leave the monastery and return to the world, and that he who was above that age might also leave it with impunity if he liked, but such a one was not to be compelled to leave. If any one left the monastery, to him the abbot was to give the dress of a

[1] A letter of Cranmer to Cromwell (Jenkyns, Cranmer's Remains, i. 156), who was asked by the former to settle a doubt that had been raised, supplies the clause in the injunctions to which the author refers: "Item quod nullus deinceps permittatur profiteri regularem observantiam aut vestem suscipere religionis per confratres hujus domus gestari solitam, nisi vicesimum suæ ætatis annum compleverit. Et si, qui jam sub vicesimo anno completo in veste hujusmodi infra hanc domum jam inducti sunt, et si qui alii sub vicesimo quarto anno existentes discedere velint, illam quamprimum se exuant. Et magister hujus domus suo sumptu vestibus sæcularibus et honestis ad præsens ornet et ad amicos suos chariores cum viaticis competentibus transmittendos curet." Cranmer says to Cromwell, "I will not take upon me to make any exposition herein, but such as you shall make, by whose authority the injunctions were given." The letter is dated Nov. 18, 1535.

secular priest, instead of the habit of the order, and about eight pieces of gold; but the nuns were to wear the dress of women living in the world.[1] Finally, all monks and all nuns, of what order soever, were to deliver into the hands of the king's agents all the ornaments of price belonging to their churches, together with the relics of the saints.[2] Lee, indeed, in order to discharge correctly the duties laid upon him, tempted the religious to sin, and he was more ready to inquire into and speak about uncleanness of living than anything else.

That visitation had for its end to enable the king to destroy every monastery the possessions of which he coveted. Accordingly, on the 4th of February, after the publication of the enormities of the religious,[3] partly discovered and partly invented, all the monasteries the

[1] Hooper, in a letter to Bullinger from Strasburg (Original Letters, No. 21), whither he had fled from justice, says: "Our king has destroyed the Pope, but not Popery; he has expelled all the monks and nuns, and pulled down their monasteries; he has caused all their possessions to be transferred into his exchequer; and yet they are bound, even the frail female sex, by the king's command, to perpetual chastity. England has at this time at least ten thousand nuns, not one of whom is allowed to marry." The letter was written in 1546, after the ruin of the greater monasteries.

[2] Foxe, Acts and Monuments, v. 102, ed. Cattley. "Whereupon, the same year, the month of October, the king having then Thomas Cromwell of his council, sent Dr. Lee to visit the abbeys, priories, and nunneries in all England, and to set at liberty all such religious persons as desired to be free, and all others that were under the age of four-and-twenty years: providing withal that such monks, canons, and friars as were dismissed should have given them by the abbot or prior, instead of their habit, a secular priest's gown and forty shillings of money; and likewise the nuns to have such apparel as secular women did then commonly use, and be suffered to go where they would. At which time also from the said abbeys and monasteries were taken their chief jewels and relics."

[3] Even Latimer (Sermons, p. 123, ed. Parker Society) insinuates the dishonesty of this visitation. "I would not," said he, "that ye should do with chantry priests as ye did with the abbots when the abbeys were put down. For when their enormities were first read in the parliament house, they were so great and abominable that there was nothing but 'down with them!' But within awhile after, the same abbots were made bishops, as there be some of them yet alive, to save their pensions. O Lord! think ye that God is a fool, and seeth it not?"

revenues of which were not valued above two hundred pounds a year,[1] were by act of Parliament placed at the mercy of the king.[2]

On the 6th of January in this year queen Catherine died at Kimbolton, and was buried at Peterborough.[3] Upon her deathbed she wrote to the king to this effect: "My lord, king Henry, the love which I bear you makes me now, when the hour of my death is drawing nigh, put you in mind of your soul's salvation, which you should prefer to all things in the world. I forgive you myself, and I pray God to forgive you. I recommend to you our child, my three maids, and all my servants. Let the former be well provided in marriage; and let the latter have a year's wages in addition to what is due to them now."

The king could not refrain from tears when he read the letter;[4] but Anne Boleyn, instead of putting on mourning on the day of Catherine's funeral, put on a

[1] Stow, p. 572. "The number of these houses then suppressed was 376, the value of their lands £32,000 and more by year. The movable goods as they were sold, Robin Hood's pennyworth amounted to more than £100,000."

[2] A.D. 1536, 27 Hen. VIII. c. 28. "To have and to hold all and singular the premises, with all their rights, profits, jurisdictions, and commodities, unto the king's majesty and his heirs and assigns for ever, to do and use therewith his and their own wills, to the pleasure of Almighty God, and to the honour and profit of this realm." Stow, p. 572: "A pitiful thing to hear the lamentation that the people in the country made for them."

[3] London Chronicle, p. 9; Camden Miscellany, vol. iv. "Then dyid quene Kateryn about twelfe tide, and was beryed in Peterborow Abbey." Lord Herbert says she died Jan. 8th; but Polydore Vergil (bk. xxvii. p. 690), who was in England at the time, says with Sander, that she died "ad viii. idus Januarii"—the 8th day of January 1535, according to the calendar of those dayes, when the 25th of March was New-Year's Day. Wriothesley, in his Chronicle of England, p. 32, Camden Society, says she died "the morrowe after twelve daie, being Fridaie, and the 7th daie of Januarie;" and the editor, Mr. Hamilton, in a note, says that there is a letter to Cromwell in the Public Record Office, in which it is said that she died on the 7th, "before 2 of the clock at afternoon."

[4] Harpsfield, bk. ii. p. 137. "At the reading of which letter the king burst out a weeping. Her dead corpse was carried to Peterborough, and there interred. Before she departed at Kimbolton, she had lain two years at Bugden, passing her solitary life in much prayer, great alms, and abstinence; and when she was not this way occupied, then was she and her gentle-

yellow dress;[1] and on being congratulated on the removal of her rival, replied, "No, I am sorry, not indeed because she is dead, but because her death has been so honourable."[2] What malice! even the death of Catherine could not quench it.

It often happens that we are on the brink of ruin when we consider ourselves most secure. Anne Boleyn seemed now to be delivered from all fear of any rival. But God is just; He raised up another rival to her forthwith, and a more dangerous rival than Catherine had ever been; for the king began to grow weary of Anne, and to give his affections to another woman.

The time had now come when Anne was to be again a mother, but she brought forth only a shapeless mass of flesh.[3] The king, bent on seeing the child of Anne, went at once into her room to do so, when she, bewailing her mishap, and angry at the transference to another of the king's affections, cried out to him, "See, how well I must be since the day I caught that abandoned woman Jane sitting on your knees." The king answered her by saying, "Be of good cheer, sweetheart, you will have no reason to complain of me again,"[4] and went away sorrowing.

But when Anne saw that she had hitherto not been the mother of a boy to Henry, and that now there was

women working with their own hands something wrought in needlework, costly and artificially, which she intended to the honour of God to bestow upon some churches."

[1] Hall, 818. "Queen Anne wore yellow for the mourning."

[2] Queen Catherine was more generous, according to Harpsfield (bk. ii. p. 138), who says, "I have credibly also heard that at a time when one of her gentlewomen began to curse the lady Anne Bulleyne, she [Catherine] answered, 'Hold your peace, curse her not, but pray for her, for the time will come shortly when you shall have much need to pity and lament her case.'"

[3] Stow, p. 372. "The 29th of January, queen Anne was delivered of a man-child before her time, which was born dead."

[4] Wyatt's Memoir of Anne Boleyn, Singer's Cavendish, p. 443. "Unkindness grew, and she was brought abed before her time with much peril of her life, and of a male child dead born, to her greater and most extreme grief. Being thus a woman full of sorrow, it was reported that the king

no hope of her ever being so, she resolved to try whether, in some way or other, she, who was the wife of a king, might not become the mother of a king also. She considered that her sin would be more secret if she sinned with her own brother, George Boleyn, rather than with any other. Besides, she was a woman excessively given to pride and to self-love, and so she would have the next king of England to be a Boleyn by the father's and the mother's side. But as her incest prospered not, she gave herself up to a lewd life, having not only Norris, Weston, and Brereton, who were gentlemen, but also Mark her musician, as her companions in sin.

This wicked living could not long be kept hid from the king. Nevertheless he pretended to know nothing of it till the 1st day of May. On that day he was present at a tournament held at Greenwich, and saw Anne Boleyn, who was at a window looking on, drop her handkerchief, that one of her lovers might wipe his face running with sweat. Thereupon the king rose in a hurry, and with six attendants went straight to Westminster.[1]

But on the next day Anne was led into prison, and by Sir Thomas Boleyn[2] himself, sitting among the judges

came to her, and bewailing and complaining unto her the loss of his boy, some words were heard break out of the inward feelings of her heart's dolours, laying the fault upon unkindness; . . . he was then heard to say to her, he would have no more boys by her."

[1] Stow, p. 572. "From these jousts king Henry suddenly departed to Westminster, having only with him six persons."

[2] The accomplices of Anne—Norris, Brereton, Weston, and Mark—were tried before Anne, and found guilty of adultery. These were tried before Sir Thomas Boleyn, who therefore was one of the judges who found Anne guilty by necessary implication. But on the trial of Lord Rochford and of Anne, Sir Thomas Boleyn was not present, and cannot therefore be said to have found Anne guilty of incest. Still all these foul charges were known at the first trial, and Sir Thomas Boleyn could not have been ignorant of the effect of the first verdict. Burnet has given correctly the names of those who sat as judges of Anne Boleyn, but he has not said where he found them. The "Baga de Secretis" contains the names. See Third Report of the Deputy Keeper, 1842.

at the commandment of the king, was found guilty of adultery and incest,[1] and was beheaded May 19, having borne the title of queen not quite five months after the death of Catherine. Not long afterwards Sir Thomas Boleyn also died of grief.[2]

The very next day after the execution of Anne Boleyn the king made Jane Seymour his wife. He had loved her and preferred her to Anne even while Anne was alive. The judgments of God are not less marvellous than they are just, rewarding every one according to his works. As Anne supplanted Catherine, so Jane supplanted Anne.[3]

On the 22d day of May took place the public execution of George Viscount Rocheford, brother of Anne Boleyn, Henry Norris, William Brereton, Francis Weston,

[1] In the Archæologia, vol. xxiii., is printed a Memorial to Cromwell from George Constantyne, who was registrar of St. David's, and whose daughter was the wife of Young, archbishop of York. He was once in the service of Norris, and says that Mark Smeaton was first apprehended, and that he was examined on the last day of April. "Upon May Day Mr. Norris jousted. And after jousting, the king rode suddenly to Westminster, and all the way, as I heard say, had Norris in examination.... Mr. Norris would confess nothing to the king. . . . His chaplain told me he confessed; but he said at his arraigning, when his own confession was laid before him, that he was deceived to do the same by the earl of Hampton that now is." Of Brereton he says, "If any of them was innocent, it was he." The others "confessed, all but Mr. Norris, who said almost nothing at all." He says he heard them, and "wrote every word that they spoke." Lord Rochford said, "I desire you that no man will be discouraged from the gospel for my fall." Of Anne he says, "Her brother and she were examined at the Tower. I heard say he had escaped had it not been for a letter. . . . Now, so because that she was a favourer of God's Word, at the leastwise so taken, I tell you few men would believe that she was so abominable. As I be saved before God, I could not believe it afore I heard them speak at their death."

[2] Stow, p. 572. "After that the earl of Wiltshire and Ormond, called Sir Thomas Boloigne, had delivered the king's privy seal, whereof he was *custos*, into the king's hands, Thomas Cromwell, secretary to the king and master of the rolls, was made lord keeper of the said privy seal." Sir Thomas Boleyn died in 1538.

[3] Hall (819), with more ingenuity than candour, says, "The week before Whitsuntide the king married lady Jane." Anne Boleyn was put to death May 19, 1536, and Jane Seymour was married May 20, but Whitsuntide fell on June 4. Cranmer, on the very day on which Anne Boleyn was executed, granted a dispensation to enable Henry to marry Jane Seymour.—Chron. Materials of the new edition of the Fœdera, p. 188, where it is said that the original dispensation is in the Chapter House.

and Mark [Smeaton] because they had committed adultery with Anne Boleyn.[1]

On the 8th day of June Parliament met by the king's command, as well as the convocation of the clergy.[2] In both assemblies there were many and long debates touching matters of faith and religion, the king and the bishops striving to save the schism they had begun from issuing in the Lutheran or Calvinistic heresy. In the end a book was set forth by public authority with this title, "Articles established by the King's Highness."[3]

The first of these articles is, that in the sacrament of the Eucharist transubstantiation is to be believed; the second, that communion in one kind is sufficient for salvation; the third, that the celibacy of the priesthood must be maintained; the fourth, that vows of chastity and widowhood must be kept; the fifth, that the celebration of masses is agreeable to the law of God, and that private masses also are wholesome and necessary; the sixth, that auricular confession is necessarily to be

[1] Baga de Secretis. "Being arraigned, Smeaton pleads guilty of adultery with the queen, but as to the other charges in the indictment he pleads not guilty. And Noreys, Bryerton, and Weston severally plead not guilty." Among the judges sat Thomas earl of Wilts, and the verdict was guilty, given May 12, 1536. Stow, p. 573: "The 17th day of May, the Lord Rochford, brother to the queen, Henry Norrice, Mark Smeton, William Brierton, and Francis Weston, all of the king's privy chamber, about matters touching the queen, were beheaded on the Tower hill; the Lord Rochford's body with the head was buried in the chapel of the Tower, the other four in the churchyard there." Raynaldi Annal. Ecclesiast. ad an. 1536, n. 26: "Auxit hæc probra quod Anna Bolena Henrici spuria existimaretur, idque a pueris Parisiensibus cantillaretur atque etiam in angiportibus, valvis et plateis affixum epigramma hoc prostaret:—

"'Juno Jovis soror atque uxor, verum Anna Bolena
Et spuria Henrici filia et uxor erat.'"

[2] In the session held July 20, Edward Fox, bishop of Hereford, produced a book in which reasons were given why the king should not appear in the general council then summoned by the Pope, which reasons were approved of by Cromwell the king's vicar, and all the members of both Houses.—Wilkins, Concil., iii. 803.

[3] "Articles devised by the kinges highnes Majestie, to stablyshe Christin quietness," &c., printed by Berthelet, the king's printer, London, 1536. See note in Burnet, Hist. Ref., ii. 272, ed. Pocock. Stow, p. 373: "In the which book is mentioned but three sacraments."

retained in the Church. If any man taught otherwise, he must endure the penalties which the king's highness had decreed, with the consent of the Lords and Commons in Parliament assembled.[1]

This, in those days, was the state of religion in England: on the one hand, at variance with the Catholic faith, because men abandoned the supremacy and unity of the Chair of Peter, and all the monasteries were destroyed; and on the other hand, very much at variance, on account of these articles, with the teaching of Wicliffites, Lutherans, Zuinglians, and Calvinists.

Nevertheless, with the single exception of the men of easy principles about the court, the old nobility, as well as the people generally, not only hating heresy, but being almost universally Catholic,[2] regarded it as a matter of small moment that certain most detestable opinions should be condemned, if they could not have the Catholic religion preserved in its integrity. When, therefore, they saw that under the cloak of banishing superstition nothing else was meant but stealing the sacred vessels, the silver crucifixes, the chalices that held the blood of Christ, together with all other things by which the churches were adorned, they took up arms, first of all in the county of Lincoln, then in Northumberland, Cumberland, Durham, and York, upwards of fifty thousand men. They made it plain to all that they were about to fight for the preservation of the faith of Christ, for

[1] Rishton says that he omitted passages from the text of Sander when he gave it to his friend to be printed. That is probably the reason why in the text the six articles are represented as forming part of the book published in 1536. The six articles were passed, as it is said in the text, in Parliament, but four years later, namely, in 1540.—31 Henry VIII. c. 14.

[2] Hooper, writing to Bullinger, confesses it (Original Letters, No. 21) in offensive language: "The impious Mass, the most shameful celibacy of the clergy, the invocation of saints, auricular confession, superstitious abstinence from meats, and purgatory were never before held by the people in greater esteem than at the present moment."

on their standard were the Five Wounds, the chalice with the Host, and the name of Jesus inscribed in the centre.[1]

The dukes of Norfolk and of Suffolk, the marquis of Exeter, and other of the king's officers marched against them; but on the very day when a battle seemed imminent, a conference took place, when Henry, afraid of the issues,[2] promised the Catholic people to redress their grievances, and that no one who had been concerned in that rising should suffer for it.[3] All this the king confirmed not only by public proclamation, but also by letters under the great seal;[4] nevertheless, taking advantage of another rising—not indeed of the same noblemen, but that of Nicholas Musgrave and Thomas Gilby[5]—he put to death those whom he had pardoned[6] before. Among these were the two Lords Darcy and Hussey, Sir Robert Constable, Sir Thomas Percy, Sir Francis Bigot, Sir Stephen Hamilton, Sir John Bulmer, Sir William

[1] Latimer in a sermon thus speaks of these Catholics (Sermons, p. 29, ed. Parker Soc.): "In like manner these men in the north country, they make pretence as though they were armed in God's armour, gird in truth, and clothed in righteousness. I hear say they wear the cross and the wounds before and behind, and they pretend much truth to the king's grace and to the commonwealth when they intend nothing less; and deceive the poor ignorant people, and bring them to fight against both the king, the Church, and the commonwealth."

[2] In the report of the sermon preached by Gardiner, Dec. 2, 1554, at Paul's Cross, when the schism was apparently healed, are the following words (Foxe, vi. 578): "When the tumult was in the north, in the time of king Henry VIII., I am sure the king was determined to have given over the supremacy again to the Pope; but the hour was not then come, and therefore it went not forward, lest some would have said that he did it for fear."

[3] Stow, p. 574. "Sir Robert Aske, that was chief of the rebellion, came to London, was not only pardoned, but rewarded with great gifts."

[4] See below, note 6.

[5] Stow, p. 574. "In the same month [Feb. 1537] Nicholas Musgrave, Thomas Gilby and others stirred a new rebellion, and besieged the city of Carlisle."

[6] Lord Herbert, p. 481, ed. 1649. The contents of this pardon, dated Dec. 9, at Richmond, and sealed with the great seal, was, as our records show, "that the king granted them all a general and free pardon of all rebellion, treasons, felonies, and trespasses unto the day of the date thereof, provided that they make their submission to the duke of Norfolk and earl of Shrewsbury—the king's lieutenant—and that they rebel no more."

Lumley,[1] and Sir Nicholas Tempest; the two abbots of Jervaulx[2] and Rivaulx,[3] and the chief of them all, Robert Aske.[4]

On the 10th day of October[5] [1537], Jane Seymour gave birth to a son, who was named Edward. But the travail of the queen being very difficult,[6] the king was asked which of the two lives was to be spared; he answered, the boy's, because he could easily provide himself with other wives. Jane accordingly died soon after of the pains of childbirth, and was buried at Windsor.

On the 22d day of May [1538] the reverend father Forest,[7] of the Order of St. Francis, because he denied

[1] In the indictment (Baga de Secretis) he is called "George Lumley, late of Thwynge, . . . Esquire."

[2] A Cistercian abbey in the East Riding of York, by the river Jore, now called Ure. The abbot was Adam Sadler.—Baga de Secretis.

[3] Rivaulx, River, or Rievall, a Cistercian abbey, so called from the river Rye; also in Yorkshire.

[4] They were all put to death in the month of June 1537. Stow, p. 574: "Sir Robert Constable at Hull, near the gate called Beverley gate; Aske hanged in chains on a tower at York. . . . Lord Darcy beheaded at Tower hill, Lord Hussey at Lincoln, and the other six in number suffered at Tyborne."

[5] Edward VI. is generally said to have been born Oct. 12. Polydore Vergil says he was born "iii. idus Octobris," which is the 13th, and that Jane Seymour died two days afterwards.

[6] "All this is false," says Burnet (vol. iv. p. 572, ed. Pocock), "for she had a good delivery, as many original letters written by her council, that have been since printed, do show; but she died two days after of a distemper incident to her sex." Heylyn (Hist. Reform., p. 7) says that the common belief has always been that a surgical operation took place, which cost the queen her life. Harpsfield, writing in the reign of queen Mary, speaks of the fact as certain (Treatise of Marriage, MS., bk. iii. p. 107): "That she should die for the safeguard of the child in such manner as she did, yea, the child to be born, as some say that adders are, by gnawing out the mother's womb." So also the account of Fisher and More, printed by Mr. Pocock, Records, ii. 564.

[7] John Forest was confessor to queen Catherine. He entered the order in the seventeenth year of his age, and made his profession in the house of the Observants at Greenwich, and became provincial. It is said that he submitted to the king, but he certainly refused to make his abjuration when it was formally proposed to him. He was thrown into prison, and Latimer, in his letter to Cromwell (Remains, p. 392, Parker Society), complains that he was too gently treated: "Forest, as I hear, is not duly accompanied in Newgate for his amendment, with the White friars of Doncaster and the monks of the Charterhouse; in a fit chamber more like to indurate than to mollify; whether through the fault of the sheriff or of the jailer or both, no man could sooner discern than

the ecclesiastical supremacy of the king, was hung on a gallows by two chains around his arms : under his feet a fire was kindled, so that he was most cruelly roasted alive.

Cromwell had now for some years been creeping into the king's good graces, and he was a man after the king's own heart. Tainted with the heresy of Zuinglius, he was the author of almost all the suggestions made to the king touching the plundering of the shrines.[1] When he saw the images of the saints and the tombs of the martyrs held in honour by Christians, he felt afraid that too much honour was given to the friends of God. He then advised the destruction of the images which God had made honourable in the eyes of men by great miracles, as He had made the Probatica of old in Bethsaida, which healed the first person who went down into it on the moving of the waters by the angel, of whatever disease he had. And with these also the destruction of the

your lordship. Some think he is rather comforted in his way than discouraged: some think he is allowed both to hear Mass and also to receive the sacrament; which, if it be so, it is enough to confirm him in his obstinacy." Foxe (v. p. 180) says he was "hanged in Smithfield in chains upon a gallows, quick, by the middle and armholes, and fire was made under him, and so was he consumed and burned to death." Collier (Eccles. Hist., ii. p. 149) says he "was condemned for heresy and high treason, though by what law they could stretch his crime to heresy is hard to discover, for he was tried only for dissuading his penitents in confession from owning the king's supremacy." Latimer preached, and he announces his purpose to Cromwell in these words: "And, sir, if it be your pleasure, as it is, that I shall play the fool after my customable manner when Forest shall suffer, I would wish that my stage stood near unto Forest." The martyr received his crown after listening to the heresies of Latimer, and went home to his Father's house in the sixtieth year of his age.

[1] Cromwell employed scurrilous buffoons to bring the holy images into contempt, "in the number of whom," says Foxe (v. 403), "were sundry and divers fresh and quick wits, partaining to his family, by whose industry and ingenious labours divers excellent ballads and books were contrived and set abroad, concerning the suppression of the Pope and all Popish idolatry." Foxe then inserts in his text one of these detestable and impious ballads of Cromwell, called the "Fantasy of Idolatry," in which the following stanza is to be found :—

"At Saint Marget Patons, the Rode is gone thens
And stoele away by nyght ;
With His tabernacle and crose, with all that there was
And is gone away quygte."

shrines of the martyrs covered with gold and silver. Thus the man who pretended to abhor idols, committed manifest sacrilege.[1]

As Jacob of old, having seen the vision in his sleep, on rising set up for a title the stone he had laid under his head, pouring oil upon the top of it, and calling the place Bethel, that is, the house of God, and returning after his vow, offered there his tithes unto God;[2] and so the people who feared God, during many generations afterwards, went up to Bethel, that is, to the place which the patriarch Jacob had hallowed, carrying with them kids, to sacrifice them there unto our Lord; so the people of Christ in England went to pray in certain places where the images of our Blessed Lady and the saints had been placed, and which had been made famous by the marvellous works of God: such places were Walsingham, Ipswich, Worcester, Willesden, Canterbury, and others of the same kind. All these were destroyed and desecrated[3] by Cromwell, in order that he might obtain possession of the treasures offered there by the faithful.[4] That was not all, for he began on the 16th day of November to disturb and destroy the remaining monasteries. This was the way in which the king kept the promise he made to the people of Yorkshire when they took up arms to save the shrines from destruction.[5]

[1] Rom. ii. 22.

[2] Gen. xxviii. 12.

[3] Hall, 824. "In September, by the special motion of the Lord Cromwell, all the notable images unto the which were made many special pilgrimages and offerings were utterly taken away, as the images of Walsyngham, Ipswich, Worcester, the lady of Wilsdon, with many others."

[4] Stow, p. 575. "The images of our Lady of Walsingham and Ipswich were brought up to London with all the jewels that hung about them, and divers other images both in England and Wales, whereunto any common pilgrimage was used; for avoiding of idolatry, all which were brent at Chelsea by Thomas Cromwell, privy seal."

[5] This was the way in which Latimer spoke of the holy images, and in which Cromwell delighted. The letter of the former to the latter was sent from Hartlebury, June 13, 1538 (ed. Parker Soc., p. 395): "I trust your lordship will bestow our great Sibyll [our Lady of Worcester] to some good purpose, *ut pereat memoria cum*

One Lambert,[1] a Zuinglian, was burnt in Smithfield, November 22 [1538]. This man, convicted before Thomas Cranmer, archbishop of Canterbury, appealed to the king, who took cognisance of the cause. The matter having been argued before him, he himself publicly disputed with Lambert. But the king condemned him anew, and the sentence of death was pronounced in open court by the vicar-general of the king in spirituals—by Cromwell, who was himself a Zuinglian in disguise.

The vicar of Wandsworth, the priest who was his curate, and his servant, together with a monk whose name was Mayer, were put to death July 8 [1538];[2] and on the 14th day of November, in the same year, Hugh Faringdon, abbot of Reading, and Richard Whiting, abbot of Glastonbury, on the 1st of December, John Beche, abbot of Colchester, all Benedictines, with two priests, Rugge

sonitu. She hath been the devil's instrument to bring many, I fear, to eternal fire: now she herself, with her old sister of Walsingham, her young sister of Ipswich, with their other two sisters of Doncaster and Penrice, would make a jolly muster in Smithfield: they would not be all day in burning."

[1] John Lambert or Nicholson, according to Foxe, was born and bred in Norfolk, and perverted by Bilney, who seems to have been a Lollard. Lambert studied at Cambridge, and became chaplain to the English merchants in Antwerp. Sir Thomas More had him brought home, and the archbishop, Dr. Warham, examined and consigned him to prison, out of which he came when Cranmer was made archbishop. He then kept a school in London, and according to Foxe (v. 226), "forasmuch as priests in those days could not be permitted to have wives, he left his priesthood and applied himself to that function of teaching, intending shortly after also to be free of the Grocers, and to be married." As Lambert did not hold Luther's opinion on the Eucharist, owing probably to his Lollard training under Bilney, Barnes, another heretic, delated him to Cranmer, who was compelled to investigate the charge, and being himself more Lutheran than Zuinglian at the time, he condemned Lambert, and Lambert appealed from the inferior judge to the supreme judge, Henry VIII. The king accordingly, as supreme head of the Church of England, held a court, and after trial, ordered Cromwell to pronounce the usual sentence upon Lambert as a heretic.

[2] Stow, p. 577. "The 8th of July Griffith Clarke, vicar of Wandsworth, with his chaplains and his servant, and friar Maire, were all four hanged and quartered at St. Thomas Watering's: whose inditement I have not heard of, and therefore not able to set down the cause of their execution."

and Onion, obtained the crown of martyrdom for their denial of the king's supremacy.[1]

But lest men should imagine that the storm was directed only against those who were living on earth, and that the king dared not attack the saints in heaven, St. Thomas Beckett, archbishop of Canterbury, who for three hundred years had been numbered with the saints, and renowned for innumerable miracles, was compelled to defend himself on earth again after so many generations, and was found guilty of treason. The king thereupon forbade him to be regarded as a saint. Moreover, he made a decree in the council,[2] that any one who should either keep his feast, or mention him in his prayers, or call him a saint at all, or should suffer his name to remain in the calendar, should be treated as a capital offender.[3]

The offence for which the most holy martyr was thus severely punished was nothing else but the wealth lavished upon his tomb, and the necessity of finding

1 Harpsfield, bk. iii. p. 143. "Such as would voluntarily give over were rewarded with large annual pensions, and with other pleasures. Against some other there were found quarrels, as against Hugh Faringdon, abbot of Reading, which was there hanged, drawn, and quartered. Against Richard Whiting, abbot of Glastonbury, that was hanged on the Torr hill, beside his monastery. Against John Beche, abbot of Colchester, put also to death, which dreadful sight and hearing made some other so sore afraid that they were soon entreated to yield over all to the king's hands, and some thought they escaped fair when they escaped with their lives. So that after a few years there needed no Parliament at all for the great abbeys—they came in otherwise so thick and so roundly — but only to confirm such as had been already relinquished and yielded up to the king."

2 Proclamation (see next note): "The king's majesty, by the advice of his council, hath thought expedient to declare," that "Thomas Becket shall not be . . . called a saint."

3 The sentence may be seen in the Concilia of Wilkins, iii. 836. It is also referred to in the Bull, "Cum Redemptor noster," of Paul III., dated Dec. 17, 1538. See also the proclamation of Nov. 16 in Burnet's Records, vi. 220–222, ed. Pocock: "His images and pictures through the whole realm shall be put down and avoided out of all churches, chapels, and other places; and that from henceforth the days used to be festival in his name, shall not be observed, nor the service office, antiphones, collects, and prayers in his name read, but rased and put out of all the books, . . . upon pain of his majesty's indignation and imprisonment at his grace's pleasure."

some excuse for the pillage. The king's receiver confessed that the gold and silver and precious stones and sacred vestments taken away from the shrine filled six-and-twenty carts. We may judge from this how great must have been the wealth of which the king robbed the other shrines, churches, and monasteries. When the blessed martyr of God, in whose honour so many churches have been built, was thus dishonoured, the inhabitants of a parish in Ireland, hearing that the patron saint of their church was blotted out of the calendar, asked their bishop to tell them which of the saints they were to take for their patron. The bishop told them to take either St. Peter or St. Paul, or any other, in the place of St. Thomas. "But," asked one of them, "what if the king should drive him too out of heaven?" When another said, "Then let us dedicate our church to the Most Holy Trinity, for if any one can keep his place, it is the Most Holy Trinity;" and so they did.

In pursuance of an agreement entered into with the princes of Germany, Henry married Anne, sister of the duke of Cleves. The princess thought that everything would be safe if the king promised to make her his wife. They did not also ask him to promise not to send her away.[1] He did marry her, or rather deceived her, for

[1] Rich. Hilles to Bullinger, London, 1541. Original Letters, No. 105. "Before the feast of John the Baptist it began to be whispered about that the king intended to divorce his queen, Anne, the sister of the duke of Gelderland, though he had married her publicly with great pomp in the face of the Church on the feast of Epiphany after last Christmas. This was first of all whispered by the courtiers, who observed the king to be much taken with another young lady of very diminutive stature, whom he now has. It is a certain fact that about the same time many citizens of London saw the king very frequently in the daytime, and sometimes at midnight, pass over to her on the river Thames in a little boat. The bishop of Winchester also very often provided feastings and entertainments for them in his palace; but the citizens regarded all this not as a sign of divorcing the queen, but of adultery."

immediately afterwards he got rid of her by act of Parliament,[1] and put Catherine Howard in her place.[2]

But as the question of marriage was a source of much vexation to the king, it seemed desirable to settle it; accordingly it pleased this most chaste and watchful pastor of the Church to declare by a perpetual law the conditions for the future of a lawful marriage. After long debates in Parliament, a law was made,[3] to which all orders in the state consented, and which received the definite sanction of the supreme head, to this effect: If any two persons, whose marriage shall not be unlawful according to the law in the Book of Leviticus, shall give their consent to a marriage there and then, and shall then separate, and if afterwards either or both of them shall be married to any other person, and live together as married persons, that second marriage shall annul the first, and shall be held good against it, and no one shall be allowed to plead in any court in favour of the first marriage against the second.[4]

Now the ancient rule of the law of nations was that

1 The clergy in convocation, headed by Cranmer, first pronounced the marriage null, on the ground that the king had never given his inward consent when he publicly made her his wife (Wilkins, Concilia, iii. 854); and Parliament sanctioned the whole process by a bill introduced July 12, 1540.—Burnet, i. 450, ed. Pocock.

2 Lord Herbert, p. 527. "And now the Lady Anne of Cleves, contenting herself with the style of the king's adopted sister, the Lady Katherine Howard, daughter to Edmond, the third son of Thomas, first duke of Norfolk, and brother to the present duke, was married to the king, and presently after showed publicly as queen, August 8."

3 32 Henry VIII. c. 38.

4 Of these proceedings of the king, Richard Hilles, *ut supra*, says: "And yet what is pretended shortly after the preamble, that the commonalty of the realm have had many doubts and perplexities respecting that marriage, is altogether false. For not a man would have dared to open his mouth to mention such doubts and perplexities, even if they had existed, which is not the case. What a termination will the godly expect to this bill, which is thus founded on falsehood! It is false, too, what the statute declares, that the nobility and members of Parliament petitioned the king to refer the whole matter concerning this marriage to the consideration of his clergy; whereas it is certain that no nobleman or citizen would have dared to utter a single word about that business, either openly or in secret, until they had perceived that the

marriage was founded on consent. At this time the rule of a schismatic king began to take effect, that living together constituted a valid marriage. But the Protestants themselves were so ashamed of the law that on the death of Henry VIII. they repealed it.[1]

Sampson,[2] bishop of Chichester, and Dr. Wilson[3] were in the month of May [1540], because they had succoured certain persons who found fault with the ecclesiastical supremacy of the king, sent to prison. For the same cause Richard Farmer, a very wealthy merchant, was

king's affections were alienated from the lady Anne to that young girl Catherine, the cousin of the duke of Norfolk, whom he married immediately upon Anne's divorce."

[1] 2 & 3 Edw. VI. c. 23. "This act" of Henry VIII., says Burnet (i. 452, ed. Pocock), "gave great occasion of censuring the king's former proceedings against queen Anne Boleyn, since that which was now condemned had been the pretence for dissolving his marriage with her." This was repealed in the next reign, 2 & 3 Edw. VI. c. 23; and the following reason is given in the preamble: "Sithence the time of which act [32 Henry VIII. c. 38], although the same was godly meant, the unruliness of men hath ungodly abused the same, and divers inconveniences—intolerable in manner to Christian ears and eyes—followed thereupon; women and men breaking their own promises and faiths made by the one unto the other, so set upon sensuality and pleasure, that if, after the contract of matrimony, they might have whom they more favoured and desired, they could be content by lightness of their nature to overturn all that they had done afore, and not afraid in manner, even from the very church door and marriage feast, the man to take another spouse, and the woman to take another husband."

[2] Richard Sampson, a doctor of laws, of Trinity Hall, Cambridge; Wolsey's commissary in Tournai, A.D. 1514; archdeacon of Cornwall, 1517; dean of Windsor, 1523; prebendary of Lincoln, 1527; archdeacon of Suffolk, 1528; dean of Lichfield, 1532; treasurer of Salisbury, 1535. He was the dean of the Chapel Royal who defended the divorce and denied the jurisdiction of the Pope. The king gave him the see of Chichester in June 1536, and the bishop of London confirmed his election to the deanery of St. Paul's July 27 of the same year. His defence of the royal supremacy, printed by Berthelet, may be seen in Strype, Mem., i. ii. p. 162; and in Brown, Fasciculus, ii. 820. The king took the deanery from him in May 1540, when he sent him to prison, but not the bishopric. He was restored to the royal favour afterwards, and made bishop of Lichfield in 1543, in succession to Rowland Lee, who married Henry and Anne Boleyn. He died at Eccleshall, Sept. 25, 1554, having renounced his heresies on the accession of queen Mary.

[3] Nicholas Wilson, D.D., born in Yorkshire, and educated in Cambridge. He refused to take the oath of the succession, and was sent to the Tower with the bishop of Rochester and Sir Thomas More. Unhappily he fell away, took the oath, and in 1542 was collated to the prebend of Hoxton in St. Paul's, and died June 8, 1548.

deprived of all he had.[1] That was done, as everybody knew, by the advice of Cromwell, to whom, as a second Wolsey, the direction of all affairs of state had been now intrusted.

Sir John Neville was a Catholic, and beloved by his countrymen; but Cromwell hated him because he kept the faith, and because he was in favour with the people. So he denounced him to the king as a suspected person. Then when Sir John was playing at dice with the king, Cromwell invited him to supper; the matter had been previously arranged between Cromwell and the king. From the supper-table Sir John Neville was, by Cromwell's orders, carried away to prison, and from prison to the block.

Moreover, he laid a snare also for Lord Dacres of the north,[2] a great nobleman, and a good Catholic. But because, on the day of the trial, Cromwell could not be

1 Hall, 838. "In this month was sent to the Tower Dr. Wilson and Dr. Sampson, bishop of Chichester, for relieving of certain traitorous persons which denied the king's supremacy; and for the same offence was one Richard Farmer, grocer, of London, a rich and wealthy man, and of good estimation in the city, committed to the Marshalsea, and after in Westminster Hall was arraigned and attainted in the præmunire, and lost all his goods." Burnet (i. 567, ed. Pocock) says that Sampson and Wilson—he does not speak at all of Richard Farmer—were put in the Tower upon suspicion of corresponding with the Pope. But he retracts this indirectly in another place (vol. iii. p. 265), where he gives the substance of a letter of Richard Hilles. That writer (Epist. Tigurinæ, p. 140; Original Letters, No. 105) says: "The bishop of Chichester, and Dr. Wilson, a Papist like Eckins, were set at liberty by the king, though they had been shut out from the general pardon. The treason they had committed, as I hear, was sending alms to that Papist Abel, then brought down to the lowest misery through his long detention in a most filthy prison, and, as the Papists say, almost eaten up by worms, *vermibus fere necatus*." Stow (p. 580) says that Richard Farmer's wife and children were "thrust out of doors. Also the keeper of Newgate was sent to the Marshalsea for giving liberty to Dr. Powell and Dr. Abel, his prisoners, to go under bail."

2 Hall, 815. "The ninth day of July [1534] was the Lord Dacres of the north arraigned at Westminster of high treason, when the duke of Norfolk sat as judge. . . . He was found that day by his peers not guilty. . . . At those words, not guilty, there was the greatest shout and cry of joy, that the like no man living may remember that ever he heard."

present, being kept at home by the gout, Lord Dacres being innocent, was easily acquitted.[1] Though he knew how much he was hated by Cromwell, nevertheless, thinking it not amiss to yield to the times, he called upon him, and thanked him, as if the justice of his cause had been sustained by the goodwill of Cromwell. "Thank my legs," was the answer of Cromwell; "you should have had your deserts, if they had not kept me at home." The rude and savage man could not even dissemble his cruel temper.

The man, determined that his prey should not escape his clutches again, advised the king to make it law that a man condemned for high treason, absent and without a trial, should be regarded as no less justly convicted than a man tried and convicted by a jury of twelve men, which is the custom in England.[2] But before we go further, let us consider the justice of God, who turned this evil counsel to the ruin of its author.

[1] Baga de Secretis, bundle 6, Third Report of the Deputy Keeper, p. 234. The charge against him was "treasonable communication and alliances with the Scots," and he was tried by the Peers, the duke of Norfolk being lord high steward, July 9, 1534, and found not guilty.

[2] Foxe, v. p. 402. "Whereupon divers of the nobles conspiring against him [Cromwell], some for hatred, and some for religion's sake, he was cast into the Tower of London; where, as it happened—as it were by a certain fatal destiny—that whereas he, a little before, had made a law, that whosoever was cast into the Tower, should be put to death, without examination, he himself suffered by the same law. It is said, which also I do easily credit, that he made this violent law, not so much for any cruelty or tyranny, as only for a certain secret purpose, to have entangled the bishop of Winchester, who albeit he was, without doubt, the most violent adversary of Christ and His religion, notwithstanding, God, peradventure, would not have His religion set forth by any wicked cruelty or otherwise than was meet and convenient."

CHAPTER XVIII.

CROMWELL'S FALL—MARTYRS—THE KING WEARY OF THE SCHISM—CATHERINE HOWARD—CATHERINE PARR—MARTYRS—THE COINAGE DEBASED—SUPPRESSION OF THE CHANTRIES.

WHEN the duke of Saxony and the landgrave of Hesse, about to take up arms with some of the princes of Germany against the emperor, had formed the Smalcaldic league, they asked the king of England to become a member of it; but the emperor, having discovered their plans, prevailed upon the king to give them no countenance or support. Henry promised to do all the emperor asked of him. Moreover, when the princes of Germany applied to the king a second time to renew that league, he refused, because he would not break the promise made to the emperor. Cromwell, however, because of his adoption of their heresies, being wholly in favour of the Germans, knowing, too, that the king was afraid of the emperor, and would be glad if the latter could be embarrassed by a war, signed the treaty in the king's name without consulting the king, thinking that the king refused to do so, not from want of goodwill to the Germans, but from want of courage to show it.

The emperor complained to the king, who denied that his name had been subscribed to the league, and then the emperor sent him a copy of the treaty so signed. The king, when he saw it, was very angry with Cromwell, and resolved upon his death;[1] but as he did not like to displease the German princes, he laid other offences to his charge. Hence it was that in the marvellous justice of God, the first person who suffered according to the law which Cromwell had suggested,[2] was Cromwell himself. He was condemned in his absence and unheard, being found guilty of heresy and treason July 9, and beheaded the 20th day after[3] [July 28, 1540]. Nevertheless, the persecution of the Catholics came not to an end.

For on the 30th day of July six persons were put to death, three of whom were Catholics and three were heretics. They were carried to the place of execution through the streets upon hurdles, two and two together, a Catholic and a heretic upon the same hurdle. The cruelty of that procedure seemed to be worse than death.[4]

[1] Stow, p. 578. "The king from this time unto the day of her divorce [Anne of Cleves] was in a manner weary of his life, through his settled mislike he took of her, and his fierce wrath was kindled against all those that were preferrers of this match, whereof the Lord Cromwell was the chief; for the which, and for dealing somewhat too far in some matters beyond the king's good liking, were the occasions of the Lord Cromwell's hasty death."

[2] See note at the end of chapter xvii.

[3] Richard Hilles in a letter to Bullinger (Zurich Letters, Let. 105): "Not long before the death of Cromwell, the king advanced him, and granted him large houses and riches, and more public offices, together with very extensive and lucrative domains; and in the same way he also endowed queen Anne a short time before he beheaded her. But some persons now suspect that this was all an artifice, to make people conclude that he must have been a most wicked traitor. . . . It was from a like artifice, as some think, that the king conferred upon Cromwell's son Gregory, who was almost a fool, his father's title and many of his domains, while he was yet living in prison, that he might more readily confess his offences against the king at the time of execution. . . . There are, moreover, other parties who assert, with what truth God knows, that Cromwell was threatened to be burned at the stake, and not to die by the axe, unless at the time of execution he would acknowledge his crimes against the king, and that he then said, 'I am altogether a miserable sinner.'"

[4] Burnet (Hist. Reform., i. 474, ed. Pocock) says that the three Catholic priests "demeaned themselves towards" the three heretic priests "with the most uncharitable and spiteful malice that was possible—so that their own historian says that their being carried with them to their execution was bitterer to them than death itself." Burnet does not say how he came to know of the "most uncharitable and spiteful malice" of

The Catholics were Thomas Abel, Edward Powell, and Richard Fetherston,[1] all theologians, who having formerly defended queen Catherine in the matter of the divorce, and now refusing to acknowledge the ecclesiastical supremacy of Henry, obtained the glorious crown of martyrdom. The three heretics were Robert Barnes,[2] Thomas Gerard,[3] and William Jerome,[4] priests, who because they held the heresy of Zuinglius were by order of the king burnt in Smithfield.[5]

the three priests, of which even Foxe makes no mention. He is also unjust to Sander, who does not say that the priests felt the cruelty of being in such company, more than the three heretics felt the cruelty of being on the same hurdle with the Catholics. Foxe, however (v. 420), makes an observation which deserves to be remembered for its folly, if not for its malignity: "This was Winchester's device, to colour his own tyranny, and to make the people doubtful what faith they should trust to."

1 Richard Hilles, writing to Bullinger, from London (Original Letters, No. 105), says: "Soon after the dissolution of Parliament, namely, on the 30th of July last year, were executed six of those men who had been exempted from the general pardon. Three of them were Popish priests, whose names were Abel, Powell, and Fetherston, and who refused to acknowledge the king's new title and his authority over the clergy. They were dealt with in the usual manner, first hung, then cut down from the gallows while yet alive, then drawn, beheaded, and quartered, and their limbs fixed over the gates of the city; but the heads in general of as many priests or monks as are executed in this city are fixed on the top of a long pole, and placed upon London Bridge as a terror to others."

2 Robert Barnes, born near Lymne in Norfolk, entered the Augustinian Order in Cambridge; but he fell into heresy early, was tried and imprisoned, but escaped after recanting in 1526, and on the Continent becoming acquainted with Luther and others of the same kind, he became more and more obstinate. Notwithstanding the notoriety of his heresies, Henry VIII. employed him, till he grew weary of him, and had him burnt at Smithfield.

3 Thomas Gerard or Garret was active in circulating the writings of Luther; once curate of All Hallows, Honey Lane.

4 William Jerome was vicar of Stepney.

5 Original Letters, No. 105. "I could never ascertain," writes Hilles, "why these three gospellers were excepted from the general pardon—so that I can conjecture none more likely than that the king, desiring to gratify the clergy and the ignorant rude mob, together with the obstinate part of his nobility and citizens, appointed these three victims, as he probably considered them, as it were for a holocaust to appease those parties, or to acquire fresh popularity with them.... In the week following the burning of these preachers, were executed many others of those who had been excepted from the general pardon. The reason of their execution is unknown to me; but it was reported to have been for treason against the king. . . . It is now no novelty among us to see men slain, hung, quartered, or beheaded: some for

On the 4th day of August the prior of Doncaster, three monks, and a layman surnamed Philpott, were driven out of this world, and received into the heavenly glory of the Everlasting King, because they would not swear to the ecclesiastical supremacy of an earthly king.[1] In the same year, May 28th, at the bidding of the tyrant, Margaret countess of Salisbury underwent a blessed death.[2] She was the mother of Cardinal Pole, and sprung from the house of York, for her father was George, brother of Edward IV. The only charge brought against her was that she, being the mother of such a son, had received letters of filial duty from him without the knowledge of the king, and that she wore on her breast a picture of the Five Wounds of our Lord, which the king considered to be a sign of her affection for the men of Yorkshire, who under that standard had taken up arms in defence of the Christian faith. But the truth is, that being unable to lay his hands upon the son,[3] whom

trifling expressions which were explained or interpreted as having been spoken against the king; others for the Pope's supremacy; some for one thing, and some for another."

[1] Stow, p. 581. "4th of August [1540] were drawn to Tyborne six persons, and one led betwixt twain, to wit, Lawrence Cook, prior of Doncaster, William Horne, a lay brother of the Charterhouse of London, Giles Horne, gentleman, Clement Philip, gentleman of Calais, and servant to the Lord Lisle, Edmund Bromholme, priest, chaplain to the said Lord Lisle, Darby Gening, Robert Bird, all hanged and quartered, and had been attainted by Parliament, for denial of the king's supremacy."

[2] Stow, p. 581. "The 27th of May [1541] Margaret countess of Salisbury, sometime daughter and heir to George duke of Clarence, wife to Sir Richard Poole, knight, and mother to Cardinal Poole, was beheaded in the Tower of London, being never arraigned nor tried before, but condemned by act of Parliament."

[3] Cardinal Pole, in a letter to Cromwell, May 2, 1537, says that the king had asked the king of France to deliver him up to Henry (Burnet, Hist. Reform., vi. 186, ed. Pocock): "I was more ashamed to hear, for the compassion I had to the king's honour, than moved by any indignation, that I coming not only as ambassador, but as Legate in the highest sort of embassage that is used among Christian princes, a prince of honour should desire of another prince of like honour, 'Betray thine ambassador, betray the Legate, and give him to my ambassador's hands to be brought unto me.' This was the dishonourable request, as I understand, of the king." The letter is also to be found in Strype, Mem., i. ii. 326.

he so earnestly desired to punish because he had written a book in defence of the unity of the Church,[1] he sacrificed the mother in his place.[2]

In the year of our Lord 1541 the imperial Diet was held in Ratisbon, and thereto the king, weary, after the manner of the world, not only of the wickedness of others, but also of his own, sent Sir Henry Knyvett and Stephen Gardiner, bishop of Winchester, a man of great learning and marvellous sagacity. One of his reasons for sending them was his desire to justify his caution in matters of religion before certain princes of Germany, who were charging him with being lukewarm in his prosecution of the new gospel. But his chief reason was this:[3] He knew that if neither Catholics nor Protestants

[1] Pro Ecclesiastica Unitatis Defensione, lib. iv. The book was printed probably A.D. 1536, and was sent to the king immediately after the execution of Anne Boleyn, but not published then. Latimer, writing to Cromwell, Dec. 13, 1538 (Remains, p. 411, Parker Soc. ed.), says of this book: "God prosper you to the uttering of all hollow hearts! Blessed be the God of England, that worketh all, whose instrument you be! I heard you say once, after you had seen that furious invective of Cardinal Pole, that you would make him to eat his own heart, which you have now, I trow, brought to pass; for he must now eat his own heart, and be as heartless as he is graceless." Cranmer, also, in his answer to the "Devonshire Rebels," says, "Surely I have read a book of his making, which whosoever shall read, . . . he will judge Cardinal Pole neither worthy to dwell in this realm, nor yet to live."

[2] Lord Herbert (Life of Henry VIII., p. 532) says: "The old lady being brought to the scaffold, set up in the Tower, was commanded to lay her head on the block; but she, as a person of great quality assured me, refused, saying, 'So should traitors do, and I am none.' Neither did it serve that the executioner told her it was the fashion; so turning her grey head every way, she bid him, if he would have her head, to get it as he could." She had been attainted in 1539, then kept in prison, and put to death May 27, 1541.

[3] Burnet (Hist. Reform., iv. 578, ed. Pocock) says that "this is another ornament of the fable, to show the poet's wit; but it is as void of truth as any passage in Plautus or Terence is. For the king was all his life so intractable in that point, that the Popish party had no other way to maintain their interest with him but to comply, not without affectation in that matter." Sander had better opportunities of learning the truth on this point both in Rome and in Spain, and Gardiner confesses it (Foxe, vi. 578): "Master Knevett and I were sent ambassadors unto the emperor to desire him that he would be a mean between the Pope's Holiness and the king, to bring the king to the obedience of the See of Rome."

were satisfied with him, seeing that he fully agreed with neither, he therefore determined that his ambassadors should, in concert with the emperor, devise some means by which he might be reconciled to the Roman Pontiff, and openly observe the perfect rule of the Catholic faith, which he knew to be more true and more certain than any other. He was driven to this by the pressure of his conscience, which, as the ancients have justly observed, is equal to a thousand witnesses.[1]

But as the king wished to save his royal honour, that is, he wished to return to Catholic unity without making a public confession of sins so notorious, without doing a single act of penance, and without making restitution of the property of the Church, his good intentions came to nothing, for he loved the praise of men rather than the honour of God. Such a reconciliation would have been at variance with the canons, and would not have promoted his everlasting salvation.

But as the king himself was faithful neither to God nor to his first wife, so also his wives were not faithful to him. Catherine Howard, who had not been his wife yet two years, was found guilty of adultery,[2] and with

[1] The duke of Norfolk was examined on this point when he was put in the Tower. His answer may be seen in Burnet's Hist. Reform., vi. 274, ed. Pocock. "Also my said lord and Mr. Secretary asked me whether I was ever made privy to a letter sent from my lord of Wynchester and Sir Henry Knevet of any overture made by Grandvile to them, for a way to be taken between his majesty and the bishop of Rome, and that the said letters should have come to his majesty to Dover, I being there with him. Whereunto this is my true answer: I was never at Dover with his highness sith my lord of Richmond died. . . . It was spoken in the council that my lord of Wynchester should have said he could devise a way how the king's majesty might have all things upright with the said bishop of Rome, and his highness' honour saved. Such were the words, or much like."

[2] Stow, p. 583. "The 12th of February [1542] the Lady Howard, otherwise called queen Katherine, and the Lady Jane Rochford for being of her counsel with Thomas Culpepper, were both beheaded within the Tower of London." Of Lady Rochford the following story is told of her in "Prevarication of the Holy Church's Liberties," bk. i. ch. ii. s. 10: "There is a domestic tradition in the honourable family of the Lord Morley to this effect, viz., that the

her companions in sin, Thomas Culpepper and Francis Derham,[1] was put to death.

As these men were said to have sinned with Catherine Howard both before and after her royal wedlock, so a law is made for the prevention of the like scandal in future times, to this effect, that any woman the king might marry, believing her to be a maid, should suffer the penalties due to high treason, if being otherwise, she did not reveal her iniquity to the king.[2] However, to escape from the chances of deceit, the king took for his sixth wife Catherine Parr, the widow of Lord Latimer, and therefore married before. Catherine Parr was in one respect fortunate; the king died before he had time, as it was said he intended, to put her for heresy to death.

lady Vicountess Rochford, daughter of Henry Lord Morley, surnamed God's Cross, a learned, wise, and religious nobleman, had utterly withdrawn herself from the court and the company of the pretended queen Anne, with a resolution not to return, which purpose was diverted by earnest letters from the said Anne—whose brother the Lord Rochford was the same lady's husband—whereupon one night she was loudly called upon in her sleep—as she lay in her father's house, Hallingbury Morley, in Essex, where her chamber beareth the name Rochford to this day—by a voice which so distinctly spoke these words, 'Return not to court,' as that she awaked therewith, and looking aside, beheld, to her seeming, her own head cut off, and held up to her between one's hands, which affrighted her into a confirmation of her former resolution, which for her life and safety was so necessary; but overcome in the end by the said queen's restless importunities, she neglected all warnings, and went, though pensively, and with a kind of foreboding fearfulness, but perished with the queen."

[1] Baga de Secretis, pouch 13, bundle 1. Indictments were found against Culpepper and Derham in the counties of York and Middlesex, in the county and city of Lincoln, in Surrey and in Kent. They were tried at the Guildhall, London, where they first pleaded not guilty, then pleaded guilty before the jury retired, Dec. 1, 1541. They were put to death, according to Stow (p. 583), "at Tyborne the 10th day of December; Culpepper was beheaded, . . . Derham was quartered."

[2] 33 Henry VIII. c. 21. Richard Hilles, writing to Bullinger, Sept. 26, 1543 (Original Letters, 111), says: "Our king has within these two months, as I wrote to John Burcher, burnt three godly men in one day. For in the month of July he married the widow of a certain nobleman of the name of Latimer, and he is always wont to celebrate his nuptials by some wickedness of this kind." The king married Catherine Parr at Hampton Court, June 12, 1543. She outlived the king, married the brother of the Protector in the next reign, and died in childbed shortly before the execution of her husband.

Early in March, Jermyn Gardiner, secretary of the bishop of Winchester, and Larke, rector of Chelsea, John Ireland, a priest, and a chaplain of Sir Thomas More, and soon afterwards Ashby, suffered martyrdom because they would not acknowledge the royal supremacy.[1]

The silver coin, hitherto most pure in England, was for the first time turned into brass by the king[2]—a manifest judgment of God for the rapine and the sacrilege committed by him. The wealth taken from the monasteries was so great that even the tenth part thereof might have satisfied the greed of the most covetous king; all these treasures, the crucifixes of silver and gold, all the sacred vessels, the decorations of the altars, all the furniture of nearly a thousand monasteries,[3] their estates, farms, rents, dues, and rights, were seized by the king. Then, again, he had the tenths and first-fruits of every benefice in England; and the money brought in by the sale even of the lead, timber, and stones of the

[1] The Prevarication, etc., ch. iv. s. 12. "Likewise after the king's marriage with his sixth wife, the Lady Catherine Parr, late widow to the Lord Latimer, the said persecution raged upon German Gardiner, gent., John Larke, parson of Chelsey, John Ireland, priest, William Ashby, James Singleton, John Risby, and Thomas Rich, for they were all hanged, bowelled, and quartered for denial of the king's supremacy ecclesiastical. But when the king began to be weary of his sixth wife also, and knew not how to be rid of her, unless he should cause her to be burnt for heresy, she being a Lutheran, he began to conceive with himself that he could not in honour proceed against her as an heretic, unless also he dealt more mildly with the Catholics, and thereupon the persecution seemed to stint, for he really intended for the cause aforesaid to have taken away her life also, had not his own death prevented it." They were martyred in A.D. 1543.

[2] Stow, p. 587. "In the mean space, to wit, on the 16th of May [A.D. 1544], proclamation was made for the enhaunsing of gold to 48 sh. and silver to 4 sh. the ounce. Also the king caused to be coined base monies in great abundance, which was since that time, to wit, in the fifth year of king Edward VI., called down from 12 pence to nine pence, and from 9 pence to 6 pence; and in the second year of queen Elizabeth called into her majesty's mints and there refined."

[3] Spelman, History and Fate of Sacrilege, p. 186. "The axe and the mattock ruined almost all the chief and most magnificent ornaments of the kingdom, viz., 376 of the lesser monasteries, 645 of the greater sort, 90 colleges, 110 religious hospitals, 2374 chantries and free chapels."

monasteries. With all this he should have left his subjects free for ever from all taxes; indeed he said he should do so, but it was to make the people assent the more readily to the ruin of the monasteries. He ought therefore to have surpassed every prince in Christendom in his wealth of silver and of gold; but it was not so, for by the just judgment of God it was far otherwise with him, for within a few years after the plunder of the monasteries he was a far poorer man than either he himself or his ancestors had ever been before.[1] Yea, he alone laid heavier taxes upon the people than all the kings together had done during the five hundred years that were past.[2]

[1] Harpsfield, bk. iii. pp. 119, 120, Eyston MS. "The revenues, goods, and moveables of the said abbeys, with the said hospitals, with the great treasure that was made of the timber, bells, and leads, and the ornaments of the Church, and other furniture of the said houses, were so great that the commodity thereof seemed able and sufficient to have defended and maintained the realm against all outward and inward enemies many kings' days. And yet was the king within few years brought to great need and debt, and borrowed great sums of the merchants beyond the seas upon interest, whereof some part is yet unpaid, and the queen [Mary] that now is, is fain to take orders for it. Yea, beside the said monasteries, he levied within 14 or 15 years, and laid such exactions upon the people, of subsidies, contributions, and benevolences, when they gave it with an evil will, beside many loans, and beside the immeasurable abasing of the coin to his inestimable advantage."

[2] Richard Hilles (Original Letters, No. 105), writing to Bullinger in 1540, says: "By the authority, too, of the same Parliament, the king has imposed many burdens on his subjects. For there was granted him a fifth of all the yearly revenues of the bishops and the benefices of the clergy, in addition to the tenths, which he annually receives from them. From the laity, as well the nobility as citizens and peasantry, there was granted him the tenth of all their yearly income, patrimony, and lands; and from those who have not any patrimony or yearly revenue there was granted the king a twentieth of their moneys, goods, cattle, fruit, and all kind of property whatever. The north of England, however, where the rebellion took place immediately after the execution of queen Anne, was now excused these payments by the favour of the king. Moreover, this business was so artfully managed that the archbishop of Canterbury and the other lords spiritual—as these carnal persons are called—offered the king of their own accord the payment of this money, in the name of all the clergy, because the king had delivered them from the yoke and bondage of the Roman Pontiff. As though they had ever been, when subject to the Pope, under such a yoke as they now are, when all their property and life itself are at the king's disposal! In like man-

For when the monasteries were still standing, the preachers of a false gospel commonly asserted that no poor man would be found hereafter in England if the monasteries were once broken up [1]—if the treasures hoarded by the abbots, and the lands and farms by which a few monks were then supported, were divided among a larger number of holders. At this time not one of the monasteries is standing, and for every person who then begged his bread from door to door there are at least twenty now, and they at times can hardly obtain what they beg for in such misery.

The silver coin was then so pure that it had only one-eleventh part of alloy to make it the more easily receive the impress of the die; but after that time, by degrees

ner, too, the laity made the king a voluntary grant of this money, which they are bound by Parliament to pay under a heavy penalty. But everything is given freely and voluntarily in this country!"

[1] Harpsfield, Treatise of Marriage, bk. iii. pp. 127, 128, Eyston MS. "This prelate," says Harpsfield of Cranmer, "when the king went about to suppress the monasteries, was his chief instrument and worker. And to bury the people asleep, and to cause them to have better contentation that—as it was doubted—would not patiently and quietly bear the suppression, as it proved afterwards by the rebellion of Lincolnshire and Yorkshire, came and preached at Paul's Cross, and to sweet the people's ears with pleasant words, told them among other things that they had no cause to be grieved with the eversion of the abbeys, but should rather be very glad thereof, for the singular benefit that should redound to the whole realm thereby. And then as he had, and did many times afterwards wrongfully persuade the people in many matters by his lewd lying divinity, so now he telleth them by his vain lying rhetoric many proper imagined toys, and among others, that the king should by the suppression of the abbeys gather such an infinite treasure, that from that time he should have no need, nor would not put the people to any manner of payment or charge for his or the nation's affairs. This sermon as no wise man did believe, so myself, that chanced to be there present, have known, and the whole realm beside to their smart have felt."

And further on he thus writes: "Yea, I will now add and conclude that the only loss of the monasteries was not only for the decay of virtue, prayer, and religion, but also of the politic commonwealth inestimable and importable. I say they were the very nurseries, not only of piety and devotion, but also of the happy flourishing of the commonwealth. Where were the blind and lame and other impotent poor people fed and succoured but there? I have heard that there were more such holpen in the city of Canterbury in one day than be now in all Kent; more in Winchester in one day than be now in all Hampshire, and the like may be said of other places."

—and the work was that of the king—the coin was so debased that two ounces of silver could with difficulty be found with eleven ounces of copper or of tin.

For the better understanding of this matter we must keep in mind that Henry VIII., when he made an expedition into France, in the thirty-sixth year of his reign, for the purpose of laying siege to Boulogne, raised the value of his gold and silver coins, whereby an ounce of silver was made equivalent to four shillings of English money,[1] that is, nearly eight Spanish reals. When he had amassed as large a treasure as he could—by the taxes which he laid on the people, by the ordinary revenues of the crown, by the duties he levied at the ports, by forfeitures and escheats—he then issued a new coinage much less pure, and though it was not so much debased, yet was it of less value by one-fourth than the former; and the next coinage was much more debased still than this. In order to get the old coinage out of the hands of every one into his own, he promised those who would bring it to the mint, to render the new coin of greater value than it was commonly held to be. He then paid not only his judges, his ministers, soldiers, but also every one who sold to him the old coins, in the new coinage, which was of less value. By this trick he took from every one who had dealings with him in money, not one penny in ten, nor one penny in five, but one penny in every fourpence by way of tax. And

[1] Lord Herbert, p. 574. "Among the king's preparatives for war, that of money was the most difficult. For though he had much enriched himself with the revenues of the suppressed abbeys, and besides, received great subsidies and loans from his subjects, yet fortifications, shipping, and other provisions had exhausted his treasure. Besides, he found the money of his kingdom much drained away by his crafty neighbours, while they cried it up in their country. For remedy of which inconvenience, he both enhanced our gold from forty-five shillings to forty-eight shillings the ounce; and silver from three shillings and ninepence to four shillings: and together caused certain base moneys newly coined to be made current, though not without much murmuring."

then, when he saw the fraud prosper, he debased the coinage more and more till he filled up the measure of his days.

The Holy Ghost has warned us in the Sacred Writings that they who thus rob others of their goods[1] can never be faithful servants of Christ. Christ Himself has said, he who is unjust in that which is little, that is, in the ordering of the things of this world, is unjust also in the greater, that is, in spiritual things.[2] And the prophet Isaias cries, "Thy silver is turned into dross: thy princes are unfaithful, companions of thieves."[3] This fraud of Henry passed on to the sole heirs of the schism, as shall be shown further on.[4]

When the king had been nearly two years at war with France and Scotland—in which Boulogne was besieged and surrendered—he assembled a Parliament, November 24, 1545, by which an act[5] was passed, vesting in the king, for the term of his natural life, and giving up to his disposition, all hospitals and colleges, together with the chantries which the faithful had founded for the benefit of their souls. However, he disposed of none of them, being hindered by death.[6]

[1] Latimer, Sermons, pp. 40, 41, ed. Parker Soc. "I remember the prophet Isaiah, in what manner of wise he reproved the sons of the people, saying, . . . Thy silver is turned into 'dross.' So no doubt the fall of the money hath been here in England the undoing of men."

[2] St. Luke xvi. 10.

[3] Isa. i. 22, 23.

[4] Book ii. chapter v.

[5] 37 Henry VIII. c. 4.

[6] Heylyn, Hist. Ref., p. 12. "Towards the charges of which wars the king obtained a grant in Parliament of all chantries, colleges, hospitals, and free chapels, with the lands thereunto belonging, to be united to the crown. But dying before he had taken the benefit of it, he left that part of the spoil to such of his ministers who had the managing of affairs in his son's minority.

CHAPTER XIX.

MISERY OF THE KING—COWARDICE OF THE BISHOPS—DEATH OF THE KING.

WHEN the king saw, as the hour of death was approaching, that in his greed, or rather in his rage, he had broken away from the unity of the Church, he consulted secretly with some of the bishops how he might be reconciled to the Apostolic See, and the rest of Christendom. But behold the severity of God with those who knowingly fall into sin, or who lull themselves asleep therein! No man was found courageous enough to advise him honestly, to tell him his mind, or to show him the truth; they were all afraid because of his former cruelty. They knew that many had been put to death who had spoken their minds frankly in past times, either to him or to Cromwell, even those who had been commanded to speak. So was it now; one of the bishops, doubting whether a snare had been laid for him, replied, the king was far wiser than other men; he had, under the divine guidance, renounced the supremacy of the Roman Pontiff, and had nothing to be afraid of, now that his resolution had been confirmed by the public law of the realm.

It is said, too, that Stephen Gardiner, bishop of Winchester, persuaded him, when alone with him, to call his Parliament together, if possible, and to communicate to it a matter of that importance; if the time was too short, then to express his resolution in writing, and thereby testify to the voice of his conscience, for God would be satisfied with the mere desire of his heart, if he were in any straits which necessarily hindered the performance of the act. But as soon as the bishop had gone, the crowd of flatterers came around him, and afraid that the return of the kingdom to the obedience of the Holy See would force them to part with the ecclesiastical lands, these men persuaded him to allow no such scruples to enter his mind. It is very easy for a man not rooted and grounded in charity to break a good resolution. The king's consultation with his bishops concerning the restoration of the kingdom to the unity of the Church had no other fruit than to show openly that he who, against his conscience, had broken away from the Roman Church, and was therefore resisting the known truth, had sinned against the Holy Ghost.

As to the temper, pursuits, and habits of the king, we may say briefly that he was not unversed in learning, that he encouraged learned men, and increased the salaries of certain professors. With the exception of Cranmer, whom he made archbishop of Canterbury, to be the minister of his lust in the affair of the divorce, the bishops he named were men of learning, and very far from being bad men; many of them afterwards, during the reigns of Edward and Elizabeth, suffered bonds and imprisonment as confessors of the Catholic faith.

His reverence for the Sacrament of the Eucharist was always most profound. Shortly before he died, when about to communicate, as he always did, under one kind, he rose up from his chair, and fell on his knees to adore the Body of our Lord. The Zuinglians who were present said that his majesty, by reason of his bodily weakness, might make his communion sitting in his chair. The king's answer was, "If I could throw myself down, not only on the ground, but under the ground, I should not then think that I gave honour enough to the most Holy Sacrament."

He gave up the Catholic faith for no other reason in the world than that which came from his lust and wickedness. He rejected the authority of the Pope because he was not allowed to put away Catherine, when he was beaten and overcome as he was by the flesh. He destroyed the monasteries, partly because the monks, and especially the friars, resisted the divorce; partly because he hungered after the ecclesiastical lands, which he seized that he might have more abundant means to spend in feasting on women of unclean lives, and on the foolish buildings he raised.[1]

His understanding was acute, and his judgment solid, whenever he applied himself to the serious discussion of any question, especially in the early part of the day. After dinner he was often overcome with wine,[2] and the courtiers, the flatterers, and the heretics with whom Anne Boleyn and others, both wives and concubines, had filled the court, observed it, and then never spoke to him for the purpose of their own advantage, or for that of ruining others, but in the afternoon. Others, too, waited for the time when he took physic, for he was then more than usually cheerful; and there were those who allowed him to beat them or cheat them at dice—he was on such occasions demonstrative in his

[1] Strype, Mem., ii. ii. 353. Judge Hales, speaking of the impoverishing of the people, says: "This thing also caused the king that dead is to make so many castles and bulwarks by the seaside as he did. And his charges by these means and occasions waxing daily greater and greater, he was of necessity driven to ask and take so great subsidies and taxes of his subjects as he did."

[2] Mr. Pocock (Records, ii. 553) has printed a "Cotemporary Account of Fisher and More," written probably many years before Sander wrote, in which it is said (p. 565) that the king had become a sot in his later years: "Ac ferunt eum quotidianis fere conviviis et comessationibus studiose operam dedisse, ut multo vino obruta mens a cogitatione tot facinorum et prioris vitæ atque gloriæ memoria averteretur."

joy—and then hinting that they were ruined, begged of him in return either the goods of some innocent man, or the lead of a monastery, or the bells of a church,[1] or something of great price of that kind. It is said of one that he was not only rewarded, but raised to honours, because he gave the king a porkling well dressed, of which he was very fond; of another, because he moved the king's chair at the fitting moment away from the fire; and of another, because he behaved himself respectfully and pleasantly at dice.[2]

He restored Mary, Catherine's child, to her rank, that she might be the next in succession to his son Edward, and take precedence of Elizabeth. It is very clear from this that he was dishonest in putting away his wife, and that he did so under the influence of his passion for Anne Boleyn. He appointed, by his last will, sixteen persons to be the guardians of his son, thereby making the monarchy, as it were, an aristocracy. Shortly before he died he ordered Thomas duke of Norfolk—he was one of those who had treated the Apostolic Legates with scant respect, though otherwise a Catholic[3]—to be imprisoned for life, and had the son of the

[1] Greyfriars' Chronicle, p. 73. "Sir Myllys Patryge, knyght, the wych playd with kyng Henry the VIII. at dysse for the grett belfery that stode in Powlles Churchyarde."

[2] Stow (Survey, p. 52, ed. 1876) tells the following story: "A fair house with divers tenements near adjoining, sometime belonging to a late dissolved priory, since possessed by Mistress Cornwallies, widow, and her heirs, by gift of Henry VIII., in reward of fine puddings, as it was commonly said, by her made, wherewith she had presented him."

[3] The duke in the Tower thus writes (Burnet, vi. 275): "If I had twenty lives, I would rather have spent them all against him [the Pope] than ever he should have any power in this realm, for no man knoweth that better than I, by reading of stories, how his usurped power hath increased from time to time. Nor such time the king's majesty hath found him his enemy, no living man hath both with his heart and with his tongue, in this realm, in France, and also to many Scottish gentlemen, spoken more sore against his said usurped power than I have done, as I can prove by good witnesses."

duke, the earl of Surrey, beheaded.[1] This he did, deceived by the heretics, who took care that those Catholics should be put out of the way, for it was not believed that they had committed any offence against the king.

The king having ruined a most admirable constitution by unsatiable gluttony, was now grown so unwieldy that he could hardly enter by the doors, and was wholly unable to mount up the stairs. They lifted him up, sitting in a chair, by machinery, to the upper rooms of the palace. It was said that he had no blood left in his body, that it was corrupted into humours. When he was told that he was at the point of death, he called for a goblet of white wine, and turning to one of his attendants, said, "All is lost!"[2]

He reigned thirty-seven years, nine months, and six days, nearly twenty years of which he passed in the peace of the Church; the four years that followed were spent in strife and doubts, and the last fourteen years in open schism. Though three of his children ascended the throne in succession, yet not one of them ever raised a monument to his memory. Mary, it is true, wished to do so, but her piety stood in the way, for she could not, being a Catholic, hand on to future generations the name of one who went into schism. Edward and Elizabeth, too, who approved of Henry's apostasy and

[1] Hilles to Bullinger, Feb. 25, 1547, Original Letters, No. 118. "About one or two weeks before the death of the aforementioned king Henry, he commanded, as some say, by his will, that the duke who in this country is called the duke of Norfolk, together with his only son, who in England is called the earl of Surrey, should both of them be beheaded. The government of England, which is also confirmed by the Parliament or diet, is placed in the hands of sixteen persons, eight of whom, it is said, are bishops, until the king be grown up." The earl of Surrey was executed Jan. 19, 1547.

[2] Prevarication of the Holy Church's Liberties, ch. iv. s. 31, Eyston MS. "In his last sickness always muttering out, 'Monks and friars,' and desperately concluding his life with these his last words, 'Bryan, we have lost all!'"

schism, seem in this matter to have put away from themselves every sense of dutiful affection, unless it be that all this came to pass by the just judgment of God, that a man who scattered to the winds the ashes of so many saints, and who plundered the shrines of so many martyrs, should lie himself unhonoured in his grave.

BOOK II.

CHAPTER I.

THE ROYAL SUPREMACY—UNCHRISTIAN—EDWARD VI.—THE PROTECTOR—BOOK OF COMMON PRAYER—SIR RALPH SADLER.

WHEN God saw the people of England bent on giving up into the hands of its civil rulers the visible government of the Church, wrested from the successor of Peter, to whom our Lord had given it, He brought it most mercifully to pass in the course of His providence that the new supremacy of the Anglican Church should, in the first instance, be given to no other than Henry, the persecutor not only of Catholics, but of Lutherans and Calvinists also, and that it should not be given even upon him but in ways the most dishonourable and utterly hateful. For God did not suffer the king to become the head of the Anglican Church by any other means than by first divorcing Catherine, his most saintly wife, and putting in her place, still living, Anne Boleyn, who was related to him in the first, and more than in the first degree, yea, perhaps his own child. Moreover, after the evil deeds of Henry—and they were so many—when the English maintained that the supremacy belonged of right to the king, God, of His goodness, once more, to check their wickedness by the force of circumstances, did most compassionately provide that the supremacy recently brought in should fall the second time upon a king who was a child, too young to govern himself, to say nothing of the many priests and bishops over whom he was made to rule as supreme even in the things of God.

Then, again, when the English Protestants, thus admonished, would not amend their misdoings, God, unwearied in His goodness, brought it to pass for the third time that the successor of this boy, the supreme head of the Church of England, should be none other than a woman, who, as they had learned from St. Paul,[1] could not speak with authority in the Church, and certainly ought not therefore to be styled the supreme governor thereof. Even that, brought about by the mercy of God, wrought no amendment; and the people, according to their hardness and impenitent heart, heap up for themselves wrath in the day of wrath, and of the revelation of the just judgment of God.[2]

Oh, how marvellous the wisdom and goodness of God! how deplorable the folly and wickedness of men! For as God made His wisdom and goodness more and more manifest by leaving to the English Protestants no way of falling into sin but one that was most foul, then another more foul than that, and in the end another unutterably loathsome, so the Protestants, going further and further in their sin, fill up by degrees the measure of their iniquities. They first go from the successor of Peter to the successor of Nero, from the Pontiff to the king, from the priest to the layman, and what a layman! Then among laymen from a man to a boy, of whose deeds I am going now to speak; but from the boy they go to a woman, of whom also I shall speak further on.

[1] 1 Cor. xiv. 34.

[2] Rom. ii. 5.

The death of Henry was kept secret[1] for a few days, so it is believed; but as soon as the men in power thought it safe to make it known, they proclaimed Edward, the son of Henry and Jane Seymour, then in the ninth year of his age,[2] king of England and of Ireland. That was not all: he who was under tutors and governors like a servant, and had need of another to guide and direct him,[3] becomes the supreme head[4] on earth of the Church of England and of Ireland next after Christ, as if Christ, who by His prophets denounced "woe to the land whose king should be a child,"[5] would have intrusted the Church which He loves to be ordered and ruled, and that, too, in the last resort, by a boy, and almost an infant. But so it pleased God by these circumstances to make it plain to all how great was the wrong done by the king—no one before him had ever done so[6]—when he

[1] Richard Hilles, writing from Strasburg to Bullinger, Feb. 25, 1547 (Original Letters, No. 118), says "I have no later news to tell you of than that it is certain that our king in England died on the 28th of January, and that on the following Monday his only son was publicly proclaimed king."

[2] The king was in his tenth year, and Burnet observes upon this mistake, "that it shows how little this author considered what he writ, when in so public a thing as the king's age he misreckons a year."

[3] Galat. iv. 1, 2.

[4] Burnet writes upon this: "He says king Edward was not only declared king of England and Ireland, but made supreme head of the Church, and upon this runs out to show how incapable a child was of that power. This is set down in such set terms as if there had been some special act made for his being supreme head of the Church, distinct from his being proclaimed king, whereas there was no such thing; for the supremacy being annexed to the crown, the one went with the other." This "shows how little" Burnet "considered what he writ;" for Sander never said what is attributed to him, but that which Burnet thinks he ought to have said, namely, that by becoming king he became also supreme head, &c.—"*fit summum ecclesiæ Anglicanæ et Hibernicæ in terris caput.*"

[5] Eccles. iv. 16.

[6] Harpsfield, Treatise of Marriage, bk. iii. p. 115, Eyston MS. "After this divorce he was most ugly, deformed, and transformed into a quite contrary monstrous shape, so far forth that he took upon himself—the first pestilent pernicious precedent that ever was before or since showed in any realm of Christendom, and wherein he is yet alone—he took upon him, I say, to be supreme head of the Church of England, in all causes as well ecclesiastical as temporal, neither is it to be marvelled if he thus fell into schism and heresy." Cardinal Pole had also told the king, in his letter of July 15, 1537, written from Venice (Strype,

assumed this title; and if in him the assumption of the title was the highest folly, it was a greater folly still to transmit it to his heir, who was a youth not yet of age.

After the proclamation of the new king, when it was thought that the first thing to be done was to execute the last will of the king who was dead, it came to pass, by the marvellous justice of God, that the first thing done was to treat that will as a nullity. Henry VIII., by destroying the monasteries, churches, and altars which had been built for the worship of God, had wickedly set aside innumerable wills devoutly made, and could God suffer his will to be respected even for an instant by those in whom he most trusted? The king had appointed sixteen guardians with equal rights for the protection of his child in his ninth year, in order that there might not be wanting persons to defend the king in his tender years, if any powerful nobleman attempted to usurp the kingdom or wrong his son.[1]

Some of these guardians were Catholics, and therefore desirous of bringing the kingdom back again into the unity of the Church, more especially as they knew the king's mind to have been so disposed, and particularly when death had come near to him. Others, however, seeing that a much greater present gain was to be made by robbing the Church than by restitution of stolen goods, not only dissented from their colleagues, but resolved to go on with the schism.

Accordingly, Edward Seymour, king Edward's uncle, at that time earl of Hertford, but soon after duke of

Mem., i. ii. 304), that the title of supreme head was a burden "which no other prince beside in their realms, feeling the displeasure of God, dare venture to take upon them, nor ever did since the Church began."

[1] The words of the will are, "That none of them presume to meddle with any of our treasure, or to do anything appointed by our said will, alone, unless the most part of the whole number of the co-executors do consent, and by writing agree to the same." The will is printed in Rymer's Fœdera, vi. p. 3, p. 142.

Somerset,[1] made himself the sole and only guardian of the king,[2] and protector of the kingdom, in violation of the will of the late king. Some of his co-executors encouraged him, some connived at his doings, while others, under the influence of fear, dared not stand up against him, Thomas Lord Wriothesley, who was lord chancellor at Henry's death, alone opposing him openly.[3] There could be no doubt that this man, commissioned by no one, but coming in his own name, would indeed admirably execute his office. Being a Calvinist, he had nothing more at heart than to pollute and defile still more that wretched and disfigured form of religion which Henry had commanded to be observed. Henry, it is true, destroyed all the monasteries, plundered the wealthiest shrines of the martyrs, and threw down also certain statues and pictures of the saints which God had made miraculous; but he had left, nevertheless, in cities and towns, in colleges, in villages, a very large number of churches unrifled, which our forefathers had built; and he had preserved their furniture undamaged, crucifixes, pictures, vessels, vestments. He also held in honour the seven sacraments, and checked and suppressed almost every heresy except that which related to the supremacy of the Roman Pontiff and the religious orders.

In the first place, this new protector of Edward, and

[1] Edward Seymour, brother of Jane Seymour, was made Viscount Beauchamp of Hache, June 5, 1536, immediately after the marriage of his sister, and in the following year, Oct. 18, 1537, earl of Hertford. He was made a baron on the 15th, and on the next day, the 16th, of Feb. 1547, made duke of Somerset.

[2] The lords of the council in a letter to the king (Burnet, v. p. 279) thus speak: "The protectorship and governance of your most royal person was not granted him by your father's will, but only by agreement, first amongst us the executors, and after, of others, and upon condition he should do all things by advice of your council."

[3] Burnet charges Sander with saying that "king Henry when he was dying had made Wriothesley lord chancellor;" but the words of Sanders are that he left him in office —"*quem Henricus summum regni cancellarium reliquerat.*"

the faction that clung to him, held the winds throughout the whole kingdom "that they should not blow upon the land;"[1] that is, they forbade the bishops and the priests to preach in any church, in order that "when the little ones asked for bread, and there was no one to brake it unto them,"[2] the deadly poison of Lutherans and Calvinists, who alone were allowed to preach, might be the more eagerly quaffed by the people consumed with thirst.[3]

In the second place, all the images of Christ our Saviour, of the Virgin Mother of God, and of the prophets were utterly destroyed, the pictures defaced and the statues burnt, thereby showing against whom war was declared, and against whom they were fighting. In the place of the cross of Christ, which they threw down, they put up the arms of the king of England,[4] namely, three leopards and three lilies, having for supporters the outstretched feet of a serpent and a dog. It was like a declaration on their part that they were worshippers, not of our Lord, whose image they had comtemptuously thrown aside, but of an earthly king, whose armorial bearings they had substituted for it.[5]

1 Apoc. vii. 1.

2 Thren. iv. 4.

3 Burnet (Hist. Reform., v. p. 588, ed. Pocock) says, "So falsely has our author stated the matter;" but he admits that such a prohibition was made in the beginning of the second year of the king. A proclamation to that effect was published by Fuller, and copied from him by Wilkins (Concilia, iv. p. 30); but that proclamation begins by saying that a prior proclamation had been made, which had been too much disregarded: "Whereas the king's majesty hath by proclamation inhibited and commanded that no manner of persons, except such as was licensed by his highness, the lord protector, or by the archbishop of Canterbury, should take upon him to preach," &c.

4 Stow, Survey, p. 75, ed. 1876. "Three leopards passant, gardant; which were the whole arms of England before the reign of Edward III., that quartered them with the arms of France, three fleur-de-lis."

5 Dr. Martin, addressing Cranmer at Oxford in 1556, thus speaks (Foxe, viii. 56): "But if you mark the devil's language well, it agreed with your proceedings most truly; for, 'Cast Thyself downward,' said he, and so taught you to cast all things downward. Down with the Sacrament, down with the Mass, down with the altars, down with the arms of Christ, and up with a lion and a

In the third place, the Calvinists, not satisfied when they had wrought all this mischief, abolished by an act of Parliament [1] the awful sacrifice of the Body and Blood of our Lord, which had of ancient times, from the dismissal first of the catechumen and then of the faithful, received the name of the Mass, Missa. There was no other way to the plundering of the chalices, the silver pixes, the crucifixes, the ewers, and other sacred vessels, the candlesticks of silver and of brass, the sacred vestments of woven gold, the silk banners, the money given for the provision of wax, oil, and everything else used in the worship of God. And lastly, it was the only excuse to give for seizing upon the money and lands given for the maintenance of that worship, and for converting them into the profane uses of private persons.

In the fourth place, communion under both kinds was sanctioned by a law.[2]

dog." So also Harpsfield, bk. iii. p. 110: "Then our churches were more like to the Jews' synagogues—the image and the cross of Christ, with the image of His Blessed Mother, and all His holy saints, being defaced and broken, the altars overthrown, and the Precious Body of Christ villainously prophaned—than to Christian churches. The wall all bepainted like the Jews' temple with places of Holy Scripture, and yet worse than the Jews' temple, for that the meaning of those authorities was to make the world believe that to pray to the saints, to pray for the dead, to worship Christ's Body in the Blessed Sacrament, was nothing but plain superstition and idolatry. Then should you have seen in the place where Christ's Precious Body was reposed, over the altar, and instead of Christ's crucifix, the arms of a mortal king, set up on high with a dog and a lion, which a man might well call the abomination of desolation standing in the temple that Daniel speaketh of." Grindal (Remains, p. 134), in the reign of Elizabeth, ordering the destruction of the altar stones and the taking down of the cross from the roodloft, "required a convenient crest" to be placed in the crossbeam. It was a principle of the Lollards to place the king in the room of the Pope, for as early as A.D. 1395 they wished to make the white hart, which was the cognisance of Richard III., to be the distinction of a priest.

[1] 2 & 3 Edw. VI. c. 1, suppressed the Missal and Breviary, substituting for them the Book of Common Prayer.

[2] 1 Edw. VI. c. 1, enacts "that the said Most Blessed Sacrament be hereafter commonly delivered and ministered unto the people within this Church of England and Ireland, and other the king's dominions, under both the kinds, that is to say, of bread and wine, except necessity otherwise require."

In the fifth place, divine service was ordered to be said in the vulgar tongue, a singularly absurd order, the pretence being that when the divine office was used in the churches of England, the people might understand and be able to answer Amen. Now the people of Wales, Cornwall, and Ireland hardly understood a word that they heard, for their language is very different from that of the English. But if the divine office were said in Latin, the priests at least, who know that language, might have explained to the people much of that which they were reciting. The fitting place for the language of any country is in the sermons of the priests, and that has been always the usage in the Church. Now, when the English prayers were said in Wales, Cornwall, and Ireland, it came to pass that less profit was obtained from the use of the vulgar tongue than had been obtained when the use of the Latin tongue prevailed.[1]

In the first Parliament of the king's reign the form prescribed for the administration of the Eucharist differed but slightly from the Catholic Mass, in order that the

[1] Bucer, writing from Cambridge, at Pentecost 1550, to Calvin (Original Letters, No. 253), thus describes the result: "The bishops have not yet been able to come to an agreement as to Christian doctrine, much less as to discipline, and very few parishes have pastors qualified for their office. Most of them are sold to the nobility; and there are persons even among the ecclesiastical order, and those too who wish to be regarded as gospellers, who hold three or four parishes, and even more, without ministering in any one of them; but they appoint such substitutes as will be satisfied with the least stipend, and who for the most part cannot read English, and who are in heart mere Papists. The nobility, too, have in many parishes preferred those who have been in monasteries, who are most unlearned and altogether unfit for the sacred office; and this merely for the sake of getting rid of the payment of their yearly pension. Hence you may find parishes in which there has not been a sermon for some years; . . . and even our friends are so sparing of their sermons, that during the whole of Lent, which, nevertheless, they still seem to wish to observe, with the exception of one or two Sundays, they have not once preached to the people, not even on the day of the commemoration of Christ's death, or of His resurrection, or of this day. Sometimes, too, many of the parochial clergy so recite and administer the service that the people have no more understanding of the mysteries of Christ than if the Latin instead of the vulgar tongue were still in use."

people might suppose that nothing had been taken away, and believe that the words formerly said in Latin had been translated into the vulgar tongue.[1] Accordingly the canon of the Mass from beginning to end was copied almost word for word. The sign of the holy cross was retained, at least that which the priest makes with his hand. But all the Protestants were not of one mind. Those whose sole aim was the riches of the Church cared very little for the sign of the cross made in the air; but those who could not endure that the image and representation of the death of Christ should even in that way be held in honour,[2] very soon obtained the suppres-

[1] 2 & 3 Edw. VI. c. 1. Hooper, writing to Bullinger, Dec. 27, 1549 (Original Letters, No. 36), thus describes the issues: "The archbishop of Canterbury entertains right views as to the nature of Christ's presence in the supper, and is now very friendly towards myself. . . . Like all the other bishops in this country, he is too fearful about what may happen to him. There are here six or seven bishops who comprehend the doctrine of Christ as far as relates to the Lord's Supper with as much clearness and piety as one could desire, and it is only the fear for their property that prevents them from reforming their churches according to the rule of God's Word. The altars are here in many churches changed into tables. The public celebration of the Lord's Supper is very far from the order and institution of our Lord. Although it is administered in both kinds, yet in some places the supper is celebrated three times a day. Where they used heretofore to celebrate in the morning the Mass of the apostles, they now have the communion of the apostles; where they had the Mass of the Blessed Virgin, they now have the communion, which they call the communion of the Virgin. Where they had the principal or high Mass, they now have, as they call it, the high communion. They still retain their vestments and the candles before the altars. In the churches they always chant the Hours and other hymns relating to the Lord's Supper, but in our own language. And that Popery may not be lost, the Mass priests, although they are compelled to discontinue the use of the Latin language, yet most carefully observe the same tone and manner of chanting to which they were heretofore accustomed in the Papacy."

[2] Hooper disliked the new service because it was Lutheran rather than Zuinglian. Thus he writes to Bullinger, March 27, 1550 (Original Letters, No. 38): "It is no small hindrance to our exertions that the form which our Senate, or Parliament as we commonly call it, has presented for the whole realm, is so very defective and of doubtful construction, and in some respects manifestly impious. . . . I am so much offended with that book, and that not without abundant reason, that if it be not corrected, I neither can nor will communicate with the Church in the administration of the supper. Many altars have been destroyed in this city [London] since I arrived there."

sion of these ceremonies, the removal of the canon of the Mass, and in its place a new liturgy.[1] This changeableness on the part of the Protestants for some time kept back the ignorant people from accepting their doctrines, for they used to say, "Let us first see where they are going to—where they will stand and remain."

Spiritual questions were discussed in Parliament as if the assembly were a synod of bishops—questions even of ecclesiastical law. Among others a cause of marriage was thus settled.

Matthew Barrow, an artisan, went abroad, leaving his wife and the mother of his children behind. The wife was once a laundress in the service of Cromwell, in whose service also at the time was Ralph Sadler, a man not unknown.[2] I do not know why Matthew Barrow went abroad, but some people thought that he suspected the honour of his wife, and that he therefore left her to avoid the sight of what he could neither endure nor check. When he had been absent some years his wife heard that he had died, and then Sir Ralph Sadler married her. Matthew at last came home again, and finding his wife married to another, claimed her; but Sadler, who by this time had children by her, refused to part with her. The dispute was carried to the highest court, to Parliament itself, in the reign both of Henry and his son Edward. The judgment of that court was, that the woman, who was in the first place the wife of Matthew Barrow, and again of

1 The first Book of Common Prayer, printed in 1549, represented the Lutheran opinions, and was extremely disliked by the Wicliffite or Zuinglian preachers. It was therefore abolished, and the second Book of Common Prayer was put forth in 1552, teaching the Lollard opinions, which by this time had recovered themselves against those of Luther.

2 He was a servant of Cromwell when Cromwell himself was in the service of Cardinal Wolsey. "Sir Rafe Salder," says Cavendish (p. 270, ed. Singer, 1827), "now knight, was then his clerk, and rode with him" when he quitted his master to become the servant of Henry VIII.

Sadler, and the mother of children by both, should for the future be regarded not as the wife of her first husband, Matthew, but of the second, who was Sadler.[1] Of the two, Sadler had the greater influence and wealth, and so to him, contrary to the truth of the gospel, was given the wife of a man still living, in order to establish a new law of marriage, as a new law of divine service had been established already.

[1] Upon this Burnet (vol. v. p. 593, ed. Pocock) says: "This is, as far as I can learn, a forgery from the beginning to the end. And it seems Sadler, that was a privy councillor in queen Elizabeth's time, did somewhat that so provoked Sander that he resolved to be revenged of him and his family by casting such an aspersion on him." But as Burnet gives no proof of the "somewhat," nor even attempts it, the story need not be a forgery wrought in malice. The doctrine of marriage held by men at that time may well have been made use of in the affairs of Sir Ralph Sadler. The commission appointed, first by Henry VIII. and then by Edward VI., to reform the laws of the Church, proposed that the second marriage of the party deserted should stand good, notwithstanding the fact that the first husband or wife was still alive. See Reform. Legum, tit. de adulteriis et divortiis, c. 8, 9.

Sir Walter Scott, in his Life of Sir Ralph Sadler, prefixed to the "State Papers and Letters," Edinburgh, 1809, says that "Mr. Sadler became the husband of the widow of one Ralph Barrow, who does not seem to have been a person of high rank, although no good grounds have been discovered for the scandal with which Sanders and the Catholic writers have stigmatised this union. That she was a woman of credit and character must be admitted, since Lord Cromwell, to whom she was related, not only countenanced this marriage, but was godfather to two of their children." Sadler was Cromwell's servant, and Cromwell's kindred were not persons of high rank, and he may well have a laundress among them; and most certainly his notions about the validity of the bond of marriage were not strict. As for Burnet, he denounced the history of Poynet in the same way, and upon no authority.

CHAPTER II.

DESTRUCTION OF THE ALTARS—CRANMER'S CHANGES—LATIMER—EXECUTION OF LORD SEYMOUR—THE RISINGS IN THE WEST AND IN NORFOLK.

MEANWHILE the English Catholics, and especially the more learned among them, who hoped for the repression of the schism of Henry VIII., at least after his death, were blaming themselves for not having more resolutely set their faces against it when it began; they were living wretchedly in great misery and grief, for they saw now that the schism was so far from dying out that it had grown into a much more deadly heresy. St. John Chrysostom,[1] writing against the heathens who denied the Divinity of Christ, uttered the praises of the ancient faith of this country, which he specially commended for this, that altars had long ago been raised in Britain in honour of Christ. These are his words: "Churches have been built and altars raised in the British Isles." But now, after the lapse nearly of twelve hundred years, those very altars are thrown down and destroyed, not by pagans, but by men who call themselves Christians. What must any one, on reading that Homily of St. John Chrysostom, have felt when he saw this destruction? He must have wept and moaned, for if the altars of Christ were of old signs of Christian belief, the ruin of the altars must be a sign of antichristian unbelief.

Men now were discussing matters of faith in every

[1] S. Jo. Chrysost., Op., i. p. 575, ed. Bena.

workshop, tavern, and alehouse: every gossiping old woman, every silly old man, every wordy declaimer, as St. Jerome[1] complained of old—in short, every one took up the sacred books, pulled them to pieces, taught them to others before they had been taught them themselves. Some discoursed to women, others learned from women what they taught to men; and the Apocalypse especially, in which there are as many mysteries as there are words, was in everybody's mouth. The Protestants proved their opinion from it, and took passages therefrom utterly irrelevant, which they interpreted in their own sense, boldly explaining to others what they did not understand themselves. It is so in the beginning of all sects, and accordingly the English people did nothing else at this time but hear or preach some new thing.

Stephen, bishop of Winchester; Edmund Bonner,[2] bishop of London; Cuthbert Tunstall, bishop of Durham; Nicholas Heath,[3] bishop of Worcester; and [George] Day,[4] bishop of Chichester—all of these venerable prelates resisted these innovations as well as they

[1] Ep. liii. ad Paulinum, tom. i. p. 275, ed. Villars.

[2] Edmund Bonner, native of Worcestershire, educated at Broadgates Hall, Oxford, into which he was admitted about A.D. 1512. In 1525 he took the degree of doctor in law. He was one of the king's chaplains, commissary of Cranmer, and in 1535 was made archdeacon of Leicester. He was very zealous in promoting the divorce, and—so he tells us himself—behaved insolently to the Pope. He accepted the bishopric of Hereford from the king, and then that of London, and was consecrated April 4, 1540. He was not a bishop, for he received no Bulls. He accepted all the changes in religion, and even the English services in the beginning of the reign of Edward VI. But he did not accept everything, and was put in prison, deprived of the see, which was given to Ridley, who threw down the altars.

[3] Nicholas Heath was consecrated with Bonner, without Bulls, to the see of Rochester, from which Henry VIII. removed him to Worcester, A.D. 1543. He was thrown into prison, and Hooper was put in his place, A.D. 1551. Queen Mary set him free, and then he confessing his guilty share in the schism, was reconciled to the Church, and made archbishop of York, A.D. 1555.

[4] George Day, master of St. John's College, and then provost of King's College, Cambridge, consecrated by Cranmer in schism May 6, 1543. He submitted to all the changes that was made till he was ordered to throw down the altars. That he refused to do, and Edward VI. took his bishopric from him.

could. But on the other side, and in the defence of heresy, stood Cranmer, archbishop of Canterbury, raised from the house of Anne Boleyn, as I said before,[1] to the archbishopric; and with him all those who were made bishops by Edward VI.—Ridley,[2] Hooper,[3] and Poynet,[4] superintendents[5] of London, Gloucester, and Winchester. Others held a middle course—though nothing of the kind is allowable in the service of God—hoping, it is true, for the triumph of the Catholic faith, but at the same time professing heresy, lest they should lose anything for the sake of Christ.

Hitherto, indeed, Cranmer himself had been a Henrician, that is, a follower of Henry VIII., from whose instructions he never dared to depart even a hair's breadth in anything. So long as the king lived, Cranmer heard

[1] See bk. i. chap. xv. p. 109.

[2] Nicholas Ridley, born in Northumberland, and educated at Cambridge, proctor of the university in 1534, and in 1540 master of Pembroke Hall. Cranmer made him vicar of Herne, and prebendary of Canterbury. In 1545 he was one of the prebendaries of Westminster, and in 1547 vicar of Soham, on the presentation of his college. Edward VI. made him bishop of Rochester in the same year, and licensed him to hold with Rochester the two vicarages of Herne and Soham, and the two prebends of Canterbury and Westminster, and April 1550 translated him to London, having first deprived Bonner of the see.

John Hooper, born in Somerset, was educated at Oxford; but betraying early his heretical opinions, wandered abroad, and became a friend of Bullinger, and others of the same sort, and married, though a priest. He returned to England in May 1549, and found his "father still alive, and though not a friend to the gospel, yet not an enemy to it."—Original Letters, 39. He was made chaplain to the duke of Somerset, and preached constantly against the faith. He demurred to the ecclesiastical dress on being made a bishop, but he yielded, and held the two sees of Worcester and Gloucester, as Foxe (vi. 643) says, he "abhorred nothing more than gain." He fed the poor in his palace at Worcester, but "being before examined by him or his deputies, of the Lord's prayer, the articles of their faith, and ten commandments."—Foxe, vi. 644.

[4] John Ponet or Poinet was born in Kent, and died at Strasburg about the 10th of August 1556. See below, p. 208.

[5] This was the word used instead of bishop by the sectaries: Elizabeth Young, in her examination in 1558, is asked by Dr. Martin, "What do ye call Scory?" who was a bishop in the days of Edward VI., and answers, "Our superintendent."—Foxe, Acts and Mon., viii. p. 540. And Strype (Mem., ii. ii. p. 141) confesses that "the word superintendent began to be affected, . . . and the rather perhaps being a word used in the Protestant churches of Germany. This the Papists made sport with."

Mass every day, and on certain days even said it himself. His greatest distress was that he could not show abroad as his wife the woman who was living with him. The king would not allow him to do so. He must therefore keep her secretly in his house. When he went abroad, he was compelled to carry her from place to place hidden from sight in a chest.[1]

But when the king died, Cranmer ceased to be a Henrician, and became wholly a Lutheran, knowing at the same time that Henry had been a most earnest opponent of Luther. He printed and published a catechism,[2] dedicated to Edward VI., wherein he taught

[1] Harpsfield, Treatise of Marriage, bk. iii. p. 98. "The archbishop of Canterbury was married in king Henry's days, but kept his woman very close, and sometimes carried her about with him in a great chest." When the palace in Canterbury was in danger of destruction by fire, "he caused the chest with all speed to be conveyed out of danger, and gave great charge of it, crying out that his evidences and other writings which he esteemed above all worldly treasure were in the chest. All this I heard out of the mouth of a gentleman that was there present." "His brother also, the archdeacon, was likewise married, and kept privily his woman; and being thereof examined by Dr. Thirlby, that was afterwards bishop of Ely, and had commission from the king for the examination of such matters, swore upon a book that he was not married. And indeed he might truly have sworn that he was never lawfully married." The 18th of December 1543, says Stow (p. 585), "the archbishop of Canterbury's palace at Canterbury was brent, and therein was brent his brother-in-law and other men." The Three Conversions of England, vol. ii. chap. vii. p. 371: "It happened at Gravesend, where the bishop lay one night, his chests were brought a land and put in a gallery. And this among other being much recommended to the shipmen, as containing precious stuff belonging to my lord's grace, they severed that from the rest and put it up and long against the wall in my lord's chamber, with the woman's head downward, which putting her in jeopardy to break her neck, she was forced at length to cry out. And so the chamberlain perceiving the error, took her forth foully disfigured, and as good as half dead. This is a most certain story, and testified at this day by Cranmer's son's widow, yet living, to divers gentlemen her friends, from whom myself had it." Cranmer seems to have kept his wife in secret till the year 1550, when he showed her openly; for that must be the explanation of the letter of Stumphius to Bullinger (Original Letters, 223): "There is also the greatest hope as to religion, for the archbishop of Canterbury has lately married a wife."

[2] Catechismus, that is to say, "a shorte instruction into Christian religion for the syngular commoditie and profyte of children and yong people. Lond. by Nycolas Hyll for Gwalter Lynne, 1548." The book is a translation of the translation made by Justus Jonas into Latin of a German catechism, and John Burcher

that every Christian who received the Eucharist received in his mouth the very true Body and Blood of Christ, either under, in, or with the bread.[1] But a few months had hardly gone by when the miserable man found out that the protector of the king, the duke of Somerset, was a Calvinist, not a Lutheran.[2] What was he to do? He recasts the catechism, changes his language,[3] and he who was once a Henrician, then a Lutheran, becomes a Calvinist.[4]

in a letter, Oct. 29, 1548, to Bullinger (Original Letters, 298), thus speaks of the fruits it brought forth: "The archbishop of Canterbury, moved, no doubt, by the advice of Peter Martyr and other Lutherans, has ordered a catechism of some Lutheran opinions to be translated and published in our language. This little book has occasioned no little discord, so that fightings have frequently taken place among the common people on account of their diversity of opinion, even during the sermons. The government, roused by this contention, have convoked a synod of the bishops to consult about religion." John ab Ulmis, writing to Bullinger from London, Aug. 18, 1548 (Original Letters, 185), says, "He has lately published a catechism in which he has not only approved that foul and sacrilegious transubstantiation of the Papists in the holy supper of our Saviour, but all the dreams of Luther seem to him sufficiently well-grounded, perspicuous, and lucid."

[1] Cranmer admits the fact (Jenkyns, ii. 440). "And in a catechism by me translated and set forth," he says, "I used like manner of speech, saying that with our bodily mouths we receive the Body and Blood of Christ." But he goes on to say that he did not mean it. "Which my saying," he adds, "divers ignorant persons, not used to read old ancient authors, nor acquainted with their phrase and manner of speech, did carp and reprehend for lack of good understanding."

[2] Foxe, viii. 34, repeats this statement. "During all this meantime of king Henry aforesaid, until the entering of king Edward, it seemed that Cranmer was scarcely yet thoroughly persuaded in the right knowledge of the sacrament, or at least was not yet fully ripened in the same; wherein shortly after he being more groundedly conformed by conference with bishop Ridley, in process of time did so profit in more ripe knowledge, that at last he took upon him the defence of that whole doctrine, that is, to refute and throw down, first the corporal presence, secondly the phantastical transubstantiation, thirdly the idolatrous adoration."

[3] In his examination at Oxford, Cranmer is thus addressed by Dr. Martin (Jenkyns, iv. 96): "Then there you defended another doctrine touching the sacrament, by the same token that you sent to Lynne your printer, that whereas in the first print there was an affirmative, that is to say, Christ's body really in the sacrament, you sent then to your printer to put in a 'not,' whereby it came miraculously to pass that Christ's body was clean conveyed out of the sacrament." To this Cranmer answered, "I remember there were two printers of my said book, but where the same 'not' was put in I cannot tell." See also Foxe, viii. 57.

[4] John ab Ulmis, writing to Bullinger from Oxford, Nov. 27, 1548, says that Cranmer was at that time a Zuinglian or Calvinist; these are

Many Protestants resented this, and therefore assigned the first rank in preaching the gospel, not to Cranmer, but rather to Hugh Latimer,[1] a heretic loose of tongue, whom they everywhere called the Apostle of the English, as if he had been the first who preached to them the true gospel of God. They knew not that even Latimer himself had been at first a Lutheran, and not a Calvinist. Latimer, moreover, admitted publicly at Oxford that he continued a Lutheran even to his old age, and that his conversion to Calvinism was the work of Thomas Cranmer more than of any other man, brought about a few years ago before his death.[2]

his words (Original Letters, 186): "That abominable error and silly opinion of a carnal eating has been long since banished and entirely done away with. Even that Thomas [Cranmer] himself, about whom I wrote to you when I was in London, by the goodness of God and the instrumentality of that most upright and judicious man Mr. John à Lasco, is in a great measure recovered from his dangerous lethargy." Hooper, writing to the same Bullinger, from London, Dec. 27, 1549 (ibid. 36), says, "The archbishop of Canterbury entertains right views as to the nature of Christ's presence in the supper, and is now very friendly towards myself." Strype (Life of Cranmer, bk. ii. c. 25) seems to assign but one change of opinion, and that due to the influence of Ridley. But the words of Cranmer, by him there quoted, show that the archbishop was a Lutheran only a short time before the publication of this catechism. "I confess of myself," says Cranmer, "that not long before I wrote the said catechism, I was in that error of the real presence, as I was many years past in many other errors—as of transubstantiation, of the sacrifice propitiatory," &c. Cranmer speaks of two errors he held successively, "that of transubstantiation and that of the real presence." By the real presence he means Lutheranism, into which he was seduced by Ridley. There is therefore no reason for rejecting the account in the text. Cranmer, urged by Ridley, accepted Lutheranism and entertained Peter Martyr; but afterwards, under the direction of the Pole à Lasco, held the Zuinglian or Calvinistic opinion on the Eucharist.

[1] Hugh Latimer, born probably A.D. 1491, in Thurcaston, Leicestershire, was educated at Cambridge, where he took his degrees as a zealous Catholic, and was cross-bearer of the university. He was perverted by Bilney, and at last, when known to be deep in heresy, was brought by Cranmer to preach at the court. Henry VIII. gave him the bishopric of Worcester, and he was consecrated by Cranmer Sept. 26, 1535, Gardiner assisting, but without Bulls or any sanction whatever of the Pope. He resigned his see in 1539, because he could no longer bear the constraint of Henry VIII. and the six articles.

[2] Traheron, writing from London, Sept. 28, 1548, to Bullinger (Original Letters, 151), says: "You must know that Latimer has come over to our opinion respecting the true doctrine of the Eucharist, together with the archbishop of Canterbury and the other bishops who heretofore seemed to be

The protector, the duke of Somerset, had a brother, Thomas Seymour, admiral of the fleet, who had married Catherine Parr, the last wife of Henry VIII., after the king's death.[1] Between her and the wife of the protector there sprung a quarrel about precedence, and the quarrel was not confined to the wives, it passed on to the husbands.[2] And as the rivalry grew from day to day, and as the protector's wife gave her husband no rest, matters came at last to this: the protector, who, though he ruled the king, was yet ruled by his wife, must put his brother to death,[3] that he might satisfy his ambition without let or hindrance. But as Thomas Seymour was innocent of everything for which he deserved to die, except heresy, and as the protector, himself a heretic, could not lay that to his brother's

Lutherans." In the Disputation of Oxford, April 1554, Latimer said (Remains, p. 265, ed. Parker Society), "I have long sought for the truth in this matter of the sacrament, and have not been of this mind past seven years; and my lord of Canterbury's book hath especially confirmed my judgment herein." He then, in answer to the question that he was a Lutheran, says, "No, I was a Papist; for I never could perceive how Luther could defend his opinion without transubstantiation." It seems that Latimer, in spite of his Lutheranism, never quite denied the doctrine of the Eucharist while Henry VIII. lived.

[1] Edward VI.'s Journal (Burnet v. 5, ed. Pocock) says, "The lord Seymour of Sudeley married the queen, whose name was Katerine, with which marriage the lord protector was much offended." Heylyn (Hist. Reform., p. 71) says, "That they might appear in greater splendour, he took into his hands the episcopal house belonging to the bishop of Bath and Wells, which being by him much enlarged and beautified, came afterwards to the possession of the earl of Arundel, best known of late times by the name of Arundel House."

[2] Foxe, vi. 283. "Now it happened—upon what occasion I know not—that there fell a displeasure betwixt the said queen and the duchess of Somerset, and therefore also in the behalf of their wives displeasure and grudge began between the brethren."

Sir John Hayward reports the like story in his Life of Edward VI.; but Strype, without any authority (Mem., ii. ii. 188), writes: "And verily all this is the less to be credited, viz., the controversy between the two wives for precedency, and the duchess of Somerset's setting her husband upon this mischief, because it is taken from lying Sanders, or at the best from vulgar report."

[3] Foxe, vi. 283. "As many there were who reported that the duchess of Somerset had wrought his death, so many more there were who . . . affirmed . . . that the fall of the one brother would be the ruin of the other."

charge, it was necessary to have recourse to falsehood. A charge is contrived without difficulty by another Jezebel; but the difficulty lay in making it public. They betake themselves to this new apostle of the English, Hugh Latimer. The protector persuaded him to denounce his brother as a traitor to the people in one of his sermons. Hugh Latimer, whose apostolate was that of lying, undertook the task. He went into the pulpit and said that Thomas Seymour had plotted against the life of the king, and therefore deserved to suffer death.[1] The people now did not shout as usual; it was ashamed of its own apostle, when it heard him falsely accusing an innocent man. Thomas Seymour, however, was found guilty of treason, and beheaded March 20 [1549].[2]

Many also in these days wrote admirable treatises in defence of the Catholic faith. Dr. Peryn,[3] of the Order

[1] John Burcher (Original Letters, 301), in a letter to Bullinger, March 12, 1549, says that the admiral "entered in the dead of night" a room close to that of the king with the intention of committing murder, and on the next morning, January 19, was committed to the Tower. Whether the story be true or not remains a question. Hooper (Original Letters, 29), writing to Bullinger, says "He was beheaded and divided into four quarters; with how much unwillingness he suffered death, Master John Utenhovius, who is the bearer of this letter, will fully explain to you by word of mouth." Latimer (Sermons, pp. 161, 162, ed. Parker Society) says "that he died very dangerously, irksomely, horribly. . . . But surely he was a wicked man; the realm is well rid of him: it hath a treasure that he is gone. He knoweth his fate by this, he is either in joy or in pain."

[2] The warrant for the execution was signed, among others, by the brother, the duke of Somerset, and Thomas Cranmer, archbishop of Canterbury. Upon this Burnet (Hist. Reform., ii. p. 187, ed. Pocock) says, "One particular seemed a little odd, that Cranmer signed the warrant for his execution, which being in a cause of blood was contrary to the canon law." He then proceeds to show his sense of that law, and ends by saying, "It seems that Cranmer thought his conscience was under no tie from those canons, and so judged it not contrary to his function to sign that order." Cranmer had released himself from other canons beside those, and it would be difficult to say what canons he held to be binding on him.

[3] William Peryn, born in Shropshire, and educated in Oxford, fled to the Continent in the beginning of the schism, and returned in the year 1543. He seems to have stained his profession in 1547 by his recantation of a sermon in defence of the doctrine of images. "In June," says

of St. Dominic, Dr. Smith,[1] the king's professor of theology in the University of Oxford, and Stephen, bishop of Winchester, surpassing all others in acuteness. When the Homilies, written in English, were brought to him, in which the doctrine of justification by faith only was wickedly and impiously set forth, he at once objected to them, saying that there was heresy in the Homilies, and that they ought never to be read in the hearing of the people.

And as he held this language, not only in private, but in the pulpit also, and most vehemently resisted, both by word of mouth and by writing, the heresy of Calvin and of Luther, not only in the matter of justification, but on very many other points, especially that of the Eucharist, he was thrown into prison on the last day of July.[2]

In the next year, about the feast of St. John the Bap-

Strype (Mem., ii. i. 61), "one Perin, a Black Friar, recanted in the parish church of St. Andrew, Undershaft, London."

[1] Richard Smith, born in Worcestershire, became a fellow of Merton College in Oxford in 1527, rector of Cuxham, then principal of St. Alban's Hall, reader of theology in Magdalene College, and finally master of Whittington College, London. When Henry VIII. founded the professorship of theology in Oxford, Dr. Smith was the first who held the chair. In the reign of Edward VI. he abandoned all his preferments, but was restored in the second year of queen Mary, made one of her chaplains, and also a canon of Christ Church. He lost all his preferments when Elizabeth obtained the throne, and was committed to the care of Matthew Parker at Lambeth, by whose persuasion he was brought again to make another recantation, if the account be true in the Life of Parker, De Antiquit. Britan. Eccles., 552, ed. Drake. He escaped at last and went abroad, was one of the first professors in the University of Douai, where he died July 9, 1563. Jewell, writing from Salisbury, June 1, 1560, to Peter Martyr, says he heard that Smith is in Wales "keeping a hired tavern." He had said in a former letter to the same person, written March 20, 1559, that he had been deprived of his professorship in Oxford for uncleanness of life. Both stories rest on the credit of Jewell. He is also said to have recanted more than once.

[2] This seems to be an error; it should have been June. Edward VI. in his Journal (Burnet, v. p. 7, ed. Pocock) wrote, "Upon St. Peter's Day the bishop of Winchester was committed to the Tower;" but it was not on that day. On that day the bishop preached before the king, and on the following day, June 30, was committed to the Tower. He had been in the Fleet also the year before, from Sept. 25 till the 7th day of Jan. 1548.

tist, the people of Cornwall and Devonshire,[1] when they saw their children baptized in a new fashion of which they had never heard before, and not in the ancient way to which they and their fathers had been accustomed;[2] when they saw that the sacrifice of the Mass had been utterly suppressed, and the altars, not those of Jupiter or Diana, but of God Almighty and the one Mediator Jesus Christ, everywhere thrown down and destroyed, they took it most grievously to heart, and flew to arms for the defence of the faith, and laid siege to Exeter. But while driving back with their arrows the troops of horsemen brought from Cleves,[3] they fell into disorder

[1] John Burcher in a letter to Bullinger, Aug. 25, 1549 (Original Letters, 306), says: "In the western part of England, which is divided into Cornwall and Devonshire, these rebels assembled in the months of June and July last, to the numbers it is believed of 16,000 men. The leaders of the rebels in the first place proclaimed deliverance to the people from the injustice and oppression of the nobility, who, partly by force and partly by fraud, had converted to their own use the pastures which formerly had been common. And for this cause the rebellion extended through all parts of England."

[2] Baptism was not only administered in English, but the administration was restricted to Sundays and other holy days. The sixth article of the "demands of the people" was: "We will that our curates minister the sacrament of baptism at all times, as well in the week day as on the holy day."

[3] Prevarication of the Holy Church's Liberties, chap. iv. s. 16, Eyston MS. The earl of Warwick, afterwards duke of Northumberland, "adviseth the protector to make a further progress in the English schism, thereby as well to ratify the Church lands already gotten, as to make a further sport of the Church's dowry; and because this could not be done without great difficulty, to call in some foreign forces, not directly in show for such a purpose, as too distasteful to the people, but under pretence to fetch the young queen of Scots in person for a wife to the king, according to a treaty begun by king Henry VIII. The protector conformeth himself to the advice, calleth in mercenary Germans; and, to blind the people, goeth personally into Scotland with a well-ordered army; being a manner of wooing not well liked by the earl of Huntley and other the Scots."

Burnet (Hist. Reform., iii. 329, ed. Pocock) says: "The true secret of it on both sides was this: the bulk of the people of England was still possessed with the old superstition to such a degree that it was visible they could not be depended on in any matter that related to the alterations that were made, or were designed to be made; whereas the Germans were full of zeal on the other side, so that they might well be trusted to: and the princes of Germany, who were then kept under by the emperor, so that they neither durst nor could keep their troops at home, but hoped they might at some better time have an occasion to use them, were willing to put them in the hands of the present government of England."

amid the baggage, which was left behind, either on purpose or because it could not be saved, and were routed by the troops which had fled, but now had returned to the fight. Thus the war came to an end, having no other issue than this: some of those who were concerned in it, we may believe, delivered their own souls out of heresy; it was not given them to deliver their brethren out of the slavery of Satan.

Many others, also, throughout the realm, especially in Norfolk, took up arms. The reasons they gave for their rising were the enclosures made wrongfully by the rich to the damage of the common people. Many parks of the noblemen were thrown open, fences destroyed, ditches filled, fishponds emptied, deer and rabbits stolen. Some lost their goods, and others their lives also. Thus God showed the men in power how wickedly they had done when they withdrew from the obedience of the Pope and of their fathers in God; for he who, contrary to the law, refuses to submit to his superior, is most justly disowned by his own subjects. But as the princes understood none of these things, God stirred up enemies abroad against them.

CHAPTER III.

QUARRELS OF THE EARL OF WARWICK AND THE DUKE OF SOMERSET—JOAN BOCHER—MARRIAGE OF PRIESTS—BUCER AND MARTYR—DISPUTATIONS IN OXFORD AND CAMBRIDGE.

THE French took advantage of these troubles, and attacked the forts and garrisons of the city of Boulogne, which still remained in the hands of the English; and John Dudley, earl of Warwick,[1] and afterwards duke of Northumberland, found therein a reason for censuring the government of the protector, and then having obtained the consent of the rest of the council, publicly charged him with maladministration of the state. The protector flew for safety to the castle of Windsor,[2] taking the king with him; but when he saw that the

[1] Sir John Dudley, "son to that Dudley" (Burnet, ii. 86) "who was attainted and executed the first year of king Henry VIII.'s reign," was made earl of Warwick Feb. 17, 1547, within a month of the accession of Edward VI., and Oct. 11, 1551, duke of Northumberland. He was also made earl marshall, after the execution of the duke of Somerset, and finally made himself master of the kingdom.

[2] Original Letters, No. 37. Hooper, writing from London, Feb. 5, 1550, to Bullinger, says: "On the 6th of October the king, together with the protector, fled from the palace, which we commonly call Hampton-Court, to another castle called in our language Windsor, for this reason, that the other members of the council in London had determined, as it was right they should, to make inquiry into the protector's conduct. Large numbers were collected by each party. As to myself, I determined not to interfere, because I had great enemies on both sides. The king was accompanied in his flight by his uncle the duke of Somerset, the archbishop of Canterbury, the comptroller of the household, and some of the lords of the bedchamber. All the other nobility and men of rank had lent their influence to the council, who conducted the affair in London. However, by the mercy of God, the business was at length settled without bloodshed."

whole nobility ranged themselves on the side of Warwick, and that his followers were few, he gave himself up, and was sent to prison October 14 [1549].[1] Later on, however, in the next year, on the 6th of February, he recovered his liberty, the earl of Warwick and he being reconciled. That friendship lasted but a short time, though the town of Boulogne, which was the seeming occasion of the quarrel between them, was, by the consent both of the protector and of the earl of Warwick, given up to the French on the 25th day of April.

Now, in order to bring the duke of Somerset the more assuredly within his power, the earl of Warwick promised certain persons—so it is said—whom he knew to be Catholics, to restore the Catholic religion, and to banish heresy, if they would help him to remove the protector. There was no reason for distrusting his word, for so great was his authority that he might well be able to perform his promise; besides, they knew that he hated the heresy, and that he was a man who believed either in the Catholic religion or in none. Accordingly they exerted themselves to the utmost of their power to bring down the protector and to throw him into prison. But when they reminded the earl of Warwick of his promise, he scowled at them, and told them that if they cared for their lives they would never again speak of restoring the Catholic religion.[2]

1 Original Letters, No. 37. "On the 14th of Oct. the duke of Somerset with some others was sent to the Tower of London, from whence he is not yet come out: but by the blessing of God he will be set at liberty either this evening or to-morrow."

2 Hooper, writing to Bullinger, Nov. 7, 1549 (Original Letters, 35), seems to refer to this arrangement. "My patron, who was first minister and protector, is in the Tower of London. . . . We are greatly apprehensive of a change in religion, but as yet no alteration has taken place." He writes again, Dec. 27: "We were in much alarm, and very great fear possessed the minds of the godly as to the success that the religion of Christ, just now budding forth in England, would meet with upon the fall of the duke of Somerset, who is still confined in the Tower of London. . . . No change in religion has taken place among us, and we hope that no alteration will be made hereafter."

Some of them took this exceedingly to heart, looking upon the earl of Warwick not only as a man who broke his word, but as one who used his authority oppressively, and therefore went over to the protector, whom they regarded as a man of gentler temper. Thereupon Sir Thomas Arundel, a man of influence and a Catholic, secretly visited the protector after his release from prison; but Dudley, on discovering the fact, had him, not long after, brought to the block, Sir Thomas dying in the peace of the Church.[1]

Jane Butcher, in the county of Kent, in addition to the profession of Calvinism, which she followed, denied, with Valentinus, that our Lord was incarnate of the Virgin Mary, who was but the channel through which He came into the world. Then, when she saw that the Calvinists disliked her opinion, she told them further that there was a time when even they believed that the body of Christ was in the Eucharist under the appearance of bread and wine, and that Anne Askew,[2] who denied it, was not long ago held to be a heretic and publicly burned. She, therefore, had no doubt that, as the Calvinists now believed all that Anne Askew then maintained, so before long they would believe that which she was holding now.[3] She was burned in Smithfield, London, May 12.[4]

[1] Feb. 26, 1552.

[2] Anne Askew, or Anne Kyme, recanted her heresies, before Bonner and others, March 20, 1544, and two years afterwards, in June or July 1546, being a heretic relapsed, was burned in Smithfield.—Foxe, v. 542, 550.

[3] Strype, Memorials, ii. i. p. 335. "When she was condemned to die for her denial of Christ's taking flesh of the Blessed Virgin, she said to the judges, 'It is a goodly matter to consider your ignorance. It was not long ago since you burned Anne Ascue for a piece of bread, and yet came yourselves soon after to believe and profess the same doctrine for which you burned her. And now, forsooth, you will needs burn me for a piece of flesh, and in the end you will come to believe this also, when you have read the Scriptures and understand them!' When she came to die in Smithfield, and Dr. Scory endeavoured to convert her, she scoffed at him, and said he lied like a rogue, and bade him go read the scriptures."

[4] Edward VI., in his journal, says that the execution of Joan of Kent took place May 2; so also Micronius,

Meanwhile the superintendents and their clergy, Lutherans as well as Calvinists, though some of them were religious, and others consecrated according to the Catholic rite, and therefore bound by the vow of chastity, in virtue of their ordination, according to the ancient and notorious custom of the Western Church, threw aside all sense of shame and took to themselves wives.[1] Then, when they saw that their children were not regarded as legitimate, but taken for bastards, or children born in adultery, they had recourse to the lay power of the civil parliament, petitioning it to make their children legitimate. Thereupon an act of Parliament[2] was made,

in a letter to Bullinger, from London, May 20, 1550 (Original Letters, No. 260): "A few days since, namely, on the 2d of May, a certain woman was burned alive for denying the incarnation of Christ." Cranmer pronounced her a heretic April 30, 1549, and delivered her over the same day to the secular arm; but she was "kept in hope of conversion," says the king in his journal, "and on the 30th of April the bishop of London and the bishop of Ely were to persuade her, but she withstood them, and reviled the preacher that preached at her death;" and well she might, for that preacher was Scory. The chronicle of the Grey Friars (ed. Camden Society, p. 66) says she said to Scory "that he lied like a knave." Stow (p. 604), having the chronicle probably before him, says he like, &c., omitting the offensive word. If she was burned on the 2d of May, the bishops of London and Ely had but brief conferences with her.

[1] Harpsfield, Treatise of Marriage, bk. iii. p. 99, Eyston MS.: "One Holgate, archbishop of York, a man about fourscore years of age, which had been a religious man also, married a young girl of fourteen or fifteen years of age, and yet, for three causes, she never was his wife: the one for that he had been a religious man, and had solemnly vowed chastity; the second for that he was a priest; and the third for that she was betrothed to another man, and by very force kept from him, as I have heard the party myself confess and complain in this queen's time, and that he intended to procure process out for him. But whether the archbishop's death, or some composition staid the suit, or to what end the matter came, I know not." Burnet had access to the council books, and he writes thus (Hist. Reform., iii. 344): "There was nothing that opened all men's mouths more than a complaint entered in the council book, made by one Norman against the archbishop of York, that he took his wife and kept her from him. The council gave such credit to this, that, as a letter was written to that archbishop not to come to Parliament, so they ordered a letter to be written to Sir Thomas Gargrave and Mr. Chaloner to examine the matter. What they did, or what report they made, does not appear to me. Holgate, during all the time he was archbishop of York, was more set on enriching himself than on anything else. He seemed heartily to concur in the reformation, but he was looked on as a reproach to it rather than a promoter of it."

[2] 2 & 3 Edw. VI. c. 21, sec. 2: "Be it therefore enacted . . . that all and every law and laws positive,

in which it was declared that no human law should bar the recognition for the future, as legitimate, of the children of priests. There was not much regard had to the divine law, for if anything therein seemed to be at variance with this declaration, it might be got over by a skilful interpretation.

Then when the Protestants saw that in learning and authority their ministers and superintendents were not regarded as the equals of the Catholic doctors, they sent, with the promise of higher payment, for Bucer,[1] a German by birth, and by profession a friar of the Order of St. Dominic, and at the same time for Peter Martyr,[2] a Florentine, and an Augustinian canon, then living at Strasburg. Bucer was made professor of theology in Cambridge, and Peter Martyr in Oxford, both being

canons, constitutions, and ordinances, made by authority of men only, which do prohibit or forbid marriage to any ecclesiastical or spiritual person or persons, . . . shall be utterly void and of none effect." But as the children born of these marriages were not said in the act to be children born in wedlock, people regarded the marriages with suspicion. Hence another act, 5 & 6 Edw. VI. c. 12, was passed to make the children legitimate, and to silence the clamours of those whom it calls "evil-disposed persons, perversely taking occasion of certain words and sentences in the same act comprised, have and do untruly and very slanderously report of priests' matrimony, saying that the statute is but a permission of priests' matrimony, as usury and other unlawful things be now permitted for the eschewing of greater inconveniences and evils."

[1] Martin Bucer was by birth an Alsatian, born in A.D. 1491, and perverted by reading the writings of Erasmus. He held the heresy of Luther on the Eucharist, but modified it in many ways, so that he became gradually nearer and nearer to Zuinglius and Calvin, but without adopting their more consistent heresy. He came to England accompanied by Paul Fagius, and was received on his arrival by Cranmer in Lambeth, April 25, 1549.—Original Letters, No. 159. Bucer had married a nun, and was the father of thirteen children. — Nat. Alexandr., Hist. Eccles., sæc. xv. et xvi. c. i. art. ii.

[2] Peter Martyr was born A.D. 1500, and is believed to have been perverted by reading the works of Bucer and Zuinglius. He was prior of the house of his order in Lucca, from whence he fled to Zurich, and settled at Strasburg, from which place he came to England, invited by the duke of Somerset and Cranmer. He arrived in England Dec. 20, 1547, bringing with him Bernardino Ochino, who in the following year was made a prebendary of Canterbury. Peter Martyr having stayed some time with the archbishop, went to Oxford as the king's professor of theology, and was made a canon of Christ Church in 1550.

Lutherans when they came to England.[1] Bucer remained a Lutheran to the end, and Peter Martyr held the same opinions at first, as may be seen in his writings; for in a disputation on the Eucharist, having to reply to the Zuinglian argument that Christ is in heaven, and therefore not in the Eucharist, he replied that the objection came from Satan. Afterwards seeing that the men then in power in England were Calvinists, he too went over to the opinions of Calvin.[2]

Be this as it may. Whilst he was lecturing in Oxford, many demanded of him, and that very frequently, a reason for the opinions he taught, and in particular Dr.

[1] Hooper, writing to Bullinger, April 26, 1549 (Original Letters, 30), says: "Master à Lasco will soon return into England. I greatly regret his absence, especially as Peter Martyr and Bernardine so stoutly defend Lutheranism, and there is now arrived a third, I mean Bucer, who will leave no stone unturned to obtain a footing. The people of England, as I hear, all of them entertain right notions upon that subject."

[2] This is confessed by Bucer (Gorham's Gleanings, p. 142): "I am well assured, however, that he [P. Martyr] by no means wished that the Supper of the Lord should be viewed as a mere administration of bread and wine: he acknowledges the presence and exhibition of Christ; but since the Zurich people have here [England] many and great followers, this excellent man was drawn, I hardly know how, to use the word 'signification,' although he added 'efficacious.'" Peter Martyr was charged with thus changing his opinions by Dr. Smith, and Cranmer (Jenkyns, iii. 12) thus sums up the charge as made by Dr. Smith: "Peter Martyr at his first coming to Oxford, when he was but a Lutheran in this matter, taught as Dr. Smyth now doth. But when he came once to the court, and saw that doctrine misliked them that might do him hurt in his living, he ever after turned his tippet and sang another song." Cranmer then says, by way of answer: "Of Mr. Peter Martyr his opinion and judgment in this matter, no man can better testify than I. Forasmuch as he lodged within my house long before he came to Oxford, and I had with him many conferences in that matter, and know that he was then of the same mind that he is now, and as he defended after openly in Oxford, and hath written in his book." But that is not the opinion of others, as may be seen in the two foregoing notes.

John ab Ulmis, writing to Bullinger from Oxford, May 10, 1548 (Original Letters, 184), says: "He [Martyr] has also maintained in like manner the cause of the Eucharist and holy supper of the Lord, namely, that it is a remembrance of Christ, and a solemn setting forth of His death, and not a sacrifice. Meanwhile, however, he speaks with caution and prudence, if indeed it can be called such, with respect to the real presence, so as not to seem to incline either to your opinion or to that of Luther." John ab Ulmis, who was a Zuinglian and friend of Bullinger, would not have written in this way if there had been no suspicion of Peter Martyr in his mind.

Richard Smith, who before him had sat in the chair in which he was then sitting. But he never ventured to dispute with them until he secured the presence of [Richard] Cox,[1] a heretic about the court, as his moderator, and knew that Dr. Smith, a most learned and keen disputant, had been driven away from Oxford.[2] Matters being thus arranged,[3] a disputation touching the Eucharist takes place, Peter Martyr defending the heresy of Calvin, Drs. Tresham[4] and Chedsey,[5] Catholics, oppos-

[1] Richard Cox, born at Whaddon, Bucks, A.D. 1499, educated at Eton and in King's College, Cambridge. Cardinal Wolsey placed him in the college he founded in Oxford, which he left for the headmastership of Eton. On the expulsion of the monks from Ely he was made prebendary of that church, being already an archdeacon. Afterwards he was made dean of Christ Church, and on the death of Longland, bishop of Lincoln, May 7, 1547, was elected chancellor of the university, "being in great favour," says Wood (Fast. Oxon., p. 87), "with the then king.... While the said Dr. Cox was chancellor of the university, he enacted many things that have been odious to posterity." To the deanery of Oxford he added that of Westminster, being also tutor to the king, and one of the canons of Windsor.

[2] Wood's Annals, ii. 91. "Smyth suspecting that all things would not go right on his side, that authority would back Martyr more than him, and that some tumult would be raised, did prudently abscond before the time came."

[3] Wood's Annals, ii. 92. On the departure of Smith, Peter Martyr put up a notice to this effect: "Doctor Smythus, ut in hac notissimum est academia, ad disputandum me publice provocavit. Quod cum annuissem et de quæstionibus una convenissemus tantumque expectandum tempus idoneum, abiisse dicitur."

"Cox began with an oration relating to the business to be taken in hand; that being done, the questions that were struck up with Martyr's provocation were propounded, as they follow:—

"1. In sacramento Eucharistiæ non est panis et vini Transubstantiatio in Corpus et Sanguinem Christi.

"2. Corpus et Sanguis Christi non sunt corporaliter aut carnaliter in pane et vino, neque ut alii dicunt sub speciebus panis et vini.

"3. Corpus et Sanguis Christi uniuntur pani et vino sacramentaliter."

[4] William Tresham, born in Newton, Northamptonshire, became a fellow of Merton College A.D. 1515, and registrar of the university 1523. He defended the divorce, and was made one of the canons of the first foundation of Christ Church A.D. 1532, and in 1546 a canon on the new foundation. In 1540 he was installed prebendary of Lincoln, and in 1542 became rector of Bugbrooke, where he died A.D. 1569, deprived of all his preferments. During his residence in Oxford he was twice vice-chancellor of the university.

[5] William Chedsey was a Somersetshire man, scholar and fellow of Corpus Christi College, Oxford, and chaplain of Dr. Bonner, bishop of London. He obtained the prebend of Twyford in St. Paul's in 1548, which he exchanged for that of Chiswick in 1554, according to Tanner, who refers to Bonner's register; but Le Neve is silent. In 1556

ing. When three days had been spent in that disputation, Cox, the moderator and a Calvinist, seeing Peter Martyr more hardly pressed than he expected, and almost driven from his chair by the stamping of feet and the clapping of hands, said that he had been summoned to London, and therefore could no longer remain as moderator in the disputation. He spoke highly of Peter Martyr, as if he had been victorious in the struggle, and then having exhorted the others to lead peaceable lives, brought the disputation to a close.[1] The disputation was after-

he was archdeacon of Middlesex, canon of Windsor, canon of Christ Church 1557, and in 1558 elected president of his college, Corpus Christi; and in 1559 was deprived of all he had, Elizabeth being queen. After the disputation with Peter Martyr, he began to "preach openly at Oxford against the steps of the Reformation that were made and making. Wherefore, March 16 [1550], he was committed to the Marshalsea for seditious preaching, where he lay till Nov. 11, 1551, and then he was ordered to be brought to the bishop of Ely's [Goodrich], where he enjoyed his table and an easier restraint."—Strype's Cranmer, bk. ii. chap. 21. "After his deprivation of the presidentship, he was, for denying the queen's supremacy in ecclesiastical matters, clapped up in prison, called the Fleet, in London, where he died about the year 1561."—Wood, in the Account of Corpus Christi College.

[1] The disputation was begun May 28, 1549, and, according to Strype and others, lasted four days, and not three, as is said in the text. But the statement in the text is supported by the confession of Cox himself, who in putting an end to the contest on the fourth day, said, "Peregimus quatuor dimidiatos dies in excutiendis duabus questionibus;" so that it seems he closed the disputation in the beginning of the fourth day, when only two out the three questions had been discussed. "To whom the laurel was given," says Wood (Annals, p. 93), "let others judge from their disputations that are, if true, printed, though that of Chedsey is not altogether agreeable to the MS. which is in Corpus Christi College Library, given thereto by him, if I mistake not. The Protestant writers say it was given to Martyr, the Roman Catholic to their party; and that also Dr. Smyth put him to silence divers times before he left Oxford. The truth is, had not Cox the moderator favoured Martyr, and helped him at several dead lifts, he had been shamefully exposed to the scorn of the auditory. But so it was that authority backed him, and favoured little or nothing the other party. Much more I could say of this matter, but I forbear, lest I seem partial. . . . All that I shall say is that such irreverence was before and at this time used by the generality of the Protestant theologists in their disputations, preachings, readings, and discourses concerning the sacrament of the Body and Blood, as also by the vulgar in their common talks, rhymes, songs, plays, and gestures, which sober and impartial men did abhor to hear, that an act of Parliament was a little before this time made to repress it, which being not rightly understood by the Academians, or else that they

wards published by Peter Martyr, but, as is the custom of heretics, not honestly. Certainly the university regarded him as twice beaten: once when he refused to dispute with Dr. Smith, then in this disputation, when he could not reply to the arguments of those who disputed with him. A disputation held in Cambridge between the theologians of that university and Bucer had a like result.[1]

were too nice in the observance of it. . . . For whereas the sacrament was lately delivered unto such communicants in a small round wafer called commonly *sacramentum altaris,* and that such parts thereof that were received from time to time were hanged over the altar in a pyx or box: those zealous ones in hatred to the Church of Rome reproached it by the odious names of 'Jack-in-a-box,' 'round-robin,' 'sacrament of the halter,' and other names so unbecoming the mouths of Christians that they were never taken up by the Turks or infidels," &c.

[1] Foxe (vi. 335) says that the conclusions to be disputed were—

"1. The canonical books of Holy Scripture alone do sufficiently teach the regenerated all things necessarily belonging unto salvation.

"2. There is no Church in earth which erreth not in manners as well as in faith.

"3. We are so justified freely of God, that before our justification it is sin, and provoketh God's wrath against us, whatever good work we seem to do. Then being justified, we do good works."

CHAPTER IV.

DOCTORS AND CONFESSORS—FECKENHAM—JOLIFFE—CRISPIN AND MOREMAN—DR. WATSON—ANTONIO BUONVISI—HARPSFIELD—CARDINAL POLE—GARDINER.

PUBLIC disputations on the Eucharist, as a sacrifice and as a sacrament, were held not only in the Universities of Oxford and Cambridge, but in many other places also, especially between Hooper, the superintendent of Gloucester, and Dr. Feckenham,[1] who excelled in theological learning; between Harley,[2] the superintendent of Hereford, and Henry Joliffe,[3] a Catholic priest. The frivolous objections of Harley were solidly overthrown by the bishop of Winchester, to whom the disputation was brought when he was in prison. Peter Martyr also had gathered together not a few objections against the doctrine of the Eucharist, and had written a book in which they were contained; these, too, the bishop refuted, and the refutation was published under the name of Marcus Constantius, that the real author might not

1 John Howman was born at Feckenham in Worcestershire, and became a Benedictine in the abbey of Evesham. He went from the abbey to Gloucester Hall, Oxford, being then only eighteen years old, and his studies completed, returned to Evesham. On the dissolution of the abbey, 1535, he returned to Oxford. In 1569 he was one of Bonner's chaplains. He was often imprisoned under Edward VI., and in the reign of queen Mary was made dean of St. Paul's, and then on the refounding of Westminster was made abbot. Queen Elizabeth turned him adrift, and shut him up with the other prisoners in Wisbeach Castle, where he died in 1585.

2 John Harley was of Magdalene College, Oxford, bishop of Hereford in 1553, and expelled the next year; being a married man.

3 Henry Joliffe was of Clare Hall, Cambridge, proctor of the university 1536, and prebendary of Worcester 1544. He was made dean of Bristol 1554, and died in exile 1573.

be discovered, and the severities of his prison be made still harder to bear.

There is also on the same question a learned book by Dr. Langdale,[1] who unravelled the captious sophistries of Ridley directed at the Eucharist. Must I speak of the sermons and the writings of those most grave priests Crispin and Moreman,[2] and of their imprisonment also? Of the admirable sermons of Henry Cole,[3] and of his long imprisonment borne for the Catholic faith? Of the constancy and the patient endurance of Thomas Watson[4] before he became bishop of Lincoln, and of his colleague Dr. Seton?[5]

[1] Alban Langdale, born in Yorkshire, and educated at St. John's College, Cambridge, was made rector of Buxted, Sussex, in 1556, being then archdeacon of Chichester. He was deprived of all he had under queen Elizabeth. The book is "Confutatio Catholica Nicolai Ridlæi determinationis de Eucharistia. Paris, 1556."

[2] Cranmer, in his answer to the eleventh demand of the Devonshire insurgents in 1549, thus speaks of these priests: "And to declare to you plainly the qualities of Crispin and Moreman, and how unmeet they be to be your teachers, they be persons very ignorant in God's Word, and yet thereto very wilful, crafty, and full of dissimulation. For if they were profoundly learned, and of sincere judgments, as they be not, they might be godly teachers of you." Moreman was one of the disputants in convocation, A.D. 1553, against Philpot.

[3] Henry Cole, born at Godshill, Isle of Wight, educated in Winchester school, whence he proceeded to New College, Oxford, being admitted fellow of the house 1523. He went to Italy to perfect himself in civil law, and on his return, 1540, practised in the Court of Arches, being made a prebendary of St. Paul's. He was elected warden of New College, Oct. 4, 1542, having been ordained deacon in the beginning of that year; then rector of Newton Longville. He had favoured the Reformation during the lifetime of Henry VIII., but on the accession of Edward VI. resigned all his preferments. On the accession of queen Mary he was made archdeacon of Ely 1553, dean of St. Paul's, London, 1556, and in the next year vicar-general of Cardinal Pole, archbishop of Canterbury. He preached the sermon at the burning of Cranmer, and on the accession of Elizabeth was deprived of all his benefices, imprisoned first in the Tower, and then in the Fleet, where he died Feb. 4, 1579, in the eighty-seventh year of his age.

[4] Thomas Watson, master of St. John's College, Cambridge, Sept. 28, 1553; dean of Durham, Nov. 18, in the same year. In 1557 he was made bishop of Lincoln, from which see he was driven by Elizabeth, June 25, 1559, and made a prisoner first in London, then in Wisbeach Castle, where he died Sept. 27, 1584. His sermons on the seven sacraments, with a biographical notice, have been recently edited by the Rev. T. E. Bridgett, of the Congregation of the Most Holy Redeemer.

[5] John Seton or Seyton was of St. John's College, Cambridge, and

Time would fail me if I were to speak by name of all those who in these days, on account of the Catholic faith, were driven out of their benefices or their colleges, and then were made to suffer the more grievous pains of bonds and imprisonment. John Storey,[1] a doctor of

one of the chaplains of Gardiner, and made a prebendary of Winchester 1553.

[1] John Storey was educated in Hinksey Hall, Oxford, and in 1537 was principal of Broadgates Hall. He was vicar-general of Bonner 1539, sitting also in the House of Commons. Soon after uttering the words in the text in his place in Parliament, he fled the country, but returned in the reign of Mary, and, according to Tanner, was made chancellor of London. When Elizabeth came to the throne, his life and liberty were threatened. Parkhurst, the Protestant bishop of Norwich, writing to Bullinger, May 31, 1562 (Zurich Letters, No. 48), says, "Story, that little man of law, and most impudent Papist, has been arrested, as I understand, in the west of England, 'in his barrister's robes.'" The words of Parkhurst are "*more aulico*," and according to the "Declaration of the Life and Death of John Story, London, 1571," he was "taken in the west country riding before a mail in a frieze coat like a serving man, and was apprehended in the highway by one Mr. Ayleworth, one of the queen's servants," and sent to prison. He made his escape, however, and went to Louvain with his wife and children. But he was soon troubled with many fears, for he thought he had done wrong in escaping from death, whereby he lost the crown of martyrdom. He wanted much to return, and consulted Dr. Sander, who, however, would not take it upon himself to advise or sanction his return. The greater part of his time he now spent in the Carthusian monastery, and if his wife had consented, would have entered religion. Some of his kindred made their escape from England and came to him, who was already poor, having lost all he had, and he knew not what to do to provide for himself, his wife, children, and grandchildren. He was then offered the place of searcher of ships, and though his friends dissuaded him from undertaking that employment, unfitting him, his poverty prevailed. The merchants who traded in contraband goods, finding their gains lessened, determined to be revenged; and they suborned one of his friends, who deceived him and inveigled him on board a ship ready to sail. "After he had entered the ship," writes Horn to Bullinger (Zurich Letters, No. 98, 1st series), "and was prying about in every corner, and had just gone down into the interior of the vessel, they suddenly closed the hatches" and sailed for England. He was then placed in the Lollard's tower, and afterwards lodged in the Tower. May 26, 1571, he was arraigned in Westminster Hall. He declined to plead or defend himself, beyond saying that he was not a subject of the queen. The judges condemned him to death, and the night before his martyrdom he was allowed to have Dr. Feckenham, the abbot of Westminster, with him. June 1st he was drawn on a hurdle to Tyburn from the Tower, where he was hung, drawn, and quartered because he would not acknowledge the supremacy of Elizabeth and deny the supremacy of the Pope. Cecil, the earl of Bedford, and Lord Hunsdon were present at the martyrdom. "His head," says Stow, p. 669, "set on London Bridge, and his quarters on the gates of the city."

canon and civil law, went into exile because, while speaking in Parliament in defence of the faith, he ventured at last to repeat the words of Solomon,[1] "Woe to thee, O land, whose king is a child."

An Italian, Antony Bonwise,[2] lived in England, a great merchant, great not only in his wealth, but much more so in his reputation as a man of integrity and honour. He had always had a great respect for Sir Thomas More; and now, seeing even the traces of the Catholic faith being removed from England, went to live in the University of Louvain, not indeed to carry on his business as a merchant of this world, but to attend to the business of the next. Louvain was then the nearest harbour of the faith to which Englishmen driven out for the faith might run for refuge. There he gathered around him and comforted those who were in exile for the faith, especially the physician John Clement[3] and his wife, John Storey, and that great light of all England, Nicholas Harpsfield,[4] who after-

[1] Eccles. x. 16.

[2] Antonio Buonvisi was, according to Dod (vol. i. p. 201), "a native of Lucca, who resided several years in London, where he assisted Sir Thomas More with many conveniences while he was prisoner."

[3] John Clement, educated at Oxford, was tutor to the children of Sir Thomas More. He returned to Oxford about A.D. 1519, and was professor of Greek on the foundation of Cardinal Wolsey, and applied himself later to medicine, and was a fellow of the College of Physicians in London. He went abroad in the reign of king Edward, returning under Mary, when he practised medicine in Essex, and finally into exile on the accession of Elizabeth. He had married Margaret, brought up by Sir Thomas More with his own children, and died in Mechlin July 1, 1572, nearly two years after his wife, who went to her rest July 6, 1570. He once complained to Dr. Stokesley, bishop of London, of the corruption into which men had sunk. The answer of the bishop was, "*Vendidimus primogenita*" ("we have sold the right of our primogeniture"), "meaning," says Harpsfield (Treatise of Marriage, bk. iii. p. 136, Eyston MS.), "of the removing of the obedience of the See Apostolic."

[4] Nicholas Harpsfield, born in London, educated at Winchester and New College, Oxford, of which house he became a fellow A.D. 1535; principal of White Hall, 1544; professor of Greek, 1546; in exile for the faith during the reign of Edward VI. He returned A.D. 1553, took his degree of doctor of laws, and practised in the Court of Arches. Archdeacon of Canterbury 1554, being then a prebendary of St. Paul's; judge in the Court of Arches, dean of the

wards in the reign of Elizabeth suffered a lengthened imprisonment; also John Boxall,[1] a man of great learning and honour, and the lawyer, William Rastall,[2] with his wife, who died in Louvain.

Reginald, Cardinal Pole, was then living in Rome—hope of England, glory of the Roman Church, and light of Christendom. He had written four books, full of learning, in defence of the unity of the Church, and addressed them to Henry VIII. Not reaping therefrom the fruit he expected, he wrote a fifth book,[3] addressed to Edward VI., king of England, for he would leave nothing undone that he considered to be for the welfare of his country. After the death of Paul III., who had made him a cardinal, he might have been elected to the sovereign Pontificate if he had desired that great dignity, for nearly two-thirds of the votes were given him;[4] but he chose to forego that high eminence, chiefly for the sake of gaining the more abundant merit of not seeking it, and that he might reserve himself for the task of restoring his most cherished country, by his per-

peculiars of Canterbury, 1558. On the death of Mary he refused to acknowledge the supremacy of the crown, and was thrown into prison, wherein he was kept for more than twenty years, released, not by the queen, but by death, in 1583.

[1] John Boxall, a member of queen Mary's council, dean of Peterborough, Norwich, and Windsor. "On the 4th of March, Boxall, a notorious Papist and secretary to queen Mary, died at Lambeth."—Parkhurst's Letter to Bullinger, Aug. 10, 1571; Zurich Letters, No. 99, 1st Series.

[2] William Rastall, a nephew of Sir Thomas More, whose sister was his mother; his wife was Winifred, daughter of John Clement. She died in Louvain at the end of his first exile, July 7, 1553. He returned to England, and was one of the judges under queen Mary. He went into exile again under Elizabeth, and died at Louvain, aged fifty-seven, Aug. 27, 1565.

[3] Reginaldi Poli, Cardinalis Britanni, Epistola ad Edw. VI., Angliæ regem. Printed by Schelhorn in his "Amœnitates Ecclesiasticæ," vol. i., and in the "Bibliographia Critica" of Fr. Michael de St. Joseph, vol. iv. p. 24.

[4] Vita Reginaldi Poli, p. 21. Venet., 1563. "De eo cum suffragia recenserentur, inventa sunt xxviii. atque in his Gallorum duo quæ illum Pontificem Max. declararent, ita ut ad Pontificatum consequendum duo omnino deessent. Id Polo magnæ voluptati fuit."

sonal labours, to the unity of the Church.[1] Richard Pate,[2] also, bishop of Worcester, lived in Rome, as did Thomas Goldwell,[3] now bishop of St. Asaph, and Maurice Clenock,[4] afterwards bishop elect of Bangor.

[1] Harpsfield, Treatise of Marriage, bk. iii. p. 133, Eyston MS. "I add here that the great integrity and modesty of the said Cardinal, free from all importunate ambition of all worldly honour, wherewith the other prelate [Cranmer] was overwhelmed and drowned, is otherwise also more notable, as of one that refused the very high and supreme dignity of the Papacy of Rome, whereto he was by the Cardinals lawfully elected, for whose consent they stayed their election of any other person two whole months, a thing that was never read or heard of, I trow, before in any Pope's election, and yet could they not win his consent. This thing as it is of itself most notable, so it should be to us Englishmen most comfortable. For unless I be greatly dedeceived, one of the greatest causes of his refusal proceeded from the fatherly tender love he bore to this his native country, whose reformation he desired of all other things, and would reserve himself free, if ever God did send a meet time, to help forward in his own person that holy work and business of our reformation, whereof it seemed he was not without hope, but looked and longed for it, and hoped to be a worker therein."

[2] Richard Pate. Godwin (De Præsulibus Angl., p. 470) says that Pate was made bishop of Worcester in 1534, and that he was sent abroad on an embassy, and never returned to take possession of the see he had accepted. Wharton says nothing of this. Neither Stubbs nor Godwin gives the date of his consecration. Strype in his Mem., iii. i. 257, writes thus: "This Pate had lived abroad many years, and had long been attainted under king Henry VIII. for taking the bishopric of Worcester from the Pope. He had holden a secret correspondence with the Pope, and was excepted out of the last general pardon under king Edward VI. But now [A.D. 1554] his attaint was taken off, and he restored to his see of Worcester, long since bestowed on him by the Pope, but never enjoyed till now." He was made bishop of Worcester in July 1541, and was at Trent in 1552, taking his place, according to his consecration, between the bishop of Syracuse and the bishop of Strasburg, as is shown by Nicholas Pseaume, bishop of Verdun—"Hugo, sacræ Antiquitatis Monumenta," p. 323. His name is disfigured there by the copyist into "Richardus Palus, episcopus Wormiensis."

[3] Thomas Goldwell, born in Kent about 1500, and educated at All Souls College, Oxford, rector of Cheriton, near Canterbury, 1531. He left England in the beginning of the schism and entered the family of Cardinal Pole, where he was for a time, and then became a Theatine. He came back on the accession of Mary, and was made bishop of St. Asaph. On the accession of Elizabeth he went again into exile, returned to Rome, where he lived in great honour and veneration till his death, April 3, 1585, the last of the bishops of England. See the account of his life by the Rev. Fr. Knox, D.D., of the London Oratory.

[4] Maurice Clenock, born in Wales, educated in the University of Oxford, "where he chiefly applied himself to the canon law, and was about six years professor in that faculty; at the same time a progress in divinity and proceeding doctor. In queen Mary's reign he was a prebendary of York, almoner and sec-

Towards the end of the fourth year of the reign of Edward VI., on the 17th day of December [1550], the tide in the Thames, departing from the natural course, rose and fell three times within the space of nine hours.[1] People regarded it as a portent, and connected it with the unjust harassing of Stephen bishop of Winchester,[2] especially as he was taken then by water, when that unusual tide occurred, to make his defence of the faith. Be that, however, as it may, Gardiner, who had resolutely spoken everywhere in defence of the faith, was a month or two afterwards deprived of his see, and a Calvinist, Poynet by name, translated from Rochester, was put in his place.

retary to Cardinal Pool, as also chancellor of the Prerogative Court of Canterbury. Upon the decease of William Glyn, bishop of Bangor, who died in May 1558, Dr. Clenock was nominated by the queen his successor, but was never consecrated. After queen Elizabeth ascended the throne, he was obliged to surrender all his preferments, for refusing to comply with the court measures."—Dod, Church Hist., vol. i. p. 513.

[1] Greyfriars' Chronicle: "The 15th day of December 1550 was brought from the Tower of London unto Lambeth the bishop of Winchester, then being Dr. Stephen Gardiner, . . . and the 18th day following, thither again, and that same day was two tides at London Bridge within the space of five hours." The Chronological Historian, by W. Toone, Esq., i. 163: "The Thames ebbed and flowed three times in nine hours below the bridge."

[2] The bishop was a prisoner in the Tower, from which he was taken to the court in Lambeth Palace, in which sat as commissioners of the king, Cranmer, Ridley, Thirlby bishop of Ely, Holbeach bishop of Lincoln, Sir William Petre, Sir James Hales of the Court of Common Pleas, Dr. Griffith Leyson, Dr. John Oliver, Richard Goodrich and John Gosnold, Esquires. They opened their court Dec. 15, 1550, and sat till Saturday, Feb. 14, 1551. On that day, in their twenty-second session, they sentenced him to the loss of his bishopric—notwithstanding his formal appeal "to the king's majesty" made before they pronounced their decision—"by authority of a commission by the high and mighty prince, our most gracious sovereign lord Edward VI., king of England, France, and Ireland, defender of the faith, and of the Church of England and also of Ireland, in earth the supreme head." Foxe, Acts and Monuments, vi. ed. Cattley, contains a full report of the process.

CHAPTER V.

DEBASING OF THE COIN—PONET—HOOPER.

In the fifth year of king Edward, by a public proclamation, July 9th [1551], the silver coin throughout England was lessened one-fourth in value, and forty days afterwards another fourth part was taken away from the value of all the silver coin current. Henceforward every pound in silver was to pass for half the former value, every shilling and every penny to pass current as if they were coins of sixpence and one halfpenny. Thus a man to-day possessed of one hundred pounds in money lost fifty pounds in forty days, though he had not suffered shipwreck, though he had not been taken by the enemy and robbed, and though no person whatsoever had cheated him.[1] Such taxation was never made before, namely, that every man without exception should pay the half of all the money he had in his possession. The people, indeed, never imagined that they were paying more than one-half, when, meanwhile, they were in reality paying to the last farthing, and therefore paying even more than the whole.

For the right understanding of this matter we must keep in mind that after the beginning of the schism

[1] Edward VI. in his journal (Burnet, v. 41) says, under July 9, "Proclamation made that a testorn should go at 9d. and a groat at 3d. in all places of the realm at once." Strype (Memorials, ii. i. 486) adds, "And in August . . . the teston was again cried down from ninepence to sixpence, the groat from threepence to twopence, and the twopence to a penny, the penny to an halfpenny, and the halfpenny to a farthing."

Henry VIII. began to turn into dross the silver money of pure coinage. Then they who made the schism of Henry still more grievous, lowered continually the intrinsic value of the coin till at last there were hardly more than two parts of silver left, instead of twelve. Again, as it became impossible to issue money that was more worthless and more debased, when the people had paid their money according to one price, and when they should have received that money back again at the same price, lo! a proclamation is made that they are to receive what they had paid only at half the former value. Certain coins, too, of the king, issued at a certain value, were taken, some at one-fourth, others at one-sixth of that first value. He who will take all these frauds into account will easily see that the English people were robbed more than once in the course of a few years of all their money.[1]

To this was added intolerable extortions by the more powerful everywhere; these people, foreseeing the coming depreciation of the coin—they were the advisers of it—paid their debts to their creditors, and their wages to their servants, and bought estates, paying for them in money one day which they knew would on the morrow be current for less than one-fourth its nominal value. All these wrong-doings God, in His infinite mercy, permitted, that the people might learn even in this way what unjust stewards of the grace of God and of His heavenly gifts they must be who could not honestly administer their temporal affairs. The words of truth are, "He who is unjust in little, is unjust also in the greater. If then you have not been faithful in the unjust mam-

[1] Hooper, writing to Bullinger, April 8, 1549 (Original Letters, 28), says, "A new gold coinage is now being struck in England of a purer standard than that which was coined under the late king; but what is increased in one way is diminished in another, for the standard weight of the crowns is diminished by nearly a fourth part."

mon, who will trust you with the true?"[1] The truth taught in the gospel, then, is this: they who so wickedly cheated the people in worldly things never could be true and faithful stewards of the mysteries of God. And yet these were they who had the sovereign direction of sacred things; we must, therefore, not be surprised if they taught the people heresy instead of the Catholic faith.

In the same year [1551] a certain disease, called the sweating sickness, raged in England; in the city of London alone eight hundred persons died of it within a week,[2] and many thousands throughout the country. Ford,[3] the second master of Winchester school, perverted Joliffe, the head boy, and made him a Calvinistic heretic. He in his turn brought over the other boys, for the

[1] St. Luke xvi. 10, 11.

[2] Burcher, writing to Bullinger, Aug. 3, 1551 (Original Letters, 321), says, "A pestilence called the sweating sickness has been prevalent in London. More than nine hundred died in one week." "It grew so much," says Edward VI. (Burnet, v. 41), "for in London the 10th day there died 70 in the liberties, and this day [July 11] 120." Heylyn (Hist. Ref., p. 110, ed. 1661) says, "And that which was most strange of all, no foreigner which was then in England—four hundred French attending here, in the hottest of it, on that king's ambassadors — did perish by it: the English being singled out tainted and dying of it, in all other countries, without any danger to the natives." Stow (p. 605) says, "This sickness followed Englishmen as well within the realm as in strange countries, wherefore this nation was much afeared of it, and for the time began to repent and remember God, but as the disease relented the devotion decayed. The first week died in London 800 persons."

[3] Strype (Memorials, iii. i. 276), "Mr. William Ford, sometime scholar, and after usher of Wickham College beside Winchester," he was supposed to be a destroyer of images as early as 1535 or 1536.

Prevarication of the Holy Church's Liberties, chap. iv. s. 21, Eyston MS. "One Ford had infected one Jolife, a forward young man in Winchester College, with Calvinism, and Jolife spread his infection of heresy to others. But Jolife, with all those that adhered to him, were—as it was then noted — taken away with the sweating sickness, and such others as were converted from their errors by one White, a devout and religious man, all which, nevertheless, the statists had not the grace to make use of, for Dudley earl of Warwick, during the commitments of the protector, had said to Sir Antony Brown, afterwards Viscount Mountacute, moving him amongst others for the restoration of Catholic religion, that albeit he knew the Roman religion to be the true religion, yet seeing a new religion was begun, run dog, run devil, he would go forward."

most part, to his opinion. God visited this Joliffe and others, some of whom were of kin to him, and the rest his friends, and brought this sickness upon them. Then He brought them to salutary penance through the preaching of that most saintly man John White,[1] and soon after took them away by death. All the other boys, nearly two hundred in number, were either converted to the Catholic faith or so strengthened therein, that in after-life, by telling the story of this divine visitation, they brought many others back from the heresy of Calvin to the unity of the Catholic Church.

Poynet,[2] in possession of the see of Winchester, though he wished to be considered a bishop, thought it a little matter to take a wife; so he took away from her husband the wife of a butcher[3] who was still living, and who by

[1] John White, born in Fornham, educated at Winchester and New College, Oxford, of which he became a fellow in 1527. He was made head-master of Winchester in 1534, and soon after warden; bishop of Lincoln in 1554, and in 1556 translated to Winchester, from which see he was driven by Elizabeth, 1559. He preached the sermon at the burial of queen Mary, and in doing so, says Sir John Harington (Briefe View, &c., p. 60, ed. 1653), "fell into such an unfeigned weeping that for a long space he could not speak." He died at South Warnborough, Jan. 11, 1560.

[2] John Poynet or Ponet was born in Kent and educated at Cambridge. He was one of Cranmer's chaplains, who gave him the benefice of St. Michael, Crooked Lane, London. He held also the vicarage of Ashford, the rectory of Towyn, Merionethshire, and a canonry in Canterbury, all of which he kept, with the bishopric of Rochester, which Edward VI. gave him in 1550. On the deprivation of Gardiner in that year the king gave him Winchester, but only in name, for, according to Strype (Mem., ii. ii. 166), he had but "2000 marks a year settled upon him: the rest of the temporalities of this rich bishopric was taken into the king's hands, who bestowed most of the good manors and lands thereof upon several of his courtiers." Ponet was in the rebellion of Wyatt, but seeing that it was failing, "he took his leave" (says Stow, p. 620) "of his secret friends, and said he would pray unto God for their good success, and so did depart, and went into Germany, where he died." He is said to have died at Strasburg, Aug. 11, 1556.

[3] Chron. of the Greyfriars, p. 70, ed. Camden Society. "And the xxvii. day of the same monyth [July 1551] the byshoppe of Wynchester that was than, was devorsyd from hys wyffe in Powlles, the whyche was a bucheres wyff of Nottynggam, and gave here husband a sartyne mony a yere dureynge hys lyffe as it was jugydde by the law." See also Machyn's Diary, p. 8. Burnet (v. 603, ed. Pocock) charges Sander

process of law obtained restitution of her. Some time afterwards a nobleman speaking to Gardiner, partly in jest and partly in mockery, said, "Perhaps you expect some day to recover your bishopric." Gardiner replied, "Why should I not expect? the butcher has recovered his wife." Gardiner's bishopric and the butcher's wife had been taken possession of by one and the same man.

There was also another false prophet, in bad odour not only for his hypocrisy, but for his heresy as well. When he was but a private person he used to slander the Catholic bishops,[1] reproaching them with the state they kept, and their possession of too abundant riches.[2] He, made a superintendent[3]—for so these Calvinists call by a Latin name those whom our forefathers, using a Greek word, called bishops[4]—took to himself two bishoprics at once, the sees of Gloucester and of Worcester.[5]

with the inventing of this story, and calls it a "forgery." Ponet is the author of the Short Catechism published in the reign of Edward VI. in Latin and in English, and ordered by the king to be used, having been "written," says the king, "by a certain godly and learned man." The Catechism has been reprinted in the volume of "The Two Liturgies," by the Parker Society.

[1] Micronius to Bullinger, May 29, 1559 (Original Letters, 260): "Only he stirred up some lazy noblemen and bishops against himself, especially because he exhorted the king and council to a more complete reformation of the Church."

[2] Micronius, writing from London, Aug. 14, 1551, to Bullinger (Original Letters, 265), says of Hooper: "I pray you to exert your influence in recommending to him meekness and gentleness. Exhort Mistress Anna, his wife, not to entangle herself with the cares of this life. Let her beware of the thorns by which the word of God is choked. It is a most dangerous thing for one who is in the service of Christ to hunt after riches and honours. Your admonitions will have much weight with them both."

[3] Christopher Hales, writing from London to Rodolph Gualter, May 24, 1550 (Original Letters, 99), says, "Hooper was made bishop of Gloucester two days since, but under godly conditions, for he will not allow himself to be called Rabbi, or my lord, as we are wont to say; he refuses to receive the tonsure, he refuses to become a pie, and to be consecrated and anointed in the usual way."

[4] Strype, Memorials, ii. ii. 141. "The bishops had exercised so much dominion and rigour, and been such "Papalins," that the very name of bishop grew odious among the people, and the word 'superintendent' began to be affected and come in the room; and the rather, perhaps, being a word used in the Protestant churches of Germany. This the Papists made sport with."

[5] The bishopric of Worcester was

Miles Coverdale[1] also, after a long residence in Germany, returned to England, drunk bodily through his intemperate indulgence in wine, and mentally through his excessive affection to heresy. The man hearing that the University of Oxford was earnestly devoted to the Catholic faith, and unwillingly giving way to heresy, went to Oxford,[2] promising himself great things, and purposing to bring about the perversion of many. He mounted the pulpit and told the people, expecting wondrous things, that he was about to speak on the very gravest of questions—the Sacrament of the Altar. He began by saying that he was one in whom they could

by far the better endowed, but Hooper obtained a royal dispensation, on taking possession of Worcester, to hold Gloucester *in commendam;* and Foxe (vi. 643) defends the process by saying that Hooper "so ruled and guided either of them, and both together, as though he had in charge but one family."

[1] Miles Coverdale was born in the parish of Coverham, in the North Riding of Yorkshire, and entered the Augustinian House, Cambridge, of which Barnes, burned at Smithfield A.D. 1540, was afterwards prior. He employed himself much in translating the Scriptures, and was afterwards diligent in the service of Cromwell searching out the priests who had not mutilated the Breviary and the Missal by blotting out the names of St. Thomas of Canterbury and of the Pope. On the death of Cromwell he fled the country, and kept a school in Bergzabern, and married. He returned in the reign of Edward VI., and was made one of the royal chaplains. He accompanied the troops sent down to Devonshire, when the people rose in defence of the faith, and became vicar-general of the bishop of Exeter. The bishop soon after resigned, and Coverdale was put in his place. In the reign of Mary he was ordered into prison, but the king of Denmark interceded for him, and he was allowed to go abroad. John Macbee, a Scotch preacher in Denmark, having married a sister of Coverdale's wife, had prevailed upon the king to interpose his good offices on his behalf. On the accession of Elizabeth he returned again, and was employed in the consecration of Parker, but never readmitted to be a bishop. He accepted the benefice of St. Magnus, London Bridge, and died in Feb. 1569, aged eighty-one. On his being made bishop of Exeter, he received from Edward VI. a licence to preach, and also a licence to him "and Elizabeth his wife, during their lives, with five or six at their table, to eat flesh and white meats in Lent and on other fasting days."—Strype, Memorials, ii. ii. 266. See Rymer, Fœdera, vi. iii. 214.

[2] Peter Martyr, writing to Bullinger from Oxford, April 25, 1551 (Original Letters, No. 232), says that Hooper "was here with me at Oxford three days before Easter, together with Michael Coverdale, a most effective preacher, and one who deserves well of the gospel. Both of them preached to our people at Oxford, and attended my public exposition of the Epistle to the Romans."

rightly place the utmost confidence touching this controversy. He knew, he said, that the Catholics believed in transubstantiation, that the Lutherans taught the impanation of Christ, that the Zuinglians held the sacrament to be but a type and figure of Christ, and that Calvin allowed it to be only a certain virtue and power; but he, Coverdale, putting all human authority on one side, divesting himself of every prejudice, and following no party, had for fourteen years seriously examined the matter, not in the light of human tradition, but in that of the Divine writings alone.

Gravely uttering this, he seemed to think himself a wise man; others thought him silly; the more learned, however, thought he was mad. Now, as the sensual man does not understand the things of the Spirit of God,[1] and as that which reveals to us the things that are not seen is the one faith of Jesus Christ,[2] which faith is by hearing—hearing by the word of Christ,[3] not the word read only, but the word openly preached, which has gone forth into every land—and as the mystery of the Eucharist is the most spoken of, is every day present to the faithful, as it were in their hands and in their mouths, it must be granted that the man who confesses that he has cast away the Catholic faith preached and believed in the house of God, who has been fourteen years without a definite belief in that mystery, and who has therefore been all that time an unbelieving infidel, must be like a madman if he asks people to believe what he says on the ground that he has been without belief himself.

St. Paul, it is true, says that the Scriptures can instruct unto salvation;[4] but how? He answers, by the faith which is in Christ, for otherwise the Jews imagined that they had life in the Scriptures. But because they

[1] 1 Cor. ii. 14. [2] Heb. xi. 1. [3] Rom. x. 17. [4] 2 Tim. iii. 15.

had not the faith of Christ, their table, whereat they thought they were feeding on the Scriptures, became a snare before them.[1] Yea, that is the true reason why no heretic can understand the sacred writings; for while he is searching the Scriptures for the purpose of ascertaining what he is to believe, he is not in possession of the faith he is seeking, nor without the faith has he the understanding of the Scriptures. Hence it comes to pass that such a one ruins himself and those who listen to him.[2]

When, then, the Catholic doctors and priests spoke in this way, and reminded others of the truth, the Catholic faith was so advanced in the University of Oxford that men were found there who by speaking and writing denied openly the ecclesiastical supremacy of Edward VI. How could he be the supreme head and governor of the Church of England? he who was but a boy, differing in nothing from a servant, a child in understanding and judgment, in civil matters necessarily under a guardian.[3] Christ gave His Church to be fed and ordered not by children but by men, and then not by every man, but by men who can rightly "exhort in sound doctrine, and reprove them that gainsay it."[4]

Among those who thus thought there were two men who deserve to be remembered: one was Gilbert Lever,[5] a man almost illiterate, he went to prison rather than take the oath of supremacy to a boy; the other was in years a youth, but in courage an old man—Richard Brittain,[6] he maintained, not by word of mouth only, that

[1] Psalm lxviii. 23.

[2] 2 Tim. ii. 14.

[3] Gal. iv. 1; 1 Cor. xiv. 20.

[4] Tit. i. 9.

[5] In the margin, "Who to this day has much to suffer for the Catholic religion."

Prevarication, chap. iv. s. 20. "Gilbert Lever, Richard Brittain, and other Oxonians, for preaching and writing against the supremacy and proving the authority of the Pope by the testimony of all the ancient fathers: some of them were condemned, others committed."

[6] Richard Brittain was of New

the Roman Pontiff, as the successor of St. Peter, is the sovereign head of the whole Church, and in that dignity the sole Vicar of Christ, but also by writings, which he presented to his judge, proving his faith and confirming it by the testimony of the Scriptures and the ancient fathers. And he, too, was kept in prison for the sake of Christ.

Edward Seymour the protector, the chief leader of the Calvinists also, who had put his own brother to death,[1] is now for the second time sent to prison, and his wife with him;[2] he was charged with an attempt on the life of John Dudley, formerly earl of Warwick, but at this time duke of Northumberland.[3] It is said that the duke

College, Oxford, and at the age of twenty-four, by reading Catholic books, recovered the faith, and defended the authority of the Pope. He was tried, and at his trial confessed more amply still, for which he was sent to prison. His only food was bread, to which on feast days he added a little broth. His great austerities and constancy in the faith won others over—among whom Sander was one—who visited him in prison, and resolved, if the opportunity arose, to contend for the faith as he had done. He obtained his liberty on the accession of Mary, and not long afterwards died in the Order of St. Francis.

1 Francis Bourgoyne, writing to Calvin from London, Jan. 22, 1552 (Original Letters, No. 347), says, "It was notorious to every one in this kingdom that he was the occasion of his brother's death, who having been convicted on a charge of treason which no one could prove against him by legal evidence, and of which when brought to execution he perseveringly denied the truth, was beheaded owing to his information, instigated by I know not what hatred and rivalry against his brother."

2 Micronius, writing to Bullinger from London, Nov. 7, 1551 (Original Letters, No. 266), says, "The disturbance which suddenly took place here on the second imprisonment of the duke of Somerset, his wife, and other noble persons, greatly distressed our minds." He was sent to the Tower, according to Strype (Memorials, ii. i. 497), on the 15th day of October.

3 Micronius, writing to Bullinger, March 9, 1552 (Original Letters, No. 267), says: "Various grounds have been assigned for this procedure. The real cause, however, as I understand from persons worthy of credit, was his having formed a conspiracy against some of the council, which is a capital offence. For the king's council, after the first imprisonment of the duke of Somerset, with the view of uniting them more closely to each other, passed a law to this effect, that any one of the king's council who should plot in secret against another of that body, should suffer death by hanging as a felon. And as Somerset was said to have offended against this law, he was arrested on the 16th of October, and on the following day his wife, together with many other of the nobility who were thought to have been privy to this conspiracy. . . .

of Somerset—well aware, and knowing by experience before he was put in prison, that Warwick hated him with all his heart—was persuaded by others to kill Warwick, and for that end went to his house under the pretence of paying him a visit. Finding that his enemy was in bed, he obtained access to his room as if for the purpose of renewing their friendship; but though protected by a coat of mail secretly worn, and though his friends also who accompanied him were in the next room, provided with concealed arms, nevertheless at the last moment he did not venture to strike his enemy lying defenceless on his bed, and came away without accomplishing his purpose. He was then betrayed by one of his own servants,[1] and afterwards condemned to death under a law[2] by which any one devising the murder of a member of the king's council, though he should do nothing more, was to die a murderer's death.

When the protector Seymour, who ruled the king himself, was put out of the way by Dudley, against the king's will as it was said, everybody saw at once that Seymour, who was a weak man, never attained to his great honours by his own sagacity and skill, but rather through the craft of Dudley. Dudley knowing the man to be mean-spirited, more intent upon heaping up riches than on building up an honourable reputation, thought he could easily make use of him for the furtherance of all his plans, and then ruin him whenever he pleased. It was convenient for Dudley, who was not a man of very great weight at the death of Henry VIII., to make use of one who was of greater importance than he was in removing out of his way those who seemed likely to

He was, however, beheaded on the 22d of January, to the great grief of the people."

[1] Burnet, Hist. Ref., ii. 305. "But Sir Thomas Palmer, though imprisoned with him as a complice, was the person that ruined him."

[2] 3 & 4 Edw. VI. c. 5. The trial of the duke took place in Westminster Hall, Dec. 1, 1551.

thwart his schemes, and then to be able without much difficulty to ruin him through whom he had ruined the others.

Accordingly, seeing that Edward Seymour, the king's uncle, was the fittest instrument for his purpose, he helped to advance him with all his might. Then by his aid he brought about the destruction of Thomas Seymour, his brother, a man of great capacity; that done, he allied himself with the duke of Suffolk,[1] who was regarded as the next in power to the protector, and then ruined the protector himself. Then, at last, as if he thought very little of having raised himself from a moderate estate and condition [2] to the highest rank and honour—those of a duke—he resolved to mount up even to the royal throne.

For when he saw king Edward wasting away,[3] he felt confident that after the two children of Henry VIII.—Mary, the daughter of Catherine, and Elizabeth, the daughter of Anne Boleyn—the right to the crown must devolve upon Frances duchess of Suffolk,[4] for he made

[1] Henry Grey, marquis of Dorset. He married Frances, daughter of Charles Brandon, duke of Suffolk, by his wife Mary, sister of Henry VIII. He was created duke of Suffolk Oct. 10, 1551, a few days before the arrest of the duke of Somerset. His daughter, Jane Grey, became the wife of Guilford Dudley, the fourth son of the duke of Northumberland.

[2] Burnet, Hist. Reform., ii. 86. "He was son to that Dudley who was attainted and executed the first year of Henry VIII.'s reign."

[3] Stow, p. 609. "In the month of January [1553] the king fell sick of a cough at Whitehall, which grievously increased, and at last ended in a consumption of the lights."

[4] Burnet, Hist. Reform., ii. 301. "The next in the will were the heirs of the French queen by Charles Brandon, who were the duchess of Suffolk and her sister, though I have seen it often said, in many letters and writings of that time, that all that issue by Charles Brandon was illegitimated, since he was certainly married to one Mortimer [Margaret, daughter of John Nevil, marquis Mountague, widow of Sir John Mortimer], which Mortimer lived long after his marriage to that queen, so that all her children were bastards. Some say he was divorced from his marriage to Mortimer, but that is not clear to me." Julius Terentianus (Original Letters, 182), writing Nov. 29, 1553, says: "A few days before his death the king made a will at the instigation of Northumberland, by which he disinherited both his sisters, and appointed the Lady Frances, wife of the duke of

no account of the other Mary who was queen of Scotland. Accordingly he persuaded Edward to disinherit Mary and Elizabeth, partly on the ground that they were not born in lawful wedlock—that, however, could not be supposed of both—and partly on the ground that they might be married to foreigners, to whom he should not like to make England subject; and lastly, to save the Calvinistic teaching, which during the king's infancy had flourished, from being rooted out under Mary. He advised the king to make Jane, one of the daughters of the duchess of Suffolk, his heir. Matters being thus arranged, his own son, Guilford Dudley, and Jane are betrothed in the month of May, and through him he trusts to possess himself of the sovereign power.

King Edward departed this life[1] July 6 [1553], on the day and the month in which Sir Thomas More,

Suffolk, to be his heir. She declined it, and the kingdom was made over to her daughter Jane, who had been married two months before to the Lord Guilford, the third son of the duke of Northumberland."

[1] Julius Terentianus, Original Letters, 182. "The most godly Josiah, our earthly hope, died on the 6th of July; of consumption, as the physicians assert; by poison, according to common report; for this is rumoured by the Papists for the purpose of exciting a general hatred against Northumberland; nor, to tell the truth, were there wanting many and strong suspicions: but still, if I may say what I think, I believe the Papists themselves to have been the authors of so great a wickedness, for they have expressed no signs of sorrow, and no inquiry has been made respecting so great a crime." He does not say how the "Papists" could have come near enough to the person of the king so as to administer poison to him. The belief in the poisoning of the king was common among the Protestants, and is witnessed to by Burcher in a letter to Bullinger from Strasburg, Aug. 16, 1553 (Original Letters, 325): "That monster of a man the duke of Northumberland has been committing a horrible and portentous crime. A writer worthy of credit informs me that our excellent king has been most shamefully taken off by poison. His nails and hair fell off before his death, so that, handsome as he was, he entirely lost all his good looks. The perpetrators of the murder were ashamed of allowing the body to lie in state and be seen by the public, as is usual; wherefore they buried him privately in a paddock adjoining the palace, and substituted in his place, to be seen by the people, a youth not very unlike him whom they had murdered. One of the sons of the duke of Northumberland acknowledged this fact."

fountain of honour and of justice, was beheaded a few years before by his father's orders ; and so it came to pass that all might see, who rightly consider the course of this world, that Henry paid in the death of his eldest son the penalty of the death of that great man, but yet did not satisfy the Divine justice, because he had not done penance for his sin according to the will of God.

BOOK III.

CHAPTER I.

LADY JANE GREY—ACCESSION OF MARY—CONDEMNATION OF CRANMER—ARRIVAL OF CARDINAL POLE—PETITION OF PARLIAMENT — ABSOLUTION AND RECONCILIATION OF THE KINGDOM.

On the fourth day after Edward's death,[1] that is, on the 10th of July, Jane, daughter of Frances duchess of Suffolk, and granddaughter of Mary, sister of Henry VIII., was openly and publicly proclaimed queen under the will of king Edward; meanwhile every one, not shouting for joy as the custom is on such occasions, but rather murmuring in secret, and execrating the unjust deed.[2] Jane, however, with her husband, Guilford Dudley, went by water to the Tower of London, as one taking possession of the royal throne. Many of the nobles also were there with her, for the duke of Northumberland had brought them thither either by fear or by fraud. He, indeed, had brought it to pass that nearly every man of weight throughout the realm had given his consent to the duke's will, and that in writing.

[1] Edward died July 6. On the 8th the lord mayor was sent for to Greenwich and told of the will by which the succession was changed, when he and those who were with him, says Stow (p. 609), "were sworn and charged to keep it secret."

[2] Burnet, Hist. Reform., ii. p. 380. "There were very few that shouted with the acclamations ordinary on such occasions."

Sir Francis Englefield, who was in the household of Mary, refused to sign anything against the interests of his mistress, and was committed to prison; but if the duke of Northumberland had returned successful, he would also have lost his life.

Meanwhile Mary, the daughter of Henry and of Catherine, the lawful heir to the throne, had fled for refuge to Framlingham Castle in Suffolk,[1] and there the people from all parts of the country flocked around her at once with incredible speed and zeal.[2]

Dudley, the duke of Northumberland, having brought certain troops together, marched out against Mary; but the nobles, learning that throughout the realm Mary's rights were upheld not only by the people, but by the principal personages of the country, and that Dudley's army was wasting away by desertion, deprived Jane of the throne on the ninth day[3] of her occupation of it, and Mary obtained her rights. The next day the duke of Northumberland, already abandoned by his followers, surrendered at Cambridge, and on the 22d day of August next died on the block; but before he died he renounced all his heresies, and sincerely professed the Catholic faith, moved thereunto by Nicholas Heath,[4] then bishop of Worcester, and afterwards archbishop of

[1] Stow, p. 616. "The Lady Mary was fled to Framlingham Castle in Suffolk, where the people of the country almost wholly resorted to her."

[2] Julius Terentianus, Original Letters, No. 182. "Mary, who had most faithful councillors, by their advice went, as though defenceless, into Norfolk, where she is received and hailed as queen with general applause. . . . Almost the entire nation rise to her assistance; first of all the people of Norfolk and Suffolk, and then those of Oxfordshire, Buckinghamshire, Berkshire, and Essex. A portion too of the nobility, who had given in their adhesion to Jane merely for the purpose of deceiving her, revolt from her forthwith, and exert all their energies in behalf of Mary."

[3] Ibid. "Thus Jane was queen for only nine days, and those most turbulent ones. After some days Mary made her entry with great triumph into the city, to take possession of the Tower; on entering which she immediately set at liberty the bishop of Winchester, the duke of Norfolk, Lord Courtney, and the widow of the duke of Somerset.

[4] Consecrated in schism bishop of Rochester, by Gardiner, Sampson, and Skip, April 4, 1540, and translated to Worcester A.D. 1543, without any Bulls or lawful authority.

York. To his clear understanding and profound judgment the Catholic faith alone seemed true, but he was blinded by his ambition. He saw that by pretending to be a heretic he had at least some chance of making himself a king, and that he had none whatever if he professed the Catholic faith. He preferred a kingdom obtained by heresy to subjection in the Catholic religion.

After a schism which lasted twenty years, God gave the victory in a marvellous way to Mary, the Catholic princess, over almost all the nobles of the realm, and that without shedding one drop of blood.[1] It was a manifest miracle wrought before all the world in favour of the Catholic faith.

Mary, then, the daughter of Catherine, entered in triumph the city and Tower of London, and at once restored to freedom and to their former rank, Edmund bishop of London, Stephen bishop of Winchester, Cuthbert bishop of Durham, all the other Catholics who were in prison for the profession of the faith, together with Thomas duke of Norfolk, and William earl of Devon.[2] She rejected the title of the profane ecclesiastical supremacy, and resolved to restore the ancient rights and reverence due to the Apostolic See, which she had always honoured, even at the risk of her life, in the days of her father and brother, and sent for Cardinal Pole.

She married Philip, son of the emperor Charles V.

[1] Foxe himself confesses it (vi. 388): "God so turned the hearts of the people to her, and against the council, that she overcame them without bloodshed, notwithstanding there was made great expedition against her both by sea and land."

[2] Stow, p. 613. "The queen entered the city through Aldgate, up to Leadenhall, then down Grace Street, Fenchurch Street, Mark Lane, Tower Street, and so into the Tower, where Thomas duke of Norfolk, Dr. Gardiner, late bishop of Winchester, Edward Courtney, son and heir to Henry marquess of Exeter, the duchess of Somerset, prisoners in the Tower, kneeling on the hill within the same Tower, saluted her grace, and she came to them and kissed them, and said, 'These be my prisoners.' On the next morrow, Edward Courtney was made marquess of Exeter, and the other forenamed prisoners pardoned, and discharged in the queen's chamber."

There were very grave reasons in favour of that marriage, but the chief was this: the prince would be a help to her in bringing the kingdom back again to the faith and obedience of the Church.

Wyatt made a sedition in Kent for the purpose of thwarting the marriage and the reconciliation of the kingdom by renouncing heresy, but the queen overcame him, not so much by the valour of her troops as by her own admirable faith.

The duke of Suffolk renewed the war,[1] was taken prisoner and beheaded. The queen sent succours to her husband, who was laying siege to St. Quintin,[2] and thereby lost Calais through the negligence or the treachery of her own subjects.[3]

Cranmer archbishop of Canterbury, who had pronounced sentence of divorce against her mother, against all justice, was found guilty of high treason;[4] the sentence was confirmed in Parliament, and by his own confession. In the hope of saving his life,[5] he pretended to be a

1 Collier, Eccles. Hist., ii. p. 360. "When Wyat's insurrection broke out in Kent, the duke of Suffolk, with his two brothers, Lord John and Lord Leonard Grey, rode down into Warwickshire and tried to raise the country against the Spaniard." He was tried by the Peers, Feb. 17, 1554, and found guilty, suffering the penalty of death on the 21st.

2 Stow, p. 631. "The 18th of August [1557] the town of St. Quintins was taken by king Philip with the help of Englishmen."

3 Stow, p. 632. "The loss of this town seemed strange to many men of great experience; the same town being so many years so strongly fortified with all munitions that could be devised, should now in so short space be taken of our enemies without fight or slaughter of any man more than Sir Antony Agar." P. 634: "The 2d of July, the Lord Wentworth and divers others that had been governors of Calais, were attainted of treason, being then in France." P. 639: "The 22d of April [1559] William Lord Wentworth, late deputy of Calais, was arraigned at Westminster upon an indictment of treason . . . for the loss of Calais, but he was acquit by his peers."

4 Stow, p. 617. "The 13th of November, Dr. Cranmer, archbishop of Canterbury, Lady Jane, that was before proclaimed queen, and the Lord Guilford, her husband, and the Lord Ambrose Dudley were arraigned at the Guildhall of London and condemned of treason." Parliament, 1 Mar. c. 16, confirmed the attainder of the duke of Northumberland, Cranmer, and others.

5 Burnet, ii. 535. "He was dealt with to renew his subscription, and then to write the whole over again, which he also did; all this time

Catholic, and signed his recantations seventeen times with his own hand. In the end his hypocrisy was discovered, and certain bishops having degraded him from all ecclesiastical rank, delivered him up to the secular arm, when he was burnt in Oxford by order of the queen.

The devotion, prudence, and firmness shown by the queen in the restoration of the Catholic religion throughout all her dominions, ought not, I think, to be forgotten; they are matters that redound to the everlasting honour of that most saintly woman, and to the shame and punishment of a sinful and unhappy people, that afterwards returned so readily to its vomit.

In the very beginning, with the consent of Parliament, she repealed the impious laws of her brother against the Catholic faith, abolished the heretical religion, sent away the teachers of the sect,[1] and restored

being under some small hopes of life; but conceiving likewise some jealousies that they might burn him, he writ secretly a paper containing a sincere confession of his faith, such as flowed from his conscience, and not from his weak fears." Harpsfield thus writes of his end (Treatise of Marriage, bk. iii. p. 130, Eyston MS.): "Now to what end he came, it is so late done and so notorious, that I need say nothing in it, only this I will tell you, that in all his life he never showed more inconstancy and mutability, nor more dangerous to his soul than at his very end; for whereas he had by writing recanted and revoked his heresies and given out many copies thereof signed with his own hand, whereby if he had continued he might have saved his poor soul. Lo! suddenly the same day that he saw he should needs die, he revolted, and reverted with the dog to his pestilent vomit. So this revocation was only for an outward show, while he was yet in some hope to get thereby pardon for his temporal life, whereof, when he was in despair, he discovered his crooked dissimulation, and desperately both cast away his body and soul. And as he entered his first preferment—as you have heard—with devilish dissimulation, so he ended his wretched life in the same. This, lo! is the pillar of this divorce. This is he that adventured to take upon him the Pope's authority, and to give judgment againt the lawful marriage, which though it had been unlawful, yet had his sentence been unlawful for lack of competent jurisdiction. And yet if his jurisdiction had been competent, there is no goodly wise man that might justly think [him] a meet person to commit such a weighty matter unto. And thus end we with this prelate made at the bearstake. Six copies of his recantations were published by Cawood, and may be seen in Strype, Mem., iii. i. 392, and in Jenkyns' Works of Cranmer, iv. p. 393.

[1] "The queen's proclamation for the driving out of the realm strangers and foreigners" may be seen in Foxe,

the Breviary and the Missal throughout England and Ireland, and all other places of her dominions; it was done without difficulty, and it was done at once in the first Parliament of her reign. But the reparation of the fearful breach which Henry VIII. had made when he withdrew from the communion of the Apostolic See and of the Church throughout the world, and the restoration of the ancient observance of ecclesiastical obedience and submission in her dominions, must be a painful and laborious work; nor could it be rightly done without the grace and goodwill of the Pope. For that end, therefore, Cardinal Pole, dear to the queen for many reasons, was invited over at once. The Pope, Julius III., readily consented to the queen's request, and sent the Cardinal, furnished with the fullest powers, as Legate *a latere* to the king and queen and the whole realm. For before this Philip had landed in England, the marriage had taken place,[1] and the reconciliation of the kingdom was earnestly promoted by the authority of the king and the queen.

On the 12th of November [1554] Parliament assembled in London,[2] and recalled Cardinal Pole, who had

vi. p. 429. "The queen our sovereign lady, understanding that a multitude of evil-disposed persons, being born out of her highness's dominions, in other sundry nations, flying from the obeisance of the princes and rulers under whom they be born, some for heresy; some for murder, treason, robbery; and some for other horrible crimes, be resorted into this her majesty's realm, and here have made their demurrer, and yet be commorant and lingering, partly to eschew such condign punishment as their said horrible crimes deserve, and partly to dilate, plant, and sow the seeds of their malicious doctrine and lewd conversation among the good subjects of this her said realm, on purpose to infect her good subjects with the like. Insomuch as beside innumerable heresies which divers of the same, being heretics, have preached and taught," &c.

[1] Philip and Mary were married by Gardiner in the cathedral church of Winchester, July 25, 1554.

[2] Stow, p. 625. "The 12th of November the Parliament began at Westminster. The 24th of November Cardinal Poole came out of Brabant into England, and was received with much honour; he was by Parliament restored to his old dignity that he was put from by king Henry, and shortly after came to the Parliament-house, where the king, queen, and other states were present. Then he declared the cause of his legacy, and exhorted them to return to the com-

been for some time in Brabant. On the 23d day of the same month he entered the city in great state, and on the fifth day thereafter went to the assembly of the Estates, called there the Parliament, and in the presence of the king and the queen made known the reasons why the Pope had sent him as his Legate, urged a return to the communion of the Church, the restoration of his lawful jurisdiction to His Holiness the Pope, the successor of the prince of the apostles, who in his compassion was ready to receive them back. He also reminded them that they should give thanks unto God, who had given them such a king and such a queen. At the conclusion of his address he left the house.

Then the bishop of Winchester, who was also the lord chancellor,[1] spoke to the same effect, and urged them at great length to return to unity and peace, and to give most hearty thanks unto God, who in His infinite compassion had raised up a prophet who was of their own race, the most eminent Cardinal, wholly devoted to their welfare.

On the following day the two Houses of Parliament,[2] after hearing the speech and demands of the Legate, and consenting thereunto, petitioned the king and the queen to intercede with him on their behalf. In their petition they said that they were very sorry for the schism, for the refusal of obedience to the Apostolic See, and for their assenting to laws made against it; for the future they would be subject to the Pope and to the queen, and

munion of the Church, and to restore the Pope his due authority. Secondly, he advertised them to give thanks to God, that had sent them so blessed a king and queen."

[1] He was made chancellor Aug. 23.

[2] Stow, p. 625. "The next day the whole court of Parliament drew out a form of supplication, the sum whereof was that they greatly repented them of all that schism that they had lived in, and therefore desired the king, queen, and Cardinal that by their means they might be restored to the bosom of the Church and obedience of the See of Rome."

would do all they could for the repeal of those laws in the present Parliament. They were most earnest in their petition for release from the censures they had incurred, according to the laws of the Church, through their schism, and for their restoration into the bosom of Christ's Church, as penitent children, that for the rest of their lives they might, in the obedience of the Roman Pontiffs and See, serve God to the glory of His name and the increase of their own prosperity.[1]

Two days afterwards [November 30], in the presence of the king, the queen, and the Legate, the lord chancellor stood up and gave an account of the resolutions of both Houses of Parliament in answer to the demand of the Legate. That done, he presented the humble petition of both houses, in writing and under seal, to the king and the queen, praying them at the same time to accept it. The king and the queen having opened the paper, returned it to the chancellor that it might be read. Whereupon the chancellor demanded of all those then present, as representing the whole realm, whether they agreed in that petition. They answered that they did;

1 This petition was afterwards embodied in the statute 1 & 2 Philip and Mary, c. 8, sec. 2. "We, the Lords spiritual and temporal and the Commons assembled in this present Parliament, representing the whole body of the realm of England and the dominions of the same, in the name of ourselves particularly, and also of the said body universally, in this our supplication, directed to your majesties, . . . do declare ourselves very sorry and repentant of the schism and disobedience committed in this realm and dominions aforesaid against the said See Apostolic, either by making, agreeing, or executing any laws, ordinances, or commandments against the supremacy of the said See, or otherwise doing or speaking, that might impugn the same: offering ourselves and promising by this our supplication that, for a token and knowledge of our said repentance, we be and shall be always ready, under and with the authorities of your majesties, . . . to do that shall lie in us for the abrogation and repealing of the said laws and ordinances in this present Parliament, as well for ourselves as for the whole body whom we represent, . . . set forth this our most humble suit, that we may obtain from the See Apostolic, . . . as well particularly as generally, absolution, release, and discharge from all danger of such censure and sentences as by the laws of the Church we be fallen into."

thereupon the king and the queen rose and presented it to the Legate, who read it.

Then the Legate, having read the petition of both houses, brings forth in turn the Bull of his faculties as Legate; that also is read, in order that all might know that the Pope had given him power to absolve them.

After this the Legate preached to them, and saying how pleasing unto God is penance, and how the angels are glad when the sinner repents. Having illustrated this by many examples, he gave thanks unto God, who had breathed into them a spirit willing to be reformed. Then he stood up—the king and the queen rising and falling on their knees—and prayed God to pour down His mercy upon them, to look with compassion on His people, and to forgive them their sin; and then saying that he had been sent by the sovereign Pontiff, the Vicar of Christ, to absolve them, blessed the whole assembly and absolved it.

They went then to the chapel, where they gave thanks unto God, singing His praises, followed by tokens of joy and gladness, according to the custom.[1]

[1] Stow, p. 625. "The next day, the king, queen, and Cardinal being present, the lord chancellor declared what the Parliament had determined concerning the Cardinal's request, and offered to the king and queen the supplication before mentioned, which being read, the Cardinal, in a large oration, declared how acceptable repentance was in the sight of God, &c. And immediately making prayer unto God, by authority to him committed, absolved them. When all this was done, they went all unto the chapel, and there singing *Te Deum* with great solemnity, declared the joy that for this reconciliation was pretended."

CHAPTER II.

SERMON OF GARDINER—DEATH OF MARY—ACCESSION OF ELIZABETH.

On the 2d day of December[1] the king and the Legate, with almost all the chief personages of the whole kingdom, went to St. Paul's, where the bishop of Winchester, the lord chancellor, preached a sermon from that most famous pulpit of St. Paul's Cross.[2] He told the people, after a devout preface, with what sincerity the three estates, representing the whole kingdom, had placed themselves under obedience to the Apostolic See; with what charity the Legate of our most holy lord the Pope had received them, and absolved them from their sins and from the censures they had incurred. He then exhorted them all to give continual thanks unto God for a grace so great, to His Holiness the Pope, and to the king and queen, their most religious sovereigns. Not long after this, ambassadors were sent to Rome on the part of the king and the queen, and of the people, who on behalf of the whole realm were to promise dutiful obedience to the Apostolic See.[3]

[1] The first Sunday in Advent, 1554.

[2] Stow, p. 625. "The 2d of December Cardinal Poole came from Lambeth by water and landed at Paul's Wharf, and from thence to Paul's Church, with a cross, two pillars, two poleaxes of silver borne before him. He was there received by the lord chancellor, with procession, where he tarried till the king came from Westminster by land at eleven of the clock, and then the lord chancellor entered Paul's cross and preached a sermon, taking for his theme these words: 'Fratres, scientes quia hora est jam nos de somno surgere.'" The substance of the sermon may be seen in Foxe, vi. 577.

[3] These were the Viscount Montague, the bishop of Ely, and Sir

But the sins and the sacrilege of Henry VIII., and the wickedness of the people, were such that they could not be thus lightly expiated, and therefore this calm did not last. The queen having reigned five years and four months, changed the earthly for the heavenly kingdom; unhappy in this, that being the child of Henry VIII., no child might be born of her. It was the will of God that Henry VIII., for his sins and for the schism, should be thus severely punished; for though when he died he left three children living—Edward, Mary, and Elizabeth—yet of none of them might a child be born and reared. But still more unhappy did she regard herself in that she was forced to leave the kingdom to Elizabeth, not only her rival and a bastard, but one whom, notwithstanding her dissimulation, she suspected to be a heretic, and always feared would be a plague to the state and to religion.

I must now explain briefly how and by what title Elizabeth came to the throne.

Mary, it is true, made more than one effort to shut her out from the succession, either on the ground of heresy or on that of treason—for she had done many things against her sister and the state—or on the clearer ground of her tainted birth, for the pretended marriage of Henry and Anne, with the issue thereof, was, as we have said before, distinctly declared unlawful by a judicial decision of Clement VII. The like decision was made in Parliament afterwards by commandment of the king when he was in a calmer mood.[1] Besides, the

Edward Carne. Sir Richard Morison, writing to Bullinger from Strasburg, Aug. 23, 1555 (Original Letters, No. 75), thus speaks of them: "Our ambassadors, who went to Rome for the purpose of bringing back the wolf upon the sheep of Christ, are now with the emperor."

[1] 28 Henry VIII. c. 7. Mary and Elizabeth are declared bastards, and the crown is settled upon the issue of Jane Seymour; the oath in favour of Elizabeth is dispensed with, for the new oath is to this effect: "And in case any other oath be made or hath been made by you to any person or persons, that then ye do repute the same as vain and annihilate."

king released his subjects from the observance of the oath which they had taken in favour of Anne and her child, and, moreover, declared in Parliament that Anne never was, and never could have been, his wife, for certain reasons communicated by him, as he said, under the seal of secrecy, to the archbishop of Canterbury.[1]

And though in the thirty-fifth year of his reign,[2] having obtained authority from Parliament to nominate his successors, he willed that Elizabeth should have a place in the order of succession to the throne; nevertheless, neither her own birth nor the marriage of her father and mother was by any subsequent law sanctioned or made lawful either by Henry her father or by herself. Her right to the throne, therefore, stands on the act of Parliament, and not upon any title which is hers by right of birth, nor has she any better title at this day.

On the other hand, the two Houses of Parliament, in the first year of the reign of queen Mary,[3] declared the marriage of Henry and Catherine valid, and the issue thereof, by human and divine law, to have been born in lawful wedlock; repealing at the same time all acts,

[1] Cranmer, who, May 28, 1533, had pronounced the marriage of Henry and Anne Boleyn to be good, pronounced that very marriage, May 17, 1536, a nullity; that is, the marriage never was good: "*Prorsus et omnino fuisse nullum, invalidum et inane, viribus quoque et effectu juris semper caruisse et carere, ac nullius fuisse et esse roboris seu momenti.*" He did this for certain reasons, true, just, and lawful, lately brought to his knowledge; but he does not recite those reasons, nor does he say that they were brought to his knowledge in the course of the trial. He does not even say who revealed them. But in the act of Parliament (28 Henry VIII. c. 7) it is said that "certain just, true, and lawful impediments, unknown" at the time, "were confessed by the said Lady Anne before" Cranmer "sitting judicially." The reason of the invalidity of the marriage must be some secret sin, for all honest and lawful impediments to the marriage were perfectly well known at the time it was made. The former marriage with Catherine, and the engagement with Percy, even if it were a contract, were not "unknown," and could not be the grounds on which this marriage "was never good."

[2] 35 Henry VIII. c. 1.

[3] In the second session of Parliament, but in the first year. 1 Mariæ, c. 1.

processes, and sentences to the contrary. The marriage of Anne, therefore—for Catherine was still living—could not be valid, and her issue must be bastard, and incapable, naturally, of succeeding in any way according to the municipal law, which gives bastards no title to the crown of England; and to this day this law has not been repealed even by Elizabeth herself. She, it is true, claimed the throne as her right, and willed that everybody should acknowledge her right in her first Parliament, but she never grounded her right upon anything else than on the power of Parliament; she never claimed the crown as her birthright. Care was taken afterwards to make it a capital offence to deny the right of the king and the estates of the realm to give the kingdom to whom they pleased.[1] No word was ever uttered for the purpose of making her legitimate, or clearing away the taint of her birth; on that point the silence was complete.

But to return. Mary, who knew too well that the child of Henry and Anne Boleyn was a child born in adultery and worse, and therefore unworthy of the crown, was never satisfied with that law on which the title of Elizabeth to the throne was grounded. But as she alone, of her own authority, could not repeal that law without the consent of the Lords and Commons, she was forced to be content with doing that which was in her power to do. Many, she knew, held that most iniquitous and deadly opinion, namely, that it was better for them to be governed by a bastard and a heretic, provided he were one of themselves born in the country, than by a foreigner, however good and lawful his title. This perverse opinion has often brought upon England, and on many thriving countries, the most severe chastisements of God. Under these circumstances,

[1] 13 Eliz. c. 1.

the best course to follow was most prudently followed by Mary. At the approach of death she sent some of her council to Elizabeth, to ask her, among other things, two things in particular: the payment of the queen's debts; the money borrowed of her subjects, which she had spent in the public service, and for which she had pledged her royal word. The second was, not to allow the Catholic religion, now settled in England, to be destroyed or undermined. Elizabeth, who had always pretended to be a Catholic during her sister's reign—and had once, in the presence of some of the council, wished the earth might open and swallow her up, if she was not so in truth—with her usual hypocrisy gave her most solemn promise to do that which the queen asked of her, and never performed it.[1]

Mary died.[2] God had raised up this most saintly woman, and placed her in the midst of the Anglican schism as a faithful sign, to the great consolation of

[1] Edwin Sandys, afterwards a bishop under Elizabeth, thus describes this in a letter to Bullinger, Dec. 20, 1558 (Zurich Letters, No. 2): "Mary not long before her death sent two members of her council to her sister Elizabeth, and commanded them to let her know in the first place that it was her intention to bequeath to her the royal crown, together with all the dignity that she was then in possession of by right of inheritance. In return, however, for this great favour conferred upon her, she required of her these three things: first, that she would not change her privy council; secondly, that she would make no alteration in religion; and thirdly, that she would discharge her debts and satisfy her creditors. Elizabeth replied in these terms: 'I am very sorry to hear of the queen's illness; but there is no reason why I should thank her for her intention to give me the crown of this kingdom. For she has neither the power of bestowing it upon me, nor can I lawfully be deprived of it, since it is my peculiar and hereditary right. With respect to the council, I think myself,' she said, 'as much at liberty to choose my counsellors as she was to choose her own. As to religion, I promise this much, that I will not change it, provided only it can be proved by the Word of God, which shall be the only foundation and rule of my religion. And when, lastly, she requires the payments of her debts, she seems to me to require nothing more than what is just, and I will take care that they shall be paid, as far as may lie in my power.'" It is possible, certainly, that Sandys may have believed the account he gives to be true.

[2] The queen died on Thursday, Nov. 17, 1558.

the Catholics, that they might not be discouraged and crushed under the burden of heresy. Cardinal Pole[1] also, on the same day, and about twelve hours after the queen, departed this life. Then came the hour of Satan, and the power of darkness took possession of the whole of England.[2]

[1] Edwin Sandys, to whom Elizabeth gave the bishoprics successively of Worcester, London, and York, thus announces these facts to Bullinger in a letter from Strasburg, Dec. 20, 1558 (Zurich Letters, No. 2): "We yesterday received a letter from England, in which the death of Mary, the accession of Elizabeth, and the decease of Cardinal Pole is confirmed. That good cardinal, that he might not raise any disturbance, or impede the progress of the gospel, departed this life the day after his friend Mary—*Maria sua.* Such was the love and harmony between them that not even death itself could separate them. We have nothing therefore to fear from Pole, for dead men do not bite."

[2] St. Luke xxii. 53.

THE ANGLICAN SCHISM RENEWED UNDER ELIZABETH.

THE CONTINUATION OF THE HISTORY.

BY THE

REV. EDWARD RISHTON, B.A.

OF BRASENOSE COLLEGE, OXFORD,

MISSIONARY PRIEST OF THE SEMINARY OF DOUAI.

BOOK IV.

SYNOPSIS.

THE author of the foregoing history had also written the story of some of the years of Elizabeth; but as he is no longer living, others are preparing a more exact account of the life, manners, and government of this woman, to be published in due time. At present we give but briefly the story of her doings against the Church, that seeing the claws of the lioness, people may recognise her when a fuller account shall be given.

The government of the Church was given by Christ to the apostles and their successors, and especially above all others to Peter, the high priest and Pope; but the English Protestants maintain that the government of the Church ought to be in every country in the hands of the laymen by whom those countries are governed. God, therefore, for the refutation of this heresy, brought it about that the government of the Church in England should fall first into the hands of no other layman than Henry VIII., who was a most impious and sacrilegious tyrant; then after him into those of the boy Edward; and then of Elizabeth, a woman.

Henry was not, but he might have been—for his age and sex allowed it—a minister of the Word of God, by which the Church is chiefly ordered, and a judge in sacred things. Edward neither was nor could be a minister of the Word, for his youth forbade it, though his sex allowed it. But Elizabeth, on account of her sex, never could be a minister of the Word, without which the government of the Church becomes impossible. Hence it has come to pass that, according to the teaching of Protestants, the highest place in the government of the Church is filled by one who not only is not in possession of it—this applies to Henry and Edward also—but by one who never can possess it; and this applies to Elizabeth alone, and has been pointed out by St. Chrysostom in these remarkable words: "When the government of the Church is in question, that is a work which, because of its greatness, cannot belong to a woman."[1] For as there are men in the Church as well as women, and as in the beginning God made the woman out of the man, and for the sake of the man, man is therefore by the law of nature the head of the woman; so also Christ is the head of the man, and God the head of Christ.[2] Now, as it never can come to pass that Christ should govern God, or any man govern Christ, so also it can never be that a woman may govern either the man or the Church of Christ, in which there are men at all times, rightly and orderly, in those things which are the things of God and of Christ.

When Satan was about to disturb the blessed order which God had established, he put the woman forward as one who was to teach man how to break the laws of God, and he set her up as the teacher and guide of man, to the utter ruin of the whole human race. But the Son of God, whom the Father hath appointed to judge and re-establish all things, has repeated His command, that the woman should be subject to man. The apostle Paul calls that command a law, saying that it prevails in ecclesiastical matters; and his words are, "Let women hold their peace in the churches; for it is

[1] De Sacerdotio, lib. ii.; Op., tom. i. p. 372, ed. Ben.
[2] 1 Cor. xi. 3.

not permitted them to speak, but to be subject, as also the law saith."[1] If then by the law, not the law of Moses, but the law of God, proclaimed in Paradise, the woman in the Church must be subject, how can she be the governor of the Church in which her duty is to be subject? Moreover, the apostle, according to the law of nature, forbids the woman to pray or prophesy with her head uncovered:[2] that is to be a perpetual token of her subjection. She is reminded by the ceremonial of the rite that the female sex has no authority in the administration of sacred things, and that the woman must be as it were unseen in the divine solemnities. If she will not keep this law, that is, if she will not be covered, saith the apostle, "let her be shorn; for if it be a shame to a woman to be shorn or made bald, let her cover her head,"[3] if not because of men, who are generally present in churches, yet at least because of the angels, who are never absent; whether by angels we understand the priests of Christ and the ministers of His sacraments,[4] with St. Ambrose,[5] or those blessed spirits who ever guard and defend the churches as the fortresses of God.

But the woman, who is of man and for man created—whom Satan places over man in the things of God, but whom Christ subjects again to man in those things, and who because of the angels chiefly is commanded to be covered—is, according to the teaching of Protestants, rightly placed, not only in authority over men in the Church generally, but over the very angels themselves—whose lips keep the knowledge of God, and from whose mouth we seek His law[6]—and that not in the lowest rank, not in the second or the third, but in the very highest rank, next unto Christ Himself, with juris-

[1] 1 Cor. xiv. 34.
[2] 1 Cor. xi. 3–16.
[3] 1 Cor. xi. 6.
[4] 1 Cor. iv. 1.
[5] Lib. de Mysteriis, c. 2.
[6] Malach. ii. 7.

diction in ecclesiastical affairs: there never has been any blasphemy in the world, if this be none.

It was not without reason that the apostle said of women laden with sins that they were more easily deceived than others by heretics.[1] Experience shows that women, eager in the pursuit of anything, especially if that thing be wrong, are more eager and more dangerous than men in that pursuit, and that men always are most easily and most fatally ensnared by them. St. Jerome[2] has observed that nearly every heresy before his day had been spread by the help of women whom their followers worshipped almost with divine honours. We read of the Pepuziani,[3] heretics of most impure lives, that they treated women with such respect as to give to them alone the ministration of their sacred rites and sacraments. Finally, all men see that this unhappy generation, and that most abandoned sect, have their Athalia,[4] Maacha,[5] Jezabel,[6] Herodias,[7] Selene,[8] Constantia,[9] and Eudoxia.[10]

But Elizabeth has surpassed them all, she has taken upon herself the supremacy in the things of God, over even bishops and priests. We shall now speak of her ecclesiastical supremacy and administration.

[1] 2 Tim. ii. 6.

[2] Ep. 133, ad Ctesiphontem, s. 4, ed. Vallars.

[3] S. Augustin. de Hæresibus, c. 27. "Pepuziani . . . tantum dantes mulieribus principatum ut sacerdotes quoque apud eos honorentur."

[4] Athalia, daughter of Achab and the wife of Joram king of Juda. She put to death as many as she could of the royal family, and made herself queen. See 4 Kings xi. 1.

[5] Maacha, wife of Roboam and mother of Abiam, his son and successor. She was a priestess of impious and filthy rites. 3 Kings xv. 13.

[6] Jezabel, wife of Achab. She was not a Jewess, and persecuted Elias, and slew the prophet. 3 Kings xvi. 31; xviii. 23.

[7] Herodias, the incestuous wife of Herod Antipas, and the mother of Salome, who at her suggestion asked for the head of St. John Baptist. St. Matt. xiv. 3–10.

[8] Selene, or Helene, a woman of evil life, the companion of Simon Magus. Tertullian, De Anima, c. 34.

[9] Constantia, daughter of Constantine the Great, who for her cruel and ruthless temper was called Megæra. Ammian. Marcellin., lib. xiv. c. 1.

[10] Eudoxia, the wife of the emperor Arcadius, and the persecutor of St. John Chrysostom.

CHAPTER I.

HYPOCRISY OF ELIZABETH—CECIL—OATH OF SUPREMACY — HEADSHIP OF THE CHURCH — DELUSION OF THE CATHOLICS.

On the death of Mary, Elizabeth ascended the throne, another daughter of Henry VIII., being the child of his concubine Anne Boleyn, and born in the lifetime of Catherine his wife, whom he had put away. Elizabeth, though she professed the Catholic faith in all things while her sister lived, now, under the pressure of the fear, suggested by certain treacherous heretics whom she admitted into the council, that because she was the issue of a marriage condemned by the Church and the sovereign Pontiff, a doubt might be raised touching her birth and her title to the throne—for the sacred canons were against her—refused to submit to the ecclesiastical laws, and made up her mind to change at the first opportunity the form of religion and of the government of the Church.[1]

She made her purpose manifest at once in many ways,

[1] Heylyn, Hist. Reform., iii. p. 107. "In this Parliament [the first of Elizabeth] there passed an act for recognising the queen's just title to the crown, but without any act for the validity of her mother's marriage, on which her title most depended. For which neglect most men condemned the new lord-keeper, on whose judgment she relied especially in point of law; in whom it could not but be looked on as a great incogitancy to be less careful of her own and her mother's honour than the ministers of the late queen Mary had been of hers."

but especially by silencing the Catholic preachers.[1] She allowed the heretics to return to the country from the several places to which they had banished themselves,[2] and ordered a bishop, about to say Mass in her presence, and standing in his vestment before the altar, to abstain from elevating the Host at the consecration.[3] In consequence of these proceedings, the archbishop of York, who, now that the Primate, Cardinal Pole, was dead, would have had to crown her, refused to do so, as did the other bishops also, with one exception, and he almost the youngest of them.[4]

At her coronation, by the advice of men who, for the

[1] Jewell, writing to Peter Martyr, Jan. 26, 1559 (Zurich Letters, i. No. 3), says, "The queen has forbidden any person, whether Papist or Gospeller, to preach to the people. Some think the reason of this to be that there was at that time only one minister of the Word in London, namely, Bentham, whereas the number of Papists was very considerable." The proclamation of the queen is printed by Wilkins (Concil., iv. 180), who took it from Strype. Richard Hilles, writing to Bullinger from London, Feb. 28, 1559 (Zurich Letters, ii. No. 8), says, "With respect to religion, silence has been imposed upon the Catholic preachers, as they are called, by a royal proclamation, and sufficient liberty is allowed to the Gospellers to preach three times a week during this Lent, before the queen herself, and to prove their doctrines from the Holy Scriptures."

[2] Jewell says (Zurich Letters, i. No. 3) in a letter to Peter Martyr, written Jan. 26, 1559, "All we hear is, that their return was very acceptable to the queen, and that she has openly declared her satisfaction."

[3] Dod (ed. Tierney, ii. 124) says that the bishop was Heath, the lord chancellor and archbishop of York; but Mr. Tierney refers to Cardinal Allen, who says the bishop was Oglethorpe of Carlisle. In the depositions made before Alexander Riarius, Curiæ Cameræ Apostolicæ Generalis Auditor, Feb. 7, 1570, the Reverend Edmund Daniel, dean of Hereford, testified as follows (Laderchius, iii. 204): "Scio insuper et adfueram cum Regina Elizabeth in sacello esset sub anno 1559 ubi Missam celebrante episcopo Carleolense, dum cantores Gloriam in Excelsis canebant, ipsa unum qui a secretis ei erat, ad eumdem episcopum misit, qui præciperet ne Hostiam elevaret. At episcopus, ut accepi, respondit, se juxta Catholicæ Ecclesiæ consuetudinem Hostiam elevare velle. Quare regina, antequam Evangelium diceretur, discessit, et ipse a secretis mihi dixit quod discesserat ne videret Sacramenti elevationem. Et decanus, reginæ nomine præcepit mihi, ut die S. Stephani celebrare deberem, sine tamen elevatione. Quod quidem facere recusavi. Quare illa postea sacellanum suum, Minter appellatum, misit, qui absque elevatione celebravit; et videbam reginam quæ aderat huic, quia ego quoque aderam, et præfatus presbyter non elevavit."

[4] Owen Oglethorpe, president of Magdalene College, Oxford, was con-

purpose of obtaining a crown, thought it lawful to lie and dissemble, to swear and to forswear, she took the usual oath of Christian kings, prescribed by tradition and by law, in the most solemn way, to defend the Catholic faith, and to guard the rights and immunities of the Church. That was done in order that at a later time her possession of the crown might not be called in question. She was also anointed, but she disliked the ceremony and ridiculed it; for when she withdrew, according to the custom, to put on the royal garments, it is reported that she said to the noble ladies in attendance upon her, "Away with you, the oil is stinking!"

There were certain men about her either of the new religion or of none, and among these was William Cecil,[1] one of the councillors of Edward VI., a man supple in mind, counsel, and conscience. Shortly before this he had assumed the appearance of a Catholic with so much cunning as to offer his services, not without the expectation of reward, to queen Mary and to Cardinal Pole. They refused to have anything to do with him, and so he went over to Elizabeth, and now, on her accession, hoped to rise to the highest honours in the state, especially if she abolished the old religion, declined the counsels of the old nobility and the prelates, and listened to him and his friends. The unhappy queen yielded, and so he enriched himself and his friends, and embroiled the kingdom more and more, so that there was

secrated bishop of Carlisle on the feast of the Assumption, 1557. Under Edward VI. he had professed heresy. Burnet, v. 312, ed. Pocock: "I did never preach," he says, "or teach openly anything contrary to the doctrine and religion set forth by the king's majesty. . . . The foolish and lately-received doctrine concerning the sacraments, and namely the attribute of transubstantiation, I do not like, and I think it not consonant to the Scriptures and ancient writers."

[1] Cecil was in the service of the duke of Somerset originally as master of requests, being the first, according to Camden (Annales rerum Anglicarum, p. 774, ed. Hearne), on the authority of Cecil himself, who bore that title in England; others say that he was simply the duke's secretary. He was made Lord Burghley, Feb. 25, 1571.

no hope of good left, and brought himself and the queen and the country into such misery by his greed that there is no way of escape.

Soon afterwards, chiefly by the advice of Cecil, she, being a woman, would have herself styled, by an act of the Parliament then assembled, the supreme governor of the Church[1] of these realms, even in things spiritual. With the exception of the lay peers, all persons were bound to acknowledge her title upon oath. It was not thought proper to call her the head of the Church, because Calvin[2] had disapproved of the assumption of that title by her father Henry VIII. These are the words of the accursed oath:—

"I, A. B., do utterly testify and declare in my conscience that the queen's highness is the only supreme governor of this realm, and of all other her highness's dominions and countries, as well in all spiritual or ecclesiastical things or causes as temporal; and that no foreign prince, person, prelate, state, or potentate hath, or ought to have, any jurisdiction, power, superiority, pre-eminence, or authority ecclesiastical or spiritual within this realm; and therefore I do utterly renounce and forsake all foreign jurisdictions, powers, superiorities, and authorities."[3]

[1] Sandys, writing to Parker, April 30, 1559 (Burnet, Hist. Reform., v. 505, ed. Pocock), thus speaks: "The bill of supreme government of both the temporalty and clergy passeth with a proviso that nothing shall be judged heresy which is not condemned by the canonical Scriptures and four general councils. Mr. Lever wisely put such a scruple in the queen's head, that she would not take the title of supreme head. The bishops, as it is said, will not swear unto it as it is, but rather lose their livings." Parkhurst writes to Bullinger, May 21, 1559 (Zurich Letters, i. No. 12), "The queen is not willing to be called the head of the Church of England, although this title has been offered her; but she willingly accepts the title of governor, which amounts to the same thing. The Pope is again driven from England, to the great regret of the bishops and the whole tribe of shavelings. The Mass is abolished."

[2] Calvin, Comment. in Amos, c. vii. 13. "Erant enim blasphemi qui vocarent eum [Henricum VIII.] summum caput ecclesiæ sub Christo."

[3] 1 Eliz. c. 1. The oath is continued in these terms: "And do pro-

Beside others who are to take this oath, all archbishops, bishops, ecclesiastical officers, and the whole of the clergy, are expressly bound. If any one refuses, he forfeits, at the first refusal, his benefices, all his goods and chattels, and is to be kept in prison for the rest of his life. If the oath be refused the second time, the penalty of the recusant is death after the manner of traitors.[1]

Now, when the less instructed in these matters found that the word "head" which was in the first act of Parliament had not been inserted in the oath, they in their simplicity rejoiced that people had not gone to such lengths as to give to a woman that which they thought might be honourably yielded—as they thought formerly—to Henry and Edward, who were men. Thereupon very many persons, not Calvinists only, but some Catholics also, somehow imagined that the taking of this oath was more excusable.

Others, seeing more clearly, discerned the trick, or, may one say, the blundering of the lawmakers, and pointed out that the meaning was the same whether the queen was called head or governor, that there was no difference of sense in the difference of words: that the terms of the oath carried the impiety, and the usurpation of the sovereign ecclesiastical jurisdiction, much farther than the mere title of head given to the two kings. It is necessary, they said, to admit and swear, according

mise that from henceforth I shall bear faith and true allegiance to the queen's highness, her heirs and lawful successors, and to my power shall assist and defend all jurisdictions, privileges, pre-eminences, and authorities granted or belonging to the queen's highness, her heirs and successors, or united and annexed to the imperial crown of this realm. So help me God, and by the contents of this book."

[1] 5 Eliz. c. 1, s. 8. "Shall suffer and incur the dangers, penalties, pains, and forfeitures ordained and provided by the statute of provision and Præmunire," &c.

S. 11. "For the same second offence and offences shall forfeit, lose, and suffer suchlike and the same pains, forfeitures, judgment, and execution as is used in cases of high treason."

to this oath, that the queen's power in spiritual and ecclesiastical things is not less than her power in the temporal affairs of the realm; indeed, many thought that, according to the act of Parliament, the queen might have claimed the priestly power, even that of administering sacraments.

The queen, learning that some people had this scruple against taking the oath, ordered the publication of a certain exposition or correction of it, in her first visitation of the clergy, namely, that she neither desired nor claimed any authority greater than that granted by Parliament [1] to her father and her brother with the title of head of the Church, so that the title, head of the Church—the giving of which to a woman seemed not long ago to be dishonourable and unreasonable—was more modest and less offensive than its present substitute. Thus politicians, when they presume to meddle with sacred things, show that they understand neither the words nor the matter of their discourse.

[1] Injunctions given by the queen's majesty, A.D. 1559 (Wilkins, Con., iv. 188): "The queen's majesty being informed that in certain places of the realm, sundry of her majesty's subjects being called to ecclesiastical ministry of the Church, be, by sinister persuasion and perverse construction, induced to find some scruple in the form of an oath which by an act of the last Parliament is prescribed to be required of divers persons for their recognition of their allegiance to her majesty, which certainly never was ever meant. . . .

"And further, her majesty forbiddeth all manner her subjects to give ear or credit to such perverse and malicious persons which most sinisterly and maliciously labour to notify to her loving subjects how, by words of the said oath, it may be collected that the kings or queens of this realm, possessors of the crown, may challenge authority and power of ministry of divine service in the Church, wherein her said subjects be much abused by such evil-disposed persons. For certainly her majesty never doth or will challenge any authority than that was challenged and lately used by the said noble kings of famous memory, king Henry VIII. and Edward VI."

CHAPTER II.

THE ROYAL SUPREMACY—LEGISLATION OF ELIZABETH.

In order that foreigners unversed in our affairs may understand the present condition of the state, I shall now show in a few words wherein, according to the acts of Parliament, this spiritual or ecclesiastical supremacy, given to this woman, and to the two kings her predecessors, chiefly consists.

In the first place, here are the words of the act of Parliament:[1]—

"Such jurisdictions, privileges, superiorities, and pre-eminences, spiritual and ecclesiastical, as by any spiritual or ecclesiastical power or authority hath heretofore been, or may lawfully be, exercised or used, for the visitation of the ecclesiastical state and persons, and for reformation, order, and correction of the same, and of all manner of errors, heresies, schisms, abuses, offences, contempts, and enormities, shall for ever, by authority of this present Parliament, be united and annexed to the imperial crown of this realm."

"And that your highness, your heirs and successors, kings or queens of this realm, shall have full power and authority . . . to assign, name, and authorise . . . such person or persons . . . as your majesty . . . shall think meet, to exercise . . . under your highness . . . all manner of jurisdictions, . . . to visit . . . and amend all such errors, heresies, schisms, abuses . . . whatso-

[1] 1 Eliz. c. 1, s. 17, 18.

ever, which by any manner of spiritual or ecclesiastical power . . . can or may lawfully be reformed."

It is enacted also that the clergy may not meet in synod unless summoned by the king's writ, nor make nor execute any canon, law, or constitution, ordinance provincial or other, without the "royal assent and licence to make, promulge, and execute such canons, . . . upon pain of every one of the said clergy doing contrary to this act, and being thereof convict, to suffer imprisonment and make fine at the king's will."[1]

No person "shall depart out of the king's dominions to or for any visitation, congregation, or assembly for religion, but that all such visitations, congregations, and assemblies shall be within the king's dominions."[2]

Moreover, all bishops must be made by the royal authority only, not on the nomination or by election of any other; and the episcopal jurisdiction and authority must be held and exercised at the queen's pleasure, received from her only, or by authority derived from her majesty.[3]

The queen empowers not only her own bishops and ecclesiastical persons to use this their jurisdiction under herself in all spiritual things and over all spiritual persons; she empowers laymen as well, making them her commissaries or vicars, to exercise every kind of spiritual jurisdiction; and appeals are often carried to them from the bishops themselves.

But how complete is the dependence upon her, for all their spiritual authority and jurisdiction, of those vicars and the bishops themselves, may be seen in their official letters; in which it is confessed, to our amazement, that

[1] This clause was enacted first under Henry VIII.—25 Henry VIII. c. 19, being the statute of the submission of the clergy. The act was repealed under Philip and Mary, and now revived by this statute of 1 Eliz. c. 1, s. 6.

[2] 25 Henry VIII. c. 21, s. 20, repealed under Philip and Mary, and revived by the statute of 1 Eliz. c. 1, s. 8.

[3] 25 Henry VIII. c. 20, repealed under Philip and Mary, revived 1 Eliz. c. 1, s. 9. See also 8 Eliz. c. 1.

holy orders must be given by no other authority than that of the crown. Thus, according to the former legislation, the king wrote to a certain archbishop, "Inasmuch as all authority to declare the law, and all manner of jurisdiction, whether ecclesiastical or civil, is derived from the royal authority, as it were from the supreme head, . . . we authorise you by these letters, remaining in force during our good pleasure, to confer holy orders upon those who are of your diocese."[1] The archbishop in his turn writing to his clergy, when he had anything to command, said, "We, N., by the divine permission, archbishop of Canterbury, primate of all England, sufficiently and duly authorised by the king's majesty;" or thus, "We command you on behalf and in the

[1] These are the terms of the faculties granted by Henry VIII. to the bishops. Burnet (iv. 410) has printed the faculties of Bonner bishop of London, issued Nov. 12, 1539. The king begins by saying that the royal jurisdiction is the source of the ecclesiastical: "Quandoquidem omnis jurisdicendi auctoritas atque etiam jurisdictio omnimoda, tam illa quæ ecclesiastica dicitur quam sæcularis, a regia potestate, velut a supremo capite, et omnium infra regnum nostrum magistratuum, fonte et scaturigine, primitus emanavit." The king then says that he had made Cromwell his vicar-general and official principal, but as Cromwell had so much to do, and could not personally attend to all the matters within the king's jurisdiction as supreme head, he therefore made Bonner another vicar: "Tibi vices nostras sub modo et forma inferius descriptis conmittendas fore, teque licentiandum esse decernimus." Bonner, as the king's vicar, is authorised to ordain priests, to collate them to benefices, and to institute them on the presentation of others, and to make a visitation of the diocese. The same doctrine is taught in the "Reformatio Legum, de Officio et Jurisdictione." These faculties were granted to the other bishops, to Gardiner and Tunstall—Edward VI. walked in the ways of his father; and Cranmer's faculties, by which he is authorised to hold ordinations, may be seen in Wilkins, Concil., iv. 2. And even at this day the same doctrine lives. King William IV., in his letters-patent appointing the first bishop of Australia, gives to him "and his successors, bishops of Australia, full power and authority to admit into the holy orders of deacon and priest respectively any person whom he shall," &c.; and in the patents of the other bishops it is said that "they may perform all the functions peculiar and appropriate to the office of bishop" within their dioceses. When a bishop was sent to India, it was enacted in Parliament, 53 Geo. III. c. 155, s. 53, "that such bishops shall not have or use any jurisdiction, or exercise any episcopal functions whatsoever, . . . but only such jurisdiction and functions as shall or may from time to time be limited to him by his majesty, by letters-patent under the great seal of the United Kingdom."

name of the king, whose representative we are in this matter."[1]

But the very Protestants themselves have become long ago ashamed of these most foolish laws; they have attempted to hide the baseness of them from people unacquainted with English affairs, by saying that nothing is meant by them beyond a declaration that the king or queen is supreme over ecclesiastics as well as over laymen. But the facts hitherto mentioned remove at once this cloak of iniquity, for it is plain that by this law the king or queen is supreme, not only in civil affairs, over all his or her subjects of every rank, but in the things of God also, over ecclesiastical persons, supreme, just as he or she is supreme over the civil judges in matters relating to the public peace and government of the kingdom.

This is not all their folly; they say that this spiritual jurisdiction is a part of the kingly authority, not granted now for the first time, but restored and given back to the crown as its ancient rights.[2] This is nothing else but saying either that heathen princes who were not possessed of that spiritual power were not real kings, or that Catholic kings, whether those now reigning in other Christian lands, or those who reigned in England before the schism, were not true and perfect kings, but kings who reigned with diminished rights; or it is saying that our Lord made no distinction between the things of God and the things of Cæsar, or that there is no difference between the rights of the king and the rights of the priests, between the Church, which is the mystical body of Christ, and a secular society; or lastly, between

[1] Wilkins, Concil., iv. 22. These terms are used by Cranmer, ordering the destruction of the images of the saints, Feb. 24, 1548.

[2] The words of the statute 1 Eliz. c. 1, s. 1, are, "For the restoring and uniting to the imperial crown of this realm the ancient jurisdictions, authorities, superiorities, and pre-eminences to the same of right belonging and appertaining." See note 1 on the preceding page.

those whom the Holy Ghost has made rulers in the Church of God and the human institution, which has for its immediate end the comforts and repose of this life. But we must pass on, and leave these matters in the hands of God, who will judge the cause of His Church, and make their princes like Oreb and Zeb, Zebee and Salmana, who said, "Let us possess the sanctuary of God for an inheritance."[1]

When the queen had appropriated this authority to herself and her heirs, abolishing at the same time that of the Apostolic See, she took to herself, as the chief minister in divine things, the first-fruits and the tithes of all spiritual revenues;[2] in other words, she claimed the whole of the first year's profits of every benefice, and all the property of the monks and friars which her sister had restored.[3] She appointed vicars and commissaries in spirituals, provided herself with a special seal to be used in ecclesiastical affairs; the laws made for the punishment of heretics[4]—and they were much to the

[1] Ps. lxxxii. 12, 13.

[2] Stow, p. 636. "Queen Elizabeth, in this her first Parliament, holden at Westminster the 20th of this month of January, expelled the Papal supremacy, resumed the first-fruits and tenths, repressed the Mass, and for the general uniformity of her dominions established the Book of Common Prayer in the English tongue, forbidding all other."

[3] Stow, pp. 638, 639. "In the month of July, the old bishops of England then living were called and examined by certain of the queen's majesty's council, where the bishops of York, Ely, and London, with other to the number of thirteen or fourteen, for refusing to take the oath touching the queen's supremacy and other articles, they were deprived from their bishoprics. And likewise divers deans, archdeacons, parsons, and vicars deprived from their benefices, and some committed to prison in the Tower, Fleet, Marshalsea, the King's Bench. Commissioners were likewise appointed for the establishing of religion throughout the whole realm. Also the houses of religion by queen Mary, as the Priory of St. John of Jerusalem by Smithfield, the nuns and brethren of Sion and Sheen, the black friars in Smithfield, the friars of Greenwich, were all suppressed: the abbot and monks of Westminster were put out, a dean, prebends, and canons placed there, and so named the College of Westminster, founded by queen Elizabeth."

[4] 1 Eliz. c. 1, s. 15. "That one act and statute made in the first and second years of the late king Philip and queen Mary, entituled 'An Act for the reviving of three statutes made for the punishment of heresies,' and also the said three statutes men-

purpose then—were repealed, and no man was to be accounted a heretic, and no opinion or proposition to be condemned as heretical, unless condemned by the four general councils, or at least another council which had decided the question by the authority of the Scriptures, or, which is the chief point, by the high court of Parliament.[1]

Finally, the queen decreed a change of religion and belief: it was a change wrought according to her will and the will of her councillors. She took away the daily sacrifice, with the solemn prayers and the administration of the sacraments; she prescribed a new worship, new ceremonies, and the prayers in the vulgar tongue; for the most part after the Lutheran fashion, but with one exception, the destruction of the sacred images,[2] though the legislators, with their ministers and followers, were more inclined at the time and afterwards to the Calvinistic opinions. All this the queen brought about by

tioned in the said act, and by the same act revived, and all and every branches, articles, clauses, and sentences contained in the said several acts and statutes, and every of them, shall be, from the last day of this session of Parliament, deemed and remain utterly repealed, void and of none effect to all intents and purposes."

[1] 1 Eliz. c. 1, s. 36. "Provided always, and be it enacted, . . . that such person or persons to whom your highness, your heirs or successors, shall hereafter, by letters-patent under the great seal of England, give authority to have or execute any jurisdiction, power, or authority spiritual, or to visit, reform, order, or correct any errors, heresies, schisms, abuses, or enormities by virtue of this act, shall not in anywise have authority or power to order, determine, or adjudge any matter or cause to be heresy, but only such as heretofore have been determined, ordered, or adjudged to be heresy, by the authority of the canonical Scriptures, or by the first four general councils, or any of them, or by any other general council, wherein the same was declared heresy by the express and plain words of the said canonical Scriptures, or such as hereafter shall be ordered, judged, or determined to be heresy, by the high court of Parliament of this realm, with the assent of the clergy in their convocation, anything in this act contained to the contrary notwithstanding."

[2] Stow, p. 640. "On the eve of St. Bartholomew, the day and the morrow after, &c., were burned in Paul's Churchyard, Cheap, and divers other places of the city of London, all the roods and other images of the churches; in some places the copes, vestments, altar-cloths, books, banners, sepulchres, and roodlofts were burned."

the help of laymen only, for she was opposed by every one of the bishops, who in Parliament are the first who give their opinions, and certainly they alone should have been listened to in matters of faith—all the clergy of the province of Canterbury then assembled in convocation in London also refusing their consent.

But as this nation stands now almost alone in this, that heresies and sects of perdition were brought in, not as in France, Scotland, Belgium, and other countries, through popular tumults, but in a legal way, at the commandment of its kings, it may be as well to explain here how it was that the queen obtained the consent of both Houses of Parliament to the changes she made, for without their consent she had not the power to make any changes whatever in religion.

CHAPTER III.

THE PARLIAMENTARY ELECTIONS — COWARDICE OF THE PEERS — THE ACT OF UNIFORMITY — THE CATHOLICS DRIVEN OUT OF THE COUNTRY.

THE English Parliament consists of two houses: that of the nobility, namely, the prelates and the lay lords, and is called the Upper House; the other, that of knights, representatives of counties, and burgesses, representatives of cities, of the more important towns, and of the people, and is called the Lower House. The election of the members of the Lower House, in every county and borough, was so managed that those only were elected who were ready to make changes in the belief and religion of the country, and hence it was that the queen had no difficulty in obtaining their consent to everything that she proposed to do.[1] Now, in the Upper House sat the bishops, all most learned men and most faithful confessors, and very many were influenced by their eloquence and opinions. With them sat many lay peers, who in that very place but three years before, in the presence of the Legate of His Holiness, and on behalf of the whole realm, made a common profession of faith and obedience, and who were now ashamed to withdraw from it so soon, at the wish and pleasure of a woman. They too were present in the house who so

[1] Butler, Memoirs, i. 272. "Five candidates were nominated by the court to each borough, and three to each county; and by the sheriff's authority the members were chosen from among these candidates; a measure which appears to discover apprehensions in the court that the general sense of the people was contrary to the Reformation."

lately had gone as ambassadors to Rome to obtain the reconciliation of the kingdom, and they solemnly warned the Peers not to apostatise from the faith and communion of Christendom and of their own ancestors, nor to allow themselves to be branded with everlasting disgrace for levity and inconsistency in matters touching their salvation.[1] In consequence of this there was a long struggle in the Upper House, and its consent was obtained with great difficulty.[2]

The Catholic religion could not have been set aside at that time but for the cunning of the queen, who won the Peers over to her side: some she flattered, to others she made promises, and some she bribed; even their kindred were not neglected. One peer was won over by the expectation of marrying the queen, held out to him by Elizabeth herself,[3] and another by the offer of a dis-

[1] Sir Antony Brown, now Viscount Montague, according to Camden, (Eliz., p. 36), "acriter instabat magno Angliæ dedecori esse, si ab Apostolica Sede, cui nuper se submisse reconciliarat mox deficeret. . . . Majorem etiam in modum etiam atque etiam obtestando contendit, ut a Romana Sede non secederent, cui Christianam fidem primum acceptam et perpetuo conservatam debent."

[2] Sir Simonds d'Ewes, Journals of Parliament, p. 23. "On Saturday the 18th day of March [1559] the bill for the restoring of the supremacy to the imperial crown of this realm, and repealing divers acts of Parliament made to the contrary, with certain provisoes added thereunto by the Lords, was read the third time: "*et conclus. dissentientibus Archiepiscopo Eboracen., Comite Salop., Vicecomite Mountacuto, Episcopo Londin., Episcopo Winton., Episcopo Wigorn., Episcopo Landaven., Episcopo Coven., Episcopo Exon., Episcopo Castren., Episcopo Carleol., et Abbas* [sic] *de Westm., et prædicta billa est commissa attornato et sollicitatori reginæ in Domum Communem deferend.*"

[3] This was the earl of Arundel. In the "Crudelitatis Calvinianæ de Morte Comitis Northumbriæ," at the end, is the following account of this: "Ac primus quidem præcipuusque totius ordinis qui authoritate sua præcipue hoc effecit dux fuit Norfolciensis, qui paucis post annis, ab illis ipsis quibus ea in re gratificatus fuerat, capite fuit perridicule mulctatus; cujus etiam nunc filius ac hæres carceribus tenetur. Socer autem qui illum ad hoc induxerat, ambitione quadam potiundi reginæ matrimonio sibi promisso, despectus postea ac illusus, æreque alieno ac infamia exhaustus contemptibilissime moritur. Cætera nobilitas quid exinde sit passa, et quid in posterum passura videatur, nisi Deus misertus fuerit, universus orbis fere videt ac loquitur." The earl repented in his later days; for (Life of the Countess of Arundel, p. 180) "he was so happy as to be reconciled sometime before his death to the Catholic Church, and to receive the holy sacraments

pensation in the matter of marriage,[1] which he could not so easily obtain from the Pope. And yet after all, the schismatics obtained their end against the Catholics only by three votes.[2] Elizabeth gained her object, neglected her suitor, and shamefully mocked him. She would remain a virgin, she said, and on her tombstone should be written, "Here lieth Elizabeth, queen for many years, and all her life a virgin."[3]

The other great nobleman, the duke of Norfolk, whom she won over by her blandishments, she afterwards persecuted in many ways, had him falsely accused, and then beheaded. That was, as many said, the just judgment of God upon him; indeed, a grave and pious London matron is said to have visited the duke, and to have spoken to him with great frankness. "When your grace," she said, "gave your vote—formerly given, and as you were bound to give it, for the defence of the Church and the Catholic faith—unto heretics and for the ruin of religion, you had probably forgotten that you and your family, brought to the very

and rites thereof by the persuasion and procurement of the Lord Lumley, his son-in-law."

1 Sir Simonds d'Ewes, Journals, p. 25. House of Lords, March 21, 1559.—"At which hour the lord-keeper and divers other lords being set, the bill for ratification of the marriage between the duke of Norfolk and the Lady Margaret, now his wife, and for the assurance of certain lands for her jointure, with a new proviso added by the Commons, *conclusa est*, being read *tertia vice dissentientibus Archiepiscopo Eboracen., Episcopis Londin., Winton., Landaven., Castren, Carleol., et Abbate de Westm.*"

2 Butler, Histor. Memoirs, vol. i. chap. xxiii. "The bill was finally carried by a majority of three voices. The Catholics had particularly relied on an active opposition to it from the duke of Norfolk and the earl of Arundel, whose daughter he had married; but both voted for the bill, and the duke used all his proxies, which were numerous, in its favour. It passed the Commons without a division."

3 Stow, p. 637. Elizabeth, in answer to the petition of her first Parliament, said, "And in the end this shall be for me sufficient, that a marble stone shall declare that a queen having reigned such a time, lived and died a virgin." So also in a letter to the emperor (Burnet, vi. 442) she says, "Non invenimus in nobis voluntatem ullam deserendi hanc solitariam vitam, sed potius, juvante Deo, libentem animi inductionem in eadem diutius porro vita perseverandi."

brink of ruin by the heretics, had been, by queen Mary of most blessed memory, saved and raised to its present rank: well! because you have done this, loving the praise of men more than the glory of God, God will punish you, and the rest of the old nobility who have had a share in this sin, by means of these very heretics and upstarts."

During the discussion on the supremacy, the Peers said, among other things, that they could not take the oath with a good conscience; so she—and this helped her exceedingly—took care to make an exception in favour of the lay lords, provided they made the taking of the oath compulsory on the bishops at least, the ecclesiastics, and some others. Thereupon many of the Peers, thinking themselves safe under this provision, cared very little for the bishops and the clergy, and left them to the mercy of this impious legislation. This is the result whenever divine things are handled in human and secular assemblies which have not received from God the promise of the spirit of truth, judgment, and justice.

It is said of Henry VIII., when he resolved to seize the possessions of the monasteries and of the religious, that he easily obtained his object in Parliament from the lay peers and the prelates, who thought that they had but scanty interest in any legislation touching monastic houses and religious persons;[1] accordingly the regular

[1] Harpsfield, bk. iii. p. 142. "Woe! therefore, even for very civil and politic causes, to the said prelate [Cranmer] that made the lewd lying sermon for the destruction of the said abbeys. Woe! therefore, to them that procured the spoil and eversion of them. Woe! be even to the great abbots themselves that winked at the matter, yea, and gave their consent to the suppressing of the lesser, thinking to keep and preserve their own still, which they could not do long after, for all the fair and flattering promises made unto them, and for all that many of them—to their great charges and impoverishment—procured and purchased the continuance of their houses under the great seal, as I have heard some of them report, only they got the benefit that Polyphemus promised to Ulisses, that is, he would be so gracious and favourable to him that he would spare him and eat him last of all his fol-

clergy, abandoned by the lay lords and by the bishops, speedily became the prey of the tyrant. Afterwards, indeed, and especially in the Parliaments of Elizabeth, God permitted it, and it was easily brought about—when the bishops and all the clergy had been attacked, and the ecclesiastics being for the most part abandoned to the rapacity of a woman, by the lay lords—that the lay lords themselves in their turn also should be abandoned, in reparation for the wrong which they had done before, and that religion should be most shamefully trodden under foot. We ourselves have already seen, and our children will also more clearly see, and wonder at, the chastisements which have befallen the lay lords for their deeds.

A law[1] was now made that on a certain day, namely, the feast of St. John the Baptist, A.D. 1559, every one who said Mass, every one who heard Mass, every one who procured the celebration of the divine office in the

lowers. But yet Ulisses by policy got himself out of danger, but these men could by no means provide but that their abbeys were at length eaten and devoured as well as the lesser. All those which being under the clear yearly value of two hundred pounds, or not above, were given to the king by act of Parliament. But as for the residue, they came to the king's hands by one means or other, and that without any act of Parliament at all."

[1] 1 Eliz. c. 2. This is called the Act of Uniformity.

Grindal, writing from London, May 23, 1559, to Conrad Hubert (Zurich Letters, ii. No. 8), says: "Now at last, by the blessing of God, during the prorogation of Parliament, there has been published a proclamation to banish the Pope and his jurisdiction altogether, and to restore religion to that form which we had in the time of Edward VI. If any bishops or other beneficed persons shall decline to take the oath of abjuration of the authority of the bishop of Rome, they are to be deprived of every ecclesiastical function and deposed. No one after the feast of St. John the Baptist next ensuing, may celebrate Mass without subjecting himself to a most heavy penalty. It is therefore commonly supposed that almost all the bishops, and also many other beneficed persons, will renounce their bishoprics and their functions, as being ashamed after so much tyranny and cruelty exercised under the banners of the Pope, and the obedience so lately sworn to him, to be again brought to a recantation, and convicted of manifest perjury. We are labouring under a great dearth of godly ministers; for many who have fallen off in this persecution, are now become Papists in heart; and those who had been heretofore, so to speak, *moderate* Papists, are now the most obstinate."

ancient way, every one who administered any sacrament according to the Roman rite, was to be heavily fined; that is, the first offence against that law was to be visited by a fine of one hundred marks,[1] and imprisonment for six months if it be not paid.

For the second conviction under the statute the fine was to be four hundred marks, and if not paid, the imprisonment was to be for one year; and for the third conviction the penalty was imprisonment for life, and the forfeiture of all goods and chattels.[2]

The result of this act was that on the day fixed the public celebration of Mass ceased throughout the whole realm. But as the bishops, with one exception,[3] refused to assent to this iniquity, as I have already said, and to say that they believed in their consciences that the queen alone was the supreme governor of the Church under Christ, they were soon after deprived of their dignities, and committed either to prison or to the custody of divers persons; so that they are now, all of them, worn out by the weariness of their miserable treatment.[4]

[1] *Ducentos aureos.* This penal legislation seems to have moved Jewell to great merriment, for he thus writes to Peter Martyr from London, March 5, 1560 (Zurich Letters, i. No. 30): "There is nothing, however, of which they [the Catholics] have any right to complain; for the Mass has never been more highly prized within my memory; each being now valued, to every individual spectator, at not less than two hundred crowns."

[2] 1 Eliz. c. 2, s. 9–13.

[3] This was Antony Kitchen, consecrated May 3, 1545, in the lifetime of Henry VIII. and of Cranmer, and without Bulls.

[4] Jewell, writing to Peter Martyr, Feb. 7, 1562 (Zurich Letters, i. No. 43), says, "The Marian bishops are still confined in the Tower, and are going on in their old way." Again to Bullinger, Feb. 9 (ibid., 44): "Some few of the bishops who were furious in the late Marian times, cannot as yet, in so short a time, for very shame return to their senses. They are therefore confined in the Tower lest their contagion should infect others." Cox bishop of Ely, writing to Peter Martyr, Aug. 5, 1562 (ibid., 49), says: "The heads of our Popish clergy are still kept in confinement. They are treated, indeed, with kindness, but relax nothing of their Popery. Others are living at large, scattered about in different parts of the kingdom, but without any function, unless perhaps where they may be sowing the seeds of impiety in secret."

To preserve the names of these illustrious confessors from oblivion, I give them here. In the first place stands Nicholas [1] archbishop of York, and shortly before this lord chancellor of England, Edmund [2] bishop of London, Cuthbert [3] bishop of Durham, John [4] bishop of Winchester, Thirlby [5] bishop of Ely, Turberville [6] bishop of Exeter, Bourne [7] bishop of Bath and Wells, Pole [8] bishop of Peterborough, Bayne [9] bishop of Lichfield, Cuthbert [10] bishop of Chester, Oglethorpe [11] bishop of Carlisle. Thomas Goldwell, [12] bishop of St. Asaph, in great sanctity and full of days, however, lived in Rome for six-and-

[1] Nicholas Heath. See bk. ii. chap. ii. p. 179, note 3.

[2] Edmund Bonner. See bk. ii. chap. ii. p. 179, note 2.

[3] Cuthbert Tunstall. See bk. i. chap. x. p. 64, note 3. He was now committed to the custody of Parker at Lambeth Palace, where he died Nov. 18, 1559.

[4] Dr. John White. See bk. ii. chap. v. p. 208, note 1.

[5] Thomas Thirlby, born at Cambridge, where he was educated, and became master of Trinity Hall. He was bishop of Westminster while that see lasted, then of Norwich and of Ely. He was put under the care of Parker at Lambeth Palace, where he died Aug. 26, A.D. 1570.

[6] James Turberville, educated at New College, Oxford, consecrated Sept. 8, 1555. It is said that he was allowed to live in peace with his relatives.

[7] Gilbert Bourne was fellow of All Souls, Oxford, and archdeacon of London, consecrated April 1, 1554. The see had been stripped almost bare, but he recovered some of the estates. Deprived by Elizabeth, he was consigned to the custody of Gregory Dodds, dean of Exeter, and died at Silverton Sept. 10, 1569.

[8] David Pole was fellow of All Souls, dean of the Arches, archdeacon of Derby and of Salop, consecrated bishop of Peterborough Aug. 15, 1537. Heylyn (Hist. Reform., 115) says "he died upon one of his own farms in a good old age;" but according to Le Neve, "he died at London in June 1568," and he had held his preferment during the reign of Edward VI.

[9] Ralph Bayne, born in Yorkshire and educated at St. John's College, Cambridge. He was for some time professor of Hebrew in the University of Paris. Consecrated Nov. 18, 1554, he was deprived by Elizabeth in June 1559, and died at Islington Nov. 18 of the same year. His body was laid in the church of St. Dunstan.

[10] Cuthbert Scott, educated at Christ's College, Cambridge. Elizabeth put him in the Fleet prison, but he made his escape and went to Louvain, where he died.

[11] Owen Oglethorpe, president of Magdalene College, Oxford, A.D. 1535, and canon of Windsor in 1540. Having resigned the presidency of Magdalene Sept. 27, 1552, he was again elected president Oct. 31, 1553, and in the next year was made dean of Windsor. He was consecrated bishop of Carlisle Aug. 15, 1557, and deprived in 1559. He died the same year, Dec. 31, and was buried in St. Dunstan's-in-the-West.

[12] Goldwell. See bk. ii. chap. iv. p. 203, note 3.

twenty years afterwards. It is not long since he went to his rest in our Lord by a most blessed and holy death. To these, on account of his unvarying constancy and partnership in bonds, must be added Feckenham[1] abbot of Westminster, who having confessed a good confession, in this very year slept in our Lord in peace.

The better part of the clergy followed in the footsteps of their prelates; very many of them, high dignitaries in the Church, were either thrown into prison or banished the realm, while heretics usurped their dignities and filled their places. Very many religious also, of divers orders, fled the country. Three monasteries[2] of men and women departed, leaving not a single member behind. Many persons too of high rank, of both sexes, followed their example, even to bonds and the loss of their possessions. The very flower of the two universities, Oxford and Cambridge, was carried away, as it were, by a storm, and scattered in foreign lands.[3] Some three hundred persons, of all conditions, went away at once into different parts of Europe, but especially to the Belgian universities, where a most abundant harvest is gathered, to be sown again in the barren lands of England, there to grow at last, so we hope, to be the salvation of all its people.[4]

[1] Feckenham. See bk. ii. chap. iv. p. 198, note 1.

[2] The Friars Observant from Greenwich, the Carthusians from Richmond, and the Brigettine nuns from Sion.

[3] Jewell, writing to Bullinger, May 22, 1559 (Zurich Letters, i. 14), says: "Our universities are so depressed and ruined that at Oxford there are scarcely two individuals who think with us, and even they are so dejected and broken in spirit that they can do nothing. That despicable friar Soto and another Spanish monk, I know not who, have so torn up by the roots all that Peter Martyr had so prosperously planted that they have reduced the vineyard of the Lord into a wilderness. You would scarcely believe so much desolation could have been effected in so short a time."

[4] The queen's visitors appeared in Oxford about the end of June 1559, removed the Catholics, and put the heretics in their places. The result was that in the act of 1560, according to Wood (Annals, ad an. 1561), "was none in divinity, and but one in the civil law, three in physic, and eight in arts, and in

Some of these wrote books both in Latin and in English, wherein they clearly and vigorously defended many doctrines of the Catholic religion against the heretics.[1] Among these a distinguished place is occupied by Nicholas Harpsfield—who in prison wrote, among other works, an admirable book against the centuriators of Magdeburg, publishing it, however, in the name of Cope[2]—Nicolas Sander,[3] and—they are still living—William Allen[4]

the act this year [1561] not one in divinity, law, or physic. The students also were so poor and beggarly that many of them were forced this and the year following to obtain licence under the commissary's seal to require the alms of well-disposed people."

[1] One of the articles issued by Grindal previous to his proposed visitation of the province of Canterbury in 1576, being the eighteenth of Elizabeth, is as follows: "Whether there be any person or persons, ecclesiastical or temporal, within your parish, or elsewhere within this diocese, that of late have retained or kept in their custody, or that read, sell, utter, disperse, carry, or deliver to others, any English books, set forth of late years at Louvain, or in any other place beyond the seas, by Harding, Dorman, Allen, Saunders, Stapleton, Marshall, Bristow, or any of them, or by any other English Papist, either against the queen's majesty's supremacy in matters ecclesiastical, or against true religion, and Catholic doctrine now received and established by common authority within this realm; and what their names and surnames are."—Art. 41 in Grindal's Remains, p. 169.

[2] See before, bk. ii. chap. iv. p. 201, note 5. The book referred to is "Dialogi Sex contra Summi Pontificatus Monasticæ Vitæ Sanctorum, Sacrarum Imaginarum Oppugnatores et Pseudomartyres. Antverpiæ, 1566."

Alan Cope was born in London, and became fellow of Magdalene College, Oxford, in 1549. He went into banishment in 1560, and proceeded to Rome, where he was made one of the canons of St. Peter's. He was a friend of Harpsfield, who sent to him the book referred to in the text in order to have it published. Alan Cope, because his friend was in prison, and because it was most certain that his hardships would be multiplied, even if his death might not be hastened, gave his own name to the book, and hid the name of the author under the letters—

A. H. L. N. H. E. V. E. A. C.,

that is, Auctor hujus libri, Nicolaus Harpesfeldus. Eum vero edidit Alanus Copus. Alan Cope died in Rome A.D. 1580.

[3] The author of the book to which this continuation of Rishton is added.

[4] Cardinal Allen, whose name is in benediction, was born in Lancashire, and educated at Oxford, where he became principal of St. Mary Hall, a place in the gift of Oriel College, of which he was one of the fellows. On the death of Mary he withdrew to Louvain, and on his return to England denounced the practice of the Catholics who frequented the heretical services to avoid the penalties. He went abroad again, and founded the College of Douai and Rheims, being thereby the founder of the English missions, and another St. Gregory to this country. He was made canon of Cambrai, then of Rheims. He shrunk from accepting the dignity of the cardinalate under Gregory XIII.,

and Thomas Stapleton,[1] by whose labours their countrymen who had been deceived are returning daily in unnumbered crowds, by the grace of Christ, into the bosom of the Church.

but had to yield to Sixtus V., who raised him to that dignity by the title of St. Martin in Montibus, Aug. 7, 1587. In 1589 he was appointed archbishop of Mechlin, but he never took possession of the see. He died in Rome, Oct. 16, 1594.

[1] Thomas Stapleton, born at Henfield, Sussex, in the month and year of the martyrdom of Sir Thomas More, educated first at Canterbury, then at Winchester and New College, Oxford, of which house he was a fellow A.D. 1554. He was a prebendary of Chichester when Elizabeth came to the throne, and, forced to quit the country, took refuge in Louvain. He was for some time catechist at Douai, but, recalled to Louvain, he was made regius professor of theology and canon of St. Peter's there, where he died Oct. 12, 1598, having lived for two-and-forty years in exile for the faith.

CHAPTER IV.

THE LAWYERS — THE COUNTRY GENTLEMEN — CATHOLICS FREQUENT THE HERETICAL ASSEMBLIES — LACK OF MINISTERS IN THE NEW RELIGION.

BESIDE the two most ancient universities already spoken of, abounding once in learned men, especially in theologians, but now, as in days of heresy, merely the nursing mothers of grammarians and preachers of novelties, England possessed, in London,[1] very honourable schools, in which for the most part the sons of princes, noblemen, and of the more wealthy of the people, studied the statute and common law. Out of these schools generally come those who administer justice in the courts, and manage the affairs of the kingdom—men, if any, prudent, grave, and honoured. These so hated the change of religion, foreseeing the dangers into which it would bring the state, that very many of them, at the time and afterwards—for they cherished the faith and the ancient tradition—were removed from the administration of justice and of public affairs. Their places were filled, not indeed by heretics, for among the lawyers heretics

1 The Third University of England, by G[eorge] B[uck], knight, London, 1631, at the end of Stow's Chronicle, chap. ix. "Now follow in their order the colleges, houses, or inns of the professors of our laws of England, who have within and about the city fourteen houses, which our judicious Camden styleth discreetly colleges, *collegia juris consultorum*, which are commonly called Inns of Court and Inns of Chancery. . . . And because that by ancient custom and by old orders of the Houses of Court and Chancery, all those which were admitted into these houses were and ought to be gentlemen, and that of three descents at the least, . . . for no man can be made a gentleman but by his father."

were very few, but by men who submitted to Cæsar and went with the times, giving the second place to God. In all ranks they who did so were many, and they proved more ruinous to the state than the heretics themselves.

Of the three parties into which Englishmen might be divided, one party was at the time not so very much given to heresy; it neither desired the change of religion nor approved of it after it was made, and it liked it still less afterwards when it had tasted of its fruits. For beside the very large number of the nobility, of which I have spoken before, the greater part of the country gentlemen was unmistakably Catholic; so also were the farmers throughout the kingdom, and in that kingdom they are an honourable and wealthy people. They all hated the heresy. Not a single county except those near London and the court, and scarcely any towns except those on the sea-coast, willingly accepted the heresy; and even in those places the heretics were the lazy and the luxurious—young men, bankrupts and spendthrifts, women laden with sins, and people of that kind.

We all observed when we were young, especially in the universities, that persons fell more readily into heresy if they were troublesome to their masters, disobedient to parents and superiors, faithless to their lords, or given to any other grave sin. Putting these aside, though the others were almost all Catholic at heart, nevertheless they thought they might to some extent outwardly obey the law, and yield to the will of the queen; if in so doing there was any sin, that must be laid at the queen's door, not at theirs, for they were of opinion that the straits they were in somehow or other might be held to excuse them.

This opinion was adopted also by the lower clergy,

simple and parish priests, not a few canons of cathedral or collegiate churches, who in their hearts hated the heresy, and for a time, listening to the voice of conscience, refrained from the use of the new service. So general was this, that after the day appointed by the statute on which the true sacrifice was to cease and the false rites were to begin, many churches throughout the kingdom remained shut for some months; for the old priests would not willingly use the schismatical service, and the new ministers were not yet numerous enough to serve so many places.[1]

Before long, the queen, upon whom fell the care of all the churches, held a visitation,[2] and made inquiries touching the beneficed clergy who on the appointed day had not adopted in their parishes the parliamentary rites; thereupon many of these, fearing the loss of their goods and of their benefices, submitted. In the place of those who refused to conform she put ministers of the new creation, who were to discharge the duties thereof. She also compelled the people to frequent the churches as before, and according to the act,[3] inflicted a fine of one shilling upon every one who should be absent on holy days. And thus by force or fraud it

[1] Jewell to Peter Martyr, Aug. 1, 1559 (Zurich Letters, 1st series, No. 16): "Now that religion is everywhere changed, the Mass priests absent themselves altogether from public worship, as if it were the greatest impiety to have anything in common with the people of God."

[2] The injunctions of the queen may be seen in Wilkins, Concil., iv. 182, and the articles of inquiry, ibid., p. 189. Among the latter is the following: "Whether you know any man in your parish secretly or in unlawful conventicles say or hear Mass, or any other service prohibited by the law." The commission of the northern visitors is given by Burnet (Hist. Reform., v. 533, ed. Pocock), from whom Wilkins (Concil., iv. 193) has copied it. Those visitors, all except one, being laymen, received from the queen power to deprive the old priests, and to put in their places men who would conform to the new religion. That commission was signed on the very day, June 24, 1559, on which the Missal and the Breviary were to be superseded by the Book of Common Prayer.

[3] 1 Eliz. c. 2, s. 14. "Twelve pence to be levied by the church-wardens of the parish, . . . of the goods, lands, and tenements of such offender, by way of distress."

came to pass that the largest portion of the Catholics yielded by degrees to their enemies, and did not refuse from time to time publicly to enter the schismatical churches to hear sermons therein, and to receive communion in those conventicles.

At the same time they had Mass said secretly in their own houses by those very priests who in church publicly celebrated the spurious liturgy, and sometimes by others who had not defiled themselves with heresy; yea, and very often in those disastrous times were on one and the same day partakers of the table of our Lord and of the table of devils, that is, of the blessed Eucharist and the Calvinistic supper. Yea, what is still more marvellous and more sad, sometimes the priest saying Mass at home, for the sake of those Catholics whom he knew to be desirous of them, carried about him Hosts consecrated according to the rite of the Church, with which he communicated them at the very time in which he was giving to other Catholics more careless about the faith the bread prepared for them according to the heretical rite.[1]

[1] The Lives of Philip Howard and Anne Dacres, his Wife, p. 170. "Before the promulgation of the Council of Trent's declaration concerning the unlawfulness of being present at the Protestant service, sermons and the like, here in England, the Lady Monteagle was accustomed to have Protestant service read to her by a chaplain in her house, and afterwards to hear Mass said privately by a priest. But as soon as she understood the unlawfulness of this practice, she would never be present at the Protestant service any more. And once urged by the duke of Norfolk, with whom she lived a while before her death, and at whose house she died, to do something contrary to the profession of her faith, though she much esteemed and respected him, yet her answer was so sound and resolute that he never mentioned the like any more, but gave her full liberty to have all the assistance desired before and at her death. Wherein she was more happy than her daughter the duchess, who dying not long before her in childbed, though she desired to have been reconciled by a priest, who for that end was conducted into the garden, yet could not have access unto her, either by reason of the duke's vigilance to hinder it, or at least of his continual presence in the chamber at the time." Fr. Persons also, in "A Briefe Apologie," p. 2, speaks of the "division of opinions about going to the heretical churches and services, which most part of Catholikes did follow for many yeares."

I write this that other nations, made wise by the things they see among us, may learn how heresies begin and grow, and be on their guard in time against pestilences of this kind.

Meanwhile the queen and her ministers considered themselves most fortunate in that those who clung to the ancient faith, though so numerous, publicly accepted, or by their presence outwardly sanctioned, in some way, the new rites which they had prescribed. They did not care so much about the inward belief of these men, or if they did, they thought it best to dissemble for a time. They were not a little pleased that even priests were found who did not shrink from the new service; for they were at first afraid that they would not be able to persuade them to accept it, contrary to the example and commandment of their bishops and the voice of their own conscience. The new ministers were not enough; more than thirty thousand parishes must be supplied.[1] And they thought it would bring them into discredit if the churches should for the most part be suddenly shut, and all divine service interrupted; perhaps, too—and this is peculiar to all heretics—they preferred at first, the more easily to deceive the people, the services of true priests to those of the false.[2]

[1] Rishton has here repeated a popular misconception about the number of parishes in England and Wales. It is probable that the number of parish churches never exceeded half that sum, and that the estimate in the "Douai Diary," p. 93, may be correct, namely, that the number of parish churches was 9285. But Simon Fish, in his "Supplication for Beggars," said that there were "52,000 parish churches" in England.

[2] Thomas Lever, writing to Bullinger, July 10, 1560 (Zurich Letters, 1st series, No. 35), says, "Many of our parishes have no clergyman, and some dioceses are without a bishop. And out of that very small number who administer the sacraments throughout this great country, there is hardly one in a hundred who is both able and willing to preach the Word of God." Jewell to Martyr, Nov. 6, 1560 (ibid., No. 38): "We are only wanting in preachers, and of these there is a great and alarming scarcity. The schools also are entirely deserted."

It was thus that these things were done in England, and soon after, too, in those parts of Ireland which recognised the queen's authority, where in the same way she laid the yoke of heresy on the people against their consciences, for the people of that country are before all things Catholics.[1]

[1] Renehan, Collections on Irish Church History, p. 12. "When Elizabeth issued a *congé-d'élire* for the election of Adam Lofthouse, the chapter of Armagh dispersed themselves throughout the country, and the dean could not find a sufficient number to comply with the injunction. Nay, to the end of his life, and for years afterwards, there could not be found in—except a few of the large towns—more than ten or fifteen places through the entire province of Ulster, either persons to attend, or a minister of any kind to perform, the Protestant service. The consequence was, the churches fell into decay, and the parsons in after-times called for Parliament aid to repair them. When Elizabeth issued a commission to inquire into the ecclesiastical state of Ireland, there could scarcely be found a church or an officiating clergyman. The Catholic priests were ejected from their churches, many of them preferred to say Mass for their people in private places to exposing themselves to imprisonment or death; on the other hand, very few Irishmen abandoned their religion, and the inferior benefices were not sufficiently tempting for the English apostates."

CHAPTER V.

THE CREATION OF THE PROTESTANT BISHOPS—THE OLD TITLES RETAINED—MARRIAGE OF THE NEW CLERGY—PARLIAMENTARY SANCTION OF THE PROTESTANT ORDINATIONS—MARRIAGE OF THE CLERGY.

MEANWHILE the governor of the Church applies herself to the creation of new bishops and clergy of her sect.[1] In the distribution of offices and ecclesiastical rank, and in the very form of government, the queen paid no heed to the Zuinglian or Calvinistic model, nor indeed did she accurately copy that of the Lutherans; but she wished to be regarded as one that was more of the Lutheran than of any other heresy, not only in ceremonial, but also in her way of believing. She pretended to a certain moderation; for as she had been considered a Catholic not long before, she was not willing at once to appear as a heretic of the worst kind. Accordingly that seditious assembly, which is called the Consistory, and those degrees or ministries of elders, ministers, and the rest, she put on one side. But whether it was her own act or the result of the advice of others, she resolved

[1] Jewell to Simler, Nov. 2, 1559 (Zurich Letters, 1st series, No. 22): "As to your expressing your hopes that our bishops will be consecrated without any superstitious and offensive ceremonies, you mean, I suppose, without oil, without the chrism, without the tonsure. And you are not mistaken; for the sink would indeed have been emptied to no purpose if we had suffered these dregs to remain at the bottom. Those oily, shaven, portly hypocrites we have sent back to Rome, whence we first imported them; for we require our bishops to be pastors, labourers, and watchmen. And that this may the more readily be brought to pass, the wealth of the bishops is now diminished and reduced to a reasonable amount," &c.

that it would be more for the honour of her spiritual prelates, more for the splendour of her temporal kingdom, and lastly, more for the security of the sect, that the clergy she was instituting should, according to the arrangements of the old Church, consist of archbishops, bishops, priests, and even deacons—for they allow no order lower than this.

In the same way the cathedral and collegiate churches were to have, as before, provosts, deans, archdeacons, chancellors, canons, and other officers, according to the custom of each place. All these men were to retain the titles of the ancient dignities and honours, the possessions of the old clergy, and almost all the privileges which they had both in Church and State. Moreover, the religious woman made an effort to have Religious of her belief, for she asked that illustrious confessor the abbot of Westminster [1] not to allow his monks to go away because of the change, and to assure them of her kindly feelings towards the monastery; that she wished them to remain there, and to pray for her, celebrating divine service according to the order of her laws. But those good men saw no reason why they should forsake the rule of St. Benedict to keep that of Calvin.

The queen is in the habit of boasting before strangers and the foreign ambassadors that the clergy of her sect are held in honour, and are not mere starvelings like those of Geneva, and other Churches of the kind, not so well ordered as hers; and that she had not gone so far from the faith of other princes and of her own ancestors as many think. The better to keep up this fraud, she retained for some years on the table, which she had set up in the place of the altar, in her chapel, two wax

[1] Stow, p. 628. "The 21st of November [1556], John Fecknam, late dean of Paul's in London, was made abbot of Westminster, was stalled, and took possession of the same; and fourteen monks more received the habit with him that day of the Order of St. Benet."

candles, which were never lighted, with a silver crucifix between them.[1] And then in order to please the Catholics, and to impose the more easily upon foreigners, she used to say from time to time that she was forced, not by her own convictions, but by the clamours of her subjects, to make a change of religion, but that she had practised great moderation in making it.

Let us return to the principal question. She gave away the ecclesiastical dignities and offices to Lutherans and Calvinists, but more especially to the latter.[2] They had come from Savoy and other countries, into which they had fled, to divide the spoils. They came with the utmost speed, who not long before, after the

[1] Jewell, writing to Peter Martyr from London, Nov. 16, 1559 (Zurich Letters, 1st series, No. 24), says: "That little silver cross, of ill-omened origin, still maintains its place in the queen's chapel. Wretched me! this thing will soon be drawn into a precedent." Then, Jan. 6, 1560, Sampson writes to the same person (ibid., Let. 27): "O my father! what can I hope for, when the ministry of the Word is banished from court? While the crucifix is allowed, with lights burning before it, the altars indeed are removed, and images also, throughout the kingdom, the crucifix and candles are retained at court alone." Parkhurst, Protestant bishop of Norwich, writing to Bullinger, April 26, 1563 (ibid., No. 5), says: "I wrote you word that the cross, wax candles, and candlesticks had been removed from the queen's chapel; but they were shortly after brought back again, to the great grief of the godly. The candles heretofore were lighted every day, but now not at all." In a letter to Rodolph Gualter, March 4, 1568, Parkhurst gives this further account of the crucifix: "About the beginning of November, a certain youth, under the influence of great zeal for God, entered the queen's chapel, and threw down on the ground, with great force, the golden cross, together with the images connected with it: then stamping on it with his feet, he broke it in pieces, in the sight of all who were assembled for common prayer, for it was done publicly. From that time no cross has been seen there; it was abolished, and it will for ever be abolished as a mischievous thing."

Mr. Gorham, who translated and published this letter in his "Reformation Gleanings," p. 435, has softened the fierce language of the Protestant bishop, which, however, he has given in a note: "Abiit et abitura est in perpetuum in malam crucem." Heylyn (Hist. Reform., p. 124) gives a more probable account of the destruction of the crucifix, wrought by the queen's fool "at the solicitation of Sir Francis Knolles, the queen's near kinsman by the Careys, and one who openly appeared in favour of the schism at Frankfort."

[2] Horn to Rodolph Gualter, Aug. 10, 1576 (Zurich Letters, 1st series, No. 129): "As she has always abominated Popery from her infancy, so also will she never admit Lutheranism, which is a great disturber of Christianity."

fashion of Calvin, hated the proud and antichristian prelates with their domineering authority; these men having usurped the honours and the goods of the Church, behaved themselves more violently, more tyrannically, more greedily, and more insolently than the true owners could have done or we have imagined. They forgot the form of prayers and the plan of government to which they had been accustomed in Geneva, and which they had promised their teachers there to introduce into England, submitting themselves like slaves to the supremacy and directions of the queen,[1] for that was the road to the greatest gain.[2]

But, however, to soothe their offended friends, they obtain for the Calvinists—French, Flemish, and Walloon

[1] George Withers to the Elector Palatine (Zurich Letters, 2d series, No. 62, p. 163): "But the ministry is in fact nothing at all, nor is there any discipline. For those persons cannot be said to be ministers of Christ, but servants of men, who can do nothing according to the prescript of the Word, but are obliged to act in every respect at the nod of the queen and the bishops. What must we say when most of them are Popish priests consecrated to perform Mass?"

[2] George Withers thus writes to the Elector Palatine (Zurich Letters, 2d series, No. 62): "Then on the expulsion of the Popish bishops, new ones were to be appointed in their room, and most of these were of the number of those who had been exiles. These at first began to oppose the ceremonies; but afterwards, when there was no hope otherwise of obtaining a bishopric, they yielded, and, as one of them openly acknowledged, undertook the office against their conscience." Parkhurst, writing to Bullinger, Aug. 23, 1560 (ibid., 1st series, No. 37), says, "Many pious persons are quite satisfied; as for myself, a few things still remain unsatisfactory, but I hope for an improvement." That improvement never came, for Pilkington, who was bishop of Durham in 1573, thus complains (Zurich Letters, 1st series, No. 110): "We endure, I must confess, many things against our inclinations, and groan under them, which if we wished even so much, no entreaty can remove. We are under authority, and cannot make any innovation without the sanction of the queen, or abrogate anything without the authority of the laws; and the only alternative now allowed us is, whether we will bear with these things or disturb the peace of the Church." Grindal, also from London, writing to Bullinger, Aug. 27, 1566 (Zurich Letters, 1st series, No. 73), says: "We who are now bishops, on our first return, and before we entered on our ministry, contended long and earnestly for the removal of those things that have occasioned the present dispute. But as we were unable to prevail either with the queen or the Parliament, we judged it best, after a consultation on the subject, not to desert our churches for the sake of a few ceremonies, and those not unlawful in themselves," &c.

—the use of certain churches in London,[1] where these might pray by themselves, and celebrate their supper in the most pure and reformed way. Afterwards there was a sharp quarrel between those churches and the new synagogue of England.[2] Some of the French preachers were afterwards compelled to quit the country, and some of that brotherhood were burnt;[3] for people of the foulest morals from divers nations soon joined themselves to those churches under the pretence of their Calvinism.

However, they seize with eagerness and without scruple upon the bishoprics and other ecclesiastical prelacies, even though they knew that the true bishops in communion with the whole of Christendom were still living,[4] deprived of their dignities for no reason and by no lawful authority; though they possessed a certain knowledge that the churches, the sees and the offices

[1] Wilkins, iv. 204. Elizabeth directed the lord treasurer to assign the church of the Augustin Friars for the use of the strangers, but the bishop of London was to appoint the preachers or ministers, and Edmund Grindal applied to Calvin for directions. Calvin sent over Nicolas des Gallars, who accordingly came, was received by Grindal, and settled by him as the pastor of the French congregation in London. See Zurich Letters, 2d series, No. 21. But in 1568 (Wilkins, iv. 254), the queen, by proclamation, orders these strangers to be examined, doubting lest that among such numbers there may be some who are guilty of "rebellion, murders, robberies, or suchlike."

[2] Heylyn (Elizabeth, p. 133) says the foreigners were allowed "to have a church unto themselves, and in that church not only to erect the Genevian discipline, but to set up a form of prayer which should hold no conformity with the English Liturgy. . . . What else is the setting up of a presbytery in a Church founded and established by the rules of Episcopacy, than the erecting of a commonwealth or popular estate in the midst of a monarchy? Which Calvin well enough perceived, and thereupon gave Grindal thanks for his favour in it, of whom they after serve themselves upon all occasions."

[3] Heylyn (History of the Presbyterians, p. 280) records the burning of two Dutchmen in Smithfield, July 2, 1575.

[4] The Catholic bishops were made a mockery; for thus writes Jewell to Peter Martyr, Feb. 7, 1562 (Zurich Letters, 1st series, No. 43): "The Marian bishops are still confined in the Tower, and are going on in their old way. If the laws were but as vigorous now as in the time of Henry, they would submit themselves without difficulty. They are an obstinate and untamed set of men, but are nevertheless subdued by terror and the sword."

had not been founded by other, or for other, than Catholic men. But they looked upon all these as some one did upon kingdoms, who said that they belonged to the first person who could make them his own. The queen by her letters-patent granted these dignities, but those who accepted them must be ordained by certain persons, and in a certain way, according to the laws of the realm.

Henry VIII., who was the wicked root, made a law, when he withdrew the kingdom from the Church and the Apostolic See, that no one chosen to be a bishop should apply, in order to his consecration, for the Papal Bulls or the Apostolic mandate, but should provide himself only with the royal licence, and thereupon, ordained by three bishops with the consent of the metropolitan, and not in any other way, should be recognised as a true bishop, in virtue of the act of Parliament[1] made in imitation of ancient canons. In the consecrations under that act, the king retained the old ceremonial with the solemn anointing, according to the tradition of the Church; but Edward VI., going on from bad to worse, suppressed it, and put in its place certain prayers which were Calvinistic, preserving, however, in force the former enactments touching the number of bishops present at the laying on of hands on the bishop elect. This new legislation was set aside by Mary, and renewed by Elizabeth; hence it became necessary for these prelates of the queen to be ordained in this way, namely, that with the consent of the metropolitan, two or three bishops should be present and lay hands upon them.

But now, when these superintendents were to be

[1] 25 Henry VIII. c. 20, s. 5, A.D. 1534. Cranmer applied for and obtained his Bulls; but no bishop afterwards during the reign of Henry either applied for or obtained them, and all those who were from that time forth consecrated, were consecrated in heresy and schism till the days of queen Mary, who restored the ancient observances.

created, the affair became ridiculous; they could find no Catholic bishops to lay hands upon them, and in their sect there were neither three nor two bishops, nor was there any metropolitan whatsoever, having previously received episcopal consecration, to give his consent or to lay his hands upon them. They did not betake themselves either to their neighbours, the Lutheran or Calvinistic Churches, for the purpose of obtaining the services of a bishop, for perhaps there were none among them. They importuned an Irish archbishop,[1] then a prisoner in London, to succour them in the straits they were in. They promised to set him at liberty, and to reward him for his services, if he would preside at their ordination. But the good man could not be persuaded to lay hallowed hands upon heretics or be a partaker in the sins of others.

Being thus utterly destitute of all lawful orders, and generally spoken of as men who were not bishops, for by the laws of England they could not be, they were compelled to have recourse to the civil power to obtain in the coming Parliament the confirmation of their rank from a lay authority, which should also pardon them, if anything had been done or left undone, contrary to law, in their previous admission to their offices; and this was done after they had been for some years acting as bishops without any episcopal consecration.[2] Hence their name of parliamentary bishops.

[1] The application to the Irish archbishop is not denied by Mason (Vindic. Eccles. Anglican., lib. iii. c. 9), who recites the story in the objection, but takes no notice of it in his reply. Dr. Dowdall, archbishop of Armagh, died in 1558, and was succeeded, according to Gams (Series Episcoporum, p. 207), by Donat. O'Teig, who died in 1562, and he by Richard Creagh, who was a prisoner in London before the eighth of Elizabeth, when the statute was made declaring the consecrations of the bishops good.—Renehan, Collections, p. 11.

[2] 8 Eliz. c. 1, s. 4. "That all acts and things heretofore had, made, or done by any person or persons, in or about any consecration, confirmation, or investing of any person or persons elected to the office or dignity of any archbishop or bishop within this realm, or within any other the

Whatever those false bishops may be, or by what means they were so made, they came out of their dens and lairs lions and wolves, strong to seize their prey, to domineer over clergy and laity, and to plunder them by ways that were new and never heard of before. First of all the queen held her own visitation throughout the whole realm, then the metropolitans made another each in his province, and the bishop a third in his diocese: during these visitations the Catholics were most rigorously sought out and punished, and marvellous reforms were made.

Among the articles of inquiry were these:[1] Is Mass anywhere still said? Is the sacrament reserved? Are there any churches in which the divine service newly ordered is not said? Are there any altars unbroken and undefaced? Is the choir made level with the floors of the nave of the church? Do the windows or the walls preserve any traces of images? How many chalices, pyxes, and crucifixes are left? Of what material? The

queen's dominions or countries, by virtue of the queen's majesty's letters-patent or commission, sithence the beginning of her majesty's reign, be, and shall be, by authority of this present Parliament, declared, judged, and deemed, at and from every of the several times of the doing thereof, good and perfect to all respects and purposes; any matter or thing that can, or may, be objected to the contrary thereof in any wise notwithstanding."

[1] The Queen's Injunctions, A.D. 1559 (Wilkins, iv. 182), require "the whole Bible of the largest volume in English, and within twelve months next after the said visitation the Paraphrases of Erasmus also in English;" and the destruction of "all shrines, coverings of shrines, all tables, candlesticks, trindals, and rolls of wax, pictures, paintings, . . . so that there remain no memory of the same in walls, glass windows, or elsewhere within their churches and houses." And that the churchwardens of every parish "shall deliver unto our visitors the inventories of vestments, copes, and other ornaments, plate, books," &c. In the articles of the queen's visitation, A.D. 1559 (Wilkins, iv. 189), it is asked whether "they minister the holy communion any otherwise than only after such form and manner as it is set forth by the common authority of the queen's majesty and the Parliament." And also, "Whether you know any man in your parish, or in unlawful conventicles, say or hear Mass, or any other service prohibited by the law." Grindal, also, in York, A.D. 1571 (Wilkins, iv. 269), directs "all altars to be pulled down to the ground, and the altar stones defaced and bestowed to some common use; and roodlofts altered."

people were compelled to provide Bibles in English, most falsely translated by heretics, and defiled with impious notes, the "Institutions" of Calvin, and books of the same kind, and to place copies in every church, where any one might read them; lastly, they made inquiries concerning the life of the parish priests, whom they generally advised to marry betimes.

The new clergy of England, partly apostates [1] and partly laymen, as it is a very spiritual clergy,[2] turned its thoughts at once to marriage, and strove hard to obtain a legal sanction for the marriages of bishops, canons, and others of the ministry, and for the legitimacy of their children; but it could not obtain it, for their marriages were regarded as a dishonour to the ministry and a danger to the state. Edward VI., it is true, removed by an act of Parliament all hindrances canonical and civil to the marriage of clerks and even of religious, but that law was repealed under queen Mary. And now a cry is raised for the repeal of the act of Mary, but nobody listens. Nevertheless, in every part of the kingdom, the ministers, not certain, as they say, of the gift of chastity, without law, but with licence, or, as they speak, with the Scriptures on their side, but so explained as to favour sin, marry once, twice, yea, even three times, contrary to the canons, and the custom not of the Latins only, but of the Greeks also. The result is that, having large families to support and provide for, they are very hard upon the people, and miserably dilapidate their benefices.

[1] Perceval Wiburn (Zurich Letters, 2d series, p. 358) says, "The English clergy consist partly of the Popish priests, who still retain their former office, and partly of ministers lately ordered by some bishop there."

[2] Strype, Annals, i. i. 265. "Another inconvenience the want of clergymen now brought was the ordination of illiterate men to be readers, which likewise many were offended at. These readers had been tradesmen, or other honest well-disposed men, and they were admitted into inferior orders, to serve the Church in the present necessity by reading the common prayer and the homilies and orders unto the people."

They were either careless or unlucky from the very first in the choice of wives, for almost all of them married women of tainted reputation; the weaker brethren were therefore scandalised, and the Catholics laughed. Then the queen interposed her authority, and every woman about to be married to a clerk, even if he were a bishop, was to be approved of by certain persons.[1] And yet after all, this was not a sufficient safeguard for their honour and their needs; for many of them said they could not live without wives any more than they could live without food, for the yoke of celibacy was an unbearable burden. Even the Protestants, to say nothing of Catholics, would not give them their daughters in marriage; for they regarded it as something disgraceful to be, or to be said to be, the wife of a priest. Then, according to the law of the land, those marriages are not yet lawful, the issue are bastards,[2] and the wife and children obtain neither

[1] Queen Elizabeth's Injunctions (Wilkins, iv. 185, 186). "Because there hath grown offence and some slander to the Church by lack of discreet and sober behaviour in many ministers of the Church, both in choosing of their wives and indiscreet living with them, . . . no manner of priest or deacon shall hereafter take to his wife any manner of woman without the advice and allowance first had upon good examination by the bishop of the same diocese, and two justices of the peace of the same shire. . . .

"And for the manner of marriages of any bishops, the same shall be allowed and approved by the metropolitan of the province, and also by such commissioners as the queen's majesty thereunto shall appoint.

"And if any master or dean, or any head of any college, shall purpose to marry, the same shall not be allowed but by such to whom the visitation of the same doth properly belong, who shall in any wise provide that the same tend not to the hindrance of their house."

In a proclamation, dated Aug. 9, 1561 (Wilkins, iv. 227), the queen "willeth and commandeth that no manner of person, being either the head or member of any college or cathedral church within this realm, shall . . . be permitted to have within the precinct of any such college his wife or other woman to abide and dwell in the same, or to frequent and haunt any lodging within the said college."

[2] Dr. Sandys, writing to Parker, April 30, 1559 (Burnet, v. 506, ed. Pocock), says, "Lever was married now of late: the queen's majesty will wink at it, but not stablish it by law, which is nothing else but to bastard our children." Laurence Humphrey and Sampson, in a letter to Bullinger, July 1566 (Zurich Letters, 1st series, p. 164), says, "The marriage of the clergy is not allowed and

rank nor honour in the state from the rank of the father, which is inconsistent with the nature of a real marriage. Neither archbishop nor bishop, nor any other prelate, if married, can give any rank or precedence to his wife, who is no better than an unmarried woman.

Accordingly the queen herself never receives these women in court, not even those who are said to be the wives of archbishops. The wives of the nobility avoid them also, and they confine themselves to the houses of those who have taken them into them. These marriages being attended by these inconveniences, hardly any honest woman could be found who would become the wife of even the highest dignitaries, who were therefore forced to marry whom they could get.[1]

The civil magistrate checked these men in other ways. The fellows of colleges in the universities are very many, well fed, with abundance of leisure, and grown up; well, these men also wished to have wives, but it was found to be inconvenient, and the privilege was granted to the heads of colleges only, but upon this condition, that the wives were to live outside the college and very rarely enter its gates.[2]

sanctioned by the public laws of the kingdom, but their children are by some persons regarded as illegitimate."

[1] Harpsfield, Treatise of Marriage, bk. iii. p. 100. "It would pity a man at the heart to hear of the naughty and dissolute life that these yokel priests led with others also beside their pretended wives, wherein the women were nothing behind for their parts, and to hear of the strife, contentions, and debates that were among them. Among other there was one in Kent, which all to beat her yokemate with a wash-betle or battledore, upon whom he complained grievously to the judges at the sizes, and the more to aggerate his injury, showed them openly the said battledore. Many like stories and frays were daily heard of at that time, and many of those women would say to the said priests, being reproved of them for their vicious living, 'Why, knave, thinkest thou that, if I had been an honest woman, I would ever have married with thee?'"

[2] Perceval Wiburn thus sums the matter (Zurich Letters, 2d series, p. 359): "The lords bishops are forbidden to have their wives with them in their palaces; as also are the deans, canons, presbyters, and other ministers of the Church within colleges or the precincts of cathedral churches."

CHAPTER VI.

DESTRUCTIVE TENDENCIES OF THE NEW CLERGY—HONOUR PAID TO THE QUEEN—CECIL'S FAST—THE QUEEN CORRECTS THE PREACHERS—VIOLATION OF TREATIES—ENCOURAGEMENT OF FOREIGN REBELS—THE NUNCIO OF THE POPE NOT ALLOWED TO LAND IN ENGLAND.

Now as many of these new-fashioned clerks, to avoid superstition, wished to appear in public, and to minister in the church in the ordinary dress of a layman,[1] the queen issued her orders on the apparel and dress of ecclesiastics. She strictly enjoined the use of a cope in the administration of their Eucharist,[2] and of a surplice in the reading of the other prayers,[3] and forbade them to appear abroad without a gown and cap.[4] Even the bishops must wear a rochet.[5]

Hereupon arose a great dispute among these brethren;[6]

[1] Laurence Humphrey, the queen's professor of theology, and president of Magdalene College, Oxford, and the biographer of Jewell, asks Bullinger, Feb. 9, 1566 (Zurich Letters, 1st series, No. 68), "whether laws respecting habits may properly be prescribed to churchmen, so as to distinguish them from the laity in shape, colour, &c."

[2] Wilkins, Concil., iv. 186. The Injunctions of 1559 require "all archbishops and bishops, and all other," &c., "shall use and wear such seemly habits, garments, and such square caps as were most commonly and orderly received in the latter year of the reign of king Edward VI." But in the Advertisements of 1564 (ibid., iv. 248), "in the ministration of the holy communion in cathedral and collegiate churches, the principal minister shall use a cope."

[3] Wilkins, iv. 248. "Every minister saying any public prayers . . . shall wear a comely surplice with sleeves."

[4] Ibid., iv. 249. "All inferior ecclesiastical persons shall wear long gowns of the fashion aforesaid, and caps as before is presented."

[5] Ibid., iv. 249. "All archbishops and bishops do use and continue their accustomed apparel."

[6] Jewell writes to Bullinger from Salisbury, Feb. 24, 1567 (Zurich Letters, 1st series, No. 77), "It is

they would not submit to the queen, and sent messengers and letters to their brethren in France, Germany, Switzerland, and the Savoy, especially to Theodore Beza[1] and Peter Martyr,[2] requesting their opinion and advice. They wished to know whether, now that they were free in Christ, they could lawfully undergo this yoke of slavery.[3] Those men might answer, advise, or determine as they pleased; the queen deprives every recusant of his rank and benefice,[4] for there is no appeal from the

quite certain the queen will not be turned from her opinion, and some of our brethren are contending about this matter, as if the whole of our religion were contained in this single point; so that they choose rather to lay down their functions, and leave their churches empty, than to depart one tittle from their own views of the subject." Horn also (ibid., No. 64) says, "It was enjoined us, who had not then any authority to make laws or to repeal them, either to wear the caps and surplices or to give place to others. We complied with this injunction, lest our enemies should take possession of the places deserted by ourselves. But as this matter has occasioned a great strife amongst us, so that our little flock has divided itself into two parties, . . . I beg of you," &c.

[1] Beza writes to Bullinger (Zurich Letters, 2d series, No. 53), "Our distressed brethren seek the consolation, advice, and prayers of those churches by whose love they were formerly refreshed, and hope also to be refreshed at the present time. Some of them, I admit, are rather hard to please, but in so much affliction it is difficult to keep within bounds. . . . From the statement, that you will receive in detail from this our brother, of which also he has left a copy here with me, you will learn that the Papacy was never abolished in that country, but rather transferred to the sovereign."

[2] Peter Martyr generally recommended his friends to obey the queen, and to keep their places; but he had not been so obedient himself, for thus he writes to Sampson (Zurich Letters, 2d series, No. 14), "As to myself, when I was at Oxford, I would never wear the surplice in the choir, although I was a canon; and I had my own reasons for doing so." He advised Sampson (ibid., No. 11) to "retain the function of preaching, . . . and to declaim against rites which are full of offence and occasions of falling."

[3] Humphrey, *ut supra*, asks Bullinger "whether those persons who have till now enjoyed their liberty can with a safe conscience, by the authority of a royal edict, involve in this bondage both themselves and the Church."

[4] Miles Coverdale, Humphrey, and Sampson, in their letter to Beza and others (Zurich Letters, 2d series, No. 50), says: "Out of doors must be worn the square cap, bands, a long gown, and tippet, while the white surplice and cope are to be retained in divine service. And those who refuse to comply with these requirements are deprived of their estates, dignities, and every ecclesiastical office—namely, brethren by brethren and bishops, whose houses are at this time the prisons of some preachers; who are now raging against their own bowels; who are now imposing these burdens not only on their own persons, but also on the shoulders of

supreme head of the Anglican to foreign synagogues, however much they might be reformed. The queen retained many of the ancient customs and ceremonies at the persuasion of her ministers, and against the will of the new clergy, partly for the honour and illustration of this new Church, and partly for the sake of persuading her own subjects and foreigners into the belief that she was not far, or had not gone far, from the Catholic faith. In this matter she behaved with great cunning in her relations with her lovers, suitors, and allies, whether at home or abroad, who were for the most part Catholics. She would raise hopes in them that she might perhaps return to the faith of her predecessors. But her chief reasons, though not all, were these: she knew that the ministers of the new sect, under the pretence of avoiding superstition, would by degrees destroy, in Church and state, all order, good manners, policy, and civilisation itself—yea, and even their own religion—by their savage rudeness, if the civil power did not put some check upon them. Certainly it contributed in a very great degree to the establishing and building up of this heresy that it was not left to the discretion of the clergy; for it would have long ago vanished in smoke, carried away by this evangelical liberty, if human policy had not sustained and kept it in order.[1]

others; and this too at a time when, in the judgment of all learned men, they ought to have been removed and abolished altogether." John Abel, in a letter to Bullinger (ibid., No. 49), says, "Five preachers have lately been deprived and sent as prisoners, two of them to Master Horn, bishop of Winchester; two to Dr. Cox, bishop of Ely; and one to Master Parkhurst, bishop of Norwich, . . . so long as the queen and her council shall think fit."

[1] Jewell, writing to Peter Martyr (Zurich Letters, 1st series, No. 9), says, "The scenic apparatus of divine worship is now under agitation; and these very things which you and I have so often laughed at are now seriously and solemnly entertained by certain persons, for *we* are not consulted, as if the Christian religion could not exist without something tawdry." The language of Cox, bishop of Ely, is still more frightful; writing to Peter Martyr (Zurich Letters, 1st series, No. 28), he says, "We are only constrained,

For a long time she retained the organs, the ecclesiastical chants,[1] the crucifix, copes, candles, and principally for this reason, that the clergy, in these garments, might come forth in procession to receive her whenever, either for business or pleasure, she made her public entry into any city, as was her custom often to do. For the same reason, too, the bells were spared, that they might be rung whenever, in her progress, she passed by a church; but principally on her birthday and on the day of her coronation, which days are kept with more solemnity throughout the kingdom than the festivals of Christ and of the saints. Indeed the Protestants were compelled by law to keep in some way or other almost all the ancient holy days of the Church; but they have shown their spite more especially against the feast of Corpus Christi, the Assumption, Nativity, and Conception of our Lady, which they have utterly suppressed.[2] And to show the greater contempt for our Blessed Lady, they keep the birthday of queen Elizabeth in the most solemn way on the 7th day of September, which is the eve of the feast of the Mother of God, whose nativity they mark in their calendar in small and black letters, while that of Elizabeth is marked in letters both large and red. And, what is hardly credible, in the church of St. Paul, the chief church of London—whether elsewhere or

to our great distress of mind, to tolerate in our churches the image of the cross and Him who was crucified: the Lord must be entreated that this stumbling-block may at length be removed."

[1] Edwin Sandys, bishop of Worcester, asked convocation in A.D. 1563 (Wilkins, iv. 239) to move the queen to the effect "that all curious singing and playing of the organs may be removed." Four years later, Grindal and Horn, also bishops, writing to Bullinger (Zurich Letters, 1st series, No. 75), say, "We do not assert that the chanting in churches, together with the organ, is to be retained, but we disapprove of it, as we ought to do."

[2] Wilkins, iv. 239. Sandys proposed in convocation, A.D. 1563, "that all saints, feasts, and holy days bearing the name of a creature, may, as tending to superstition, or rather gentility, be clearly abrogated; or at least a commemoration only reserved of the said saints by sermons, homilies, or common prayers, for the better instructing of the people in history."

not is more than I can tell—the praises of Elizabeth are said to be sung at the end of the public prayers, as the Antiphon of our Lady was sung in former days.

The Protestants are forced also somehow or other, even now, to keep the fast formerly observed, though they do it very much against their will, for they complain loudly that the ordering of matters of this sort is contrary to Scripture and the liberty of the gospel. But the queen, for the relief of their consciences herein, makes a proclamation at the beginning of Lent every year,[1] that the fast is ordered to be kept not for the sake of religion, penance, or devotion, but simply for the good of the state; in order by the greater consumption of fish to furnish the fishermen, a large class of men in the island, with a livelihood, and to have during the rest of the year a more abundant supply of fleshmeat, and in particular for the necessary provisioning of the fleet.[2]

Not deeming the abstinence of Friday and Saturday to be a sufficient support of the navy, the queen instituted a fast to be kept every Wednesday,[3] now commonly known as Cecil's fast, because it is regarded as

[1] Collier, Eccles. Hist., bk. iv. p. 476. "The queen concurred with the archbishop [Parker], for this year there was a strict proclamation for the keeping of Lent, which was likewise the constant custom of this reign."

[2] The Second Part of the Homily of Fasting. "But first an answer shall be made to a question that some may make, demanding what judgment we ought to have of such abstinences as are appointed by public order and laws made by princes and by the authority of the magistrates upon policy, not respecting any religion at all in the same. As when any realm in consideration of the maintaining of fisher-towns bordering upon the seas, and for the increase of fishermen, of whom do spring mariners to go upon the sea, to the furnishing of the navy of the realm, whereby not only commodities of other countries may be transported, but also may be a necessary defence to resist the invasion of the adversary."

[3] 5 Eliz. c. 5, s. 14. "From the feast of St. Michael the Archangel, in the year of our Lord God 1564, every Wednesday in every week, throughout the year, which heretofore hath not by the laws or customs of this realm been used and observed as a fish-day, and which shall not happen to fall in Christmas week or Easter week, shall be hereafter observed and kept, as the Saturdays in every week be, or ought to be; and that no manner of person shall eat any flesh on the same day, otherwise than ought to be upon the common Saturday."

his invention. Though the people, who despise these public fasts, are liable to heavy fines,[1] very few observe them, and certainly not the bishops and the rest of the clergy, who are very much ashamed to find themselves under the law of fasting. But the queen herself easily grants a dispensation in writing, upon cause assigned, to the lords and others, and the archbishop of Canterbury also on the payment of fees.[2]

In short, the queen lays down for her clergy a rule of life, outside of which they dare not move, not only in those things which Protestants call indifferent, but in all matters of faith, discipline, and doctrine, in virtue of that supreme spiritual power with which she is invested:[3] she suspends her bishops when she pleases,[4] she grants a licence to preach,[5] either to those who are ordained

[1] 5 Eliz. c. 5, s. 15. The penalty for eating flesh on the fish-days is the forfeiture of three pounds or three months' imprisonment without bail or mainprise.

[2] Zurich Letters, 2d series, p. 360. The State of the Church of England, by Perceval Wiburn. "He [the archbishop] has also the Court of Faculties, where, on the payment beforehand of a pretty large sum of money, licences are obtained for non-residence, plurality of benefices, dispensations for forbidden meats on the third, fifth, and sixth holiday [the translator probably meant Wednesday, Friday, and Saturday], the vigils of the saints, Lent, and the ember days of the four seasons." These dispensations issued out of the Court of Faculties, and Grindal, when he had possession of Canterbury, gives an account of its processes. The archbishop's commissary with a registrar constituted the court, but the fees paid in this way, one-half to the queen, the other half divided between the lord chancellor and his registrar, the archbishop, the commissary, and the registrar. Thus, if the fee were £9, the queen had £4, 10s., the archbishop £2, the lord chancellor £1, his registrar 10s., the commissary of the court 10s., and the registrar 10s."—Grindal's Remains, ed. Parker Society, p. 446.

[3] Pilkington, to whom she gave the see of Durham, writing to Gualter, July 20, 1573 (Zurich Let., 1st series, No. 110), complains as follows: "We endure, I must confess, many things against our inclinations, and groan under them, which, if we wished ever so much, no entreaty can remove. We are under authority, and cannot make any innovation without the sanction of the queen, or abrogate anything without the authority of the laws; and the only alternative now allowed us is, whether we will bear with these things or disturb the peace of the Church."

[4] She suspended Grindal archbishop of Canterbury. See Wilkins, Concilia, iv. 289.

[5] Injunctions of the Queen, s. 8; Wilkins, iv. 183. "They shall admit no man to preach within any their cures but such as shall appear unto them to be sufficiently licensed thereunto by the queen's majesty, or the archbishop of Canterbury or York

according to her rite or to simple laymen, and in the same way at her pleasure reduces whom she will to silence. To show her authority in these things, she occasionally, from her closet, addresses her preacher, and interrupts him in the presence of a large congregation, in some such way as this : "Mr. Doctor, you are wandering from the text, and talking nonsense, return to your subject." [1]

This, then, is the way in which religion is administered in England at this time. I will now say nothing—for it must be reserved for another work and another occasion—of civil affairs and the like, nor of the queen's suitors foreign and domestic, whom she encouraged, and who in their turn were masters in court and council ; nothing of the many noble personages—English, Scotch, Austrian, Swede, and French [2]—whom she from the very beginning of her reign to this day deluded, nor how both Houses of Parliament,[3] who often begged her, for

in either of their provinces, or by the bishop of the diocese, or by the queen's majesty's visitors."

[1] Heylyn, Hist. Reform., p. 124. "Particularly when one of her chaplains, Mr. Alexander Nowel, dean of St. Paul's, had spoke less reverently in a sermon preached before her of the sign of the cross, she called aloud to him from her closet window, commanding him to retire from that ungodly digression, and return unto his text."

[2] Jewell, writing to Peter Martyr from London (Zurich Let., 1st series, No. 9), says, "Nothing is yet talked of about the queen's marriage, yet there are now courting her the king of Sweden, the Saxon, and Charles the son of Ferdinand, to say nothing of the Englishman Pickering." Ibid., No. 14 : "The public opinion, however, inclines towards Sir William Pickering." Camden (Annales, p. 67) adds James earl of Arran, a Scotchman.

[3] Jewell to Bullinger, Feb. 24, 1567 (Zurich Let., 1st ser., No. 77) : "We have assembled within these few months the Parliament of the whole kingdom. . . . The question respecting the succession was likewise brought forward. . . . This question occupied the minds of all parties for a month or two ; for the queen was unwilling that any discussion should take place upon the subject, while every one else was exceedingly anxious about it : and the contest was carried on with great earnestness and ability on both sides. What next? After all, nothing could be done ; for the queen, who is a wise and cautious woman, suspects that when her successor is once determined upon, there may hence arise some danger to herself. For you know the saying, that there are more worshippers of the rising than of the setting sun." See also Sir Simonds d'Ewes, Journals, p. 107.

the sake of the succession and the safety of the realm, to choose a husband either among her own subjects or among strangers, were either satisfied or mocked by her assertion that she was resolved to live and die a virgin ; nor will I speak of the great scandal which she gave not only to Catholics, but to the people of her own sect, by this pretence of a single life, which was the ruin of the state, and by her ecclesiastical supremacy, which was the ruin of the Church.

But there is one thing, and it belongs in a special manner to the subject of my book, which ought not to be passed over in silence. The queen and her politicians understood at once, as soon as their sect and religion had been set up, that many of her subjects would be very much disturbed by the changes wrought in Church and state ; that she would find a stern judge in the Pope, and that the emperor and the most powerful Christian kings would withdraw from her. Then, being thus severed in faith and communion from the whole world, she would not be long safe against her own subjects or her neighbours. There was, therefore, no security for her but in inflicting a like calamity as soon as possible upon the neighbouring countries,[1] France and Scotland and Flanders, that all the Catholic sovereigns being fully occupied with their own affairs, might have no time to attend to those of others.[2]

[1] See the "Desire for Alteration of Religion" (Burnet, v. 497). Among other suggestions is this : First, for France, "to practise a peace, or if it be offered, not to refuse it : if controversy of religion be there amongst them, to kindle it. . . .

"Scotland will follow France for peace, but there may be practice to help forward their division, and specially to augment the hope of them who inclined them to good religion," *i.e.*, to Protestantism.

[2] Hilles, writing to Bullinger from London, July 31, 1562 (Zurich Let., 2d series, No. 38), says, "The queen appears to be considering the evils that may possibly be hanging over us, and is apprehensive lest any misfortune should arise to the realm by reason of negligence and inactivity ; that is, lest any foreign prince, in the event of the disorders which still exist in France being settled, should be stirred up by the Roman Pontiff, or any other foreign Papists who

Accordingly all the treaties between England and the great monarchs of Christendom were at once either openly violated or observed only in appearance; those of recent date, as well as the older treaties, were dealt with in the same way. Then, to the unutterable dishonour of England, and to their everlasting shame, the queen and her councillors made a league with those who were in rebellion against all those sovereigns, with the men who were traitors to their country and plagues of the world.[1] In Scotland they are the confederates of James the bastard,[2] Morton,[3] and others against queen Mary; in France they are leagued together with the admiral, and men of the same kind,[4] most detestable tyrants, against the most Christian kings, three brothers in succession; in Flanders they ally themselves against the most mighty and just sovereign, Philip, with the scourge of God the reprobate prince of Orange.[5] In a word, they send troops into their countries, lay waste their borders, take their cities, plunder their treasuries; they send out pirates,[6] who commit grievous depreda-

adhere to him, to find some occasion of quarrel against her."

[1] Jewell, writing to Bullinger, Aug. 14, 1562 (Zurich Letters, 1st series, No. 50), says: "Our queen . . . gradually withdrew her alliance with the Guises, and not obscurely intimated her determination to assist the prince of Condé. The duke of Guise was very angry at this, . . . and declared by a public proclamation that the queen of England was planning intrigues against the kingdom of France, and that she alone had occasioned those disorders."

[2] James Stewart, earl of Murray, and prior of St. Andrews, was a natural child of James V.

[3] James Douglas, earl of Morton. This nobleman, on the murder at Dumbarton of the last archbishop of St. Andrews, made an apostate Carmelite friar bishop, and thereby took the revenues of the see into his own hands.

[4] The admiral Gaspar de Coligni. The queen had bound herself (Camden, Annales, p. 93) to pay the prince of Condé, Rohan, the admiral, and others "an hundred thousand angels," to send over into France six thousand men, whereof three thousand should be employed for the defence of Dieppe and Rouen."

[5] William of Nassau-Dillembourg obtained possession of the principality of Orange under the will of a cousin, who had it in right of his wife, forsook the Catholic faith, and founded the republic of Holland, in rebellion against the king of Spain, who put a price upon his head.

[6] Francis Drake, John Hawkins, and Oxenham.

tions, and in every country urge the people into rebellion. By means of their barbarous religion spreading like a pestilence, they have brought their neighbours the Scots to ruin, and their queen into that most miserable condition, utterly undeserved, in which we see her at this moment. In France they have been poison to unnumbered souls, and brought kings, still in their youth, into extreme peril. Lastly, they have corrupted almost the whole of Belgium; they have made themselves the accomplices, the leaders, and the protectors of the seditious heretics in every nation, to the end that the disorder raging throughout Christendom might be made still greater. All this they did in order that, through the misfortunes of other sovereigns and other countries, they might themselves live in peace at home, and by the scattering far and wide of the poison of their heretical corruption, secure to themselves a longer continuance in their sect.[1]

While the whole island was in this way going to destruction, France in distress, and all the northern nations in danger, Pius IV.[2] offered the ordinary remedy of the Church for so great an evil. Hitherto the convocation of a general council had met with many hindrances, but now, after laborious efforts, and with the assent of almost all the princes of Christendom, he summoned it to meet in Trent. He sent a Nuncio,[3]

1 Heylyn, Hist. Reform., p. 163. "For well she knew that if the Hugonots were not encouraged underhand, and the Guisian faction kept in breath by their frequent stirrings, they would be either hammering some design against her in her own dominions, or animate the queen of Scots to stand to her title and pretensions for the crown of England. Upon which general ground of self-preservation, as she first aided those of Scotland for the expelling of the French, and the French Protestants from being ruined and oppressed by the house of Guise, so on the same she afterwards undertook the patronage of the Belgic Netherlands against the tyranny and ambition of the duke of Alva, who otherwise might have brought the war to her own door, and hazarded the peace and safety of her whole estate."

2 John Angelo di Medici, elected Dec. 26, 1559, died Dec. 9, 1565.

3 Dod, ed. Tierney, ii. 147. "Where-

who was to travel through Lower Germany to England, to represent to Elizabeth her errors, and to persuade her not to ruin herself and her illustrious realm out of hatred to the Pope. He was also to say that, if on account of her doubtful birth she was afraid that her title to the throne might, on the part of the Church or the Pope, be questioned, the matter could be easily settled, for the Apostolic See is indulgent. The queen would neither listen to the Nuncio nor allow him even to land in England.

Soon afterwards the Pontiff, to leave no means untried, sent another Legate[1] to persuade the queen to allow some at least of her own bishops to attend the council, and to enter into conference with the Catholics, promising them liberty of speech and the safety of their persons. That Legate, too, was disdainfully refused. The mock prelates also, aware of their own weakness and ignorance, were very urgent with the queen that none of them should be sent to the council.[2]

fore about May 1560 he sent his Nuncio as far as Flanders with orders to pass over into England, and exhort the queen to return back into the bosom of the Catholic Church. . . . This design being imparted to the queen and council, they entered into a consultation about it. . . . The negative being resolved upon, the Nuncio proceeded no further than Calais." The Nuncio was Vincent Parpaglia, abbot of St. Saviour's, and the refusal to receive him disposes of the story that he was the bearer of a message from the Pope to the effect that the Pope was willing to reverse the sentence against the marriage of Henry and Anne Boleyn, thereby bastardising queen Mary, and to sanction the changes which Elizabeth had made in the divine offices, on the condition of acknowledging the jurisdiction of the Pope. See Camden, Annales, p. 73.

[1] The abbot Martinengo, sent over in 1561. Of him, Jewell, writing to Peter Martyr, Feb. 7, 1562 (Zurich Letters, 1st series, No. 43), says, "The Pope's Nuncio is still loitering in Flanders, for he cannot yet obtain a safe-conduct to come over to England."

[2] Jewell, writing to Peter Martyr, Feb. 7, 1562 (Zurich Letters, 1st series, No. 43), says: "Our queen has fully made up her mind not to send any representative to the council, as to the existence or locality of which we are totally ignorant: certainly, if it is held anywhere, or has any being at all, it must be very secret and obscure. We are now thinking about publishing the reasons which have induced us to decline attendance."

CHAPTER VII.

THE EMPEROR INTERCEDES ON BEHALF OF THE CATHOLICS—MARY QUEEN OF SCOTS—THE EARLS OF NORTHUMBERLAND AND WESTMORELAND.

LETTERS, too, at this time were brought to Elizabeth from the Catholic sovereigns, and especially from the emperor Ferdinand, who in most affectionate terms entreated her not to forsake the fellowship, in matters of faith and religion, of all Christian princes, and even of her own forefathers; not to set her own opinion, and the opinion of certain men who were of yesterday, neither many nor learned, above the judgment of the Church. If, however, she had made up her mind to continue in the sect she had adopted, in spite of the decision of the sovereign Pontiff and a general council, or the example of her Christian fellow-sovereigns, that in that case she would at least, out of her natural kindliness and goodness, proceed no further against those learned and pious men, the Catholic bishops, who were in her prisons, but rather set them free, seeing that they had done nothing against her majesty or against the state; the only offence laid to their charge being their perseverance in the communion, and their profession, of the ancient faith, which is the faith of all nations, and which, said the emperor, "is also mine." Lastly, he earnestly begs of her to let them and the other Catholics have the use of some of the churches in the kingdom, wherein they may meet together for the worship of God according to the rites of the Catholic religion. But even he could gain nothing, and matters in England went daily from bad to worse.[1]

It was discussed in the council whether Elizabeth, on account of her unendurable obstinacy, should not be publicly denounced as a heretic, seeing that she was according to law an excommunicated person. Nothing, however, was done, for the emperor, whose son she had led to hope and expect to be her husband, obtained from the fathers a respite; for he told them that when she was married to a Catholic husband, she must come to a better mind. But she deceived this suitor as she had deceived others, and was day by day more obstinate, and to the Catholics more cruel.

At this time Mary queen of Scots resolved upon flight. She had been harassed by the treachery of English heretics, and the unutterable cruelty of her own subjects: she had been shut in a prison and compelled to resign. She lost her husband by a most iniquitous murder, and then was herself accused of the crime.[2]

[1] Camden, Annales, p. 52. "Hoc tempore quum imperator et Catholici principes crebris litteris intercederent ut clementer cum episcopis abdicatis ageretur, et templa in urbibus seorsim Pontificiis permitterentur, respondit [Elizabetha] . . . Templa autem in quibus sua divina officia seorsim celebrent, salva republica et illæso honore atque conscientia concedere non posse. . . . Permittere vero templa cum ritibus diversis, præterquam quod legibus parliamentaria auctoritate sancitis aperte repugnet, nihil aliud esset quam religionem ex religione serere, mentes bonorum varie distrahere, factiosorum studia alere, religionem atque rempublicam conturbare, et divina humanaque commiscere." . . . The queen made her own conscience, it seems, the rule of the conscience of others; but at the same time, while refusing this questionable boon to the Catholics, she granted it to all the foreign heretics, and gave the crypt of Canterbury Cathedral to the French Protestants, who are in possession of it at this day.

[2] Grindal to Bullinger, Aug. 29, 1567 (Zurich Letters, 1st series, No. 81): "The queen by a solemn public instrument resigned her royal dignity to the prince her son. . . . The queen is still kept in the closest confinement, and there are those who think it will be perpetual. It is reported that there were found in Bothwell's writing-desk some letters written in the queen's own hand, in which she exhorted Bothwell to accelerate the death of the king her husband. How true this may be, I know not." Camden, Annales, 141: "Tandem mortis terrore injecto, eam inauditam compulerunt tribus

She might easily have made her way into the territories of some Christian king, and there were among the Scotch nobles some who begged her to do so. But the letters, messengers, and presents of Elizabeth prevailed, she was invited to pass over the Border into England, and troops were promised her, by the help of which she was to recover her kingdom.[1] But as she had not thoroughly learned that they are not to be trusted who have abandoned the faith of Christ, she went to England against the will of her people, to another prison, to be guarded there by other soldiers.

Not long after her arrival, Mary was placed in the custody of the earl of Shrewsbury,[2] who treated her always with excessive harshness because of her unwavering profession of the Catholic faith; but afterwards, when she was placed in the charge of others, who were more merciless than the earl, her life was a death rather than life, for she was tormented in various and unseemly ways, and made the butt of false accusations wholly undeserved.[3] She was herself a queen, not a

diplomatibus chirographum apponere, quorum primo regnum cessit filiolo vix 13 menses nato."

[1] Blackwood, Martyre de Marie Stuart, c. xii. p. 588, ed. Paris, 1644. "Elle portoit avec elle le gage d'amitié que la royne d'Angleterre, sa sœur, luy avoit envoyé, et les lettres qu'elle luy avoit escrites, pleines d'honnestes offres de faveur et de secours en sa necessité. Et incontinent qu'elle fut sortie de Lochleven luy ayant renvoyé par un gentilhomme expres un diamant qu'autrefois elle avoit receu d'elle pour token et gage d'amitié, elle luy reïtera les promesses que Trogmorton son ambassadeur luy avoit faictes avec asseurance de secours contre ses rebelles, et mesmement s'il plaisoit a sa majesté de se retirer en Angleterre, qu'elle viendroit jusques sur la frontière pour la recevoir et assister en personne de tout son pouvoir." Jewell, writing to Simler, Aug. 13, 1562 (Zurich Letters, 1st series, No. 52), says, "The queen of Scotland, niece of the duke of Guise, has within these few days, by way of courting the favour and friendship of our queen, sent her a most splendid and valuable diamond, enclosed and fixed in a plate of gold, and set off with some flattering and elegant verses."

[2] George Talbot, earl marshal; he died in 1590.

[3] Jewell, writing to Bullinger, Aug. 7, 1570 (Zurich Letters, 1st series, No. 91), thus speaks of the queen: "The queen of Scots, an exile from her country, is, as you know, here in custody, with sufficient honour indeed, yet so as that she cannot raise any disturbances. This is she to whom Pope Pius not

subject of Elizabeth, nor bound by her laws, but, nevertheless, she could not obtain—what is not refused to foreign princes and their ambassadors—a priest to say Mass or to administer the sacraments, that she might serve God as her forefathers had done; and the privation was a heavier affliction than exile and a prison.

This treatment of the queen of Scots was strange and barbarous, for she was of all people the nearest in blood to Elizabeth, and also her invited guest; nevertheless, for these seventeen years, notwithstanding the most earnest entreaties, she was never once allowed to speak to her, or even to see her.

But to return. Not very long after the arrival of Mary, many noblemen, weary of heresy and of the government, especially in the northern counties, took up arms in their own defence against the heretics and the upstarts who had led Elizabeth into her madness. Foremost among these were Thomas earl of Northumberland, and Charles earl of Westmoreland,[1] two illustrious men of the old nobility. But as the rest of the Catholics, on the ground that the Pope had not published the sentence of excommunication, and had not released them from their allegiance, did not join them, they were easily defeated by the queen's troops, and driven into Scotland.[2] There the earl of North-

only freely promises Scotland, but England likewise; for he hopes that a woman, a Catholic, a murderer of her husband, and an adulteress, will have great influence in the restoration of Popery! We are preparing a fleet, and have troops in readiness."

[1] The earl of Westmoreland fell into honest hands in Scotland, and was enabled to make his escape into the dominions of the emperor in Flanders, where he lived, but in poverty, for some years, dying, according to Camden (p. 424), in 1584 or 1585.

[2] Grindal, writing to Bullinger from London, Feb. 18, 1570 (Zurich Letters, 1st series, Let. 87), says: "At the beginning of November two earls, those of Northumberland and Westmoreland, collected troops and raised a rebellion in the counties of York and Durham, for the purpose of restoring the Catholic religion, falsely so called. Their army consisted of twelve hundred cavalry and four thousand infantry. . . . The queen then collected an army of twenty-four thousand men, consisting both of cavalry and infantry,

umberland was afterwards betrayed and sold to his enemies.[1] When he was brought back to England they offered him his life, if he would give up the faith. He refused the offer, and ended his days by a glorious martyrdom in York. Those who had followed him, as well as those who had followed the earl of Westmoreland, were diligently sought after everywhere, in order that they might be put to death.

and which the rebel army had not the courage to resist. So that on the 16th of Dec. the rebels disbanded their infantry. . . . The two earls themselves fled into Scotland with a hundred chosen troops. But Northumberland was taken prisoner by the regent of Scotland, where he still remains in confinement. Westmoreland, who is a young man, and with the spirit of a Catiline, is living among free-booters in the wilds of Scotland. Thus was this rebellion suppressed within forty days, and without bloodshed, except that five hundred of the rebels were afterwards executed, and many are still kept in prison awaiting a like punishment. The rebel army had on their colours the Five Wounds, as they are called, and the representation of a cross, with this inscription, '*In hoc signo vinces.*' They performed their Masses in every church ; the Bibles, moreover, translated into our language, which are found in all our churches, they either tore in pieces or committed to the flames. They ransacked the property of the bishop of Durham, and that of all the pastors and ministers ; but they put no one to death." Richard Hilles (ibid., 86) says, "They not only threw down the communion-tables, tore in pieces the Holy Bible and godly books, and trod under foot the printed Homilies, but also again set up the blasphemous Mass as a sacrifice for the living and the dead."

[1] Stow, p. 673. "Thomas Percie, earl of Northumberland, late of Topcliffe, who had been before attainted by Parliament of high treason, as being one of the principal conspirators in the late rebellion ; since fled into Scotland as is aforeshowed, being there taken, was sent to Berwick in the month of July, and delivered to the Lord Hunsdon, then captain or governor of that town, and was now on the 22d day of August beheaded at York about two of the clock in the afternoon, on a new scaffold set up for that purpose in the market-place." The earl of Morton, who had been befriended by him when he was himself an exile, sold him for money—*pacta pecunia.*—Camden (p. 266) to Lord Hunsdon, Elizabeth's cousin.

CHAPTER VIII.

THE SEMINARIES—BULL OF ST. PIUS V.

WHILE the affairs of England were in this state, some, out of the remnant of those who were driven out of the schools at home, came together in Douai,[1] and were formed into a college there under the direction of Dr. William Allen, then the king's professor of theology in that university. Philip, the generous king of Spain, protected them in their banishment, supplied their wants, and gave them the means of continuing their

[1] The college was founded in 1568, and in 1575 His Holiness Gregory XIII. (Dod, ed. Tierney, ii. 161) "gave orders that an allowance of a hundred Roman crowns should be paid monthly for its subsistence out of the treasury of the Holy See. This was afterwards augmented to an annual pension of two thousand crowns, which is continued to this day."

Collegii Anglo-Duaceni Diarium, i. 3. "Anno Domini nostri Jesu Christi millesimo quingentesimo sexagesimo octavo, cum hoc egregium opus, divina fretus misericordia et benignitate, inchoaret reverendus Dominus, Dominus Guilielmus Alanus doctus et pius sacerdos, postea sanctæ Romanæ Ecclesiæ Cardinalis presbyter, Angliæ nuncupatus — primos sui collegii alumnos habuit sex Sacræ Theologiæ studiosos sibi subditos, quatuor quidem Anglos, et duos Belgas. Qui omnes ex piorum quorundam abbatum et aliorum benefactorum eleëmosinis, industria Domini Alani collectis, vixerunt in unis simul ædibus in Universitate Duacensi.

"Angli erant isti: Richardus Bristous, Vigorniensis; Joannes Martialis, postea canonicus Insulensis; Edouardus Risdenus, postea Carthusianus; Joannes Whitus. Belgæ autem Joannes Ravastonus, Simon Colierius.

"Huic porro cœtui continenter se adjunxit Dominus Morganus Philippus, venerabilis sacerdos, quondam ejusdem Alani in Universitate Oxonienis præceptor, nunc vero in hoc saneto opere, et vivus coadjutor et moriens insignis benefactor."

Morgan Philips was one of the disputants at Oxford when Peter Martyr attempted the defence of his heresies in May 1549 (bk. ii. ch. iii.) He was made principal of St. Mary's Hall in 1546, and resigned in 1550. In the beginning of queen Mary's reign he was made precentor of St. David's, and on the accession of Elizabeth went abroad, and died at Douai, 1577. Cardinal Allen was the fourth principal of St. Mary's Hall in succession to Morgan Philips.

studies. The college prospered as time went on, supported at first by the alms of good people, and afterwards by the munificence of the Apostolic See. Many admirable priests were trained in it, who from time to time were sent to England, there to revive the Catholic faith; and on the other hand, the men of goodwill were received within its walls who came from England to learn the truth. So that soon after the foundation of the college there was a great change in men's minds, as well as a great many conversions, in England.

The college was so hateful to the heretics, that they obtained the expulsion of its members from Douai, by the help of the Belgians, without much difficulty, the Belgians being at this time a prey to sedition.[1] But afterwards, in the providence of God, and by the permission of the most Christian king, the college was removed to Rheims,[2] where it flourishes at this day. It has grown into ample proportions, and ecclesiastical studies are thriving within it. In order to gather in a more abundant harvest, Pope Gregory XIII.,[3] of most blessed memory, founded another college in Rome itself, in the ancient hospital of our nation, endowing it at the

[1] Dod, ed. Tierney, ii. 165. "Those that have searched into the bottom of the affair tell us that all the disturbance was occasioned by the Huguenots, who, out of hatred to religion or for the hopes of plunder, lay privately in the town, and instilled such notions into the common people, as if the English that resided amongst them were in the French interest."

[2] Ibid., p. 164. "They arrived at Rheims, March 27, 1578. The rest followed by degrees, excepting two or three persons that were permitted to remain in the house, which they kept possession of for fifteen years, till the college returned again to Douay."

The writer of this fourth book was sent from Douai to Rheims to learn the dispositions of the university there, as it seems from the Douai Diary, *ad ann.* 1576, p. 113: "Eodem die [Nov. 10, 1576] ad Academiam Remensem hinc a nobis missi sunt D. Writtus, Sacræ Theologiæ baccalaureus, et D. Rishtonus, S. Theolog. studiosus, ut et illius loci commoditatem et Academiæ erga nos voluntatem explorarent. Qui eo accedentes humanissime recepti sunt, et omnia nobis, si adventaverimus, ad nostram voluntatem libentissimis animis paratissima fore promissa sunt."

[3] The Bull *Quoniam divinæ bonitati* is dated April 23, 1579, and may be seen in the Appendix to Dod, ed. Tierney, ii. p. cccxxxvii.

same time with ample revenues, and placing it under the care and direction of the Fathers of the Society of Jesus. These two colleges have in our days sent to the English harvest more than three hundred priests, who have also watered with their consecrated blood the field of our Lord in that country.

One thing there is in this matter marvellous to observe, and which we can assign to nothing else but to the finger of God. While even in Catholic countries there are many who become priests only for honour and gain, the members of these colleges—among whom are noblemen and eldest sons not a few—without any hope of reward, yea, rather with the loss of their heritage, with the certainty of disgrace, danger, and even death, so eagerly desire and receive the priesthood, that no fear of shame or of loss, no persuasion of kindred and of friends according to the flesh, can shake their holy resolution.

The councillors of Elizabeth at first despised the poor beginnings of the seminary of Douai. They thought, and they said so too, that those who might be trained in the college, or even become priests, would, compelled by want or tempted by gain, return some day to England, accept a benefice, and minister in the Anglican churches according to the laws and teaching of the state. But if any among them should be obstinate, and refuse to conform, they would be able to do nothing; for what could a few poor and homeless men —such is the judgment of the world—do against their new Church, which was under the protection of so mighty a queen,[1] guarded by such severe laws, watched

[1] Hooker, Dedication of the fifth book of his "Ecclesiastical Polity," p. 11, ed. Oxon., 1836. "Her especially, whose sacred power with incomparable goodness of nature hath hitherto been God's most happy instrument, by Him miraculously kept for works of so miraculous preservation and safety unto others, that as 'By the sword of God and

over by such diligent ministers, and so effectually defended on every side? But before many years were over it was observed that very many young men, possessed of great gifts, went from the schools and the universities to the colleges beyond the seas, and came back before long as priests to their native land, where by preaching, by their writings and example, by the ministration of the sacraments in secret, by reconciling men to the Church, by withdrawing them from schism, and from their attendance upon the sacrilegious rites of the heretics—for many Englishmen at that time, men who in their hearts believed aright, had thus defiled themselves through fear of the laws—they made a great impression upon innumerable souls. Then the queen's advisers, when they saw this, and that the country, the towns, the universities, the houses of the nobility, and even the court itself, were full of converts, began to bewail their mistake, and by cruel laws,[1] by every human means and contrivance, and by spreading terror far and near, to set themselves against the work, which we believe to be the work of God.

The Catholic Church was governed, when the seminary was founded, by Pius V., another Phinees, who with the utmost diligence pursued heretics, Turks, and other unbelievers with a zeal wholly beseeming the sovereign Pontiff. He is, as I believe, the first who authorised not only the members of the seminary, but the other most learned priests to go to England, and who gave them diverse spiritual powers necessary for the furtherance of so good a work. He issued an Apostolic Brief, and placed all the missioners, to avoid dissensions, under

Gideon' was sometime the cry of the people of Israel, so it might deservedly be at this day . . . the true inscription, style, or title of all Churches as yet standing within this realm, 'By the goodness of Almighty God and His servant Elizabeth we are.'"

[1] 27 Eliz. c. 2. "An act against Jesuits, seminary priests, and other suchlike disobedient persons."

the direction of Allen. Then in the same spirit of fortitude in which he formed the Holy League against the Turk, the most cruel enemy of Christ, and with the help of the Catholic king and other states, undertook that most glorious war against him, he pronounced against Elizabeth sentence of excommunication and deposition in the following words:—

"Sentence declaratory of our sovereign Lord the Pope Pius V. against Elizabeth, pretended queen of England, and the heretics who abet her, whereby all subjects are declared released from the oath of allegiance, and every other bond, and those who hereafter shall obey her, bound by the bond of anathema.

"PIUS, Bishop, servant of the servants of God, in memorial of the matter.

"The sovereign jurisdiction of the one holy Catholic and Apostolic Church, outside of which there is no salvation, has been given by Him, unto Whom all power in heaven and on earth is given, the King who reigns on high, to but one person on the face of the earth, to Peter, prince of the Apostles, and to the successor of Peter, the Bishop of Rome. Him He has set up over all nations, and over all kingdoms, to root up and destroy, to waste and to scatter, to plant and to build, to the end that he may maintain in the unity of the spirit the faithful people bound together by the bond of charity, and present them unto Him their Saviour perfect and without loss.

"In the discharge of this duty, We, whom God of His goodness has called to the government of His Church, shrink from no labour, striving with all Our might to preserve in their integrity that very unity and the Catholic religion, which are now assailed by so many storms, by His permission from Whom they come, for our correction, and for the trial of the faith of His children. But the wicked are so many, and are growing so strong, that there is no part of the world which they have not attempted by their evil doctrines to corrupt; among others labouring for this end is the servant of iniquity, Elizabeth, the pretended queen of England, with whom, as in a safe refuge, the worst of these men have found a secure retreat.

"This woman having taken possession of the kingdom, unnaturally claims for herself the place, the great authority and jurisdiction of the sovereign head of the Church throughout all England, and has involved in miserable ruin that kingdom so lately recovered to the Catholic faith and piety.

"She has forbidden by the strong hand of power the observance of the true religion, overturned by the apostate Henry VIII., and by the help of the Holy See restored by Mary, the lawful queen, of illustrious memory. She has followed after and accepted the errors of heretics. She has driven the English nobles out of the royal council, and filled their places with obscure heretics. She has been the ruin of those who profess the Catholic faith, and has brought back again the wicked preachers and ministers of impieties. She has done away with the sacrifice of the Mass, the Divine Office, fasting, the distinction of meats, celibacy, and the Catholic rites. She has ordered the use of books, containing manifest heresy, throughout the realm, and the observance by her subjects of impious mysteries and ordinances, according to the rule of Calvin, accepted and practised by herself.

"She has dared to take away their churches and benefices from the bishops, the parish priests, and other Catholic ecclesiastics, and has given them with other ecclesiastical goods to heretics. She has made herself a judge in ecclesiastical causes. She has forbidden the prelates, clergy, and people to acknowledge the Church of Rome, or to obey its mandates and the Catholic constitutions. She has compelled many to take an oath to observe her wicked laws, to renounce the authority of the Roman Pontiff, to refuse to obey him, and to accept her as the sole ruler in temporal and spiritual matters. She has decreed pains and penalties against those who do not submit to her, and has inflicted them upon those who continue in the unity of the faith and obedience.

"She has thrown Catholic prelates and parish priests into prison, where many, worn out by sorrows and their protracted sufferings, have ended their days in misery.

"All this being notorious and known unto all nations, and so confirmed by very many grave witnesses, as to leave no room for palliation, defence, or concealment, sin being added to sin, and iniquity to iniquity, the persecution of the faithful, and the ruin of religion daily growing more and more at the suggestion and under the direction of Elizabeth aforesaid, whose will is so obstinate and whose heart is so hardened that she has set at nought not only the charitable prayers and counsels of Catholic princes entreating her to return to a better mind and be converted, but also Our own by her refusal to allow the Nuncios of the Holy See to enter the realm, We, having recourse, by necessity compelled, to the weapons of justice, are unable to control Our grief that We must proceed against one whose predecessors have rendered signal services to Christendom.

"Relying then on His authority who has placed Us on this sovereign throne of justice, though unequal to the bearing of so great a burden, We declare, in the fulness of the apostolic power, the aforesaid Elizabeth a heretic, and an encourager of heretics, together with those who abet her, under the sentence of excommunication, cut off from the unity of the Body of Christ.

"Moreover, We declare that she has forfeited her pretended title to the aforesaid kingdom, to all and every right, dignity, and privilege; We also declare that the nobles, the subjects, and the people of the kingdom aforesaid, who have taken any oath to her, are for ever released from that oath, and from every obligation of allegiance, fealty, and obedience, as We now by these letters release them, and deprive the said Elizabeth of her pretended right to the throne, and every other right whatsoever aforesaid: We command all and singular the nobles, the people subject to her, and others aforesaid, never to venture to obey her monitions, mandates, and laws.

"If any shall contravene this Our decree, We bind them with the same bond of anathema.

"Seeing that it would be a work of too much difficulty to send these letters to every place where it is necessary to send them, Our will is that a copy thereof by a public notary, sealed with the seal of an ecclesiastical prelate, or with the seal of his court, shall have the same force in courts of law and everywhere throughout the world that these letters themselves have if they be produced and shown.

"Given at St. Peter's in Rome, in the year of the Incarnation of our Lord one thousand five hundred and sixty-nine, on the fifth of the calends of March,[1] in the fifth year of Our Pontificate.

CÆ. GLORIERIUS.
H. CUMYN."

[1] Feb. 25, 1570, according to the present computation, for St. Pius began the year on the 25th of March.

CHAPTER IX.

FURY OF THE QUEEN AND PARLIAMENT—PENAL LEGISLATION —ROWLAND JENKS—RISE OF THE PURITANS—THE SOCIETY OF JESUS—CONVERSIONS—MARTYRS.

ONE or two persons of greater zeal, because they made known and defended the Apostolic Letters, were shortly afterwards condemned to a traitor's death—which they courageously underwent[1]—in London, where the Letters had been placed on the very doors of the palace of the sham bishop.[2] The rest of the Catholics continued to obey the queen, either because they did not admit the legal publication of the Apostolic Letters, and saw that the neighbouring princes and the Catholic countries had not refrained from their usual intercourse with the queen, or because they had no knowledge that the letters were issued again and confirmed by the Pope who succeeded Pius V., who died soon after the first publication,[3] or because they were afraid to stir, though they might give the other reasons for their conduct.

On the other hand, the heretics pretended to despise utterly the Bull in public, as if it were nothing more than a bugbear to frighten children, though in reality they were in great trouble, knowing well that in all time past the issues had been disastrous. It was said

[1] John Felton, of whom more will be said below. See p. 316, note 5.

[2] This was Edwin Sandys, who removed from Worcester A.D. 1570 to London, and thence to York A.D. 1577.

[3] St. Pius V. issued the Apostolic Letters Feb. 25, 1570. He died May 1, 1572, and was succeeded by Gregory XIII. May 13, 1572.

that they strove hard in Rome, through certain great personages, and in secret, to obtain the revocation of the sentence, but all to no purpose. As we read of Saul that the spirit of fear and uneasiness, rage also, and an incredible hatred of the priests of God took possession of his troubled soul when he heard the sentence which Samuel had pronounced upon him, so also was it now; from that day forth the queen and her advisers had no peace, for the prosperity of the Catholic Church thenceforward ever growing troubled them as the prosperity of David troubled Saul. It was a special source of vexation to them that this sentence was that of a Pope who, in the opinion of all good men, was a saint, and whom the Protestants themselves regarded as one of the best Popes for many generations.

The queen, made angry by the sentence, and by the daily increase of the Catholics, called a Parliament, in which savage and bloody laws were passed against those who held the ancient faith. To say that queen Elizabeth was a heretic, or schismatic, or an infidel, or usurper of the crown, was to be high treason; and it was forbidden to speak of any one as having a right to the throne during the queen's lifetime, or after her death, unless that person be the natural issue of Elizabeth. These are the very words of the statute.[1]

Next, because priests and other devout persons began about this time the practice of bringing into the country, for the comfort of Catholics, divers sacred things, it is enacted in Parliament that every one shall suffer the loss of all his goods, and be imprisoned for life,

[1] 13 Eliz. c. 1: "The natural issue of her body." Camden (Annales, ii. 241) says that he being then a young man, heard it often stated that the words "natural issue" were inserted in the act by the earl of Leicester in order that he might be able to put one of his own bastards on the throne: "*Ut aliquem ipsius ex pellice spurium pro reginæ sobole naturali Anglis tandem aliquando obtruderet.*"

who shall bring in, accept, or carry about him any sacred things usually sent from Rome as tokens of ecclesiastical communion, such as Agnus Dei, crucifixes, pictures, rosaries, or any other thing whatsoever, blessed by the Pope or by his authority. It is also made a capital offence to procure from Rome any Bulls, Briefs, Instruments, or writings of any kind whatsoever. At the same time, in order to check the salutary labours of the priests, it is made high treason to absolve any one from heresy or schism, or to reconcile any one to the Roman Church, or to be absolved or reconciled, in the sacrament of penance.[1]

Further, in the same Parliament[2] it was enacted that all those who crossed the seas on account of religion should forfeit all their goods and chattels, in order that they might not have wherewithal to subsist on so long as they lived abroad. And as many devout Catholics broke the law, or came within its meshes, they were punished: some were thrown into prison, others lost their possessions, and others were put to death, priests and lay people, men and women, high and low.

Among the memorable events of these times, in which innocent Catholics were everywhere made to suffer, is that which took place in the city and university of Oxford. One Rowland Jenks[3] was arraigned as a

[1] 13 Eliz. c. 2.

[2] 13 Eliz. c. 3.

[3] Rowland Jenks was a bookseller in Oxford, whom Camden (Annales, ii. 316) calls a man *procacis linguæ*, which means that he neither denied nor concealed his belief. He was condemned in the Black Assizes of 1577. "Judgment being passed," says Wood (Annals, ii. 188), "there arose such an infectious damp or breath . . . above 600 sickened in one night, as a physician that now lived in Oxford attesteth. . . . The number of persons that died in five weeks' space, namely, from the 6th of July to the 12th of August—for no longer did this violent infection continue—were 300 in Oxford and 200 and odd in other places, so that the whole number that died in that time were 510 persons." But among all those who died there was not one woman or child. Notwithstanding the visitation, Rowland Jenks, according to Wood (ibid., p. 192), "suffered the sentence passed upon him: went to Douai, and there became baker to the College of English seculars, and lived to be a very

Catholic, found guilty, and being but one of the common people, was condemned to lose both his ears. But the judge had hardly delivered the sentence when a deadly disease suddenly attacked the whole court;[1] no other parts of the city, and no persons not in the court, were touched. The disease laid hold in a moment of all the judges, the high sheriff, and the twelve men of the jury, whose duty it is, according to the custom of the country, to say whether a prisoner be guilty or not. The jury-men died immediately, the judges, the lawyers, and the high sheriff died, some of them within a few hours, others within a few days, but all of them died. Not less than five hundred persons who caught the same disease at the same time and place, died soon after in different places outside the city.

At this time God confounded the tongues of the heretics in England. A new sect of rigid Calvinists, namely, the Puritans,[2] by its writings and preaching, disturbed

old man, to the year 1610 and upwards, as I have been informed by one that knew him there, Mr. Jo. Mallet."

Anglo-Duacen. Diarium secundum, p. 127. "Hic [Mr. Metham] nobis enarravit Catholicum quendam [Rowland Jenks] Oxonii tanquam læsæ majestatis reum coram judicibus sisti, ibique per duos falsos testes gravissimorum verborum contra reginæ reique publicæ statum accusari, per duodecim etiam—ut mos nostræ gentis est—juratos viros criminosum inveniri, ac denique per ipsos judices condemnari; postea autem tam mortiferam tabem omnes tum judices et falsos testes, cum etiam ipsos provinciæ Oxoniensis vice-comites, duodecim juratos viros ac alios nonnullos tum nobiles cum laicos invasisse, ut qui intra bidui spatium ea morte expirarent plus quam quadringenti numerarentur."

[1] Stow, p. 681. "The 4th, 5th, and 6th of July [1577] were the assizes holden at Oxford, where was arraigned and condemned one Rowland Jenkes for his seditious tongue, at which time there arose amidst the people such a damp that almost all were smothered, very few escaped that were not taken at that instant. The jurors died presently. Shortly after died Sir Robert Bell, lord chief baron, Sir Robert de Olie, Sir William Babington, Master Weneham, Master de Olie, high sheriff, Master Davers, Master Harcurt, Master Kirle, Master Phereplace, Master Greenwood, Master Foster, Master Nash, Serjeant Baram, Master Stevens, &c. There died in Oxford 300 persons, and sickened there, but died in other places, 200 and odd from the 6th of July to the 12th of August, after which day died not one of that sickness, for one of them infected not another, nor any one woman or child died thereof."

[2] Sandys, writing to Gualter from London, Dec. 9, 1579 (Zurich Letters,

exceedingly the ordinary Protestants, whose recent royal or parliamentary belief, worship, and government were denounced as impious and superstitious in more than a hundred points. By this quarrel of the heretics the Catholics grew in number every day, and more resolute in the profession of the faith.

There was much talk at this time among the Catholics of the admirable training, order, and learning of the Fathers of the Society of Jesus, how much they were in favour with God and man. There was also a very great desire on the part of the English to profit by their labours. Earnest representations were therefore made to the superiors of the society—the Pope himself exerted his authority to the same end—that they should send some of their own subjects, especially the most distinguished Englishmen who were in the order, to labour in the British harvest; for many men of great piety and learning had during their exile entered the society.

Robert Persons and Edmund Campian,[1] men endowed with great gifts of God, were the first who were chosen. With them were sent also from both the English colleges some priests, admirably fitted for the work, who executed the mission given them by their superiors with such

1st series, No. 134), says, "These new men, whom we call Puritans, who tread all authority under foot." In a former letter to the same person, Aug. 9, 1574 (ibid., No. 124), he says, "The author of these novelties, and, after Beza, the first inventor is a young Englishman, by name Thomas Cartwright, who, they say, is now sojourning at Heidelberg." Pilkington, writing to the same person, July 20, 1573 (ibid., No. 110), says, "Not only the habits, but our whole ecclesiastical polity, discipline, the revenues of the bishops [Pilkington was a bishop], ceremonies or public forms of worship, liturgies, vocation of ministers, or the ministration of the sacraments,—all these things are now openly attacked from the press, and it is contended with the greatest bitterness that they are not to be endured in the Church of Christ. The doctrine alone they leave untouched: as to everything else, by whatever name you call it, they are clamorous for its removal. The godly mourn, the Papists exult, that we are now fighting against each other, who were heretofore wont to attack them with our united forces."

[1] Father Persons landed at Dover June 12, 1580, and Father Campian June 25, in the same year.

readiness, faith, and diligence that in a very few months, by their exhortations from house to house, by their sermons and their writings, and the ministration of the sacraments, they brought the people in countless numbers to the Church, and very many too who were illustrious for their noble birth and their great learning.

These labours are met at first with the most threatening proclamations [1] by the enemy. All the Jesuits, all the priests and students of the two foreign colleges, are declared guilty of high treason, and said to be the contrivers of divers conspiracies against the queen and the state; all parents and guardians are therefore commanded to recall those under their charge as soon as possible; merchants and others are forbidden under penalties to send money to those colleges, or to any of the members of the same; and every person whatsoever is forbidden to receive the priests into their houses, or help them in any way. These orders were issued by the sole authority of the queen,[2] but they were afterwards, as shall be shown further on, set forth and allowed in Parliament.

Then, seeing the temples and conventicles of the heretics in many places forsaken, Parliament is assembled, and a law is made "that every person above the age of sixteen years" who shall refuse to frequent the prayers, the sermons, and churches of the Protestants, shall forfeit for every month twenty pounds of lawful English money,[3] by which ruthless extortions the Catholics were afterwards marvellously plundered.

[1] Stow, p. 688. "About the 12th of January [1581] proclamation was published at London for the revocation of sundry the queen's majesty's subjects remaining beyond the seas, under the colour of study, and living contrary to the laws of God and of the realm. And also against the retaining of Jesuits and massing priests, sowers of sedition and other treasonable attempts," &c.

[2] A proclamation of the queen, dated Jan. 10, 1581, may be seen in Strype, Annals, iii. 40, and in Dod, ed. Tierney, iii. xxi.

[3] 23 Eliz. c. 1, s. 5.

It was also enacted in the same Parliament that any one who persuaded another in any way to forsake the religion now observed in England, was guilty of high treason.[1]

The pains and penalties to be inflicted on those who hear or say Mass, according to the law made in the first year of the queen's reign, are doubled,[2] and the Catholics bore it almost patiently for the love of Christ.

Meanwhile, for the better execution of these bloody laws, pursuivants and spies are sent into the houses of noblemen, and of others who kept the faith, to drag the priests, with those who entertain them and those who help them, into prison, to subject them to merciless torture, and to rob them of their property, and sometimes to put them to death. People are encouraged to betray and apprehend Jesuits and priests by the offer of large rewards, and the pardon of their crimes to men of the most worthless sort. Accordingly so many persons of all ranks are seized that new prisons are made in divers places, the existing prisons being insufficient for the priests and other Catholics upon whom they now lay hands. The venerable old man the bishop of Lincoln, the abbot of Westminster, and other confessors, still older, have been sent to Wisbech Castle,[3]

[1] 23 Eliz. c. 1, s. 2. "Shall have judgment, suffer and forfeit, as in case of high treason."

[2] 23 Eliz. c. 1, s. 4. "Every person which shall say or sing Mass, . . . shall forfeit the sum of 200 marks, and be committed to prison . . . for one year . . . Every person which shall willingly hear Mass, shall forfeit the sum of 100 marks, and suffer imprisonment for a year."

[3] Colleg. Anglo-Duaceni Diar., ii. p. 171. "Eodem tempore [Septembris 18, 1580] ex literis et quorundam sermonibus ex Anglia venientium, cognovimus reverendos in Christo patres Dominum Watsonum episcopum Lincolniensem et Dominum Flecknamum abbatem monasterii Westmonasteriensis aliosque aliquot doctos et graves viros, videlicet, Dominum Woode, Dominum Mettamum, Dominum Bluettum, Dominum Uxsbridge juris doctorem, et, quod opinor, alios quorum non sunt ad nos delata nomina, a carceribus quibus Londini inclusi tenebantur ad alium vilem et fœtidum carcerem, in loco paludoso non procul a Cantabrigia disjuncto, situm, qui quidem nostra lingua dicitur Wisbidge Castle, missos esse, ibique incarceratos."

a pestilential prison in the fens of Ely, where they have been done to death without difficulty.

Among others who at this time fell into their hands was the illustrious Father Campian.[1] A false brother, like another Judas, betrayed him.[2] He is apprehended, mocked, and laid in irons, put on the rack, and his very bones are loosened in their sockets. At the same time many persons are thrown into prison, not only the common people, but peers and gentlemen, because they had either received Father Campian into their houses or had absented themselves from the churches of the Protestants. Out of prison, in company with thieves and robbers, they are taken into court to be tried, and there heavily fined. The greatest indignities of this kind were inflicted on Lord Vaux,[3] Sir Thomas Tresham,[4] Sir William Catesby,[5] and on many others throughout the

[1] Butler's Hist. Mem., chap. xxxiii. s. 3. "On the 15th of July 1581 he was apprehended in a secret room in the house of a Catholic gentleman. After remaining during two days in the custody of the sheriff of Berkshire, he was conveyed by slow journeys to London on horseback, his legs fastened under the horse, his arms tied behind him, and a paper placed on his hat, on which in large capital letters were written the words, 'Campian, the seditious Jesuit.' He was taken to the Tower July 22, and twice tortured in secret."

Anglo-Duacen. Diar., ii. p. 181. "Hoc fere tempore [Aug. 1581], audivimus Patrem Edmundum Campianum, Georgii Elioti falsi fratris opera, ab hæreticis captum, et cum aliis decem, magno stipatum comitatu Londinum adductum fuisse. Inter autem illos decem tres erant sacerdotes, alumni nostri seminarii, videlicet, Dominus Thomas Fordus, Dominus Colingtonus, Dominus Filbeus, junior. Patris Edmundi galero—dum per plateas Londinenses, ut omnium ludibrio exponeretur, ductus est—certam quandam aiunt affixam fuisse, in qua litteris majusculis hæc verba erant inscripta: 'Hic est ille seditiosus Jesuita Edmundus Campianus.' Hunc etiam bis misere tortum o, equule carcere inclusum tenent, qui antequam caperetur, brevem sed elegantem latine scriptum contra hæreticos libellum edidit."

[2] This was George Eliot, once a servant of Lady Petre.

[3] Lord Vaux, the third baron of his family, William Vaux, who succeeded A.D. 1562. He died A.D. 1595, succeeded by his grandson, Edward Vaux.

[4] Fr. Morris, Condition of Catholics, p. 90. "Often in prison for his conscience, although he paid the statute duty besides of £20 a month for his refusing to go to church with heretics."

[5] Ibid., p. 55. "Sir William Catesby . . . being a Catholic, and often in prison for his faith, suffered many losses, and much impaired his estate." His son was Mr. Catesby, known for his share in the Gunpowder Plot.

kingdom, men admirable for their perseverance, faith, and devotion.[1]

It was not thought safe to put Father Campian and the other priests to death merely because they preached the Catholic faith, for the minds of Englishmen at this time were deeply impressed in its favour. Accordingly it is pretended, in order to have a more specious excuse, that he and others had in Rome and Rheims conspired together to kill the queen. Witnesses are sought for and suborned, men out of the very dregs of the people; and though their evidence did not hold together, and was most easily shown to be false, nevertheless Father Campian and the others are condemned to undergo a most cruel and shameful death,[2] which soon after they endured with most marvellous courage, whereby the

[1] Stow, p. 678: "The 4th of April [1574] being Palm Sunday, there was taken saying of Mass in the Lord Morley's house, within Aldgate of London, one Albon Dolman, priest, and the Lady Morley with her children; and divers other were also taken hearing the said Mass. There was also taken the same day and hour, for saying Mass at the Lady Gilford's in Trinity Lane, one Oliver Heywood, priest, and for hearing the said Mass, the Lady Gilford, with divers other gentlewomen. There was also taken at the same instant in the Lady Brown's house in Cow Lane, for saying Mass, one Thomas Heywood, priest, and one John Cooper, priest, with the Lady Brown, and divers other were likewise taken, being hearers of the said Mass. All which persons were for the same offences indicted, convicted, and had the law according to the statute in that case provided. There was also found in their several chapels divers Latin books, beads, images, patens, chalices, crosses, vestments, pixes, paxes, and suchlike." A letter of one George Gardyner to Parkhurst, in possession of the see of Norwich, written "from the Court, April 8, 1574" (Gorham, Gleanings, p. 486), gives the following account of this raid on Palm Sunday: "There was on Palm Sunday last, at one hour, at four sundry Masses in four sundry places, and out-corners of the city of London, fifty-three persons taken, whereof the most part were ladies, gentlewomen, and gentlemen. Twenty-two of them stand stoutly to the matter; whereof the Lady Morlaye and the Lady Browne, which paid before 100 marks for her first offence, are the chief. The priests glory in their doings, and did affirm that there were five hundred Masses in England that day."

[2] Stow, p. 695. "On the 20th of November Edmund Champion, Jesuit, Ralph Sherwine, Lucas Kirby, Edward Rishton, Thomas Coteham, Henry Orton, Robert Johnson, and James Bosgrave were brought to the high bar at Westminster, where they were severally and all together indicted upon high treason. . . . By a jury they were approved guilty, and had judgment to be hanged, bowelled, and quartered."

Catholics were strengthened, and all good men were edified. Even at the last moment the heretics disturbed them, urging them at least to acknowledge the supremacy of the queen, and to confess that they had wronged her, promising them their life and a pardon in return for that submission.

On the first day of December 1581 the reverend Father Edmund Campian and the venerable priests Ralph Sherwin and Alexander Bryant finished their course by a glorious martyrdom.[1]

On the 20th of May in the following year [1582] Thomas Ford, John Shert, and Robert Johnson, on the 30th of the same month William Filby, Luke Kirby, Laurence Richardson, and Thomas Cottam, all saintly and learned priests, made perfect their good confession.[2] All these were martyred in London, as before them the two priests, John Nelson in 1578,[3] and Everard

[1] Stow, p. 695. "The 1st of September [December], Edmund Champion, Jesuit, Ralph Sherwine, and Alexander Bryan, seminary priests, were drawn from the Tower of London to Tyborne, and there hanged, bowelled, and quartered."

[2] Stow, p. 695. "On the 28th of May [1582] Thomas Ford, John Shert, and Robert Johnson, priests, having been before indicted, arraigned, and condemned for high treason intended, as ye have heard of Champion and other, were drawn from the Tower to Tyborne, and there hanged, bowelled, and quartered."

"On the 30th Luke Kirby, William Filby, Thomas Cottam, and Laurence Richardson were for the like treason in the same place likewise executed."

[3] Stow, p. 684. "The 3d of February, early in the morning, John Nelson, for denying the queen's supremacy, and such other traitorous words against her majesty, was drawn from Newgate to Tyborne, and there hanged, bowelled, and quartered."

Anglo-Duacen. Diarium secundum, p. 123. "Hic nunciabat quod venerabilis sacerdos Dominus Nelsonus qui jam per annum et amplius occulte ad lucrandas Christo animas cum fratribus suis multum laboraverat, tandem ab hæreticis comprehensus pro Catholica veritate tuenda contra hæreticam pravitatem et insaniam usque ad effusionem sanguinis fortiter decertasset. Nam cum ei ista quæstio proponeretur an Angliæ regina a Catholicis aut ab ipso etiam pro hæretica haberetur, et ipse respondisset audacter—quemadmodum eam ab hæresi etiam purgarent—sentire tamen se salva conscientia non posse aliter quam quod ad minimum schismatica esset, mortis statim sententiam excepit, et paulo post crati injectus ad supplicii locum trahitur; ibi fune prius in collum imposito ad breve tempus suspenditur, deinde adhuc vivens in terram dimittitur, præciduntur

Hans in 1581,[1] with Thomas Sherwood,[2] a layman. In the country, away from London, the first martyr out of the seminaries was Cuthbert Mayne in 1577,[3] then John Payne in 1582,[4] admirable priests, and singularly zealous.

Soon after, in the same year, William Lacy, Richard Kirkman, James Thompson,[5] and in the next year William Hart[6] and Richard Thirkell,[7] gave up their blessed souls to God in the city of York, suffering with the like constancy. These were priests of great piety and learning,

genitalia, aperitur venter, viscera eruuntur, caput amputatur et baculo affigitur, membra dissecantur, ac sic excarnificatus, immani ac barbaræ crudelitati vix satisfecit."

[1] Stow, p. 695. "The 18th of July, Everard Haunce, a seminary priest, was in the sessions hall in the Old Baily arraigned, where he affirmed that himself was subject to the Pope in ecclesiastical causes, and that the Pope hath now the same authority here in England that he had an hundred years past, with other traitorous speeches, for the which he was condemned to be drawn, hanged, bowelled, and quartered, and was executed accordingly on the last of July."

The "Rheims Diary furnishes the following account of the death of Mr. Hans. Anglo-Duacen. Diar., ii. p. 181. "Ultimo Julii primum crate vectus lignea ad crucem quæ nostra lingua dicitur Tiburn, momento uno aut altero—vix quidem partibili—suspensus est; deinde viventi et vivo virilia sunt abscissa et in ignem conjecta, venterque cultro carnificis apertus, cumque viscera effusa essent, et cor jam tremulum carnifex manu attractaret, hanc supremam edidisse dictus est vocem, 'O diem felicem!' Imo plurimorum ad nos detulit consentiens fama cor ejus in ignem missum, suo eoque magno impetu ex ipsis flammis exiliisse, et cum rursus fasce coopertum lignea in ignem mitteretur, secundo tanta vi latum contra fascem ascendisse, ut illum tum loco moveret, tum in fumo ipso hærere tremulum faceret."

[2] Stow, p. 684. "The 7th of February, one named Sherewood was drawn from the Tower of London to Tyborne, and there hanged, bowelled, and quartered for the like treason."

Anglo-Duacen. Diarium secundum, p. 135. "Die 1ª Martii [1578] rediit ad nos ex Anglia Mr. Lous, qui nunciabat quod propter fidei Catholicæ professionem non carceres modo sed et mortem etiam sustinuisset juvenis quidam appellatus Thomas Sherwood, cujus in omnibus tormentis vox erat hujusmodi, 'Domine Jesu, nom sum dignus ut ista pro Te patiar, multo minus ea præmia recipere quæ daturum Te promisisti confitentibus Te.'"

[3] Stow, p. 682. "The 30th of September [1577] Cuthbert Mayne was drawn, hanged, and quartered at Launceston in Cornwall for preferring Roman power."

[4] Stow, p. 695. "John Paine, priest, being indicted of high treason, for words by him spoken to one Eliot, was arraigned and condemned at Chelmsford on the last of March, and was there executed on the second day of April."

[5] Nov. 28, 1582.

[6] March 15.

[7] May 29.

condemned because they admitted themselves to be priests, and because they confessed that they had been ordained out of the kingdom by the authority of the Pope.

It is not very long since John Slade and John Body,[1] two honest laymen, were twice at different times in the city of Winchester—a thing without example in England—sentenced to death by the judge. They were condemned to death, which soon afterwards they most blessedly underwent, for no other cause than that of their refusal to accept the supremacy of the queen in ecclesiastical matters. In the same year another layman, William Carter,[2] was martyred in London.

It was no part of the duty of the priests, neither would they do so without the orders of their superiors, to discuss questions of state; but laymen had greater freedom, and James Leybourn,[3] being free, openly refused to obey the queen, as Dr. Storey,[4] Felton,[5] and Wode-

[1] Stow, p. 698. "John Slade, schoolmaster, and John Bodie, master of art, being both condemned of high treason, for maintaining the Roman power, were drawn, hanged, and quartered; Slade at Winchester on the 30th of October [1583], and Bodie at Andover on the 2d of November."

[2] Stow, p. 698. "On the 10th of January [1584], at a sessions holden in the justice hall, in the Old Baily of London, for the gaol-delivery of Newgate, William Carter, of the city of London, was there indicted, arraigned, and condemned of high treason for printing a seditious and traitorous book in English, entituled a 'Treatise of Schism,' and was for the same—according to sentence pronounced against him—on the next morrow drawn from Newgate to Tyborne, and there hanged, bowelled, and quartered." He was once in the service of Dr. Nicolas Harpsfield, formerly archdeacon of Canterbury.

[3] The valiant woman, Anne Dacres, countess of Arundel and Surrey, was a granddaughter of Sir James Labourn, and therefore near of kin to the martyr, of whom it is written in her Life, p. 176, that "he lost his for it [the faith], being put to a painful and ignominious death, hanged, drawn, and quartered at Lancaster, as I take it, in the year 1583, and twenty-sixth of queen Elizabeth, for denying her supremacy in ecclesiastical affairs." His daughter Susan was a nun, see Fr. Morris, The Troubles of our Catholic Forefathers, p. 49: "Susan Labourn, daughter to a holy martyr, for whose sake the old countess of Arundel [Anne Dacres] gave now £80 once for all to help her hither."

[4] Storey. See bk. ii. chap. iv. p. 200, note 1.

[5] Stow, p. 667. "The 8th of August [1570] John Felton was drawn from Newgate unto Paul's Churchyard, and there hanged on a gallows new set up that morning

house,[1] the priest, had done, partly because of her illegitimate birth, and partly because of the sentence of Pius V., by which she was declared to have no right to the throne. For this he suffered sharp imprisonment in Carlisle, London, Lancaster, and Manchester. He shed his blood at last in Lancaster with the utmost cheerfulness and gentleness, all who were present at his death marvelling at his courage and patience.

Nor may we fail to mention here those poor people who, not having the means to pay the fines laid upon them because they would not enter the churches nor be present at the profane services of the Protestants, were by the sentence of the judge long and piteously dragged, stripped of their clothes, and cruelly whipped through the streets of Winchester.

before the bishop's palace gate; and being cut down alive, he was bowelled and quartered."

[1] Stow, p. 677. "The 16th of June [1573] Thomas Woodhouse, a priest of Lincolnshire, who had lien long prisoner in the Fleet, was arraigned in the Guildhall of London, and there condemned of high treason, who had judgment to be hanged and quartered, and was executed at Tyborne the 19th of June."

CHAPTER X.

FATHER HEYWOOD—MARTYRS—THE PEERS ASSAILED—SEVERITY OF THE PERSECUTION.

It happened in the providence of God that Father Jasper Heywood[1] fell at this time into the hands of the persecutors. On his way to attend a conference of his brethren in France, to which he had been summoned, he was driven by an adverse wind off the coast of Normandy to an English port. There the authorities lay their hands upon him, and send him to London, where he is thrown into prison. Not many days afterwards he is taken—having been first submitted to divers interrogatories—by the lieutenant of the Tower before the judges, in the company of other priests who were made prisoners about the same time. When they were all at the door of the court, he is suddenly taken away from the rest, and lodged in a house close by during their trial. Nothing of this kind had been done before, but it is an old and really satanic trick of heretics. As he was a very learned and eloquent man, and could with the utmost ease have replied to the charges brought against them, he was therefore kept out of court for the purpose of depriving his fellow-confessors

[1] Dr. Oliver in his "Collections" says he "joined the Society at Rome, 21st May 1562. He soon attained to such a reputation for his skill in the Hebrew language, and for theological science, as to deserve the esteem and commendation of that excellent judge and patron of merit Gregory XIII. His zeal for souls induced him to accompany Fr. William Holt to England in the summer of 1581." He died at Naples, Jan. 9, 1598.

of his help, and of creating suspicion in their minds, and of the people there present, that the good father had either altogether changed his mind and his religion, or at least had given way in some thing or other to the queen. Then, that every one might the more easily believe the story, a report is spread abroad that the lieutenant of the Tower had dropped some words to that effect, and taken him back to prison, not with his companions, whom the judges had condemned to die, but by another secret door. By this wicked device it was brought about that even good people were afraid that the reverend father had yielded somewhat to human frailty. But in time that most impious fraud was detected, and people saw that the saintly confessor had been most grievously wronged; for their treacherous devices, their repeated threats, and the sore temptations by which they tried him never disturbed him. They even offered, and I heard him say so myself, to make him a bishop, if he would but yield ever so little to them.

He remained in prison, where, by messengers and letters from members of the queen's council, he was afterwards pressed to apostatise, but it was all to no purpose. The priests his companions, in pursuance of the sentence shortly before given, were led forth to the place of execution, where in great joy they perfected their confessorship in a glorious death. These were George Haddock, John Munden, John Nutter, James Fenn, Thomas Hemerford.[1]

In other parts of the kingdom also, especially in Lan-

[1] Stow, p. 698. "The 7th of February [1584] were arraigned at Westminster, John Fen, George Haddocke, John Munden, John Nutter, and Thomas Hemerford, all five found guilty of high treason, in being made priests beyond the seas, and by the Pope's authority, since a statute made *in anno primo* of her majesty's reign, and had judgment to be hanged, bowelled, and quartered, which were all executed at Tyborne on the 12th of February."

caster, York, and on the Welsh borders, many Catholics were most grievously tortured; some even were put to a dishonourable death, which is the extreme punishment of traitors or thieves, as were James Bell,[1] a priest, being then sixty years of age, and John Finch,[2] a layman, at Lancaster, and Richard White,[3] a schoolmaster, in Wales.

It would answer no purpose to recount, in this brief sketch, the offences for which these innocent persons were so inhumanly punished, for everybody knows that the true and only reason was their profession of the old religion, and their defence of the Apostolic See, and communion therewith, against the rebel children of the Church. For when they had shown without difficulty how false were the charges which were brought against them in court, they were forthwith required to reveal their more secret thoughts by means of crafty questions[4]

[1] James Bell, born at Warrington, educated at Oxford, was ordained priest in the reign of Mary, and for many years observed the state religion under Elizabeth. He was converted in 1581, and reconciled to the Church. But in Jan. 1584 he was thrown into prison by the earl of Derby, then tried for treason, which consisted in denying the royal and believing in the Papal supremacy, and being convicted, died a martyr's death April 20, 1584.

[2] John Finch, born at Eccleston, and converted after his marriage. He was tried in company with the Rev. James Bell for the same offence, that of holding the true faith, and was with him a martyr on the same day.

[3] Richard White, *i.e.*, Gwin, was born at Llanidloes, Montgomeryshire, educated at Oxford and Cambridge, became a schoolmaster, and was married. He was martyred at Wrexham, Oct. 15, 1584. A contemporary account of his life and martyrdom was published in the "Rambler," 2d series, vol. iii. pp. 233–248, and pp. 366–388.

[4] These questions are published in "A Particular Declaration or Testimony of the Undutiful and Traitorous Affection borne against her Majesty, by Edmond Campion, Jesuit, and other condemned Priests. Published by Authority. London, Christopher Barker, 1582," and are as follows:—

"1. Whether the Bull of Pius Quintus against the queen's majesty be a lawful sentence, and ought to be obeyed by the subjects of England?

"2. Whether the queen's majesty be a lawful queen, and ought to be obeyed by the subjects of England, notwithstanding the Bull of Pius Quintus, or any other Bull or sentence that the Pope hath pronounced, or may pronounce against her majesty?

"3. Whether the Pope have, or had power, to authorise the earls of

touching their future behaviour with regard to the declaratory Bull of Pius V.: whether in their judgment the sentence of the Pope was a lawful sentence; whether they believed that the Pope could depose princes, and release subjects from their allegiance; what they would do themselves, or how would they direct the consciences of others, if any one began a war on account of religion. Many other questions of the same kind were put to them. If in their replies to these questions they behaved themselves with caution and prudence, or said anything in favour of the Papal jurisdiction, their offence was said to be not one of religion, but high treason.

The queen and her advisers now were not satisfied, in their cunning cruelty, with all they had done against priests, and people of moderate fortunes who kept the faith, so they began to treat with the grossest indignities persons of higher rank, especially the peers, for they saw that these hated more and more the falsehood, the meanness, and immeasurable cruelty of the new religion. But as it was impossible for them to destroy at once every noble person who held the faith, in order to gratify the hate or the greed of each upstart courtier, they assailed them, one after another, by lying accusa-

Northumberland and Westmoreland, and other her majesty's subjects, to rebel or take arms against her majesty, or to authorise Dr. Saunders or others to invade Ireland, or any other her dominions, and to bear arms against her, and whether they did therein lawfully or no?

"4. Whether the Pope have power to discharge any of her highness's subjects, or the subjects of any Christian prince, from their allegiance, or oath of obedience to her majesty, or to their prince, for any cause?

"5. Whether the said Dr. Saunders in his book of the visible Monarchy of the Church, and Dr. Bristowe in his book of Motives—writing in allowance, commendation, and confirmation of the said Bull of Pius Quintus—have therein taught, testified, or maintained a truth or a falsehood?

"6. If the Pope do, by his Bull or sentence, pronounce her majesty to be deprived and no lawful queen, and her subjects to be discharged of their allegiance and obedience unto her; and after if the Pope or any other, by his appointment and authority, do invade this realm, which part would you take, or which part ought a good subject of England to take?"

tions and falsehoods. Thus they shamefully put to death Francis Throgmorton[1] and Edward Arden,[2] and others, men of the old religion and of ancient descent. Thus the powerful earl of Northumberland,[3] and the most devout and noble personage, William Shelley,[4] were thrown, on mere empty suspicion, into their miserable and fatal prisons. Lord Paget and Charles Arundel[5] would have been dealt with in the same way, though most innocent, if they had not saved their lives and their consciences by timely flight.

I will not stop to describe the cruelty with which they have now for some time treated the most illustrious person in the whole kingdom, the earl of Arundel,[6] the

[1] Stow, p. 698. "The 21st of May [1584] Francis Throckmorton, Esq., was arraigned in the Guildhall of the city of London, where being found guilty of high treason, he was condemned and had judgment to be hanged, bowelled, and quartered. The 10th of July next following, the same Francis Throckmorton was conveyed by water from the Tower of London to the Blackfriars' Stairs, and from thence by land to the sessions hall in the Old Baily without Newgate, where he was delivered to the sheriffs of London, laid on a hurdle, drawn to Tyborne, and there executed according to his judgment." He was the eldest son of Sir John Throgmorton, chief justice of Chester.

[2] Stow, p. 698. "Edward Arden, a squire in Parkhall, Warwickshire, Mary Arden, his wife, . . . and Hugh Hall, priest, being with other before indicted at Warwick, were on the 16th of December [1583] arraigned in the Guildhall of London, where they were found guilty and condemned of high treason. . . . And on the morrow, being the 20th of December, Edward Arden was drawn from Newgate into Smithfield, and hanged, bowelled, and quartered."

[3] Stow, p. 706. "The 21st of June [1581] Henry Percy, earl of Northumberland, in prison in the Tower of London, upon vehement suspicion of high treason, was there found dead, and also of his own devilish intent, and of his malice before pretended to have murdered himself, as more at large may appear by inquisition made by a substantial jury, taken before the coroner of London." The "substantial jury" forgot that prisoners in the Tower, such as the earl of Northumberland, were watched night and day when they brought in their verdict. See the letter concerning his death in the "Crudelitatis Calvinianæ exempla duo recentissima ex Anglia," A.D. 1585, s. l.

[4] He was sent to the Tower, Jan. 18, 1584.

[5] Camden, p. 411. "Thomas Baro Pagettus, et Carolus Arundellus aulicus, solum clam verterunt, et in Galliam se subduxerunt."

[6] Philip Howard, born June 28, 1557. His life, written by a contemporary, was published by the late duke of Norfolk in 1857.

Cornelius à Lapide, Comment. in Heb. c. x. v. 34. "Excellentissimus Arondeliæ comes, Norfolciensis ducis filius et hæres, religionis Catholicæ ergo, dum in Galliam fugam parat, captus, in Turrim Londinensem con-

eldest son and heir of the duke of Norfolk,[1] who also has been put to death by their hands stained in blood. The earl had taken to flight solely to save his conscience, but they laid hands upon him and put him in prison. They dishonour his name by shameless lying, and harass his brothers, his sisters, and all his kindred, who are all perfectly innocent.

Beside these miseries already mentioned, and the manifold extortions and molestations which they are forced to endure at the hands of most worthless men, the lay nobility are in this more unhappy than the priests: they cannot run away for conscience-sake, nor sell their estates, nor give up their goods to their wives and children, nor take them with them for their support; everything must be left behind for the exchequer and for the use of heretics: nothing more slavish and miserable can be imagined or described.

It is said that this cruelty is inflicted on all ranks of men for the safety of the queen and the state, more and more endangered—so they say—by the Catholics every

jectus et demum ad tribunal ductus et condemnatus est: post duodecim aut circiter captivitatis annos in vinculis gloriosus confessor, imo martyr obiit. Hic supremus in Anglia comes et familiæ nobilissimæ, mirum dictu et quanta amisit, et qua animi æquitate novercantis fortunæ fluctus sustinuit, in carcere enim captivus Catholicis omnibus non exemplo modo sed etiam singulari solatio fuit: nullus unquam de bonorum rapina conquerentem, nullus de carceris incommodis, de negata libertate dolentem audivit: imo conquerentes et dolentes alios ipse nunc verbis erigere, nunc mira qua pollebat comitate, consolari solebat; illi præter Deum et cælestium rerum contemplationem sapiebat nihil: pecunias quas pro sustentatione regina illi—nam juxta dignitatis gradum plus minusve in Turri captivis assignatur—concessit; tenui et parco ipse contentus cibo, inter pauperes distribuit. Alia multa dixit, fecit, sustinuit illustrissimus comes quæ antiquorum primitivæ ecclesiæ heroum factum vel æquent vel superent, et dignissima quæ æternitate consecrentur." The earl died on Sunday, Oct. 19, 1595, "*non absque veneni suspicione.*"

[1] Parkhurst, writing to Bullinger, March 16, 1572 (Zurich Letters, 1st series, No. 102), says: "The duke of Norfolk pleaded his own cause in Westminster Hall on the 16th of January from seven in the morning till night. There are many charges of treason against him, which he refuted as well as he could. The entire cognisance and jurisdiction in this cause is referred to nine earls, one viscount, and fifteen barons. All these unanimously declared him guilty, and so he is at last condemned to death." The duke was executed, June 2, on Tower Hill.

day becoming more numerous and attached to the queen of Scotland, and not at all on account of their religion. Certainly we all think so, and all sensible men think so too, who now for many years have observed that the people who now govern England are utterly regardless of religion, whatever they may pretend to be, and careful only of their own interests. This is the source of those new terrors which have laid hold of their minds, and of the suspicions which they entertain that there are people bent on the murder of Elizabeth. They are like children, afraid not only of men and things which have a real existence, but of unsubstantial ghosts and shadows. So much so that in order to ward off all dangers to the life of the queen, or to punish the authors thereof, if any such there be, they have banded themselves together, and bound themselves by oaths—a thing never heard of before, and contrary to the custom and law of the land—not only against those who may do the evil they dread, but against the very next heirs to the crown. At first this arose out of private zeal and fury, but afterwards an act of Parliament was obtained in favour of it in a certain modified form.[1]

But to return to our subject. In the midst of this cruelty exercised upon all Catholics of every rank, in order to conceal at times in some measure from foreign princes, and even the Pope himself, the severity of the persecution, and gain for themselves the reputation of being moderate and merciful, they show their mercy so

[1] Parry, the Parliaments and Councils of England, p. 227: "By an act passed in the Lords for the surety of the queen's person, an 'Association' of twenty-four of the privy council and House of Lords is formed for making inquisition after all such as should invade the kingdom, &c., or make claim to the crown of England." Camden, p. 418: "Plurimi, Leicestrio auctore, ex omni hominum ordine per Angliam ex communi charitate, dum non illam, sed de illa timuerunt, se 'Associatione' quadam mutuis votis, subscriptionibus et sigillis obstrinxerunt, ad eos omnibus viribus ad mortem usque persequendos qui in reginam aliquid attentaverint."

fraudulently, that while they are harassing, torturing, and killing one, the royal indulgence is often extended to another. Thus when there is a lucid interval or rest from the slaughter of innocent people in London, the fury of the persecution breaks out in the country with greater violence, and while they seem to allow greater freedom to some, they at the same time harass others in the most cruel way. And in order that this their cunning may the better subserve their end, they keep certain persons in the courts of princes whose business it is to insist upon, set forth, and enhance this dishonest and delusive mercy in the presence of those who are unacquainted with our affairs, and at the same time to lessen or excuse the dreadful deeds of their unmeasurable cruelty, or to explain them in a sense contrary to the faith. Hence it is that you often hear even people who are not wicked promise better things of these persecutors of the Church.

CHAPTER XI.

BANISHMENT OF THE PRIESTS—MORE PENAL LEGISLATION.

THE persecutors have in these days adopted a new course, that of banishing those whom they held in prison. This they do either because they see that they have gained nothing by slaughtering the priests, or because they think that by so doing their delusive kindness may become known in divers places, which is a thing they much desire. But most assuredly banishment for life is no strong proof of forbearance, and in truth is the most cruel punishment, when the condition of it is death if you return. Now the priests of God are in England by the command of their superiors, and out of their own great zeal for the salvation of souls; to them, therefore, this banishment must have been harder to bear than all torture and death itself, and to the Catholic people also, thus robbed of their priests, it must have been infinitely sad.

A word or two must be said of the way in which the priests were driven out of the country, for I,[1] though unworthy, had a share in this affliction, such as it was, for the name of Christ, with twenty others, for we were

[1] The Rev. Edward Rishton, the writer of this fourth book, from whom the printers obtained the MS. of Sander. He had been condemned to death on the same day with Father Campian, and was sent abroad against his will. His death, hastened by his sufferings in the Tower, took place at St. Menehould A.D. 1585. He was born in Lancashire, educated at Oxford and Douai, and was for three years in the English College in Rome, having been ordained priest at Cambrai A.D. 1577.

so many priests, and one illustrious layman,[1] who underwent this punishment.

At that time both the old and the new prisons were filled with the confessors, and in one prison, the Marshalsea—that is the name of one of the prisons of London—there were about thirty priests beside laymen. Some also of those who with Father Campian, or soon after, had been condemned to death, were kept in the Tower, and in other prisons of the city, waiting these three years for the headsman. These, but not all of them, though under the same sentence, nor yet the only ones, were chosen for banishment, and with them certain others taken out of nearly every prison in London. Others then were shut up in the many prisons throughout the land, but of these not one was released.

When the authorities had determined the day on which these prisoners were to embark, they sent to the keeper of every prison the names of those who were to be sent out of the country, with orders to inform the prisoners of the day on which they must depart, in order that they might make provision for their journey and their sustenance afterwards, for they were to be maintained at the public expense—expected by many—only so long as they were on board the vessel that carried them. But as they in the meantime were kept in prison, and allowed to speak to no one except in the presence of their jailers, they could not obtain much help for their journey, or for the endurance of the banishment to which they were driven. In this light alone, that banishment must have been regarded as most calamitous by men deprived of their all. When they were told of the queen's resolution, they laboured,

[1] Henry Orton. He had been sentenced to death, bowelling, and quartering with Father Campian and the others, Nov. 20, 1581. See bk. iv. chap. ix. p. 313, note 2.

every one of them to the utmost of their power, to obtain from their friends some provision for their needs, in the way of clothes and money.

The day came at last, though often changed, but for what purpose I do not know; and those persons who had been charged to see us transported, went from prison to prison demanding of the keepers thereof those who had been singled out for transportation. We were all brought to the ship moored in the Thames, near the gate of the Tower,[1] and ordered to go on board. Thereupon some of us, especially the reverend Father Jasper Heywood, made a public complaint in the name of all, that we ought not to be driven out of our country without cause, having committed no crime, without a legal trial and clearly not convicted. He also said that we would go no farther, and with our own consent would never forsake our country and the Catholic people who dwell therein, but would rather die there in their presence as a testimony to the faith which we and they held in common. Our country and their salvation were to us infinitely more precious than our own life.

Then, when nothing was to be gained in this way, we asked to be shown at least the letters and orders of the queen by which we are condemned to be banished for life. But nothing was shown; the vessel sailed, and we went to sea after many a farewell and with the pity of our friends.

When we had been two days at sea, and had gone far away from land, the reverend Father Jasper Heywood and others once more pressed the queen's servants with

[1] Stow, p. 700. "The 21st of Jan. [1585], Jesuits, seminarists, and other massing priests, to the number of twenty-one, late prisoners in the Tower of London, Marshalsea, and King's Bench, were shipped at the Tower wharf, to be conveyed towards France, and banished the realm for ever, by virtue of a commission from her majesty, as may more fully appear by the same commission."

great earnestness to allow them to see and read the sentence of our banishment. The men were persuaded, and showed the warrant, in which was read as follows: "The aforesaid persons, by the confession of themselves and others, found guilty of sedition and of plotting against her majesty and the state, all of them either legally convicted of those same offences, or for the like offences kept in prison, though deserving the last penalties of the law, are, under this warrant, ordered by her majesty, who in her goodness wills to deal more gently with them for this once, to be transported beyond the limits of the realm."

When they read this they all cried out in one mournful protestation, that a most false accusation had been brought against them, and that they were most grievously wronged, seeing that not one of them, or of their fellow-Catholics, had ever uttered one word that could be construed into a confession of rebellion or conspiracy against the queen or the country, and that one certainly of those whom they were taking away at the time, had been publicly acquitted, after a trial, of that most false charge. Father Heywood then spoke much to the same purpose, again and again imploring those who were in charge to take them back to England that they might be put on their trial publicly, or at least that they might be put to death for Christ, and in defence of their innocence, rather than be sent to a strange land accused of offences which they had certainly never committed. To this the answer was, that it was not within their power to do that which was asked of them, and that they must obey the orders of the queen.

We went on, consoling one another as well as we could, and rejoicing that we could bear patiently this reproach for the name of Jesus. At last, by the help of God, we landed at Boulogne, and having said farewell to those who brought us thither, we departed for different towns in France, each one according to his means. At last we all came to Rheims,[1] finding our brethren or our superiors in great distress about us in every place to which we came. They had heard the lying stories which the heretics, or those who wished us ill, had spread abroad, namely, that frightened by the dangers that were around us in England, we had of our own accord taken measures to bring about our banishment, that we had abandoned our work, or—and that was still worse—had come to some agreement with the heretics in matters of religion. But they rejoiced in our Lord when they heard the story fully related, and when many of us moreover declared their readiness to return, whenever our superiors bade us, without counting the cost. But our enemies everywhere without any restraint speak of us whom they did not put to death, but banished, as instances and evidences of the queen's kindness.[2] They persist in this, and urge it with so much shamelessness, that they will have it that the more they banish, the more must the great kindness of the queen be re-

[1] The banished priests arrived at Rheims, March 3, 1585, as appears from the following entry in the Douai Diary: "3° Martii venerunt Domini Worthingtonus, Byshop, Colingtonus, Warmingtonus, Barnes Stevenson, Rishton [the writer of this fourth book], qui cum aliis quatuordecim, paulo ante navi, inviti et reluctantes, impositi, exulare jussi sunt."

Rishton, Rerum in Turri gest. Diar., adds this to the account of his own deportation: "Non longe post quinquaginta alii, eodem exilii genere consecuti nos sunt, imposita nobis omnibus expressa capitis pœna, si unquam in patriam reverteremur."

[2] Collier, Eccles. Hist., ii. 591. "And not long after, seventy priests, some of which were condemned, and all of them under prosecution, were set at liberty and banished. Among these the most considerable were Gaspar Heywood, son of the famous epigrammatist, and the first Jesuit who set footing in England; James Bosgrave, another of the same order; John Hart, a very learned divine; and Edward Rishton, who published Sander's History, and made a supplement to it. This last, it must be said, did not make the queen a suitable return for giving him his life." Rishton's sense of the matter seems to have been different from that of Collier. But Camden (p. 412) says that Rishton was impiously ungrateful to the queen who had spared his life.

marked, and the more it must commend itself to foreign nations. The same fraud and cruelty were lately practised upon two-and-twenty prisoners taken out of the jails of York and Hull, and carried over to France; all except one being priests, and even he was a deacon. These, for the most part, were worn out not only by bonds and imprisonment, but by old age. Some of them were sixty, others seventy years old, others were still older, and one of them was eighty years of age.

Some of these, though they were very old men, had spent a great part of their life in prison; and there were those among them who for six-and-twenty years had most patiently and bravely borne all those miseries which the wickedness of so many years, and of such heretics, is wont to inflict upon prisoners.

Soon afterwards, on the 24th of September, thirty priests and two laymen,[1] brought together out of different prisons, were with the same intention driven out of the country. This is the way they think they can obtain a reputation for humanity and mercy. But it is very foolish, and nothing else but the kindness of thieves, who are wont to boast that they have given their lives to those from whom they have not taken it. It is more probable that they act thus for the purpose of burdening the seminaries, which they know to be poor, with the maintenance of so many priests. But

[1] Stow, p. 710. "On the 15th day of September, to the number of thirty-two seminarists, massing priests, and others, late prisoners in the Tower of London, Marshalsea, King's Bench, and other places, were embarked in the 'Mary Martine' of Colchester, on the south side of the Thames, right over against Saint Katherine's, to be transported over into the coasts of Normandy, to be banished this realm for ever, by virtue of a commission from her majesty."

Collegii Anglo-Duaceni Diarium, pp. 12, 13, ad anno 1585. "Hoc anno adierunt ex variis Angliæ carceribus in exilium deportati septuaginta duo sacerdotes; mense quidem Januario ex Turri et aliis carceribus Londinensibus viginti sacerdotes et laicus unus; mense Septembri ex comitatu Eboracensi et Londino alii triginta et duo alii laici."

there is no counsel against God: "The earth is our Lord's and the fulness thereof."[1]

A law too had been made in Parliament,[2] that any Jesuit or seminary priest, any other priest, deacon, or ecclesiastic, ordained by the Pope, or by any authority derived from him, after the suppression of the Catholic religion by Elizabeth, should suffer the punishment due to those convicted of high treason, if he either returned to England from abroad or remained in the country, when forty days had passed since the proclamation of the law. If there be any gentleness or mercy in this law, I know not what there is that deserves to be called wicked, cruel, or barbarous. By the former laws it was strictly enough provided that no priest should discharge any of his priestly duties. He must not say Mass nor hear confessions, nor reconcile any one to the Church, nor in any way persuade any one to accept the faith; but by this new law priests are forbidden not only to do anything against the law of the Protestants or the safety of the state, but even to remain in the kingdom, though they do nothing whatever against the state or the religion established therein.

Under this act it is not only the person who offends that suffers the punishment, and that too the most grievous of all punishments, but men of every rank, who personally commit no offence, are most unjustly condemned as traitors. By this law, and such a law was never heard of before, it is a capital offence for any Englishman to enter the Society of Jesus, or to be brought up in any school or college in any part of the world which shall be under the direction of the Society, unless, on being warned, he returns home forthwith, renounces the Catholic faith in the presence of a false bishop, and promises, having first taken the oath, to

[1] Ps. xxiii. 1.

[2] 27 Eliz. c. 2.

observe all the ecclesiastical laws which the queen has already published, or shall happen to publish in time to come.[1]

Still further, it is enacted that a father, a friend, or a guardian who shall "give or contribute any money or other relief to or for any Jesuit" or seminary priest, shall forfeit all his goods and chattels, and be imprisoned for the rest of his days.[2]

Lastly, by the same statute all the queen's subjects are forbidden to conceal or receive into their houses, or relieve any "Jesuit, seminary priest, or other such priest, either remaining in England or having returned from abroad, under pain of suffering the punishment due to murderers and thieves, which is hanging."[3]

One of the clauses of this statute I should call ridiculous rather than cruel, were it not an evidence of the silly fears of our enemies, and of the utter uneasiness of their consciences; it is to this effect, that no priest, though he renounced the Catholic faith according to the provisions of the law, and openly showed himself a heretic, may "come within ten miles" of the place where the queen shall be.[4]

[1] 27 Eliz. c. 2, s. 5, 7.

[2] Ibid., s. 6. The words of the act are, "the danger and penalty of Præmunire."

[3] Ibid., s. 4. "Shall also for such offence be adjudged a felon, without benefit of clergy, and suffer death, lose and forfeit as in case of one attainted of felony."

[4] Mr. Charles Butler (Hist. Mem., i. 388) makes the following observations upon this statute, which is simply an abuse of power: "It is observable that this act must have been purposely so worded as not to comprehend the old priests, or queen Mary's priests, as they were called, as it extended to those only who had been ordained after the feast of St. John Baptist, in the first year of her majesty's reign, and to those who received or maintained the priests so ordained. This was a part of the policy of the queen and her ministers. To avoid the imputation of an excess of severity, they always alleged that they did not meddle with the ancient Catholic clergy, or those to whom they administered the rights of religion or religious instruction, and that the whole penal code was levelled against the new priests; and this not for their religion, but because their principles—which principles they carefully instilled into all who frequented them—were not only hostile to the Protestant religion, but dangerous to her majesty's person and subversive of her government."

CHAPTER XII.

CECIL'S BOOK—CARDINAL ALLEN—MARTYRS—DUTY AND ZEAL OF THE PRIESTS—FAITHFULNESS OF THE LAITY —CONCLUSION.

NEW laws, and laws such as nobody heard of before, are made every year, and executed with the utmost severity, against Christians, subjects and members of the same state, and at the same time the robe of justice is thrown over such excessive wickedness. There are men who publish books,[1] in which they most impiously set forth and praise the sovereign goodness of the queen; her justice tempered with mercy. That is not all: following in the footsteps of the ancient persecutors of the Church, they most falsely pretend that these laws are necessarily made against and executed upon men not religious and conscientious, but men who are conspirators against the person of the queen. These false pretences have been lately laid bare on our side, by the most clear and convincing proofs in a book written against the trumpeter of this pretended British justice.[2]

The book was written with all possible moderation, and solely in defence of our innocence, nor would it have been written at all but for the provocation of the enemy.

[1] "The Execution of Justice in England, for Maintenance of Publique and Christian Peace against certain Stirrers of Sedition. London, 1583." Commonly believed to be the work of Cecil.

[2] Lord Burghley's book was answered by Dr. William (afterwards Cardinal) Allen in his "Ad Persecutores Anglos pro Catholicis," &c.

Nevertheless, a Catholic priest, Thomas Alfield, who was said to have brought copies of it into England, and a layman, Thomas Webley, by whom it was distributed, were put to death.[1] Their lives were offered them at the place of execution if they would renounce the Pope and agree with the queen. That they refused to do, and therefore clearly died a martyr's death. It is thus that these men answer our books—by hanging us.

One of the chief members of the queen's council saw and read this book as soon as it came forth, and in speaking of it to one of his friends whom he knew to be well disposed towards the Catholic faith, is reported to have said this: "I am astonished at the Papists, even the more prudent among them, why do they so earnestly, openly, and plainly make known, answer and protest against, the doings and the legislation of the queen and her ministers! Let us admit that they convict us of being in the wrong both as to religion and government, they ought to consider that, now we have gone so far, we cannot draw back with safety and honour, and that so powerful a queen cannot give way before any proofs or clamours of these poor men." These were his words.

We know that too well; and our people have not much hope that men whose hearts are hardened by the just judgment of God for their sins so many and so grievous, will ever yield to sound reason before they are

[1] Stow, p. 709. "The 5th of July [1585] Thomas Aufield, a seminary priest, and Thomas Welley, dyer, were arraigned at the sessions hall in the Old Baily, found guilty, condemned, and had judgment as felons to be hanged for publishing of books containing false, seditious, and slanderous matter, to the defamation of our sovereign lady the queen. These were on the next morrow executed at Tyborne accordingly." Thomas Alfield, a native of Gloucestershire, educated at Eton, and was a fellow of King's College, Cambridge. He went to Rheims under the name of Badger, was made priest in 1581, and came on the mission. He went abroad in January 1584, and returned in the summer, bringing with him copies of the Cardinal's book.

broken by the omnipotent arm of the Most High. Nevertheless, even those who are going to ruin must be warned, in order that their ruin may not come of our fault. The good must be encouraged, that they may persevere in the truth and in their innocence; and the rest must be strengthened, that they may not fall away under the trials of this most grievous persecution; and lastly, they must regard the public profession of Catholic truth as something not to be abandoned at the bidding of any law or through fear of any man.

We are indeed not ignorant that they who "hate Sion"[1] are not only not made better, but oftentimes made more wicked, when brought face to face with the truth. Still, not even on this account may we abandon our work, lest, having regard to temporal dangers only, we should thereby betray the souls of our brethren. These men will have no power to touch us beyond that which God shall give them for a time, for our own trial and the salvation of others. Since these holy efforts of the priests, and since the beginning of the persecution in England, we have very often seen God our most merciful Lord deliver, by strange and marvellous means, those Catholics whose lives were sought not only in England, but also abroad in their banishment. We have also seen Him preserve the seminaries of our people beyond the seas, which were assailed by cunning, violence, and fraud. Even more than this, He has by the might of His right hand saved us from the promiscuous and public massacre of all the faithful, which was the aim of the cruel words and threatenings of that fierce Aman[2] of the English, more cruel than the bear robbed of its whelps, and of his Puritanical preachers.

On the other hand, those Catholics of all ranks, whom God, in the course of His providence, to the praise of

[1] Ps. cxxviii. 5.

[2] The earl of Leicester.

His name, and for a testimony unto the truth, suffered the enemy to take, to harass, to spoil, to imprison, to fetter, to torture, and at last to slay, have, as we know, been made glad with the unutterable consolations of God, according to the greatness of their pains, wherein they rejoicing, not only bear every temporal calamity, but also stand forth as examples to their fellow-Catholics, especially to the priests, of perseverance, patience, and contempt of the world.

Hence it is that not even now, after so many murderous laws and executions, the priests nowhere abstain from the discharge of their functions; for they have learned to obey God rather than men, and to fear not those who kill the body and who cannot kill the soul, but rather Him who can destroy both body and soul into hell.[1] Him they have learned to fear, and therefore they are sent, come in, and lead apostolic and peaceable lives. They do not come to kill the queen, or to destroy the state, but to bring to both life and salvation and the peace of the Church, trusting that they shall always find an Abdias,[2] a widow of Sarephta,[3] an Onesiphorus,[4] an Alban,[5] who in spite of human laws and the wicked commandments of kings who must die, will faithfully entertain the servants of the everlasting God, and the shepherds of their souls, that by them they may be received into the everlasting tabernacles,[6] which the princes of this world can neither give nor take away.

Hitherto, God be praised, they have never failed, and,

[1] St. Matt. x. 28.

[2] Abdias, the steward of Achab, who saved the prophets from the fury of Jezabel. 3 Kings xviii. 13.

[3] The widow of Sarephta to whom the prophet Elias was sent for shelter. 3 Kings xvii. 9.

[4] Onesiphorus. 2 Tim. i. 16: "Our Lord give mercy to the house of Onesiphorus, because he hath often refreshed me, and hath not been ashamed of my chain."

[5] Alban, the protomartyr of England, who hid Amphibalus, his confessor, when the persecutors were in search of him.

[6] St. Luke x. 9.

we believe, never will, "until iniquity pass,"[1] and until all princes who say, "Let us possess the sanctuary of God for an inheritance," be as Oreb and Zeb, and Zebee and Salmana.[2]

For the present, let this suffice to show the nature of the lay supremacy, and that the supremacy of a woman, and the troubles it has brought forth; our intention was to be brief. If, however, that supremacy shall again bring forth evil upon the world, we shall not keep silence.

[1] Ps. lvi. 2.

[2] Ps. lxxxii. 12, 13.

ANNALS OF THE SCHISM.

1471. Thomas Wolsey born at Ipswich.
1477. Sir Thomas Boleyn born.
1486. Sept. 20. Arthur prince of Wales born.
1491. June 28. Henry, afterwards Henry VIII., born.
1492. Aug. 11. Alexander VI. elected Pope.
1500. Feb. 25. Charles V. born at Ghent.
1501. Oct. 8. The princess Catherine of Spain lands at Plymouth.
— Nov. 12. The princess enters London in state.
— Nov. 14. Marriage of Arthur prince of Wales with princess Catherine.
1502. April 2. Prince Arthur dies in Ludlow Castle.
— John Fisher elected lady Margaret professor of theology, Cambridge.
1503. March 10. Ferdinand I. born.
— Aug. 18. Death of Alexander VI.
— Sept. 22. Pius III. elected.
— Oct. 18. Death of Pius III.
— Nov. 1. Julius II. elected.
— Dec. 29. William Warham, bishop of London, translated to Canterbury.
1504. Nov. 26. Death of Isabella the Catholic, mother of queen Catherine.
— Nov. 24. John Fisher consecrated bishop of Rochester.
— John Fisher elected chancellor of Cambridge.
1505. John Fisher elected president of Queen's College, Cambridge.

1505. Lady Margaret, countess of Richmond and Derby, founds Christ's College, Cambridge.

1506. May 28. William Warham, archbishop of Canterbury, elected chancellor of Oxford.

1509. April 21. Death of Henry VII.

— April 22. Accession of Henry VIII.

— June 3. Henry VIII. and Catherine, his brother's widow, married by dispensation of Julius II.

— June 24. Coronation of Henry and Catherine, king and queen of England.

— Feb. 8. Thomas Wolsey made prebendary of Lincoln.

— Aug. 7. The lady Margaret, countess of Richmond and Derby, licensed by her grandson Henry VIII. to found St. John's College, Cambridge.

— Oct. 31. Nicholas West made dean of Windsor.

1511. Erasmus, professor of theology in Cambridge.

— Nov. 1. Four cardinals, with certain French bishops and abbots, meet in a schismatical council at Pisa.

1512. Jan. 16. Thomas Wolsey, prebendary of York.

— Jan. 25. Date of the charter of the foundation of Brasenose College, Oxford.

— March 3. Opening of the general council of the Lateran.

1513. May 15. Charles Brandon created viscount Lisle.

— Oct. 3. Edward Lee made prebendary of Lincoln.

— Feb. 19. Thomas Wolsey elected dean of York.

— Feb. 21. Death of Julius II.

— March 11. Election of Leo X.

— Sept. 24. Henry VIII. enters Tournai.

1514. Feb. 1. Charles Brandon, viscount Lisle, created duke of Suffolk.

— April 15. Cuthbert Tunstall succeeded Thomas Wolsey as prebendary of Lincoln.

— March 26. Consecration of Thomas Wolsey as bishop of Lincoln, at Lambeth.

— Thomas Wolsey, bishop of Lincoln, elected chancellor of Cambridge; on his refusing to accept the office, the bishop of Rochester, Dr. Fisher, who had been chancellor for the last ten years, was elected chancellor for life.

1514. Sept. 7. Thomas Wolsey created cardinal.
— Sept. 15. Cardinal Wolsey translated to the archbishopric of York.
— Oct. 10. Marriage at Abbeville of Louis XII., king of France, and the princess Mary, sister of Henry VIII.
1515. Jan. 1. Death of king Louis XII. and accession of Francis I.
— March 31. Mary, queen-dowager of France, marries Charles Brandon, duke of Suffolk.
— Sept. 28. John Voysey made dean of Windsor.
— Oct. 7. Nicholas West, bishop of Ely, consecrated at Lambeth.
— Dec. 22. William Warham, archbishop of Canterbury, resigns the great seal.
— Dec. 24. Cardinal Wolsey takes the oath of his office as chancellor of England.
1516. William Knight made prebendary of Lincoln.
— Jan. 23. Ferdinand, queen Catherine's father, dies.
— Feb. 18. The princess, afterwards the queen Mary, born at Greenwich.
1517. Feb. 3. Richard Sampson made archdeacon of Cornwall.
— March 5. Licence granted to Richard Fox, bishop of Winchester, for the foundation of Corpus Christi College, Oxford.
— March 16. Last session of the Lateran council under Leo X.
— John Longland was dean of Salisbury this year.
— Nov. 8. Death of Cardinal Ximenes.
— Dec. 15. William Knight made prebendary of St. Paul's.
1518. July 29. Cardinal Campeggio, legate of the Pope, makes his public entry into London.
— July 11. Henry Standish, friar Minor, bishop of St. Asaph, consecrated at Otford.
1519. Jan. 12. Death of Maximilian.
— April 11. John Longland made canon of Windsor.
— April 23. Richard Sampson prebendary of York.
— June 28. Charles V. elected emperor at Frankfort.
— July 18. The Cardinal of York receives the see of Bath and Wells.

1519. Aug. 31. John Voysey made bishop of Exeter by the Pope.
— Oct. 22. John Clerk made archdeacon of Colchester.
— Nov. 9. John Clerk made dean of Windsor.
— Edward Stafford, duke of Buckingham, founds the college of St. Mary Magdalene, Cambridge, called first Buckingham College.
1520. May 25. The emperor Charles V. comes to England.
— June 16. Condemnation of the heresies of Luther by Leo X.
— Oct. 23. Charles V. crowned at Aix-la-Chapelle.
— William Knight this year was made prebendary of Bangor.
1521. May 5. John Longland, bishop of Lincoln, consecrated at Lambeth.
— Oct. 11. The title of "Defender of the Faith" granted by Leo X. to Henry VIII.
— Dec. 1. Pope Leo X. died.
1522. Cardinal Wolsey seeks the Papacy, and Adrian VI. is elected, January 2.
— Jan. 17. John Stokesley made archdeacon of Dorset.
— Oct. 19. Cuthbert Tunstall, bishop of London, consecrated at Lambeth.
— Nov. 11. William Knight installed archdeacon of Chester.
1523. April 15. Parliament met at the Blackfriars, in which sir Thomas More was elected speaker of the commons.
— April 30. Cardinal Wolsey obtains the revenues of the see of Durham.
— Sept. 14. Death of Adrian VI.
— Sept. 17. William Knight made archdeacon of Huntingdon.
— Nov. 14. Richard Sampson installed dean of Windsor by proxy.
— Nov. 19. Election of Clement VII.
— Nov. 19. Edward Lee made archdeacon of Colchester.
— Dec. 6. John Clerk, bishop of Bath and Wells, consecrated in Rome.

1524\. July 29. Lorenzo Pucci, the Cardinal *Sanctorum Quatuor Coronatorum*, translated from Albano to Palestrina.

— Dec. 2. Cardinal Campeggio obtains the bishopric of Salisbury.

— May 10. Cardinal Wolsey obtains letters-patent to found his college in Oxford.

1525\. Feb. 25. Francis I. taken prisoner at the battle of Pavia.

— March 24. Thomas Winter made archdeacon of Richmond, York.

— June 18. Sir Thomas Boleyn created viscount Rochford.

— June 18. Henry Fitzroy, son of Henry VIII. and Elizabeth Blount, created earl of Nottingham, duke of Richmond and Somerset.

— June 18. Henry Courtenay made marquis of Exeter.

— Oct. 18. Edward Powell (martyr) made prebendary of Lincoln.

— Stephen Gardiner elected master of Trinity Hall, Cambridge.

— Thomas Cranmer, this year archdeacon of Taunton.

1526\. March 26. Thomas Winter made dean of Wells.

— Nov. 26. Dr. William Bennet made a prebendary of St. Paul's.

1527\. April 7. Rowland Lee made prebendary of Lichfield.

— April 22. Reginald Pole, prebendary of York.

— Nicolas Sander born at Charlwood Place, Surrey.

— May 6. The duke of Bourbon killed before the walls of Rome.

— Pope Clement made prisoner by the Imperialists, who enter Rome and sack it.

— May 17. Cardinal Wolsey as legate, with the archbishop of Canterbury and Stephen Gardiner, holds a court in his house at Westminster, and proceeds *ex officio* against the king for having married his brother's wife.

— May 21. Don Philip II., king of England, born.

— July 3. The Cardinal of York sets out on his embassy to France.

— Aug. 12. Reginald Pole elected dean of Exeter.

1527. Sept. Dr. William Knight sent to the Pope to obtain the divorce.

— Nov. 8. Edward Fox made prebendary of York.

— Dec. 9. The Pope escapes out of the hands of the Imperialists, and reaches Orvieto the next morning.

1528. Feb. Edward Fox, the king's chaplain, and Dr. Stephen Gardiner, secretary of the Cardinal of York, sent to Orvieto, where they arrive March 20, Friday, at night.

— April 1. Cranmer leaves Orvieto with despatches for England.

— April 1. Edward Fox elected provost of King's College, Cambridge.

— April 13. The commission of the legates settled.

— May 2. Edward Fox lands in England bringing with him the commission of the legates.

— May 3. Edward Fox at Greenwich gives, at the king's request, to Anne Boleyn an account of his doings at Orvieto.

— June 8. The commission of the legates to try the question of the divorce signed.

— Sept. 8. Rowland Lee installed archdeacon of Cornwall.

— Oct. 7. Cardinal Campeggio arrives in London.

— Oct. 22. The king receives the legate in state.

— Oct. 27. The two Cardinals make a ceremonious visit to the queen.

— Nov. 7. The queen declares upon oath before witnesses that her first marriage was never perfected.

— Nov. 8. Henry declares in the presence of peers and commons assembled at Bridewell that he was pursuing the divorce solely for the relief of his conscience.

1529. Jan. 11. Richard Sampson, archdeacon of Suffolk.

— Feb. The king and the Cardinal of York, having heard of the illness of the Pope, intrigue for the election of Wolsey.

— Feb. 4. Edward Lee made chancellor of Salisbury.

— March 1. Stephen Gardiner made archdeacon of Norfolk on the resignation of Thomas Winter.

1529. May 20. Issue of the king's writ to allow the Cardinals to exercise their jurisdiction.

— May 28. The Cardinals sit in the monastery of the Blackfriars.

— May 31. The commission of the legates read in open court, and the judges direct the king and the queen to be summoned to appear before them on the 18th day of June.

— June 18. The king and the queen appear in court; the queen declines the jurisdiction of the court, and appeals in due form of law to the Pope.

— June 22. Gardiner and Sir Francis Bryan arrive in London from Italy.

— June 29. The bishop of Rochester defends the queen before the legates.

— July 28. Dr. Stephen Gardiner entered on his duties as secretary of state.

— July 30. The dukes of Norfolk and Suffolk present themselves in the legatine court and press the judges to give sentence. Cardinal Campeggio adjourns till October.

— Sept. 6. The legates informed that the Pope had called the cause up to Rome in consequence of the queen's appeal.

— Oct. 5. Cardinal Campeggio takes his departure from London, and has his baggage searched at Dover by orders of the king.

— Oct. 17. Cardinal Wolsey forced to resign the great seal.

— Oct. 25. Cardinal Wolsey formally admits that he had incurred the penalties decreed in the statutes of provisors and præmunire.

— Oct. 25. Sir Thomas More made chancellor of England: the first layman who ever held the great seal.

— Nov. 1. Thomas Cromwell abandons the Cardinal of York, and rides from Esher to the court, having said to Cavendish, "I will either make or mar."

— Dec. 7. Dr. William Knight, secretary of state, made

archdeacon of Richmond, on the resignation of Thomas Winter.

1529. Dec. 8. Sir Thomas Boleyn, viscount Rochford, made earl of Wiltshire in England, and earl of Ormond.

1530. Feb. 4. Custody of the temporalities of Durham given to Cuthbert Tunstall, bishop of London.

— Feb. 21. Tunstall translated to Durham.

— Feb. 22. Clement VII. gives the iron crown to Charles V., as king of Lombardy.

— Feb. 24. The birthday of the emperor, the Pope crowns him with the golden crown of the empire.

— Feb. 30. Edward Lee, prebendary of York.

— In the beginning of Lent Cardinal Wolsey goes to the Carthusians at Richmond.

— March 25. Cuthbert Tunstall translated from London to Durham.

— April 3. In Passion week the Cardinal quits Richmond on his way to the North.

— April 10. The Cardinal is in the abbey of Peterborough.

— April 17, Easter day. The Cardinal sang high mass in the abbey.

— July 30. Letter of peers and commons to the Pope, p. 84.

— Sept. 12. Proclamation against obtaining bulls and briefs from the Pope.

— Sept. The Cardinal arrives at Cawood Castle about Michaelmas, and makes preparations for his installation in York Minster on the 7th day of November.

— Nov. 4. The earl of Northumberland, by the king's orders, arrests the Cardinal; and

— Nov. 6. Sunday, removes him from Cawood.

— Nov. 8. The Cardinal is delivered into the custody of earl of Shrewsbury at Sheffield Park.

— Nov. 22. Sir William Kingston arrived at Sheffield Park with a guard of twenty-four men to take charge of the Cardinal.

— Nov. 24. The prisoner, though very ill, sets out with his

gaoler to Hardwick Hall, belonging to the earl of Shrewsbury, and

1530. Nov. 25. Nottingham is reached by night-time.

— Nov. 26. Saturday at night the Cardinal is lodged in the abbey of Leicester, being very ill.

— Nov. 27. John Stokesley, bishop of London, consecrated.

— Nov. 29. At eight o'clock in the morning, the Cardinal, having confessed to his chaplain, and being anointed by the abbot, departed this life.

— Dec. 20. William Bennet collated to the archdeaconry of Dorset, vacated by John Stokesley, made bishop of London.

1531. Jan. 5. Clement VII. warns Henry VIII. not to marry Anne Boleyn.

— Jan. 5. Ferdinand, brother of the emperor, elected king of the Romans at Cologne, and

— Jan. 11. Crowned at Aix-la-Chapelle.

— March 22. The clergy of the province of Canterbury in their convocation acknowledge the king to be the supreme head on earth of the Anglican Church.

— March 31. Stephen Gardiner installed archdeacon of Leicester.

— April 11. David Pole, prebendary of Lichfield.

— May 4. The clergy of the province of York accept the supremacy of the king.

— Sept. 14. Death of Lorenzo Pucci, Cardinal *Sanctorum Quatuor Coronatorum*, and bishop of Palestrina.

— Oct. 30. Edward Lee made archbishop of York.

— Dec. 3. Stephen Gardiner, bishop of Winchester, consecrated.

— Dec. 10. Edward Lee, archbishop of York, consecrated.

— Dec. 27. Edward Fox installed archdeacon of Leicester on the promotion of Gardiner to the see of Winchester.

1532. March 31, Easter day. Friar Peto preached before the king at Greenwich. (See p. 112, note 5.)

— May 13. The king demands the great seal from Sir Thomas More, because he would not write in favour of the divorce.

1532. May 16. Sir Thomas More resigned the great seal.

— Aug. 23. Death of William Warham, archbishop of Canterbury.

— Sept. 1. Anne Boleyn created marchioness of Pembroke at Windsor.

— Oct. 11. The king crossed the Channel, having Anne Boleyn with him.

— Oct. 21. Meeting of the English and French kings near Calais.

— Nov. 14. The king marries Anne Boleyn secretly, queen Catherine being alive, and no sentence of divorce pronounced.

1533. Thomas Cromwell made secretary of state.

— Feb. 4. Parliament held, in which a law was made (24 Henry VIII. c. 12) that no appeals shall be made to the Pope, and that the sentence of convocation shall be "taken for a final decree" in all ecclesiastical causes in which the king and the royal family are concerned.

— March 30. Thomas Cranmer, archbishop of Canterbury, consecrated in St. Stephen's, Westminster.

— The royal assent given to the statute forbidding appeals to the Pope (24 Henry VIII. c. 12).

— April 12. Easter Eve. Anne Boleyn proclaimed queen at Greenwich.

— April 28. Death of Nicolas West, bishop of Ely, and one of the queen's advocates.

— May 23. Cranmer, at Dunstable, pronounces a sentence of divorce in favour of Henry.

— May 28. Cranmer declares the king's marriage with Anne Boleyn lawful.

— June 1. Anne Boleyn crowned at Westminster.

— June 26. Death of Mary, sister of Henry VIII., and duchess of Suffolk.

— June 29. Henry VIII. appeals to a general council from the Pope.

— July 5. Proclamation warning people not to question the lawfulness of the marriage of Henry and Anne Boleyn, nor to call Catherine queen, under pain of incurring the penalties decreed in the statutes of provisors and præmunire.

1533. Aug. 18. Henry VIII. instructs Edmund Bonner to intimate to the Pope that he, the king, had appealed from his sentence.

— Sept. 7. Elizabeth born at Greenwich.

— Oct. 11. Clement VII. lands at Marseilles.

— Nov. 8. Edmund Bonner, at Marseilles, appears before the Pope and delivers the king's appeal to a general council.

— Nov. 22. The Pope takes his departure from Marseilles.

— Nov. 25. Edward Fox made archdeacon of Dorset on the death of William Bennet.

— Dec. 10. The Pope enters Rome.

1534. Jan. 15. Parliament assembles, and enacts (25 Henry VIII. c. 19) that no canons shall be made without the king's consent; that appeals may be carried from the ecclesiastical courts to the court of chancery, and that none shall be made to the Pope.

— By the act 25 Henry VIII. c. 20, Parliament orders bishops to be made and consecrated without the leave of the Pope, and suppresses the payment of first-fruits to the sovereign Pontiff.

— By the act 25 Henry VIII. c. 21, it is ordered that the archbishops and the king shall grant the dispensations hitherto obtained from Rome.

— March 21–26. Parliament deprives the bishop of Salisbury, Cardinal Campeggio, and Jerome de Ghinucci, bishop of Worcester.

— March 23. Definitive sentence of the Pope in the cause of the divorce, and in favour of the marriage of Henry and Catherine.

— April 13. The bishop of Rochester and Sir Thomas More refused to swear that Anne Boleyn was the lawful wife of Henry VIII.

— April 19. Rowland Lee, who married the king to Anne Boleyn, consecrated bishop of Lichfield without bulls.

— April 20. Execution of Elizabeth Barton, the nun of Kent, of Edward Bocking and John Dering, Richard

Risby, Richard Masters, Hugh Rich, and Henry Gold.

1534. April 26. The bishop of Rochester sent to the Tower.

— May 2. The university of Cambridge resolves that the Pope has no more jurisdiction in England than any other foreign bishop.

— May 5. The convocation of York assembled under Edward Lee, and determined that the Pope has no more power in England than any other foreign bishop.

— May 12. Peter Vannes made archdeacon of Worcester.

— June 1. The archbishop of York certifies to the king the decision of the convocation of York.

— June 7. Declaration of the university of Oxford that the Pope has no more jurisdiction in England than any other foreign bishop.

— June 9. Proclamation by the king of the formal denial of the authority of the Pope by the bishops and clergy. The king orders the name of the Pope to be erased out of all "books in the churches."

— Aug. 11. The Friars Observant ordered out of their monasteries.

— Sept. 26. Death of Clement VII.

— Oct. 8. Thomas Cromwell made master of the rolls.

— Oct. 13. Election of Paul III.

— Dec. 19. The convocation of the province of Canterbury prayed the king to decree a translation of the sacred writings into the vulgar tongue, and declared that the Pope has no greater authority in England than any other foreign bishop according to the Scriptures.

1535. Jan. 2. The see of Rochester said by Parliament to have been vacant.

— Feb. 3. Parliament held, in which the ecclesiastical supremacy given by convocation to Henry VIII. is annexed to the crown, and the first-fruits and the first year's revenue of all benefices from bishoprics downward granted to the king to support his dignity of supreme head (26 Henry VIII. c. 1 and 3).

By c. 13 of the same year it is made high treason to say that the king is a "heretic, schismatic, infidel, or usurper."

1535. Feb. 21. Owen Oglethorpe elected president of Magdalen College, Oxford.

— Feb. 22. Peter Vannes made prebendáry of York.

— March. The dissolution of the smaller monasteries ordered in Parliament.

— In April Cranmer warns the bishop of Winchester that he is about to make a visitation of the province, and Gardiner resists because the visitation was an infringement of the royal supremacy.

— April 11. Nicholas Shaxton, chaplain of Anne Boleyn, consecrated, without bulls, bishop of Salisbury.

— April 29. The three Carthusian priors of London, Beauvale, and Axholme tried in Westminster Hall, and condemned to death, for not acknowledging the supremacy of the king.

— May 4. Martyrdom of the three Carthusian priors, of Richard Reynolds, Brigittine, of the monastery of Sion, and John Haile, vicar of Isleworth; all executed at Tyburn for refusing to accept the royal supremacy.

— May 21. Paul III. creates John Fisher, bishop of Rochester, a Cardinal.

— June 11. Three Carthusian monks, Humfrey Middlemore, William Exmew, and Sebastian Newdigate, tried and found guilty of treason, because they denied the royal supremacy.

— June 17. Trial and condemnation of the Cardinal bishop of Rochester. He was arraigned as John Fisher, clerk, not as bishop.

— June 18. Martyrdom at Tyburn of the three Carthusian monks, tried June 11.

— June 22. The Cardinal bishop of Rochester beheaded on Tower Hill.

— July 1. Trial and condemnation of Sir Thomas More.

— July 6. Sir Thomas More beheaded on Tower Hill.

— Aug. 30. Sentence of Paul III. against Henry VIII.

1535. Sept. 26. Edward Fox, Hugh Latimer, and John Hilsey consecrated bishops of Hereford, Worcester, and Rochester respectively, at Winchester by Cranmer, Gardiner, and Nicholas Shaxton.

— Oct. Visitation of the religious houses.

— Oct. 9. Edmund Bonner collated to the archdeaconry of Leicester, vacated by Edward Fox, bishop of Hereford.

— Thomas Cromwell made vicar-general of the king.

1536. Jan. 6. Queen Catherine dies at Kimbolton.

— All the bishops ordered by the king to deliver up their bulls immediately after the feast of the Purification.

— Jan. 29. Miscarriage of Anne Boleyn.

— Feb. 4. The great monasteries begin to resign themselves into the hands of the king.

— April 2. David Pole made archdeacon of Salop.

— April 30. Mark Smeaton taken to prison.

— May 1. Tournament at Greenwich. The king resolves to punish Anne Boleyn.

— May 2. Anne Boleyn committed to the Tower.

— May 12. Mark Smeaton pleads guilty; Henry Norris, William Brereton, and Francis Weston found guilty; lord Wiltshire, the father of Anne Boleyn, being one of the judges.

— May 15. Anne Boleyn and her brother, Lord Rochford, tried and found guilty.

— May 17. Execution of Lord Rochford, Norris, Brereton, Weston, and Smeaton.

— May 19. Execution of Anne Boleyn.

— May 19. Cranmer issues a dispensation to enable the king to marry Jane Seymour.

— May 20. The king marries Jane Seymour.

— June 5. Edward Seymour created viscount Beauchamp of Hache.

— June 11. Richard Sampson, dean of the chapel royal, consecrated without bulls as bishop of Chichester.

— June 16. The chief seat in the convocation of Canterbury claimed by Cromwell, as the vicar-general of the king, and granted to him.

1536. June 28. The convocation of Canterbury approved of the sentence of Cranmer against the validity of the marriage of Henry and Anne Boleyn.

— July 2. Thomas Cromwell made keeper of the privy seal, resigned by Sir Thomas Boleyn.

— July 12. Henry VIII. suspends all preachers throughout the realm; allows, however, the bishops to preach, and to have sermons preached in their presence.

— July 20. Cromwell and the convocation of Canterbury approve a pamphlet by Edward Fox, bishop of Hereford, in which Fox maintained that the king ought not to attend a general council summoned by the Pope.

— July 20. The convocation declared that the Pope could not summon a council without the express consent of princes.

— July 24. Richard Sampson, bishop of Chichester, elected dean of St. Paul's.

— Aug. 11. Order of the king to omit the observance of the holy days he had abrogated.

— Oct. Insurrection in Lincolnshire.

— Oct. 7. The Duke of Suffolk sent to subdue the insurgents.

— Oct. 7. Insurrection of the northern counties. The Pilgrimage of Grace.

— Nov. 19. The king sends his letters to the bishops, directing them how to instruct the people.

— Dec. 9. The pardon of the insurgents granted by the king under the great seal.

— Dec. 22. Reginald Pole created cardinal.

1537. Feb. Another insurrection in the north.

— May 11. John Rochester and James Walver, Carthusians, hung for not accepting the royal supremacy.

— June. Execution of the chief northern insurgents.

— In this month nine Carthusian monks were starved to death in Newgate.

1537 Oct. 10 or 12. Birth of Edward VI.

— Oct. 24. Death of the queen, Jane Seymour.

— Oct. 18. Edward Seymour, viscount Beauchamp of Hache, created earl of Hertford.

— Thomas Cromwell this year was made dean of Wells.

1538. April 24. Henry VIII. cites St. Thomas of Canterbury to hear his sentence.

— May 8. Death of Edward Fox, bishop of Hereford.

— May 22. Father Forest, confessor of Queen Catherine, burnt alive for refusing to acknowledge the king's jurisdiction in the church.

— June 5. George Day, afterwards bishop of Chichester, elected provost of King's College, Cambridge.

— June 11. Henry decrees that St. Thomas was a traitor, and orders his shrine to be destroyed, and its treasures to be taken to the exchequer.

— July 27. Thomas Cort, Franciscan, died of starvation; he denied the royal supremacy.

— Aug. 11. Destruction and plunder of the shrine of St. Thomas at Canterbury.

— Aug. 19. The bones of the martyred archbishop taken out and burnt.

— Sept. The sacred images burnt by order of Cromwell.

— Nov. 22. Lambert, a Zwinglian, condemned to death by the king as supreme head of the Church; burnt in Smithfield.

— Nov. 22. Death of Sir Thomas Boleyn, earl of Wiltshire.

— Dec. Attainder of Thomas Goldwell.

— Dec. 14. Order under the privy seal to destroy the shrine of St. Richard at Chichester.

1539. The act of the six articles passed.

— Jan. 9. Henry, brother of Cardinal Pole, beheaded.

— Feb. 3. Peter Vannes made dean of Salisbury.

— March 9. John Russell created baron Russell of Cheneys.

— April 17. Thomas Cromwell created earl of Essex.

— July. Latimer and Shaxton, through fear of the act of the six articles, give up their sees of Worcester and Salisbury.

1539. July 8. The vicar of Wandsworth and others put to death for not accepting the king's supremacy.

— July 12. The act of the six articles takes effect.

— Nov. 12. The commission authorising Bonner to execute his ecclesiastical functions issued.

— Nov. 14. The abbots of Glastonbury and Reading hanged for not accepting the royal supremacy.

— Dec. 1. The abbot of Colchester hanged for the same cause.

— Dec. 27. Anne of Cleves lands in England.

1540. Jan. 6. Henry marries Anne of Cleves.

— April 4. Edmund Bonner, bishop of London, and Nicholas Heath, bishop of Rochester, consecrated.

— May. Richard Sampson sent to the Tower for succouring those who were in prison for denying the king's supremacy. See pp. 145, 146.

— July 9. The king divorces Anne of Cleves with the consent of the bishops.

— July 9. Cromwell attainted on the charge of heresy and treason.

— July 28. Execution of Cromwell.

— July 30. Thomas Abel, Richard Fetherston, Edward Powell, priests, put to death for denying the royal supremacy, and three other priests, as heretics, namely, Robert Barnes, Thomas Gerard, and William Jerome.

— Aug. 4. Laurence Cook, prior of Doncaster, with five others, hanged and quartered for denial of the king's supremacy. See p. 151.

— Aug. 8. Catherine Howard is declared queen.

— Oct. 5. Henry Cole, prebendary of St. Paul's.

— Oct. 10. Owen Oglethorpe made canon of Windsor.

— This year Nicolas Ridley elected master of Pembroke College, Cambridge.

— Dec. 17. William Boston, hitherto abbot of Westminster, becomes dean of Westminster.

— Dec. 19. Thomas Thirlby consecrated bishop of Westminster.

1541. Jan. 3. Died, supposed to have been poisoned, John Clerk, bishop of Bath and Wells.

1541. May 28. Margaret, countess of Salisbury, mother of Cardinal Pole, beheaded; neither arraigned nor tried.

— May 29. William Knight consecrated bishop of Bath and Wells without bulls.

— July 1. Sir David Genson, Knight of St. John, put to death for denying the king's supremacy.

— Oct. 4. Order of the king directed to the bishops for destroying all the shrines in every cathedral church.

— Oct. 23. Consecration of John Chamber, bishop of Peterborough.

— Nov. 2. Cranmer reveals to the king the evil deeds of Catherine Howard.

— Dec. 1. Thomas Culpepper and Francis Derham, accomplices of Catherine Howard, pleaded guilty.

— Dec. 10. Thomas Culpepper beheaded and Francis Derham quartered at Tyburn.

1542. Feb. 12. Catherine Howard and the vicountess Rochford put to death.

— June 3. Richard Cox made prebendary of Lincoln.

— Oct. 4. Henry Cole elected warden of New College, Oxford.

— Dec. 13. Accession of Mary queen of Scots, being eight days old.

1543. Jan. 8. David Poole made archdeacon of Derby.

— Jan. 29. Death of Rowland Lee, bishop of Lichfield.

— Feb. 9. The king grants leave to all his subjects "to eat all manner of white meats" in Lent.

— March 14. Richard Sampson translated by the king from Chichester to Lichfield and Coventry.

— May 6. George Day consecrated without bulls bishop of Chichester.

— July 12. Catherine Parr, widow of lord Latimer, declared queen; the marriage being celebrated by the bishop of Winchester, Stephen Gardiner, licensed by Cranmer.

1544. Jan. 8. Richard Cox made dean of Osney, afterwards known as Christ Church, Oxford.

— March 7. John Larke, rector of Chelsea, Jermyn Gardiner, John Ireland, formerly chaplain of Sir Thomas

More, with four others, put to death for denying the supremacy of the king.

1544. March 22. The temporalities of the see of Worcester granted to Nicholas Heath, translated by the king from Rochester.

— May 16. Debasing of the coin.

— June 11. The king orders the litanies to be sung in English in the processions.

1545. Jan. 29. John Poynet, prebendary of Canterbury.

— Feb. 1. David Bethune, Cardinal-archbishop of St. Andrew's, made Legate *à latere* in Scotland.

— May 3. Anthony Kitchin consecrated, without bulls, bishop of Llandaff.

— Aug. 24. Charles Brandon, duke of Suffolk, died.

— Nov. 4. Richard Cox, hitherto dean of Osney, becomes dean of Christ Church.

— Nov. 24. Parliament assembles and gives to the king all the colleges, hospitals, and chantries that were left standing.

— Dec. 13. First session of the general Council of Trent.

1546. King Henry VIII. founds Trinity College, Cambridge.

— May 29. The Cardinal legate of Scotland murdered.

— July. Nicholas Shaxton condemned to be burned for heresy.

— July 9. Shaxton recants, and

— July 13. Is pardoned by the king: before the end of the month he preaches at the burning of Anne Askew in Smithfield.

— Aug. 6. Nicholas Sander admitted scholar of New College, Oxford.

1547. Jan. 19. The earl of Surrey beheaded in the Tower.

— Jan. 28. Death of Henry VIII.

— Jan. 31. Edward VI. proclaimed king.

— Feb. 2. Solemn obsequies of Henry VIII., begun with the vespers of the dead, and continued for twelve days.

— Feb. 14. The body of the king was carried with great pomp from the chapel to Windsor, and was placed on the night between the 14th and 15th of July in the chapel (then desecrated) of the ruined monastery of Sion, where the dog licked up the corrupted blood that flowed out of the coffin, which had burst. See p. 113, note.

1547. Feb. 15. Edward Seymour, earl of Hertford, protector, made duke of Somerset.

— Feb. 16. Thomas Seymour, younger brother of the duke of Somerset, made baron Seymour of Sudley.

— Feb. 17. Lord Seymour made admiral of England, and his elder brother, the protector, made earl marshal.

— Feb. 20. Coronation of Edward VI., Shrove Sunday.

— March 31. Francis I. dies, and is succeeded by Henry II., his son.

— May 7. Death of John Longland, bishop of Lincoln.

— July. The Anglican Homilies published.

— Sept. 23. Nicholas Ridley consecrated bishop of Rochester.

— Sept. 25. Stephen Gardiner, bishop of Winchester, sent to the Fleet prison.

— Sept. 29. Death of William Knight, bishop of Bath and Wells.

— Dec. 20. Peter Martyr, invited by the duke of Somerset and Cranmer, arrives in England, bringing with him another apostate, Bernardino Ochino.

— Dec. Parliament orders communion to be given under both kinds.

1548. Jan. 7. The bishop of Winchester released from prison.

— Jan. 27. Cranmer sends to the bishops the order of the king's council for the suppression of the candles on Candlemas Day, the ashes on Ash-Wednesday, and the palms on Palm-Sunday.

— Feb. 21. Order of the council for the destruction of the images.

— Feb. 24. The order sent by Cranmer to the bishops.

— April 23. Richard Cox made canon of Windsor.

— May 9. Bernardino Ochino made canon of Canterbury.

— May 15. The emperor publishes the *Interim*.

— June 30. The bishop of Winchester committed to the Tower.

1548. Nov. 4. Parliament meets and sanctions the book of common prayer, suppressing the missal, breviary, and other sacred books.

1549. Jan. 19. Thomas Seymour, lord Sudley, committed to the Tower.

— March 7. The book of common prayer printed.

— March 20. Thomas Seymour beheaded.

— April 25. Martin Bucer arrives at Lambeth Palace.

— May 28. The disputation at Oxford begun in which Peter Martyr defended his heresies.

— June 9. Whitsunday, the book of common prayer is used instead of the missal and breviary.

— July 7. Gilbert Bourn installed archdeacon of Bedford.

— Sept. 26. Martin Bucer and Paul Fagius obtain each an annuity of £100.

— The people rise in arms throughout the country, resenting the new religion.

— Oct. 1. Edmund Bonner deprived of his bishopric and put in prison.

— Oct. 14. The duke of Somerset committed to the Tower.

— Oct. 22. Richard Cox made dean of Westminster.

— Nov. 10. Death of Paul III.

1550. Jan. 9. Lord Russell created earl of Bedford.

— Feb. 6. The duke of Somerset released from the Tower.

— Feb. 8. Election of Julius III.

— Feb. 18. The duke of Somerset and the earl of Warwick, their wives and households, licensed by the king to eat flesh in Lent and on other fast days.

— Feb. Cranmer and his household licensed to do the same.

— March 18. Thirlby, bishop of Ely, similarly licensed.

— April 1. Nicholas Ridley translated by the king from Rochester to London.

— April 19. Edward VI. and his council refuse the princess Mary the right to have mass said in her own house.

— May 2. Jane Butcher burnt in Smithfield.

— May 13. John à Lasco arrives in England.

1550. June. Ridley destroys the altars and replaces them by tables.

— June 14. Stephen Gardiner, bishop of Winchester, promised the duke of Somerset and five others of the council to use the book of common prayer, and to see that others used it in his diocese.

— June 27. John à Lasco, his wife and children, naturalised.

— June 29. The church of the Augustinian Friars in London given over to German heretics.

— June 29. John Poynet made bishop of Rochester.

— July 3. The bishopric of Gloucester given to John Hooper, an apostate Cistercian.

— July 19. The bishopric of Winchester placed under sequestration for three months.

— Oct. 24. Peter Martyr made canon of Christ's Church, Oxford.

— Nov. 19. The bishops ordered by the king to throw down the altars.

— Dec. 15. The council orders certain chaplains of the princess Mary to be arrested for saying mass.

— This year Cranmer, who had married a niece of Osiander's wife, shows her in public as his wife.

1551. Jan. 20. Peter Martyr installed canon of Christ's Church, Oxford.

— Feb. 14. Gardiner deprived of his bishopric by the king's commissioners.

— Feb. 27 or 28. Martin Bucer died at Cambridge.

— March 8. John Hooper ordained bishop of Gloucester.

— March 18. The princess Mary appeared before the king and his council and refused to accept the new religion.

— March 20. Cranmer, Ridley, and Poynet advise the king that he might tolerate mass in the house of his sister, but that to allow it formally would be a sin.

— March 23. John Poynet translated by the king from Rochester to Winchester.

— March 24. Sir Antony Brown sent to the Fleet for hearing mass.

1551. April 26. John Scory appointed by the king bishop of Rochester.

— April 27. Dr. Mallet, chaplain of the princess Mary, sent to the Tower.

— June and July. The sweating sickness.

— July 27. John Poynet, bishop of Winchester, ordered to restore the butcher's wife to her husband. See bk. ii. chap. v. pp. 210, 211.

— Aug. 14. John Voysey resigns the bishopric of Exeter.

— Aug. 30. Miles Coverdale made bishop of Exeter.

— Sept. 10. Miles Coverdale and his wife Elizabeth licensed to eat flesh on Lent and on fast days.

— Oct. 10. Henry Grey, marquis of Dorset, father of Jane Grey, created duke of Suffolk.

— Oct. 10. George Day, having refused to destroy the images, is removed from the bishopric of Chichester.

— Oct. 10. Nicholas Heath removed from his see and put in the Fleet prison.

— Oct. 16. The duke of Somerset arrested.

— Dec. 1. The duke of Somerset tried and condemned to death.

— Dec. 20. Cuthbert Tunstall, bishop of Durham, committed to the Tower.

1552. Jan. 22. Execution of the duke of Somerset.

— April 22. Sir William Paget degraded from the order of the garter.

— April 26. John Hooper surrenders to the king the bishopric of Gloucester.

— May 20. John Hooper receives from the king the bishopric of Worcester, which with Gloucester he is to hold during good behaviour.

— May 23. John Scory translated by the king from Rochester to Chichester.

— May 24. John White, afterwards bishop of Lincoln, made prebendary of Lichfield.

— June 18. The bishopric of Lincoln, to be held during good behaviour, given to John Taylor.

— Sept. 8. Nicholas Ridley goes to Hunsdon where the princess Mary resided, and offered to preach to her.

The princess thanked him for his visit, saying, "But for your offering to preach before me, I thank you never a whit."

1552. Oct. 11. Cuthbert Tunstall deprived of the bishopric of Durham.

1553. March 1. Parliament held, in which the bishopric of Durham is dissolved.

— May 4. Edward VI. annexes the bishopric of Durham with all its rights to the crown.

— July 6. Edward VI. died at Greenwich.

— July 10. Lady Jane Grey proclaimed queen.

— July 19. Mary proclaimed queen.

— July 20. The duke of Northumberland made prisoner at Cambridge.

— Aug. 3. The queen enters London in state, and proceeds to the Tower.

— Aug. 5. The queen releases the prisoners who were in the Tower and other prisons.

— Aug. 8. Funeral of Edward VI. Gardiner said mass for him in the Tower, and Cranmer used the Protestant service at Westminster.

— Aug. 9. The bishop of Winchester leaves the Tower and enters his own house at St. Mary Overy's.

— Aug. 18. Trial of the duke of Northumberland.

— Aug. 22. The duke of Northumberland executed for treason.

— Aug. 23. Stephen Gardiner made chancellor of the kingdom.

— Sept. 1. Hooper committed to the Fleet.

— Sept. 5. Edmund Bonner resumes possession of the see of London.

— Sept. 27. Lord Paget readmitted into the order of the garter.

— Sept. 28. Thomas Watson admitted master of St. John's College, Cambridge.

— Sept. 28. John Voysey replaced in the bishopric of Exeter by royal license.

— Oct. 1. Coronation of Queen Mary.

1553. Oct. 10. Edward Courtney, earl of Devon, son of the marquis of Exeter, restored in blood.

— Oct. 18. The disputation in convocation on religion begun.

— Nov. 13. Cranmer, lady Jane Grey, with her husband, and Lord Ambrose Dudley, arraigned in the Guildhall, tried, and found guilty of treason.

— Nov. 18. Thomas Watson elected dean of Durham.

— Dec. 13. The queen orders the bishop of London, Dr. Bonner, to dissolve the convocation.

1554. Feb. 2. The rebels under Sir Thomas Wyat break into and pillage the palace of the bishop of Winchester, and destroy the library.

— Feb. 7. The rebellion quelled, and Wyat taken.

— Feb. 8. Owen Oglethorpe made canon of Windsor.

— Feb. 12. Execution of lady Jane Grey and her husband.

— Feb. 12. The earl of Devon committed to the Tower.

— Feb. 17. The duke of Suffolk found guilty of treason.

— Feb. 23. The duke of Suffolk executed.

— March 4. The queen orders the married ecclesiastics to be removed from their benefices, and all singing in processions to be in Latin.

— March 10. Order given to the lieutenant of the Tower to deliver up the bodies of Cranmer, Ridley, and Latimer, who were to be taken to Oxford, where they were to defend their heresies.

— March 10. John Feckenham elected dean of St. Paul's.

— March 15. Sir Thomas Wyat convicted of treason.

— March 18. Elizabeth sent to the Tower for her complicity in Wyat's rebellion.

— March 18. George Day recovers the see of Chichester from Scory.

— March 31. Nicholas Harpsfield made archdeacon of Canterbury.

— April 1. John White, bishop of Lincoln, James Brooks, bishop of Gloucester, Maurice Griffin, bishop of Rochester, Gilbert Bourn, bishop of Bath and Wells, Henry Morgan, bishop of St. David's, George Coates, bishop of Chester, consecrated.

1554. April 11. Execution of Sir Thomas Wyat.
— April 14. The disputation of Cranmer with the Oxford doctors begun.
— April 17. The disputation of Ridley.
— April 18. The disputation of Latimer.
— May 26. Alban Langdale made prebendary of York.
— May 31. Morgan Phillips made precentor of St. David's.
— July 10. Royal license granted to enable Cardinal Pole to exercise his authority as legate in England.
— July 19. Don Philip lands at Southampton.
— July 25. Marriage of the queen and Don Philip in Winchester Cathedral.
— Sept. 9. Henry Joliffe made dean of Bristol.
— Sept. 25. Death of Richard Sampson.
— Oct. 25. Order of Bonner to remove the texts of Scripture painted on the walls of the churches.
— Nov. 18. Ralph Bayne, bishop of Lichfield, and John Holyman, bishop of Bristol, consecrated.
— Nov. 23. Cardinal Pole makes his entry into London.
— Nov. 27. The Cardinal in Parliament.
— Nov. 28. The two houses of Parliament petition to be reconciled to the Church.
— Nov. 30. Cardinal Pole absolves the people of England *in foro externo*.
— Dec. 11. Henry Cole elected dean of St. Paul's.
1555. Jan. 29. John Hooper condemned, and delivered to the secular power by the bishop of Winchester.
— Feb. 4. Degradation of Hooper from the priesthood.
— Feb. 9. John Hooper burnt at Gloucester.
— March 5. Death of Julius III.
— March 8. License for the foundation of Trinity College, Oxford, granted to Sir Thomas Pope.
— April 9. Election of Marcellus II.
— April 16. Alban Langdale installed archdeacon of Chichester.
— April 30. Death of Marcellus II.
— May 1. License for the foundation of St. John's College, Oxford.

1555. May 12. The custody of the temporalities of St. Asaph granted to Thomas Goldwell.
— May 23. Election of Paul IV.
— Sept. 4. The princess Elizabeth fasted in order to gain the indulgence in the form of jubilee granted by Julius III.
— Sept. 8. James Turberville, bishop of Exeter, consecrated.
— Oct. 16. Burning at Oxford of Ridley and Latimer.
— Nov. 12. Death of Stephen Gardiner, bishop of Winchester.
1556. Feb. 6. The emperor Charles V. resigns.
— Feb. 24. The king and queen order the chancellor Nicholas Heath, archbishop of York, to issue a writ according to the law, for the burning of Cranmer, degraded, and delivered over to the secular arm.
— March 21. Burning of Cranmer at Oxford.
— March 22. Consecration of Cardinal Pole, archbishop of Canterbury.
— May 16. John White, bishop of Lincoln, appointed guardian of the temporalities of Winchester.
— July 15. Sir John Cheke, King Edward's tutor, recants all his heresies.
— July 16. Royal license to the dean and chapter of Winchester to elect a bishop.
— Aug. 2. George Day, bishop of Chichester, dies.
— Oct. 10. William Chedsey made archdeacon of Middlesex.
— Oct. 26. Cardinal Pole elected chancellor of Oxford.
— Nov. 21. Dr. Feckenham, dean of St. Paul's, took possession of Westminster Abbey as abbot of the same.
— Dec. 11. Henry Cole elected dean of St. Paul's.
— Dec. 24. Grant of the custody of the temporalities of Peterborough to David Poole, bishop-elect.
1557. Feb. 24. Charles V. enters the monastery of San Yusto in Estremadura.
— March 24. Thomas Watson made bishop of Lincoln by the Pope.
— May 7. John Christopherson, the queen's confessor, made bishop of Chichester.

1557. June 20. Paul IV. informs Philip and Mary that he has recalled Cardinal Pole.
— July 16. Anne of Cleves died.
— Aug. 1. The nuns of Sion resumed their monastery.
— Aug. 15. Consecration of Thomas Watson, bishop of Lincoln, David Poole, bishop of Peterborough, and Owen Oglethorpe, bishop of Carlisle.
— Nov. 21. Consecration of John Christopherson, bishop of Chichester.
1558. March 14. The emperor Ferdinand begins his reign on the resignation of his brother Charles V.
— April 24. Marriage of Mary queen of Scots and of the dauphin, Francis II.
— Sept. 7. Death of James Brooks, last bishop of Gloucester.
— Sept. 21. Death of the emperor Charles V. in the monastery of San Yusto.
— Nov. 1. Nicholas Harpsfield made prebendary of Canterbury.
— Nov. 17. Queen Mary and Cardinal Pole, the last archbishop of Canterbury, die. Elizabeth proclaimed.
— Dec. 5. Solemn burial of Queen Mary with the Catholic rites at Westminster.
— Dec. 20. Death of John Holyman, first and last bishop of Bristol.
— Dec. 22. The queen having removed the archbishop of York from the chancellorship, gives the great seal to Sir Nicholas Bacon as lord keeper.
1559. Jan. 15. Dr. Oglethorpe against law crowns Elizabeth.
— Feb. 3. Alban Langdale admitted chancellor of Lichfield.
— April 4. The bishops of Winchester and Lincoln, John White and Thomas Watson, committed to the Tower.
— May 30. Edmund Bonner deprived by Parliament of his bishopric and sent to prison.
— June 24. Cessation of the daily sacrifice by order of Parliament throughout the kingdom, according to the statute 1 Eliz. c. 2.
— July 10. Death of Henry II., king of France, and accession of his son Francis II.

1559. July 26. Edmund Grindal elected bishop of London.
— Aug. 18. Death of Paul IV.
— Sept. 9. The queen commissions Tunstall to consecrate Matthew Parker.
— Sept. 28. Cuthbert Tunstall, bishop of Durham, deprived.
— Dec. 6. The queen commissions Kitchin, Barlow, Scory, and Coverdale, with Hodgkins and Bale, to consecrate Parker.
— Dec. 26. Election of Pius IV.
1560. Jan. 12. Death of John White, bishop of Winchester.
— March 21. Edmund Grindal receives from Elizabeth the temporalities of the see of London.
— April 6. Elizabeth allows the book of common prayer to be translated into Latin and publicly used.
— May 10. Henry Cole, dean of St. Paul's, deprived, and imprisoned in the Tower.
— May 14. Edmund Grindal, bishop of London, forbids the processions of the rogation week, but allows perambulations without candles, banners, and surplice.
— June 10. Henry Cole removed from the Tower to the Fleet prison.
— Dec. 5. Death of Francis II., king of France. He is succeeded by his brother Charles IX.
1561. Aug. 21. Queen Mary returns to Scotland from France.
1563. Sept. 28. Wednesday ordered to be kept as a fast, and all Wednesdays after, by statute 5 Eliz. c. 5, § 14.
— Oct. 31. Death of Antony Kitchin, bishop of Llandaff.
— Dec. 4. Closing of the Council of Trent.
1564. July 24. Death of the emperor Ferdinand I.
— Sept. 30. Robert Dudley made earl of Leicester.
1565. May 20. Death of Miles Coverdale.
— July 29. Marriage of the queen of Scots and her cousin Darnley.
— Dec. 9. Death of Pius IV.
1566. Jan. 7. Election of St. Pius V.
— June 19. Birth of James I.
1567. Feb. 10. Murder of Darnley.
— May 15. Marriage of Mary and Earl of Bothwell.

1567. July 24. Mary queen of Scots imprisoned in Lochleven, forced to surrender the crown.
— Aug. 22. Earl of Murray made regent of Scotland.
1568. May 2. Mary queen of Scots escapes from Lochleven.
— May 13. The queen of Scots defeated by the rebels at Langside, escapes to England, and
— May 16. Lands at Workington, in Cumberland, to become the prisoner of Elizabeth.
— Foundation of the seminary of Douai by Dr. William, afterwards Cardinal, Allen.
1569. April 20. The bishop of London, Dr. Bonner, committed to the Marshalsea.
— May 20. Dr. Watson, bishop of Lincoln, Dom. Feckenham, abbot of Westminster, Henry Cole, dean of St. Paul's, and William Chedsey, archdeacon of Middlesex, committed to the Tower, and Dr. John Storey to the Fleet.
— Sept. 5. Death of Edmund Bonner, last bishop of London.
— Sept. 11. Thomas Howard, duke of Norfolk, committed to the Tower.
— Nov. 10. The earls of Northumberland and Westmoreland rise in defence of the faith, and enter Durham.
— Dec. 10. Death of William Barlow.
— Dec. 16. The two earls disband their troops and take refuge in flight.
1570. Jan. 23. Earl of Murray, regent of Scotland, shot.
— Feb. 25. Excommunication and deposition of Elizabeth.
— Aug. 8. John Felton hanged in St. Paul's Churchyard, cut down alive, bowelled, and quartered. See p. 305.
— Aug. 26. Death of Thomas Thirlby, the last bishop of Ely.
1571. May 26. Dr. John Storey condemned to death at Westminster. See bk. ii. chap. iv. p. 200.
— June 1. Dr. John Storey hanged, bowelled, and quartered at Tyburn.
1572. June 2. The duke of Norfolk executed on Tower Hill.
— May 1. Death of St. Pius V.
— May 13. Election of Gregory XIII.
— Aug. 22. The earl of Northumberland executed at York.
— Nov. 20. The puritans set up the first English presbytery at Wandsworth in Surrey.

1573. June 16. Thomas Woodhouse, priest, hanged, bowelled, and quartered at Tyburn.

— Aug. 20. The queen by proclamation orders all bishops, justices, and mayors to execute the acts of uniformity "with all diligence and severity."

1574. April 4, Palm Sunday. Fifty-three persons seized for hearing mass.

— The first missionary priests from the seminary of Cardinal Allen came this year to England.

1575. May 21. Eleven Dutch Anabaptists condemned in a consistory held in St. Paul's to be burned in Smithfield.

— July 2. Two of those condemned May 21 burnt in Smithfield.

— July 15. The queen orders John Peeters and Henry Turwert, Flemish Anabaptists, condemnned by her "inquisitors, judges, and commissaries," to be burnt.

1576. July 28. The ecclesiastical discipline of the Puritans adopted in a synod held in Guernsey, for that island, Jersey, Alderney, and Sark.

— Sept. 22. Death of the earl of Essex, supposed to have been poisoned by the earl of Leicester.

— Dec. 13. The archbishop of Canterbury, Grindal, ordered by the council to see that the ember days be observed, "as is requisite in policy for the maintenance of mariners, fishermen, and the navy of the realm."

1577. May 7. Queen Elizabeth orders the bishops to suppress "the exercise called prophesying."

— June. The queen suspends the archbishop of Canterbury.

— July 4. The black assizes begun at Oxford.

— Sept. 30. Cuthbert Mayne, protomartyr of the Seminarists, hanged, bowelled, and quartered at Launceston.

1578. Feb. 3. John Nelson, priest, hanged, bowelled, and quartered at Tyburn.

— Feb. 7. Thomas Sherwood, a layman, hanged, bowelled, and quartered at Tyburn.

1579. May 20. Matthew Hamant, a Dutch Anabaptist, burnt at Norwich.

1580. June 12. Father Persons landed at Dover.

— June 25. Father Campian landed at Dover before day-break.

— Oct. 3. The queen orders the "Family of Love" to be rooted out, and its books destroyed.

— Dec. 10. Luke Kirby and Thomas Cottam, priests, underwent the torture of the "scavenger's daughter." Blood flowing from the nostrils of the latter.

— Dec. 15. Ralph Sherwin and Robert Johnson, priests, racked in the Tower.

1581. Jan. 10. Proclamation against all priests and Jesuits, who are said to be guilty of high treason.

— Jan. 16. Parliament met, and by statute 13 Eliz. c. 1, made it high treason to be reconciled to the Church: subjected every priest who said mass to a fine of 200 marks and a year's imprisonment, and every person who heard mass to a fine of 100 marks and a year's imprisonment, and finally laid a fine of £20 a month on every Catholic, above the age of sixteen, who did not attend Protestant prayers.

— Feb. 5. From this till Whitsuntide, the lieutenant of the Tower forced the Catholics into the chapel that they might hear the heretics preach.

— March 27. Alexander Bryant, priest, taken to the Tower, tortured by the insertion of needles under his nails.

— June 21. The earl of Northumberland found dead in the Tower.

— July 15. Father Campian arrested.

— July 31. Everard Hans, priest, hanged, bowelled, and quartered at Tyburn.

— Aug. 31. Father Campian, twice tortured on the rack, is made to dispute with the heretical ministers.

— Oct. 31. Father Campian tortured the third time.

— Dec. 1. Fathers Campian and Bryant and the Rev. Ralph Sherwin hanged, bowelled, and quartered for the faith at Tyburn.

1582. April 2. John Payne, priest, martyred at Chelmsford.

— May 28. Thomas Ford, John Shert, and Robert Johnson, priests, hanged, bowelled, and quartered at Tyburn.

1582. May 30. William Filby, Luke Kirby, Laurence Richardson, and Thomas Cottam, priests, hanged, bowelled, and quartered at Tyburn.

— July 19. William Carter, printer, brought from another prison to the Tower.

— Aug. 22. William Lacy and Richard Kirkman martyred at York.

— Nov. 28. James Thompson martyred at York.

1583. Feb. 16. John Munden, priest, taken to the Tower, and kept in fetters for twenty days.

— March 15. William Hart martyred at York.

— May 29. Richard Thirkell martyred at York.

— Oct. 30. John Slade, a layman, hanged at Winchester for the supremacy of the Pope.

— Nov. 2. John Body, a layman, hanged for the supremacy of the Pope at Andover.

— Dec. 20. Edward Arden, layman, hanged, bowelled, and quartered at Smithfield for the faith.

1584. Jan. 10. William Carter, printer, hanged, bowelled, and quartered at Tyburn. See bk. iv. chap. ix. p. 316.

— Feb. 2. Robert Nutter, priest, taken and laid in the pit of the Tower for forty-seven days, twice underwent the torture of the "scavenger's daughter."

— Feb. 7. George Haddock, John Munden, John Nutter, James Fenn, Thomas Hemerford, arraigned at Westminster, and found guilty of high treason, because they had been made priests abroad.

— Feb. 12. The priests tried on the 7th hanged, bowelled, and quartered at Tyburn.

— April 20. James Bell, a priest, and John Finch, a layman, put to death at Lancaster for believing in the authority of the Pope.

— July 10. Francis Throgmorton, layman, hanged, bowelled, and quartered at Tyburn.

— Sept. 27. Death of Dr. Watson, the last bishop of Lincoln.

— Oct. 17. Richard White, layman, put to death at Wrexham for the Catholic faith.

— Nov. 10. Robert Nutter laid in the pit again, where he was kept for more than two months.

1585. Jan. 21. Deportation of twenty-one prisoners against their will, twenty priests and one layman.

— April 3. Death of Thomas Goldwell, the last bishop of St. Asaph, and the last of the bishops.

— April 10. Death of Gregory XIII.

— April 24. Election of Sixtus V.

— June 26. Death of John Scory.

— July 5. Thomas Alfield, priest, Thomas Webley, layman, hanged at Tyburn for bringing a book of Cardinal Allen into the country.

1586. Jan. 21. Edward Stransham, priest, martyred at Tyburn.

— April 20. Richard Sergeant and William Thomson, priests, martyred at Tyburn.

— April 25. William Marsden and Robert Anderton, priests, martyred in the Isle of Wight.

— June 3. Francis Ingoldby martyred at York.

— Mary queen of Scots taken to Fotheringay.

— Oct. 11. The queen of Scots tried for her life by commissioners of the queen of England.

1587. Feb. 8. Execution of Mary queen of Scots.

INDEX.